German Grammar in Context

THAMES VALLEY UNIVERSITY
Kings Road Learning Resource Centre
Kings Road, Reading, RG1 4HJ   6/7/07

Please return this item to the Issue Desk on or before the due date. Fines are charged on overdue loans.

If no-one else has reserved the item, you may extend the loan period up to three times without bringing it back. When renewing by telephone or through the learning resources catalogue, you will need your borrower barcode number and your *borrower* PIN number.

Issue Desk	0118 967 5060
24 hour automated renewals line:	020 8231 2703
Website and catalogue:	www.tvu.ac.uk/lrs

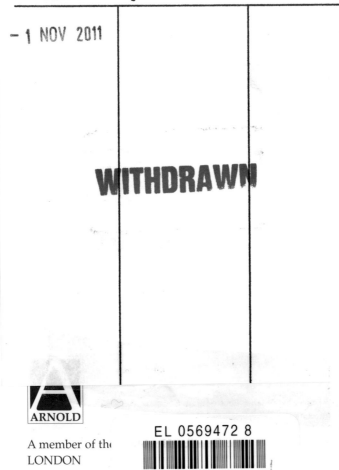

ARNOLD

A member of the
LONDON

First published in Great Britain in 2002 by
Hodder Arnold, an imprint of Hodder Education,
a member of the Hodder Headline Group,
338 Euston Road, London NW1 3BH

http://www.hoddereducation.co.uk

The advice and information in this book are believed to be true and
accurate at the time of going to press, but neither the author nor the publisher
can accept any legal responsibility or liability for any errors or omissions.

British Library Cataloguing in Publication Data
A catalogue record for this book is available from the British Library

ISBN-10: 0 340 76310 8
ISBN-13: 978 0 340 76310 0

3 4 5 6 7 8 9 10

Production Editor: Anke Ueberberg
Production Controller: Bryan Eccleshall
Cover Design: Terry Griffiths

Typeset in 10 on 14 pt Minion by Phoenix Photosetting, Chatham, Kent
Printed and bound in India by Replika Press Pvt. Ltd

What do you think about this book? Or any other Hodder Arnold title?
Please visit our website at www.hoddereducation.co.uk

Contents

Foreword

The purpose of this book is to provide an accessible text-based reference grammar of the German language for English-speaking students of German and to help consolidate their knowledge through practical exercises on a whole range of grammatical topics. It is aimed at first- and second-year undergraduate students, although more advanced students wishing to revise particular grammatical points may also benefit. As one of the main aims of the book is accessibility, grammatical terminology is kept to a minimum and only traditional terms are used. There is also a list of grammatical terms and their definitions at the beginning of the book.

The book is based on the premise that grammatical issues are more easily explained and understood within the wider context in which they appear, i.e. within whole texts, rather than in terms of isolated rules and fabricated examples. Thus, in each chapter an authentic German text is chosen which illustrates a particular grammatical feature, e.g. the past tense, the subjunctive or personal pronouns, and the necessary rules are set out in relation to the occurrence of the grammatical forms within the text. Later in the chapter, under the heading 'Discover more about . . .', supplementary rules are given which are not illustrated in the text, for the sake of completeness. Each grammatical point is explained as concisely as possible and is illustrated, if not by directly referring to the text, by the use of everyday German examples of the kind likely to be encountered and used by the student. Some of the longer chapters contain charts and tables to help the student focus on the main points in question. These usually follow the principle of 'grammar in context' in that they rarely consist of lists of isolated words but usually of words co-occurring with other forms in the language, e.g. prepositions listed with a following definite article and noun to show the case that they take. Unpredictable exceptions to rules and more complicated issues, which may be of interest to more advanced learners, are usually dealt with in footnotes.

The German texts chosen are extremely varied both in style and in subject matter, yet they have in common that they are all authentic and are examples of modern standard German. The styles range from journalistic writings to literary excerpts, from prose to poetry and drama, from scientific writings to song lyrics, and the subject matter ranges from discussions on the state of the euro to humorous dialogue transcribed from a TV chat-show, from Freud's interpretation of dreams to recipes for sausage and sauerkraut. In particular, many of the texts reflect German or Austrian life and culture.

Each chapter ends with a set of exercises designed to practise the particular grammatical topic under discussion. Some of these exercises are organised according to complexity: e.g. regular forms will be practised before irregularities and more complicated issues. The exercises are varied in style: from reformulation and gap-filling exercises, many of which are based on authentic texts themselves, to translation exercises and crosswords. In addition, the exercises in each chapter are based on a particular vocabulary topic in order to build up students' vocabulary at the same time as practising their grammar. These are useful everyday topics which students should be familiar with: food, transport, holidays, school and university subjects, careers, garden and household, hobbies and entertainment, etc. There is a key to the exercises towards the back of the book.

At the end of the main part of the book (in Appendix 3) are five revision texts, each of which deals with a number of key grammatical issues together so that students can revise the grammatical topics which they have learned earlier in the book. Each of the revision texts is followed by two sets of exercises, the first of which deals with recognising particular forms and explaining why they are used, while the second requires students to practise using the forms themselves. These are also followed by a key (in Appendix 5).

At the end of the book there is a comprehensive index covering both the main issues and the more specific grammatical problems and particular forms dealt with in the book. In the appendices are also included an alphabetical list of common irregular verbs and a set of article–adjective–noun paradigms for students to learn.

Acknowledgements

I would like to thank my colleagues in the Department of German Studies, University of Newcastle, for their support during the writing of this book, in particular Beate Müller, Anke Neibig and Jens Hentschke, on whose native-speaker intuition I have frequently called, and Nicole Böheim for her thorough reading of the final draft and her many useful comments and suggestions. I would particularly like to thank Jon West for many fruitful discussions regarding the finer points of German grammar, and Tina Fry for providing the student's perspective.

In addition, my thanks are due to the authors and publishers/media agents who very kindly allowed me to make use of their texts: Luciana Dabdab Waquil, Herbert Hertramph, Volker Vogeler; Katrin Bergel (*der Spiegel*), Alexandra Borisch (*Pestalozzi*), Claudia Brandes (*Suhrkamp Verlag*), Gernot Dallinger (*Bundeszentrale für politische Bildung*), Andreas Diel (*DeutschlandRadio, Köln*), Felix Grigat (*Forschung und Lehre*), Sylke Hemme (*Hot Action Records*), Ursula Hoog (*Frankfurter Societäts-Druckerei*), Cordula Hubert (*Oldenbourg Wissenschaftsverlag*), Traudel Jansen (*Verlag Kiepenheuer und Witsch*), B. Kasses (*Bundespressedienst Österreich*), Bettina Kaufmann (*Diogenes*), Karolin Marhencke (*Rowohlt Verlag*), Heidrun Miltzlaff (*Brigitte*), Ulrike Morgenschweis (*Bärbel Schäfer*), Kerstin Nüchter (*Akademie-Verlag*), Sabine Oppenlander (*SOA Photo Agency*), Gisela Podlech (*Fischer Verlag*), Ulrike Prechtl-Fröhlich (*Verlag Zabert Sandmann*), Antje Schillo (*DAAD Letter*), Renate Schocher (*Kurier*), Claudia Schweiger (*EM TV*), Andrea Sommer (*die Welt*), Ruth Weibel (*Liepman AG*), and Herbert Wilfart (*Katholische Bibelanstalt GmbH, Stuttgart*).

Finally I would like to thank my husband Gerhard not only for his valuable comments on Austrian German but also for his moral support and encouragement which have been much appreciated.

List of grammatical terms

Abstract noun A noun referring to an abstract concept or idea rather than to a concrete object: e.g. '**length**', '**friendship**'; *Gesundheit, Höhe*.

Accusative In German, the case used to express the direct object of the verb and also after certain prepositions: e.g. *Ich liebe **dich/den** Mann/**diesen jungen** Mann, Ein Brief <u>für</u> **meinen** Freund.*

Active A grammatical construction in which the agent of the verb is also its subject: e.g. '**He** likes me'; ***Ich** fragte ihn (contrast passive).*

Adjective A word used to describe a noun or pronoun: e.g. 'A **shy** boy', 'She is **tall**'; *Ein **großes** Zimmer.*

Adverb A word used to describe a verb or adjective: e.g. 'He got up **slowly**', They were **annoyingly** loud'; *Er spielt **gut**.*

Agent The person (or, less commonly, thing) that carries out the action described by the main verb: '**He** hit me', 'I was warned by **my friend**'; *Er wurde von **dem Lehrer** bestraft.*

Article A word meaning '**the**' or '**a**' used before nouns (*see* definite article *and* indefinite article).

Auxiliary verb A verb used together with other verbs to form different tenses: e.g. 'I **have** finished', 'He **will** come'; *Er **hat** gesagt, Sie **ist** gegangen.*

Bare infinitive In German, the infinitive used without *um* or *zu*: e.g. *Er will **spielen**.*

Case In German, a grammatical category shown by changing the forms of articles, pronouns, demonstratives and adjectives depending on their relationship to other words in the sentence (*see* accusative, dative, genitive *and* nominative).

Clause The part of the sentence which contains a finite verb (usually accompanied by a subject): e.g. '[I am hungry _{Clause 1}] but [there is nothing in the fridge _{Clause 2}]'; [*Er ist früh ins Bett gegangen* _{Clause 1}], *weil* [*er müde war* _{Clause 2}].

Comparative The form of the adjective used to compare two or more persons or things: e.g. 'You're **fatter** than me'; *Das Zimmer ist **größer** als die anderen.*

Compound (word) A word made up of two or more other words: e.g. 'house' + 'wife' = '**housewife**'; *Universität + Professor = **Universitätsprofessor**.*

Conditional A tense used to refer to hypothetical situations in the future: e.g. 'I **would buy** a new car'; *Er **würde** seinen Freund **besuchen**.*

Conditional perfect A tense used to refer to hypothetical situations in the past: e.g. 'I **would have bought** something cheaper'; *Er **hätte** es nicht gemacht.*

Conjunction A word that links clauses together: e.g. 'I came in **and** sat down'; *Er war müde, **weil** er schlecht geschlafen hatte; **Obwohl** er schlecht geschlafen hatte, war er nicht müde.*

Co-ordinating conjunction A conjunction, such as German ***und, aber, oder***, which does not affect word order (*contrast* subordinating conjunction).

Dative In German, the case used to express the indirect object of the verb and also after certain prepositions: e.g. *Ich gebe* **dir/dem** *Mann/***diesem jungen** *Mann einen Kuss, Ich gehe* <u>*mit*</u> **meiner** *Freundin aus.*

Definite article A word placed before a noun to make it definite or specific: e.g. '**the** dog'; **der** *Mann,* **die** *Tür,* **das** *Haus* (*contrast* indefinite article).

Demonstrative A word used to point out a specific person or thing and differentiate it from other members of its class: e.g. '**this** wine', '**that** bread', **dieser** *Mann,* **der** *Wagen.*

Diminutive A word with a special ending used to express smallness (and also endearment or contempt, depending on the context): '**piglet**'; **Kätzchen, Schwesterchen.**

Direct object A noun/pronoun which is the direct recipient of the action described by the main verb. It is usually expressed by the accusative case in German: e.g. 'He loves **me**'; *Sie küsst* **ihren Freund** (*contrast* indirect object).

Expanded attribute In German, a phrase of two words or more ending in an adjective which describes a following noun: e.g. *der* **für meinen Geschmack etwas zu große** *Tisch.*

Finite verb The part of the verb which may change its form (i.e. by adding an ending or changing its vowel) to show person, number and tense: e.g. 'He **works** hard'; *Ich* **liebe** *dich, Du* **bist** *gegangen, Wir* **haben** *ihn gesehen.*

Future perfect A tense used to express completed actions either in the future or as an assumption: e.g. 'He **will have finished** it by tomorrow'; *Er* **wird** *schon* **losgefahren sein.**

Future tense A tense used either to refer to future time or to express an assumption: e.g. 'John **will arrive** tomorrow'; *Er* **wird** *jetzt zu Hause* **sein.**

Gender In German nouns, the categories 'masculine', 'feminine' and 'neuter' which determine the forms of co-occurring articles, pronouns, adjectives, etc.: e.g. Masc. **der/ein Hund**, Fem. **die/eine Blume**, Neut. **das/ein** *Haus.*

Genitive In German, the case used chiefly to express possession, corresponding to English ''s' or 'of', and also after certain prepositions: e.g. *Ein Freund* **meines Vaters**, *das Haus* **der** *Nachbarin,* <u>*Während*</u> **des ersten Weltkriegs.**

Imperative The form of the verb used in commands: e.g. '**Go** away!'; **Sei** *brav!,* **Kommen Sie** *herein!*

Indefinite article A word placed before a noun to indicate that it is not specific: e.g. '**a** house'; **ein** *Freund,* **eine** *Katze* (*contrast* definite article).

Indirect object The noun/pronoun (usually a person) which is the recipient of the direct object (usually a thing). It is usually expressed using 'to' in English and the dative case in German: e.g. 'I sent the letter **to my friend**'; *Er erzählte* **den Kindern** *einen Witz.*

Infinitive In German, the part of the verb always listed in dictionaries which does not change its form to express person, number etc.: e.g. **machen, gehen, sein.**

Infinitive clause In German, a clause consisting of an infinitive preceded by *zu*: e.g. *Ich habe versucht,* **dem alten Mann** <u>**zu helfen.**</u>

Inseparable verb In German, a verb beginning with a prefix such as *be-, ent-, er-, ge-, ver-* which is never separated from the verb and does not take *ge-* in the past participle: e.g. *Es* **beginnt**, *Du hast mich* **erkannt**, *Um besser zu* **verstehen** (*contrast* separable verb).

Intransitive verb A verb not taking a direct object: e.g. 'I **stay**'; *Er* **kommt** (*contrast* transitive verb).

Irregular Not following the usual rules: e.g. 'I **thought**' (NOT *'thinked'); *Er **sang*** (NOT **singte*).

Main clause In German, a clause that does not begin with a subordinating conjunction or relative pronoun: e.g. ***Ich habe dich angerufen***, *aber **du warst nicht zu Hause*** (*contrast* subordinate clause).

Manner An expression of manner refers to *how* the action of the verb is carried out: e.g. 'He left **in a hurry**'; *Ich bin **mit dem Bus** gefahren.*

Modal verbs A set of verbs expressing a range of moods such as ability, obligation, and volition which are often used in combination with the bare infinitive form of other verbs: e.g. 'He **can** come'; *Ich **will** dich sehen; Du **musst** hier bleiben.*

Nominative In German, the case used to express the subject of the verb: e.g. ***Du*** *liebst mich,* ***Der Chef*** *kommt, Klaus ist **mein bester** Freund.*

Noun A word used to name a person, thing or concept which, in English and German, may appear after an article and may be singular or plural: e.g. 'My **friend**'; *der **Tisch**, die **Probleme**.*

Number A term used to refer to the grammatical categories of singular and plural (*see* singular *and* plural).

Object *See* direct object and indirect object.

Participle *See* past participle *and* present participle.

Passive A grammatical construction which shifts the emphasis away from the agent of the verb to the **recipient of the action** described by the verb. This recipient becomes the subject of the passive construction: e.g. '**I was asked** by him' (contrast the active 'He asked me'); *Er **wurde** vom Lehrer **bestraft*** (or, without the agent, *Er **wurde bestraft**).*

Past participle The non-finite part of the verb used in the perfect tenses and the passive: e.g. 'I have **seen** him'; *Du hast es **gemacht**, Er war **geblieben**.*

Past tense A tense used to refer to past events. In German, this is mainly used in the written language: e.g. 'He **came**'; *Ich **machte** es, Er **wartete** auf mich.*

Perfect tense A tense used to refer to past events. In German, this is mainly used in the spoken language: e.g. *Er **hat** auf mich **gewartet**.* In English, the perfect is used when the actions in the past are still relevant to the present: e.g. 'He **has arrived** (and is here now)'.

Person The grammatical category used to indicate which person or thing is being referred to. The first person refers to 'I', 'we'; the second person 'you' (singular and plural); and the third person 'he', 'she', 'it', 'they'. Person is shown on some pronouns, e.g. *ich, du, mein,* and also on verbs, e.g. *mach**e**, mach**st**, mach**t**.*

Personal pronoun A pronoun referring to one or more persons or things: e.g. 'I', 'me' 'you', 'we', 'it'; *du, dich, er, sie, es, wir, uns, Sie, Ihnen.*

Pluperfect tense A tense used to refer to events in the past which precede other events in the past (i.e. a past within a past): e.g. 'He **had expected** her to ring but she didn't'; *Er **war** lange krank **gewesen**, bevor er starb.*

Plural The grammatical category used to refer to more than one person or thing: 'My **friends**'. '**They are** here'; ***Die Probleme sind*** *noch nicht gelöst.*

Possessive A word used to denote possession: '**My** dog', '**Her** cat'; ***Unser*** *Haus, Das ist **meiner**.*

Predicative adjective An adjective used after the verb, e.g. 'He is **rich**'; *Sie sind sehr **freundlich**.*

Prefix A grammatical element attached to the beginning of a word: e.g. '**un**usual', '**ex**-husband'; ***ver**stehen, **an**rufen.*

Preposition A word, such as *in*, *on*, *under*, usually placed before nouns or pronouns to relate them to other words in the sentence: e.g. 'He hid **behind** the tree'; *Ich warte **auf** dich, Wir fahren **mit** dem Bus.*

Prepositional prefix In German, a preposition attached to the beginning of a word: e.g. **an***rufen*, **aus***gehen*, **mit***kommen*.

Present participle In English, the form of the verb ending in '-ing': e.g. 'I was **thinking**'. In German it ends in *-end* and is mainly used as an adjective or adverb: e.g. *Wir haben kein* **laufend***es Wasser.*

Present tense A tense used primarily to refer to the present (or to general/habitual occurrences and states): e.g. 'It **is** two o'clock'; *Er **spricht** Deutsch, Wir **gehen** jeden Samstag ins Kino.*

Productive A grammatical rule is productive if it still operates in the language, i.e. if it can apply to new words, such as recent technological terms or loanwords from other languages. Examples are: adding '-s' to form plurals in English, as in 'computers', 'emails', 'modems', vs. the unproductive '-en' in 'ox**en**'; and forming past participles with **ge-** . . . **-t** in German, as in *Ich habe dich **ge**email**t**, **ge**fax**t**,* vs. the unproductive **ge-** . . .**-en** in *ge*fang**en**, *ge*schlaf**en**.

Progressive forms In English, verbal constructions using the forms of 'to be' plus a present participle: e.g. 'He **is working**'. In German, the progressive aspect is expressed using words such as *eben, gerade* etc.: e.g. *Er arbeitet **gerade**.*

Pronoun A word which takes the place of a noun: e.g. 'the man → **he**' , 'the coffee → **it**'; *ein Bleistift → **einer**, dieser Rock → **dieser**, mein Bier → **meins**.*

Proper noun A noun which is the name or title of a person, thing or place: e.g. 'John', 'the *Titanic*', 'Manchester'; *Schmidt, Deutschland, Europa.*

Reflexive verb A verb whose subject and object refer to the same person or thing: e.g. '**He hurt himself**'; ***Ich dusche mich**.* These objects ('myself', 'yourself', etc.) are known as reflexive pronouns.

Relative clause A clause beginning with a relative pronoun: e.g. 'The job **that he hates**'; *Der Mann, **der im Restaurant saß**.*

Relative pronoun A pronoun that refers back to a noun or pronoun already mentioned in the sentence: e.g. 'The boy **who** was ill', 'The issue **that** was raised'; *Die Frau, **die** da sitzt, Der Lehrer, mit **dem** ich gesprochen habe.*

Sentence A group of words containing one or more clauses. In writing it begins with a capital letter and ends with a full stop: e.g. 'He speaks fluent French.' *Sie möchte Spanisch lernen, aber sie hat keine Zeit, weil sie vier Kinder hat.*

Separable verb In German, a verb beginning with a prefix such as *an, auf, aus, mit, zu* which is separated from the verb in certain grammatical constructions: e.g. *Ich **rufe** dich **an**, Du hast mir nicht **zu**ge**hört**, Ich habe keine Lust **aus**zu**gehen*** (*contrast* inseparable verb).

Singular The grammatical category used to refer to one single person or thing: '**The man**', '**A girl**'; ***Mein Freund ist** krank.*

Stem *See* verb stem.

Stress In the spoken language, emphasis placed on a particular syllable of a word: e.g. 'per**for**mance'; *ver**steh**en, **auf**stehen.*

Strong verb A verb that forms its past tense and/or past participle by changing the main vowel: e.g. 'sw**i**m – sw**a**m – sw**u**m'; *n**e**hmen – n**a**hm – gen**o**mmen.*

Subject In an ordinary active sentence, the person or thing that carries out the action described by the verb, e.g. 'She hit him', or experiences the state described by the verb, e.g. '**My friend** is ill'. In German, the subject has nominative case: e.g. *Der Lehrer fragt den Jungen, Wo ist **mein neuer Regenschirm**?*

Subordinate clause In German, a clause beginning with a subordinating conjunction: e.g. *Ich gehe ins Bett, **weil ich sehr müde bin*** (*contrast* main clause).

Subordinating conjunction In German, a conjunction such as *bevor, bis, da, nachdem, obwohl, weil* which sends the following finite verb to the end of its clause: e.g. *Ich wartete, **bis** er von der Arbeit zurückkam* (*contrast* subordinating conjunction).

Suffix An element attached to the end of a word or a stem, otherwise known as an 'ending': e.g. 'sad**ness**', 'quick**ly**'; *freund**lich**, Mein**ung**, Lehr**er**.*

Superlative The form of the adjective used to express the most extreme degree of its meaning: e.g. 'The **hottest** day'; *Der **älteste** Mann, Die **schönsten** Bilder.*

Syllable The part of a word which usually contains a vowel. The words '**man**' and *Maus* have one syllable; '**husband**' and *Katze* have two syllables; '**Germany**' and *Elefant* have three syllables.

Tense A grammatical term used to refer to relations of time: e.g. present tense, past tense, future tense.

Transitive verb A verb taking a direct object: e.g. 'I **love him**'; *Er **schreibt einen Brief*** (*contrast* intransitive verb).

Verb A word denoting an action or a state. In English and German it usually occurs with a subject and can change its form depending on its tense and the person and number of its subject: e.g. 'He **loves** me'; *Wir **spielten**, Du **warst** krank.*

Verb stem The part of the verb without any endings for person and number. In German, this usually means the infinitive minus *-en*: e.g. *mach-, les-, arbeit-.*

1 | Gender

Kommt **eine** Maus – baut **ein** Haus.

Kommt **eine** Mücke – baut **eine** Brücke.

Kommt **ein** Floh – **der** macht so!   [***Das** Kinn des Kindes kitzeln*].

Da kommt **der** Bär – **der** tappt so schwer,

5 Da kommt **die** Maus – in Hänschens Haus,

Da hinein, da hinein!   [***Die** Halsgrube des Kindes kitzeln*].

Da kommt **die** Maus – da kommt **die** Maus.

Klingelingeling!

„Ist **der** Herr zu Haus?"   [***Das** Ohr des Kindes zupfen*].

Aus: *Das ist der Daumen*. Fingerspielreime für Kinder. ©1992 Pestalozzi-Verlag.

Gender in the text

1.1   GENDER ON ARTICLES AND PRONOUNS

German nouns must have a gender, either **masculine, feminine** or **neuter**, which shows up on the articles and pronouns (and adjectives) used with the nouns in the singular. (Gender differences are not shown on the articles/pronouns in the plural.) **1.1a** and **1.1b** below give the different gender forms of the definite and indefinite articles in the nominative case.[1]

[1] See **Ch. 3** for other case forms and **Ch. 5** for gender on adjectives.

1.1a   Definite article 'the': der Mann – die Frau – das Kind (pl: die for all genders)

Common pronouns which follow the same pattern are the demonstratives **dieser**, *diese, dieses* 'this', **jener** 'that', *jene, jenes* 'that', **jeder**, *jede, jedes* 'each/every' **welcher?**, *welche?, welches?* 'which?', and the **relative pronouns** which are mostly identical to the definite articles (see **Ch. 9**).
   Some examples from the text are: masc. **der** *Bär* (line 4), **der** *Herr* (9); fem. **die** *Maus* (5, 7), **die** *Halsgrube* (6); neut. **das** *Kinn* (3), **das** *Ohr* (9). In line 4, the definite article[2] is used as a pronoun: **der** *tappt so schwer* 'it (masc., i.e. the bear) is lumbering heavily'. Similarly, **der** *macht so* (3) 'it (masc., i.e. the flea) does this'.

[2] Technically this is a demonstrative pronoun, which is identical to the definite article (see **8.2b**).

1.1b Indefinite article 'a': ein Mann – eine Frau – ein Kind (no plural)

Here, the masculine and neuter forms are identical. Common pronouns which follow the same pattern are **kein** 'not a/no' and the possessives **mein, dein, sein, unser, euer, ihr** (see **7.2**). These also have plural forms ending in -**e** e.g. *keine, meine*.

Some examples from the text are: masc. **ein** *Floh* (3); fem. **eine** *Maus* (1), **eine** *Mücke* (2), **eine** *Brücke* (2); neut. **ein** *Haus* (1). The last two examples are in the accusative case but this is identical to the nominative for all but masculine singulars (see **3.2b**).

Other points to note in the text

- Genitive case: **des** *Kindes, Hänschens* (5) (see **3.1a(iv)** and footnote 13.
- Use of *hin*- to indicate movement away from speaker: *da* **hin***ein* (6) 'in there' (see footnote 95).
- Verb first for poetic effect: *Kommt. . .* (1–3).
- Missing pronoun and *und* to create rhythm: *baut . . .* (1–2).
- Omission of final -**e** in *zu Haus* to create rhyme (9).

◢ Discover more about gender

1.2 WHICH GENDER?

It is often not possible to predict which noun will take a certain gender, particularly in the case of nouns referring to inanimate objects, and therefore when students learn individual nouns they must also remember their gender (e.g. by learning the nouns together with a definite article). There are, however, a few correlations between certain characteristics of the noun and its gender that can be given to help students remember and predict which nouns tend to take a certain gender. First, gender is often determined by the **ending** of the noun (see **Table 1**). Second, it may also be determined by the **meaning** of the noun (see **Table 2**), although it should be pointed out that, particularly with regard to the relationship between meaning and gender, we are dealing with general tendencies rather than hard-and-fast rules.

Table 1. The gender of nouns according to their endings

MASC.		FEM.		NEUT.	
-ant/-ent*	der Student	**-anz/-enz**	die Prominenz	**-chen/-lein**	das Mädchen
-ast	der Palast	**-e†**	die Phase, die Limonade	**-en** (infinitive)	das Essen
-er*	der Arbeiter	**-ei**	die Polizei	**-ett**	das Duett
-ich	der Teppich	**-ette**	die Zigarette	**-icht**	das Licht
-ig	der Käfig	**-heit/-keit**	die Schönheit	**-il**	das Wohnmobil
-ling	der Flüchtling	**-ie**	die Chemie	**-ma**	das Thema
-ist	der Polizist	**-ik**	die Musik	**-ment**	das Testament
-or	der Traktor	**-in**	die Lehrerin	**-nis‡**	das Gefängnis

MASC.		FEM.		NEUT.	
-us	der Globus	-ion	die Situation	-o	das Auto
	der Sozialismus	-sis	die Dosis	-sal‡	das Schicksal
		-tät	die Pubertät	-tel	das Drittel
		-ung	die Zeitung	-tum	das Wachstum
		-ur	die Figur	-um	das Studium

* When referring to people.
† Except for weak masculine and masculine/neuter adjectival nouns (see 3.3).
‡ In about 70% of cases.

Table 2. The gender of nouns according to their meaning

MASC.	• Males:	der Mann, der Lehrer, der Löwe, der Kater, der Stier
	• Days, months, seasons:	der Montag, der April, der Herbst, der Winter
	• Points of compass and weather:	der Norden, der Süden, der Wind, der Hagel, der Regen
	• Many drinks:	der Tee, der Kaffee, der Saft, der Wein, der Cognac (but: das Wasser/Bier)
	• Makes of car:	der Volvo, der Audi, der BMW
FEM.	• Females:*	die Frau, die Mutter, die Tochter, die Katze, die Kuh
	• Trees and flowers:	die Tanne, die Birke, die Rose, die Nelke
	• Most native rivers:†	die Donau, die Elbe, die Ruhr (but: der Rhein)
	• Nouns denoting numbers and size:	die Eins, die Zwei, die Größe, die Breite, die Länge
NEUT.	• Young persons/animals:	das Baby, das Kind, das Kalb, das Ferkel, das Küken
	• Towns, countries,‡ continents:	das Berlin, das Deutschland, das Europa, das Afrika
	• Units of measurement:	das Kilo, das Gramm, das Pfund (das or der Liter, Meter)
	• Metals:	das Gold, das Silber, das Blei, das Eisen
	• Colours:	das Rot, das Blau etc.
	• Languages:	das Deutsch, das Englisch etc.
	• Letters of the alphabet:	das A, das B etc.

* Except diminutives in -chen/-lein: e.g. das Mädchen, das Fräulein.
† Rivers outside the German-speaking area are usually masculine, unless they end in -a or -e, in which case they are feminine: e.g. die Themse.
‡ There are some exceptions to this: e.g. die Schweiz, die Türkei, der Iran.

Occasionally these two main criteria (i.e. meaning and ending of word) may conflict when determining a noun's gender. For instance, nouns in -ei are usually feminine, yet der Papagei 'parrot' is masculine because it is a male animal; nouns in -er are usually masculine when referring to people, yet die Mutter and die Tochter are feminine as they are females. Conversely, a girl is a female person, yet it is das Mädchen because of the diminutive -chen.

1.3 FURTHER NOTES ON GENDER

i) Compound words. The gender of compounds is determined by the last element: e.g. *das Haus* + *die Frau* = **die** *Hausfrau*.

ii) Abbreviations. The gender of these is determined by that of the whole word: e.g. **die** *Limo* (< *die Limonade*), **das** *Labor* (< *das Laboratorium*), despite the fact that *-o* is usually neuter and *-or* usually masculine. In the case of whole phrases, the main noun determines the gender: e.g. **die** *SPD* (< *die Sozialistische **Partei** Deutschlands*).

iii) Regional variation. The gender of some words differs depending on whether the speaker is German, Austrian or Swiss: e.g. German *die Butter, das Radio* vs. Austrian *der Butter, der Radio*.

EXERCISES

Vocabulary topic: *Tiere*.

1 Fill in the gaps with *der, die* or *das* depending on the gender of the following noun:

1 ___ Hund ist weggelaufen. Jetzt hat ___ Katze ihre Ruhe.

2 Wie viele Eier hat ___ Henne gelegt? Vier. Aber ___ Fuchs hat sie kaputtgemacht.

3 Das ist ___ Männchen und das ist ___ Weibchen.

4 Hast du ___ Lamm gesehen? Wie süß!

5 Pass auf! Hier kommt ___ Stier.

6 ___ Hahn macht jeden morgen „Kikeriki"! Das weckt uns alle auf.

7 Schau! ___ kleine Entchen sucht ___ Ente.

8 Ist ___ Igel immer noch im Garten? Nein, aber ___ Hase des Nachbarn hüpft immer noch herum.

2 Out of the 30 words below, 10 are masculine, 10 are feminine and 10 are neuter. Rearrange the words into three columns according to their gender, bearing in mind the two main factors determining gender: i) ending of word; ii) meaning of word. Place *der, die, das* in front of each word as appropriate:

Bruder	Kind	Polizist
Blume	Frühling	Höhe
Schnee	Französisch	Osten
Foto	Whisky	Erde
Regierung	Viertel	Motor
Politik	Lesen	Geräusch
Liebling	Lehrer	Freundin
Gesundheit	Natur	Fräulein
Ereignis	Tourismus	Klima
Universität	Grün	Bäckerei

☞ **For further exercises on gender see Ch. 27, Exs. 4–5 and Revision Text 4, Ex. 2.**

2 | Noun plurals

---

*Beliebte **Rezepte** für **Gäste**:* Wurstgulasch mit Sauerkraut.

Portionen: 4. **Nährwerte**: pro Portion ca 656 Kcal 50g Fett.

Zutaten: 1 Fleischwurst (400g), 100g geräucherter durchwachsener Speck,
2 **Zwiebeln**, 1 Dose Sauerkraut, 1–2 **Esslöffel** Butterschmalz, 1 Dose rote **Bohnen**,
3/4 L. Brühe, 2 **Lorbeerblätter**, Salz, Pfeffer, Zucker, gemahlene **Nelken**, 150g
5 Crème fraîche.

Zubereitung: Die Fleischwurst aus der Haut lösen, längs vierteln und in etwa 2cm dicke
Scheiben schneiden. Speck würfeln. **Zwiebeln** abziehen und in feine **Spalten**
schneiden. Sauerkraut fein schneiden. Das Butterschmalz erhitzen und Speck und
Zwiebeln darin anbraten.
10 Die Fleischwurst dazugeben und kurz mit anbraten. Die **Bohnen** auf einem Sieb unter
fließendem kaltem Wasser abspülen. Sauerkraut, Brühe, **Bohnen** und **Lorbeerblätter**
dazugeben. Bei kleiner Hitze etwa 15 **Minuten** schmoren lassen. Mit Salz, Pfeffer,
Zucker und **Nelken**pulver abschmecken. Auf **Teller** verteilen und je einen Kleks
Crème fraîche daraufgeben.

Aus: *Brigitte*, 28. Februar 2001.

Noun plurals in the text

2.1 PLURAL FORMATION

There are seven ways of forming noun plurals in German, five of which are illustrated in the above text:

1. Add **-e:**　　　　　　　*Rezept-**e*** (title), *Nährwert**e*** (line 1)
2. Add **umlaut** and **-e:**　*Gäst-**e*** (title)
3. Add **–(e)n:**[3]　　　　　*Portion-**en*** (line 1), *Zutat-**en*** (2), *Zwiebel-**n*** (3, 7, 9), *Bohne-**n***
　　　　　　　　　　　　　(3, 10), *Nelke-**n*** (4, 13), *Scheibe-**n*** (7), *Spalte-**n*** (7), *Minute-**n*** (12)
4. Add **-er:**
　(and **umlaut** the　　　*Lorbeerblätt-**er*** (4, 11)
　vowel where possible)

---

[3] -*en* is reduced to -*n* after nouns ending in -*e*, -*el*, -*er*.

5. **No change:**[4]   *Esslöffel* (3), *Teller* (13)

In addition, there are two markers which are less widely used and therefore do not occur in our text:

6. Add **umlaut** alone: e.g. *Väter*, *Läden*
7. Add **-s**:   e.g. *Fotos*, *Babys*

As it is often not predictable which plural marker a certain noun may take, this information is always given in dictionaries, along with information about the noun's gender, so that students can learn the plural form together with the singular. It is, however, of some help to note that the choice of plural marker can sometimes be predicted on the basis of gender or phonological shape of the noun. These correlations will be dealt with in **2.2** below.

> [4] When the noun plural is the same as the singular, the difference is marked elsewhere, e.g. by changing the definite article: der Teller – **die** Teller.

Other points to note in the text

- Use of infinitive as an imperative: *lösen* (6), *vierteln* (6), *schneiden* (7, 8), *würfeln* (7), *abziehen* (7), *erhitzen* (8), *anbraten* (9, 10), *dazugeben* (10, 12), *abspülen* (11), *schmoren lassen* (12), *abschmecken* (13), *verteilen* (13), *daraufgeben* (14) (see footnote 53).
- Prepositions + case: **aus** <u>der</u> Haut (6), **in** ... dick<u>e</u> Scheiben (6–7), **in** fein<u>e</u> Spalten (7), **auf** ein<u>em</u> Sieb (10), **unter** fließend<u>em</u> kalt<u>em</u> Wasser (10–11), **bei** klein<u>er</u> Hitze (12), **auf** Teller (13). (see **24.1a–b**).
- Prepositions with da(r): *darin* (9), **dazu**geben (10, 12), **darauf**geben (14) (see **7.5**).

◢ Discover more about noun plurals

2.2   **GENERAL TENDENCIES: CORRELATION BETWEEN PLURAL MARKER AND GENDER/PHONOLOGICAL SHAPE OF NOUN**

Although, generally speaking, noun plurals must be learned individually, alongside their corresponding singulars, some general tendencies in their distribution can be observed which may be helpful to the foreign learner. These are given in Table 3.

Table 3. Noun plural markers

Marker	General use	
-e	Many **masculines**	e.g. *Tage*, *Hund<u>e</u>*
	Some neuters	e.g. *Jahr<u>e</u>*
⸚e	Many **masculines**	e.g. *Bäume*, *Köpf<u>e</u>*
	Some feminines	e.g. *Händ<u>e</u>*

Marker	General use	
-(e)n	Most **feminine** nouns (over 90%)	e.g. *Frauen, Blumen*
	All 'weak' nouns (see **3.3b**)	e.g. *Jungen, Polizisten*
	Some neuters	e.g. *Ohren*
‐er	Many **neuter** nouns	e.g. *Kinder, Länder*
	A few masculines	e.g. *Männer*
	No feminines	
-	Most nouns in **-er, -en, -el** (except feminines)	e.g. *Fenster, Wagen*
	Diminutives in **-chen, -lein**	e.g. *Händchen*
¨	Some masculines in *-er, -en, -el* with an umlautable vowel:	e.g. *Brüder, Väter*
	Two feminines:	*Mütter, Töchter*
-s	Most nouns ending in a **vowel** other than *-e*	e.g. *Autos, Omas*
	Some foreign loanwords*	e.g. *Champignons*

* People's names tend to be pluralised with -s: e.g. *Die Müllers* 'the Müllers'.

2.3   COMMON NOUNS AND THEIR PLURAL FORMS

Below is a list of frequently occurring German nouns (many of which are very often used in the plural) together with their plural forms which you should learn. Examine the extent to which the plurals correspond to the general tendencies set out in **Table 3**.

der Apfel – die Äpfel	*der Garten – die Gärten*	*der Student – die Studenten*
der Arm – die Arme	*der Herr – die Herren*	*der Stuhl – die Stühle*
der Baum – die Bäume	*der Hund – die Hunde*	*der Tag – die Tage*
der Brief – die Briefe	*der Junge – die Jungen*	*der Tisch – die Tische*
der Bruder – die Brüder	*der Kopf – die Köpfe*	*der Vater – die Väter*
der Bus – die Busse	*der Mann – die Männer*	*der Vogel – die Vögel*
der Chef – die Chefs	*der Mensch – die Menschen*	*der Wagen – die Wagen*
der Finger – die Finger	*der Monat – die Monate*	*der Weg – die Wege*
der Fisch – die Fische	*der Opa – die Opas*	*der Zahn – die Zähne*
der Freund – die Freunde	*der Schuh – die Schuhe*	*der Zeh – die Zehe*
der Fuß – die Füße	*der Sohn – die Söhne*	*der Zug – die Züge*
die Blume – die Blumen	*die Minute – die Minuten*	*die Stunde – die Stunden*
die Flasche – die Flaschen	*die Mutter – die Mütter*	*die Tasse – die Tassen*
die Fliege – die Fliegen	*die Nacht – die Nächte*	*die Tochter – die Töchter*
die Frau – die Frauen	*die Oma – die Omas*	*die Toilette – die Toiletten*
die Freundin – die Freundinnen	*die Pflanze – die Pflanzen*	*die Tür – die Türen*
die Hand – die Hände	*die Sekunde – die Sekunden*	*die Wand – die Wände*
die Katze – die Katzen	*die Schwester – die Schwestern*	*die Woche – die Wochen*
die Lippe – die Lippen	*die Stadt – die Städte*	*die Wohnung – die Wohnungen*
die Maus – die Mäuse	*die Straße – die Straßen*	*die Zeit – die Zeiten*

*das Auge – die Auge**n***	*das Büro – die Büro**s***	*das Kleid – die Kleid**er***
*das Auto – die Auto**s***	*das Ei – die Ei**er***	*das Land – die L**ä**nd**er***
*das Baby – die Baby**s***	*das Fenster – die Fenster*	*das Licht – die Licht**er***
*das Bein – die Bein**e***	*das Glas – die Gl**ä**s**er***	*das Mädchen – die Mädchen*
*das Bett – die Bett**en***	*das Haar – die Haar**e***	*das Ohr – die Ohr**en***
*das Bild – die Bild**er***	*das Haus – die H**ä**us**er***	*das Rad – die R**ä**d**er***
*das Blatt – die Bl**ä**tt**er***	*das Hotel – die Hotel**s***	*das Schiff – die Schiff**e***
*das Boot – die Boot**e***	*das Jahr – die Jahr**e***	*das Tuch – die T**ü**ch**er***
*das Buch – die B**ü**ch**er***	*das Kind – die Kind**er***	*das Zimmer – die Zimmer*

Note that *das Wort* has two plural forms depending on meaning: *die **Worte*** = words used together in a phrase or sentence, *die **Wörter*** = isolated words (e.g. in a dictionary).

2.4   VERB AGREEMENT

Noun plurals in German occur with plural forms of verbs: e.g. *Der Mann **kommt*** vs. *Die Männer **kommen***. One important difference from English, however, is that **collective nouns** (i.e. singular nouns which are used to refer to a group or collection of people or things) always occur with a **singular verb** in German while English often allows a plural verb: e.g. *Seine **Familie** war sehr freundlich* vs. 'His family were very friendly'; *Die **Polizei** hat ihn verhaftet* vs. 'The police have arrested him.'

✎ EXERCISES

Vocabulary topic: *Essen*

1 Put the nouns in the following shopping list into the plural. (The gender of each noun is given in brackets):[5]

Tomate (f)	Apfel (m)	12 Ei (n)	Vollwertnudel (f)
Zwiebel (f)	Weintraube (f)	6 Brötchen (n)	2 Dose (f) Thunfisch
Kartoffel (f)	Erdbeere (f)	4 Joghurt (m/nt)	Kaffeefilter (m)
Champignon (m)	Pfirsich (m)	2 Pizza (f)	2 Kiste (f) Bier
Kraut (n)	Dattel (f)	Bonbon (m/nt)	4 Flasche (f) Wein
Gewürz (n)	Erdnuss (f)	Muesliriegel (m)	verschiedene Fruchtsaft (f)

[5] Units of measurement such as *Gramm, Kilo, Liter* (and also *Stück*) are always used in the singular after a numeral, e.g. *2 **Kilo** Orangen, 4 **Liter** Milch, 6 **Stück** Kuchen*.

2 Complete the following recipe by filling in the gaps using the appropriate plural forms of the nouns in brackets:

Couscous mit Gemüse[6] und _____ [Rosine]

1. Couscous in eine Schüssel geben. Das Wasser bis auf vier _____ [Esslöffel] langsam dazugießen und den Couscous dabei mit einer Gabel durchrühren, bis er gleichmäßig feucht ist und keine _____ [Klümpchen] bildet. _____ [Rosine] im restlichen Wasser einweichen. Beide _____ [Zutat] zugedeckt quellen lassen.

[6] 'Vegetables' is plural in English but singular in German: *das Gemüse*.

2. Couscous nach 30 _____ [Minute] mit einer Gabel durchmischen, bis er wieder locker ist. In einem Topf knapp fingerhoch Wasser aufkochen. Die Hälfte der Butter in _____ [Stückchen] teilen und auf den Couscous legen. Bei schwächster Hitze eine Stunde dämpfen.

3. _____ [Lauchzwiebel], _____ [Paprikaschote] und _____ [Zucchini] waschen und putzen. _____ [Lauchzwiebel] mit dem saftigen Grün in etwa fingerdicke _____ [Stück], _____ [Schote] in _____ [Streifen], _____ [Zucchini] in etwa fingerlange _____ [Stift] schneiden.

4. Öl erhitzen, zerkleinertes Gemüse darin anbraten. Brühe zugießen. Abgetropfte _____ [Kichererbse] und _____ [Rosine] untermischen und erhitzen.

5. Während das Gemüse gart, _____ [Mandel] grob hacken und in der restlichen Butter rösten. Joghurt mit der Pepperonicreme und etwas Salz verrühren.

6. Gemüse in die Mitte einer großen Platte geben und mit den _____ [Mandel] bestreuen. Couscous in _____ [Häufchen] um das Gemüse setzen. Joghurt dazu servieren.

Für 4 _____ [Portion]. *Pro Portion: 775* _____ [Kalorie], *3242* _____ [Joule], *11,1g* _____ [Ballaststoff], *53 mg Cholesterin. Dauert insgesamt ca. 1½* _____ [Stunde].

Aus: Barbara Rias-Bucher, *Gesünder Leben – vegetarisch Essen*. ©1991 Verlag Zabert Sandmann.

✎ FURTHER EXERCISES

3 **Complete the following crossword. All answers are in the plural** (umlauts are indicated by the letter *e* following the relevant vowel, e.g. *Männer* = maenner):

Kreuzworträtsel

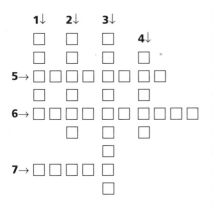

Senkrecht

1 Leute, die aus der ehemaligen DDR kommen.

2 Das, was man an den Füßen trägt.

3 Man kauft sie, um die Nachrichten zu lesen.

4 Man isst sie manchmal zum Tee oder Kaffee.

Waagerecht

5 Stücke, die vom Brot abgeschnitten worden sind.

6 Man braucht sie, um eine abgeschlossene Tür aufmachen zu können.

7 Das, was man manchmal auf dem Kopf trägt.

☞ **For further exercises on noun plurals see Ch. 3, Ex. 2, Ch. 5, Ex. 3 and Revision Text 1, Ex. 1.**

3 | Case[7]

<u>Deformiert Deutsch **das** Gesicht?</u>

Die vielen Umlaute in ihr**er** Sprache machen Deutsch**e** mürrisch und humorlos, ä,
ö und ü zögen Mundwinkel und Laune nach unten. Das behauptet **ein**
amerikanischer Psychologieprofessor.

London – Professor David Myers vom Hope College in Michigan hat demnach
5 bemerkt, dass sich **der** Mund bei **der** Aussprache deutscher Umlaute nach unten
verzieht. **Dies** führe zu ein**em** miesepetrigen Gesichtsausdruck und aktiviere
Muskeln, **die** „mit negativen Emotionen besetzt" seien. „**Das** kann **den**
Gemütszustand ein**er** Person signifikant beeinflussen", sagte Myers. „Es könnte
ein guter Grund dafür sein, dass Deutsch**e im** Ruf stehen, humorlos und
10 mürrisch zu sein." Sogar ihr**e** „Probleme, sich zuweilen mit anderen Länder**n**
in **der** Europäischen Union zu verständigen", ließen sich letztlich auf ä, ö und ü
zurückführen.

Das Englisch**e** mit sein**en** vielen e- und a-Laut**en** lasse **die** Menschen dagegen
fröhlich und hilfsbereit werden. **Die** an **der** Royal Society in Edinburgh
15 vorgestellte Theorie stieß **am** Freitag in Großbritannien auf großes Interesse.

Die „Times" und **der** „Daily Telegraph" illustrierten **die** Ausführungen **am**
Freitag auf ihr**en** Titelseiten mit Fotos ein**es** Mund**es**, **der** deutsche Umlaute
ausspricht, und ein**es** missmutig dreinblickenden Gerhard Schröder. **Die** „Daily
Mail" fragte auf Deutsch: „Sprechen **Sie** grumpy (mürrisch)?" und listete
20 deutsche Sprichwörter auf, bei **deren** Aussprache **man das** Gesicht besonders
unvorteilhaft verzieh**e**, etwa: „Unter **den** Blinden ist **der** Einäugige König." **Der**
„Daily Star" imitierte in sein**er** Überschrift ein**en** deutsch**en** Akzent: „It's the vay
ve talk zat makes us frown." (Unser**e** Sprechweise lässt **uns** so finster aussehen.)

Ein**e** Stellungnahme **der** deutschen Botschaft in London erhielt kein**e der**
25 Zeitungen. „Das ist zu wissenschaftlich", sagte **ein** Sprecher.

Aus: *Der Spiegel Online*, 25. August 2000.

---

[7] This chapter deals with case endings on articles, pronouns and nouns. Endings on adjectives are more
complex and will be dealt with separately in **Ch. 5**. A full list of article and adjective endings is given in
Appendix 2.

♀ Case shown in the text

3.1 USE OF CASE

In German, articles, pronouns, adjectives and some nouns have special endings depending on the case (nominative, accusative, genitive or dative), number (singular or plural) and gender (masculine, feminine, neuter) of the noun. Number and gender are integral features of the noun, while **case** is assigned depending on the noun's relationship to other elements in the sentence: i) to express relationships between words in a sentence, e.g. subject vs. object; ii) as a result of a particular word requiring a certain case, e.g. with prepositions.

3.1a Case expressing syntactic relationships between words

i) The **nominative** case is assigned to the **subject** of the sentence (i.e. the person or thing carrying out the action described by the verb): e.g. (with the verb underlined) *Der „Daily Star" imitierte* (21–22), *Die „Daily Mail" fragte auf Deutsch* (18–19), *Das Englische . . . lasse die Menschen* (13); (and with two different subjects) *Die „Times" und der „Daily Telegraph" illustrieren* (16).[8]

In English, the subject usually precedes the verb, but this is not always the case in German (see **26.2a**, **26.6**): e.g. *Das behauptet ein amerikanischer Psychologieprofessor* (2–3). We know that 'an American psychology professor' is the subject because he is the one carrying out the action described by the verb, i.e. 'claiming'. Similarly, where the verb is *sein* (or *werden*) the nominative is used: *Unter den Blinden ist der Einäugige König* (21), *Es könnte ein guter Grund dafür sein* (8–9). In the latter example, 'it could be a good reason for it', *es* and *ein guter Grund* are both subjects of the verb, as they both refer to the same thing.[9]

With longer sentences consisting of two or more clauses (i.e. a part of a sentence containing a finite verb of its own), there will be a subject (in the nominative case) for each finite verb: e.g. *Professor David Myers vom Hope College in Michigan hat demnach bemerkt, dass sich der Mund bei der Aussprache deutscher Umlaute nach unten verzieht* (4–6).

ii) The **accusative** case is assigned to the **direct object** of the sentence (i.e. the person or thing directly affected by the action described by the verb): e.g. *Das kann den Gemütszustand einer Person signifikant beeinflussen* (7–8), *Die „Times" und der „Daily Telegraph" illustrierten die Ausführungen* (16), *Der „Daily Star" imitierte in seiner Überschrift einen deutschen Akzent* (21–22).[10]

In English, direct objects usually follow the verb but this is not always the case in German (see **26.2b**, **26.6**): e.g. *Eine Stellungnahme . . . erhielt keine der Zeitungen* (24–25) shows that the object can come first.[11]

---

[8] The subject of a **passive** sentence is also in the nominative: e.g. *Der Daily Star wird verkauft* (see **18.2**).

[9] Contrast sentences such as *Es gibt einen guten Grund dafür*, where the verb is not *sein* and is followed by the accusative.

[10] This also applies when the subject is not mentioned, e.g. in requests: *Einen Kaffee, bitte!* (abbreviation of *Ich möchte einen Kaffee, bitte*). Similarly, expressions of time are usually in the accusative: e.g. *Ich habe ihn letzten Montag besucht*.

[11] This example from the text is misleading at first sight, as *eine* is used for the nominative and the accusative. A more obvious example would be with a masculine singular: e.g. *Den Eindruck hatte ich auch* 'I had that impression too'.

iii) The **dative** case is assigned to the **indirect object** of the sentence, i.e. the recipient (usually a person) of the <u>direct</u> object (usually a thing). This is often expressed using 'to' in English. Consider the following examples (not in the text), in which the direct object is underlined and the indirect object is in bold print: e.g. *Er gab* **dem Lehrer** <u>*einen Aufsatz*</u> 'He gave **the teacher** an essay/He gave an essay **to the teacher**', *Er erklärte* **seiner Freundin** <u>*das Problem*</u> 'He explained the problem **to his girlfriend**'.

iv) The use of the **genitive** in German is roughly equivalent to the use of the possessive *'s* in English (e.g. 'the man**'s** hat') or the use of the word *of* (e.g. 'her idea **of** a suitable partner'). The genitive tends to be used more in written and formal styles of spoken German, rather than in everyday spoken language where it is often replaced by the preposition *von* (+ dative): e.g. *ein Freund* **seines Bruders** vs. *ein Freund* **von** *seinem Bruder*. As our text is a written report it includes quite a few genitives: e.g. *den Gemütszustand* **einer Person** (7–8), *eine Stellungnahme* **der deutschen Botschaft** (24), *keine* **der Zeitungen** (24–25), *Fotos* **eines Mundes** (17), **eines** ... **Gerhard Schröder** (18), **deren** *Aussprache* (20). The last example is a relative pronoun meaning 'of which' or 'whose' (see **9.3b**).

Thus, to sum up, an example of a sentence with all cases present would be:

[**Der** Student]   *gab*   [**dem** Lehrer]   [**den** Aufsatz   **eines** Freund**es**]

SUBJ. (NOM.)   IND. OBJ. (DAT.)   OBJ. (ACC.)   'OF' GEN.

'The student gave the teacher a friend's essay'.

3.1b Case required by particular words

Certain words, most commonly prepositions, require the following noun/article/pronoun to appear in a particular case, even though there seems to be no apparent reason for this in terms of subject–object relations. In the text there are seven prepositions, all of which take a particular case: *in* + dat. *in* **ihrer** *Sprache* (1), **im** *Ruf* (9), *in* **der** *Europäischen Union* (11), *in* **seiner** *Überschrift* (22); <u>*bei*</u> + dat. *bei* **der** *Aussprache* (5); <u>*zu*</u> + dat. *zu* **einem** *miesepetrigen Gesichtsausdruck* (6); <u>*mit*</u> + dat. *mit* **seinen** *vielen* ... *Lauten* (13); *an* + dat.: *an* **der** *Royal Society* (14), *a***m** *Freitag* (15, 16–17), <u>*auf*</u> + dat. *auf* **ihren** *Titelseiten* (17); <u>*unter*</u> + dat. *unter* **den** *Blinden* (21).[12] As case is unpredictable here it must be learnt together with the individual preposition (see **Tables 21–22** for a list of common prepositions with their case).

---

[12] *An, auf, in, unter* can also take the accusative (see **24.1b** for details).

3.1c Scope of assigned case

Sometimes an accusative, dative or genitive object can consist of more than one noun (or pronoun), which means that their articles/pronouns **all** have to be marked with the appropriate case, even if some of them come much later in the sentence: e.g. *Fotos* **eines** *Mundes, der deutsche Umlaute ausspricht, und* **eines** *missmutig dreinblickenden Gerhard Schröder* (17–18); *Ich habe* **den** *Mann gesehen:* **den** *Freund von meiner Tochter* (not in text). Similarly, if a preposition has scope over more than one noun, the related articles/pronouns must all have the same case ending: e.g. *Er hat sich mit* **seiner** *Mutter,* **seinem** *Vater und sogar* **seinem** *besten Freund gestritten* (not in text).

3.2 CASE ENDINGS

In German, case is shown on articles and pronouns. It is only shown on nouns in the genitive singular masculine and neuter (-*(e)s*) [13] and in the dative plural (-*n*).[14] (For case on adjectives see **Tables 7–9** and for weak and adjectival nouns see **3.3**). **Table 4** shows case endings on definite articles and **Table 5** shows case endings on indefinite articles. As you can see, the endings are very similar for both. Students are advised to learn these different case forms in the context of a whole phrase.

---

[13] -*es* is added to words ending in -*s*, -*sch*, -*ß*, -*st*, -*t* and also tends to be added to words of one syllable (e.g. *Tages*, *Freundes*), while -*s* (without an apostrophe!) is added elsewhere (e.g. *Lehrers*), although there is variability in some one-syllable words (e.g. *Krieges/Kriegs*). Proper names, including people's names and names of countries, usually have -*s*, unless they occur with the article, in which case there is no ending: e.g. *Gerhard Schröders Kabinett* versus *eines missmutig dreinblickenden Gerhard Schröder* (18–19). From this example we can see that people's names in the genitive without an article tend to **precede** the noun. Names of countries may precede or, particularly in written German, follow the noun.

[14] -*n* is not added if the noun plural already ends in -*n*.

3.2a The definite article

Table 4. Forms of the definite article

	Masc.		Fem.		Neut.		Plural	
N		**der** *Mann*	**die** *Frau*			**das** *Kind*	**die** *Kinder*	
A	*ich sehe* **den** *Mann*	*ich sehe* **die** *Frau*	*ich sehe* **das** *Kind*	*ich sehe* **die** *Kinder*
D	*ich sage* **dem** *Mann*	*ich sage* **der** *Frau*	*ich sage* **dem** *Kind*	*ich sage* **den** *Kinder***n**
G	*das Bild* **des** *Manne***s**	*das Bild* **der** *Frau*	*das Bild* **des** *Kinde***s**	*das Bild* **der** *Kinder*

Common pronouns which follow the pattern of **Table 4** are the demonstratives ***dieser*** *diese, dieses, diesen* etc. 'this',[15] ***jener***, *jene, jenes* etc. 'that', ***jeder***, *jede, jedes* etc. 'each/every', ***welcher?***, *welche?, welches?* etc. 'which', and the **relative pronouns** which are identical to the definite articles (except for the genitive, e.g. *deren Aussprache*, and the dative plural, see **9.3**). ***Viel*** 'a lot/many' and ***wenig*** 'few' have no ending in the singular but follow the same endings as the definite article in all the plural forms: e.g. *viel Zeit* vs. *viele, vielen, viel***er** *Frauen*.

Some examples from the text are: nom. ***der*** *Mund* (5), ***die*** *„Times"* (16), ***das*** *Englische* (13), ***die*** *vielen Umlaute* (1); acc. ***den*** *Gemützustand* (7–8), ***das*** *Gesicht* (20), ***die*** *Ausführungen* (16); dat. a**m** *Freitag* (16–17) [***dem*** → -*m* after certain prepositions], ***der*** *Aussprache* (5), ***den*** *Blinden* (21), *Länder***n** (10); gen. ***der*** *deutschen Botschaft* (24), ***der*** *Zeitungen* (24–25).

---

[15] *Dies* 'this', without an ending, is used to refer to a whole idea rather than a particular noun: ***Dies*** *führe zu einem miesepetrigen Gesichtsausdruck* (6) '**this** (i.e. the pronunciation of German umlauts) leads to a grumpy look'. Similarly, *das* is used to mean 'that' in a general sense: ***Das*** *kann den Gemützustand einer Person signifikant beeinflussen* (7–8) '**that** can significantly influence a person's mood'.

3.2b The indefinite article

Table 5. Forms of the indefinite article

	Masc.			Fem.			Neut.		
N		*ein*	*Mann*		*eine*	*Frau*		*ein*	*Kind*
A	*ich sehe*	*einen*	*Mann*	*ich sehe*	*eine*	*Frau*	*ich sehe*	*ein*	*Kind*
D	*ich sage*	*einem*	*Mann*	*ich sage*	*einer*	*Frau*	*ich sage*	*einem*	*Kind*
G	*das Bild*	*eines*	*Mannes*	*das Bild*	*einer*	*Frau*	*das Bild*	*eines*	*Kindes*

i) Pronouns taking the same form. Common pronouns which follow the pattern of **Table 5** are **kein** 'not a/no' and the possessives **mein, dein, sein, unser, euer, ihr** (see **7.2**), although these also have plural forms, which the indefinite article does not have: *keine* (nom./acc.), *keinen* (dat.), *keiner* (gen.).[16]

    Some examples from the text are: nom. **ein** *Sprecher* (25), **keine** *der Zeitungen* (24–25), **unsere** *Sprechweise* (23), **ihre** *Probleme* (10); acc.: **einen** *deutschen Akzent* (22), **eine** *Stellungnahme* (24); dat. **einem** *miespeterigen Gesichtsausdruck* (6), **ihrer** *Sprache* (1), **seiner** *Überschrift* (22); gen. **eines** *Mundes* (17), **einer** *Person* (8).

> [16] Personal pronouns, e.g. *ich, du* etc., have their own case forms and are dealt with in **7.1**. See 'Other points to note . . .' for the personal pronouns in the text.

ii) Indefinite articles used as pronouns. Sometimes a noun may be omitted but still understood, e.g. 'I'm looking for a pen but can't find **one** [i.e. a pen]'. In this case, the indefinite article stands in for the noun and has the same endings as it would have had if the noun had been present: e.g. *Ich habe zwei Äpfel. Möchten Sie* **einen**? [< *einen Apfel*]. Exceptions are the **masc. nom. sg.** and the **neuter nom./acc. sg.**, which have the endings -**er** and -(**e**)**s** respectively, e.g. (not in text):

Hast du einen Bleistift? – Ja, hier ist **einer**.   [NOT *hier ist ein].

Ich habe frische Brötchen geholt. Möchtest du **eines**?[17]   [Usually pronounced (and often written) **eins**]

> [17] 'One thing' is usually rendered by *eines/eins*: e.g. *Ein(e)s steht fest, . . .* 'One thing is certain, . . .'.

Other points to note in the text

- Adjective endings: *viel**en*** (1, 13), *amerikanisch**er*** (3), *deutsch**er*** (5), *miesepetrig**en*** (6), *negativ**en*** (7), *gut**er*** (9), *Europäisch**en*** (11), *groß**es*** (15), *deutsch**e*** (17, 20), *dreinblickend**en*** (18) *deutsch**en*** (22, 24) (see **Ch. 5**).
- Expanded attribute: *die an der Royal Society in Edinburgh vorgestellt**e** Theorie* (14–15) (see **5.3**).
- Adverbs: *signifikant* (8), *missmutig* (18), *unvorteilhaft* (21) (see **5.6**).
- Personal pronouns: *Sie* (19), *uns* (23) and impersonal *man* (20) (see **7.1**).

- Subjunctive in reported speech: Konjunktiv I: *führe* (6), *seien* (7), *lasse* (13), *verziehe* (21); Konjunktiv II: *zögen* (2), *ließen* (11) (see **Ch. 17**).
- Konjunktiv II as conditional: *könnte* (8) (see **16.3**).

▲ *Discover more about case*

3.3 CASE ON NOUNS

As a rule, case is only shown on nouns in the genitive singular masculine/neuter, e.g. *des Arbeiters*, *des Hauses*, and in the dative plural, e.g. *den Häusern*.[18] However, there are also certain types of noun which always have case endings: a) adjectival nouns; b) 'weak' nouns.

[18] The dative singular ending -e can be found in older texts (see lines 8, 9 and 16 of text in **Ch. 6**), but is now regarded as old-fashioned and is only used in set phrases: e.g. *zu Hause*.

3.3a Adjectival nouns

These are nouns derived from adjectives, e.g. *der Alte* 'the old man', *der Blinde* 'the blind man', and consequently take the same case (and gender and number) endings as **adjectives** (see **5.1–5.2** for adjective endings and **5.5** for adjectival nouns). There are some examples of adjectival nouns in our text: e.g. nom. *Deutsche* (10), *das Englische*, *der Einäugige* (22), acc. *Deutsche* (1), dat. *den Blinden* (21–22), although the dative case marking is not visible in the last example as the nominative plural also ends in *-en*.

3.3b 'Weak' nouns

German has a small group of masculine[19] nouns which have the ending **-en** (*-n* after vowels and after *-r* in an unstressed syllable) in all but the nominative singular form: e.g. *der Mensch – den Menschen – dem Menschen – des Menschen – die Menschen* etc. These nouns are traditionally known as 'weak' and often refer to male humans and animals. Some common examples are (in the accusative singular):

- Most masculines with a nom. sg. **ending in -e**: e.g. *den Affe-n* 'monkey/ape', *den Bursche-n* 'lad/fellow', *den Junge-n* 'boy', *den Löwe-n* 'lion', *den Postbote-n* 'postman'.
- Most masculines with a nom. sg. **ending in a stressed suffix of foreign origin**: e.g. *-ent/-ant/-ist*: e.g. *den Student-en* 'student', *den Polizist-en* 'policeman'.
- A small group of masculines with no ending in nom. sg.: e.g. *den Bär-en* 'bear', *den Mensch-en* 'person', *den Nachbar-n* 'neighbour'.[20]

The following variations are noteworthy:

Nom.	*der Herr*	*der Name*
Acc.	*den Herrn*	*den Namen*
Dat.	*dem Herrn*	*dem Namen*
Gen.	*des Herrn*	*des Namens*
All plural forms:	*die Herren*	*die Namen*

[19] One neuter noun, *Herz* 'heart', has some weak endings; *das Herz, dem Herzen – des Herzen* (plural *Herzen*).

[20] In colloquial German the weak endings are often dropped: e.g. *den Student/Polizist/Nachbar* etc.

3.4 VERBS TAKING A DATIVE OR GENITIVE OBJECT

Some verbs always require their objects to be in the dative or, less commonly, the genitive. Some general rules can be given for this, but there is also a considerable number of verbs to which the rules do not apply, particularly with regard to dative objects, which are required by a relatively large group of verbs. This means that these verbs must be learnt together with their dative objects. **Table 6** lists some common examples.

3.4a Verbs taking a dative object

These tend to correspond with English verbs taking 'to' before the object:[21]

einfallen 'to come to mind/occur to': e.g. *Die Lösung* **fällt** <u>dem</u> *Student(en)* **ein**.
erklären 'to explain to': e.g. *Ich* **erkläre** <u>dem</u> *Polizist(en), was passiert ist.*
gehören 'to belong to': e.g. *Es* **gehört** <u>dem</u> *Chef.*
geschehen/passieren 'to happen to': *Es* **geschieht/passiert** *mein<u>em</u> Sohn.*
sagen 'to say to':[22] e.g. *Ich* **sage** <u>dem</u> *Verkäufer, was ich möchte.*
vorkommen 'to seem to': e.g. *Es* **kommt** <u>dem</u> *Lehrer* **vor**, *als ob das Kind schläft.*

Some of these take two objects at the same time: an accusative object (usually a thing) and a dative object (usually a person or animal): e.g. *Ich* **erklärte** *dem Chef meinen Plan.* Similarly, *Ich* **gab** *dem Hund einen Ball; Ich* **schenkte** *meiner Schwester ein Handy zum Geburtstag.*

---

[21] Adjectives used with 'to' also often take the dative: e.g. *dem Mann* **behilflich** 'helpful to the man'. Also: *ähnlich* 'similar to', *angenehm* 'pleasant to', *bekannt* 'known to', *dankbar* 'thankful to', *fremd* 'strange to', *klar* 'clear/obvious to', *lästig* 'troublesome', *nahe* 'close to', *wichtig* 'important to'.

[22] Verbs of saying often take the dative: e.g. *Ich sage/erzähle/antworte/widerspreche dem Lehrer.*

Table 6. Other common verbs taking a dative object

ich **antworte** *dem Lehrer*	'answer'	*ich* **helfe** *dem Kind*	'help'
ich **begegne** *dem Nachbarn*	'meet/run into'	*ich* **laufe** *dem Hund* **nach***	'run after/chase'
ich **danke** *dem Kellner*	'thank'	*es* **macht** *dem Vater* **Sorgen**	'it worries the father'
ich **drohe** *dem Kind*	'threaten'	*es* **macht** *dem Kind* **Spaß**	'the child enjoys it'
sie **fehlt** *ihrem Freund*	'her friend misses her'	*ich* **nähere** *mich dem Haus*	'approach'
ich **folge** *dem Auto*	'follow'	*der Hut* **passt** *dem Mann*	'suit/fit'
es **gefällt** *dem Chef*	'the boss likes it'	*es* **schadet** *dem Wald*	'harm/damage'
ich **gehorche** *meinem Vater*	'obey'	*es* **schmeckt** *dem Gast*	'the guest likes it'
ich **gratuliere** *dem Ehepaar*	'congratulate'	*ich* **traue** *dem Arzt*	'trust'
es **gelingt** *dem Autor*	'the author succeeds'	*es* **tut** *dem Mann* **Leid**	'the man is sorry'
ich **glaube** *dem Arzt*	'believe'	*es* **tut** *dem Patienten* **weh**	'it hurts the patient'

* Verbs prefixed with *nach-, bei-, ent(gegen)-, wider-, zu-* take the dative.

3.4b Verbs taking the genitive

These tend to correspond to English verbs taking 'of' before the object:[23]

bedürfen 'to be in need of' : e.g. *Sie **bedürfen** eines Arztes.*
sich schämen 'to be ashamed of': e.g. *Er **schämt sich** seines Benehmens.*
sich vergewissern 'to make sure of': e.g. *Er **vergewissert sich** seines Erfolgs.*

The use of the genitive here is restricted to more formal written language. In speech, prepositions (or different verbs) would be used instead: e.g. *Sie **brauchen** einen Arzt, Er schämt sich **wegen** seines Benehmens.*

[23] A few adjectives with 'of' take the genitive: *meines Fehlers* **bewusst** 'conscious of my mistake'. Also: *gewiss* 'certain of', *müde* 'tired of', *schuldig* 'guilty of', *sicher* 'sure of'.

✎ EXERCISES

Vocabulary topic: *Emotionen*

1 Put the bracketed words into the correct case:

1 Ich liebe [der Mann] [meine Schwester].
2 Ich weiß, dass [der Junge] geweint hat.
3 Sie hasst [der Chef].
4 Schlecht gelaunt ist [mein Vater] nie!
5 Er beneidet [der Freund] [das Nachbarmädchen].
6 Fröhlich gab sie [die Kinder] [ein Kuss].
7 Das ist [ein] von [die Nachbarn], nicht wahr? Er sieht sehr traurig aus.
8 Ich habe [die Assistentin] erklärt, dass [der Chef] nicht sehr geduldig ist.
9 Damit macht [der Junge] [sein Vater] sehr glücklich.
10 Das Gesicht [der Lehrer] war rot vor Wut.

2 Put the underlined nouns into the plural and change the other words in the sentence as appropriate:

Example: Leidenschaftlich gab sie dem <u>Mann</u> einen Kuss.
Answer: Leidenschaftlich gab sie **den Männern** einen Kuss.

1 Er hat Angst vor dem <u>Lehrer</u>.
2 Sie schrie den <u>Hund</u> wütend an.
3 Ich sagte der <u>Mutter</u>, dass das <u>Kind</u> böse war.
4 Verärgert erklärte ich dem <u>Arbeiter</u> die Ursache des <u>Problems</u>.
5 Warum muss die <u>Frau</u> in diesem Büro immer über ihre Gefühle reden?
6 Er macht seinem <u>Freund</u> Sorgen.

✎ FURTHER EXERCISES

3 The verbs in bold print take either an accusative object, a dative object or both. According to each verb, put the bracketed words into the correct case:

1 Ich **sagte** [die Kollegen], dass ich krank war.

2 Ich **fragte** [der Arzt], ob er mir etwas geben könnte.

3 Der Schüler wollte [der Lehrer] nicht **antworten**.

4 Er **schenkte** [sein Vater] [ein Pullover] zu Weihnachten.

5 Ich habe versucht [meine Nachbarin] zu **helfen**.

6 Es würde [meine Frau] sehr **freuen**, wenn Sie sie besuchen würden.

7 Mmm! Hast du Plätzchen gekauft? Ja, aber ich **habe** nur [ein] übrig.

8 Er **folgte** [eine] [die Studentinnen] nach Hause.

9 **Schmeckt** [die Kinder] der Saft?

10 Du musst [die Eltern] **gehorchen**!

11 Wir **suchen** [ein] von den Gästen. Er heißt Benno Andlinger.

12 Er **gratulierte** [sein Onkel] zum Geburtstag.

13 Ich bin [eine Freundin] in der Stadt **begegnet**.

14 Wir haben [ein Ausflug] **gemacht**. Es hat [die Schüler] sehr **gefallen**.

15 Wer hat [das Kind] [dieser Witz] **erzählt**?

4 Make genitive constructions out of the following (more colloquial) sentences with von. Note that particularly 3, 6 and 7 sound much better in the genitive than with von:

1 Das ist das Auto von einem Freund.

2 Das ist die Frau von Peter.

3 Es war die Idee von der Chefin.

4 Hast du die Bücher von Anna gesehen?

5 Was ist die Hauptstadt von Brasilien?

6 Ich bin mit dem Fortschritt von den Kindern sehr zufrieden.

7 Der Film handelt vom Untergang von der „Titanic".

5 Some of the following nouns are 'weak'. Add an ending only where appropriate:

1 Gestern war ich beim Nachbar__.

2 Wir zeigten dem Kunde__ unsere Ware.

3 Er gab dem Taxifahrer__ Trinkgeld.

4 Kennen Sie Herr__ Becker? Meinen Sie den Journalist__?

5 Das Kind zeichnete einen Löwe__, einen Tiger__, einen Elephant__, einen Bär__ und einen Hund__.

6 Er sprach mit dem Kommissar__ und seinem Kollege__.

7 Das ist die Wohnung des Student__.

8 Wo ist das Büro des Professor__?

6 Complete the following text by using the correct gender, number and case forms of the articles/pronouns in bold print. Some (but not all!) of the nouns in bold also need changing. If you don't know the gender of a particular noun, look it up in a dictionary. For case after prepositions see Ch. 24:

»Herr Samsa«, rief nun **d__ Prokurist** mit erhobener Stimme, »was ist denn los? Sie verbarrikadieren sich da in **Ihr__** Zimmer, antworten bloß mit ja und nein, machen **Ihr__**

Eltern schwere, unnötige Sorgen und versäumen – dies nur nebenbei erwähnt – **Ihr__** geschäftlichen Pflichten in **ein__** eigentlich unerhörten Weise. Ich spreche hier im Namen **Ihr__ Eltern** und **Ihr__ Chef** und bitte Sie ganz ernsthaft um **ein__** augenblickliche, deutliche Erklärung. Ich staune, ich staune. Ich glaubte Sie als **ein__** ruhigen, vernünftigen **Mensch** zu kennen, und nun scheinen Sie plötzlich anfangen zu wollen, mit sonderbaren Launen zu paradieren [. . .]«.

Gregor sah ein, dass er **d__ Prokurist** in **dies__** Stimmung auf keinen Fall weggehen lassen dürfe, wenn dadurch **sein__** Stellung im Geschäft nicht aufs Äußerste gefährdet werden sollte. **D__** Eltern verstanden das alles nicht so gut; sie hatten sich in **d__** langen **Jahre d__** Überzeugung gebildet, dass Gregor in **dies__** Geschäft für **sein__** Leben versorgt war, und hatten außerdem jetzt mit **d__** augenblicklichen Sorgen so viel zu tun, dass ihnen jede Voraussicht abhanden gekommen war. Aber Gregor hatte **dies__** Voraussicht. **D__ Prokurist** musste gehalten, beruhigt, überzeugt und schließlich gewonnen werden; die Zukunft **Gregor** und **sein__** Familie hing doch davon ab!

Aus: Franz Kafka, *Die Verwandlung*.

☞ **For further exercises on case after prepositions see Ch. 24, Ex. 1, and for general exercises on case see Revision Texts 1 (Ex. 2), 2 (Exs 1–2), 3 (Ex. 1), and 4 (Ex. 3).**

4 | Use of articles

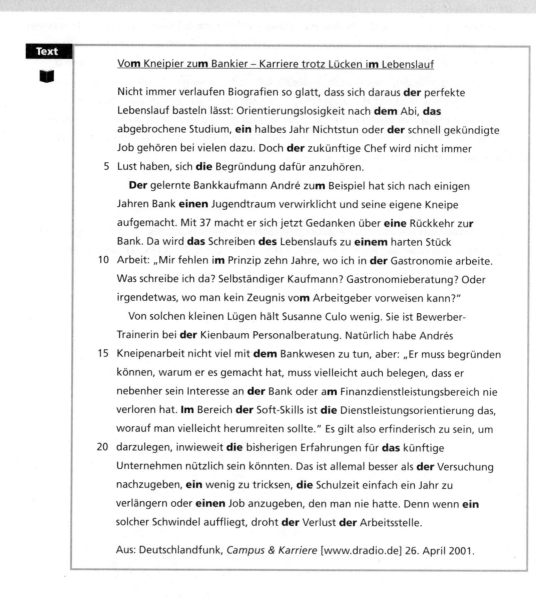

Vom Kneipier zu**m** Bankier – Karriere trotz Lücken i**m** Lebenslauf

Nicht immer verlaufen Biografien so glatt, dass sich daraus **der** perfekte Lebenslauf basteln lässt: Orientierungslosigkeit nach **dem** Abi, **das** abgebrochene Studium, **ein** halbes Jahr Nichtstun oder **der** schnell gekündigte Job gehören bei vielen dazu. Doch **der** zukünftige Chef wird nicht immer
5　Lust haben, sich **die** Begründung dafür anzuhören.

　　Der gelernte Bankkaufmann André zu**m** Beispiel hat sich nach einigen Jahren Bank **einen** Jugendtraum verwirklicht und seine eigene Kneipe aufgemacht. Mit 37 macht er sich jetzt Gedanken über **eine** Rückkehr zu**r** Bank. Da wird **das** Schreiben **des** Lebenslaufs zu **einem** harten Stück
10　Arbeit: „Mir fehlen i**m** Prinzip zehn Jahre, wo ich in **der** Gastronomie arbeite. Was schreibe ich da? Selbständiger Kaufmann? Gastronomieberatung? Oder irgendetwas, wo man kein Zeugnis vo**m** Arbeitgeber vorweisen kann?"

　　Von solchen kleinen Lügen hält Susanne Culo wenig. Sie ist Bewerber-Trainerin bei **der** Kienbaum Personalberatung. Natürlich habe Andrés
15　Kneipenarbeit nicht viel mit **dem** Bankwesen zu tun, aber: „Er muss begründen können, warum er es gemacht hat, muss vielleicht auch belegen, dass er nebenher sein Interesse an **der** Bank oder a**m** Finanzdienstleistungsbereich nie verloren hat. **Im** Bereich **der** Soft-Skills ist **die** Dienstleistungsorientierung das, worauf man vielleicht herumreiten sollte." Es gilt also erfinderisch zu sein, um
20　darzulegen, inwieweit **die** bisherigen Erfahrungen für **das** künftige Unternehmen nützlich sein könnten. Das ist allemal besser als **der** Versuchung nachzugeben, **ein** wenig zu tricksen, **die** Schulzeit einfach ein Jahr zu verlängern oder **einen** Job anzugeben, den man nie hatte. Denn wenn **ein** solcher Schwindel auffliegt, droht **der** Verlust **der** Arbeitsstelle.

Aus: Deutschlandfunk, *Campus & Karriere* [www.dradio.de] 26. April 2001.

♀ Use of articles in the text

4.1　SIMILAR USAGE IN GERMAN AND ENGLISH

By and large, definite and indefinite articles are used in much the same way in German as they are in English. Some examples from the text are:

- *dass sich daraus **der** perfekte Lebenslauf basteln lässt* (1–2)

  that **the** perfect CV can be made out of it

- *sein Interesse an **der** Bank* (17)

  his interest in **the** bank

- *besser als **der** Versuchung nachzugeben* (21–22)

  better than giving in to **the** temptation

- ***einen** Job anzugeben, den man nie hatte* (23)

  to put down **a** job that you never had

- *wenn **ein** solcher Schwindel auffliegt* (23–24)

  if such **a** trick is discovered

There are, however, a few differences, some of which depend on the context and cannot be captured in terms of a hard-and-fast rule, while others can be expressed in terms of tendencies, the most noticeable being: i) the **definite** article is used much more in German than in English; ii) the **indefinite** article is absent in certain constructions in German. These tendencies will be outlined in **4.2** and **4.3** below.

4.2 DEFINITE ARTICLE IN GERMAN VERSUS NO ARTICLE IN ENGLISH

4.2a With infinitival nouns

- *Da wird **das** <u>Schreiben</u> des Lebenslaufs zu einem harten Stück Arbeit* (9–10)

  Writing the CV becomes hard work

4.2b With nouns denoting arts, science or vocational subjects[24]

- *wo ich in **der** <u>Gastronomie</u> arbeite* (10)

  where I work in gastronomy

- *nicht viel mit **dem** <u>Bankwesen</u> zu tun* (15)

  not much to do with banking

- *im Bereich **der** <u>Soft-Skills</u>* (18)

  in the area of soft skills

[24] Yet this tends not to be the case with traditional school and university subjects, e.g. *Mathe, Physik, Geschichte, Musik,* or after the verbs *studieren, lernen* etc., e.g. *Er studiert Gastronomie.*

4.2c After nouns following prepositions, where the article is in its contracted form

It is common to use a definite article after a preposition if the article can appear in its contracted form: e.g. *i**m**, in**s**, a**m**, vo**m**, zu**m**, zu**r**.* This is particularly frequent in spoken German and in **less formal styles** of the written language. For instance, *vo**m** Kneipier zu**m** Bankier* (title) is a less formal alternative to *von Kneipier zu Bankier* 'from publican to banker'.

4.2d Instead of the possessive

German often uses a definite article when English would prefer a possessive: e.g. *Er hat eine Tätowierung auf **dem** Rücken* 'He has a tattoo on **his** back'. This is particularly the case with parts of the body and clothes, but also can be seen elsewhere. In our text there are a few occasions where a definite article may more naturally correspond to a possessive in English:

- *wo man kein Zeugnis vo**m** Arbeitgeber vorweisen kann* (12)

  where you (one) cannot produce references from **your** (one's) employer

- *inwieweit **die** bisherigen Erfahrungen . . . nützlich sein könnten* (20–21)

  to what extent **your** (one's) previous experience could be useful . . .

- ***die** Schulzeit . . . zu verlängern* (22–23)

  to extend **your** (one's) time in education

4.2e In some common set phrases with a preposition (cf. 4.2c above)

- *zu**m** Beispiel* (6)[25]   for example
- *i**m** Prinzip* (10)   in principle

> [25] This is not an absolute rule, however: e.g. *zu Fuß* 'on foot'.

4.3 NO INDEFINITE ARTICLE IN GERMAN

i) One major difference between English and German with respect to the use of the indefinite article occurs with the names of **professions, religions** and **nationalities** where the indefinite article is present in English but not in German after the verbs *sein, werden, bleiben*: e.g. 'He's **an** Englishman' versus *Er ist Engländer*. There is an example of this in the text which refers to a profession: *Sie ist Bewerber-Trainerin* (13–14) 'She is a job application trainer'. If, however, an **adjective** is used before the noun in question, the indefinite article is used: e.g. *Sie ist **eine** fleißige Bewerber-Trainerin*.[26]

ii) German usually has no indefinite article after *als* when it means 'as': e.g. *Als Kind war er immer krank* 'He was always ill as a child'.

> [26] The heading of the text also contains an example of an omitted indefinite article, i.e. before *Karriere*, although this is probably due to the fact that it is a headline and German, like English, regularly drops articles in headlines, titles, advertisements etc.

Other points to note in the text

- Verb taking dative object: *besser als **der** Versuchung nachzugeben* (22–23).
- Past participles used as adjectives: *abgebrochene* (3), *gekündigte* (3), *gelernte* (6).
- Reflexive pronoun (in the dative) used together with an accusative object: ***sich** die Begründung dafür anzuhören* (5), ***sich** . . . einen Jugendtraum verwirklicht* (6-7), *macht er **sich** jetzt Gedanken* (8) (see footnote 98, reflexives).
- Construction with *sich lassen* + infinitive (1-2) corresponding to a passive in English: '. . . that the perfect CV can be made of it' (see footnote 105, modals).
- *Da(r)*- plus preposition: *daraus* (1), *dazu* (4), *dafür* (5) (see **7.5**).
- Infinitival nouns: *Nichtstun* (3), *das Schreiben* (9) (see **27.5a**).
- Noun compounds: *Lebenslauf* (2, 9), *Bankkaufmann* (6), *Jugendtraum* (7), *Gastronomieberatung* (11), *Arbeitgeber* (12), *Bewerber-Trainerin* (13–14), *Personalberatung* (14), *Kneipenarbeit* (15), *Bankwesen* (16), *Finanzdienstleistungsbereich* (17), *Dienstleistungsorientierung* (18), *Schulzeit* (22), *Arbeitsstelle* (24) (see **27.4**).

◭ Discover more about the use of articles

4.4 PREFERENCE FOR DEFINITE ARTICLE IN GERMAN

As mentioned in **4.1–4.2** above, the definite article is used in many more contexts in German than it is in English. The most common of these are outlined below:

4.4a Days, months, seasons

Er kommt am Montag/im April[27]   He's coming on Monday/in April
Mir gefällt der Herbst besser als der Sommer   I like autumn better than summer

[27] Yet the article is not needed if no preposition is used: e.g. *Januar ist der erste Monat des Jahres.*

4.4b Meals

Habe ich das Frühstück verpasst?   Have I missed breakfast?
Was gibt es zum Abendessen?   What's for dinner?

4.4c Lakes, mountains and planets

Sie bestiegen den Mount Everest   They climbed Mount Everest
Der Luganer See ist sehr schön   Lake Lugano is very beautiful

4.4d Street names

Er wohnt in der Steinfurterstrasse   He lives in Steinfurt Street
Ich warte auf dem Berliner Platz   I'll wait on Berlin Square

4.4e Feminine and plural names of countries and regions[28]

Er kommt aus der Türkei   He comes from Turkey
Wir fahren in die Schweiz   We're going to Switzerland

By contrast, the more common neuter countries, e.g. *Deutschland, England, Frankreich, Spanien,* do not have an article, unless they are prededed by an **adjective**: e.g. *das vereinigte Deutschland* 'unified Germany'.

[28] Plural examples are *Die Niederlande* 'The Netherlands', *Die USA* 'the USA' (= *die Staaten*). With the small number of masculine countries the definite article is optional: e.g. *Er wohnt im* (or *in*) *Iran.*

4.4f Institutions and buildings

Er geht in die Arbeit/Schule/Kirche/Uni   He goes to work/school/church/university/
ins Gefängnis/in den Kindergarten   prison/nursery

4.4g Names of languages

The article is used particularly when referring to translating from one into another, or where a genitive is needed. Here, the noun declines like an adjective.

eine Übersetzung aus dem Deutschen ins Französische   a translation from German to French
die Wichtigkeit des Englischen   the importance of English

In most other contexts, the article is not used and the noun has no ending: e.g. *Er spricht/lernt Deutsch; Er sagte es auf Deutsch.*

4.4h Some abstract nouns

The use of the definite article before abstract nouns is extremely variable and context-dependent. It tends to be preferred before nouns that are frequently used and very familiar to the speaker (unless the sentence is a generalisation or saying/idiom). It also tends to be preferred after a preposition (but, again, this is not always the case):

Das *Alter spielt keine Rolle*   Age doesn't matter
*Sie würde alles für **die** Schönheit tun*   She would do anything for beauty

Abstract nouns that commonly appear with the definite article are infinitival nouns (see **4.2a**) and, to a lesser extent, nouns denoting arts, science or vocational subjects (see **4.2b**).

4.4i   Nouns in the genitive or dative when the case is to be made explicit

This is particularly common in the **genitive**, especially the genitive of feminine and plural nouns, where the definite article is the only way of expressing that case:

*die Bedürfnisse **der** Kinder*   the needs of children/children's needs
*die Probleme **der** Gesellschaft*   the problems of society

4.4j   In colloquial German, before people's names

*Hast du **den** Peter gesehen?*   Have you seen Peter?
***Der** Schumacher hat gewonnen*   Schumacher has won

In standard German, proper names are only preceded by articles when they are qualified by an adjective: e.g. *Kennst du Peter?* vs. *Kennst du **den** jungen Peter?*

4.4k   In some common phrases with prepositions

*Er geht in **die** Stadt/wohnt in **der** Stadt*   He goes to town/lives in town
*Er lag i**m** Bett/fiel aus **dem** Bett*   He lay in bed/fell out of bed
*Es hat sich mit **der** Zeit verbessert*   It's improved with time
*Was möchtest du zu**m** Geburtstag?*   What would you like for your birthday?

4.5   NO DEFINITE ARTICLE WITH INSTRUMENTS

In German there is no definite article with the names of musical instruments after the verbs *spielen, lernen* etc.: e.g. *Er spielt Klavier* vs. 'He plays **the** piano'.

EXERCISES

Vocabulary topic: *Berufe*

1 Fill in the gaps with an indefinite article only where appropriate:

1. Mein Mann war früher _____ Polizist.
2. Ich möchte _____ Deutschlehrerin an der Universität werden, weil ich selber _____ Deutsche bin und _____ Diplom in Deutsch als Fremdsprache habe.
3. Für _____ jungen Lehrer am Anfang seiner Karriere ist es sehr schwierig _____ Stelle zu bekommen genau da, wo man möchte.
4. „Er ist _____ sehr guter Pfarrer." – „Was? Er ist _____ Pfarrer? Das ist _____ Überraschung! Ich wusste nicht einmal dass er _____ Katholik ist."
5. Er ist mit _____ Ärztin verheiratet und hat _____ jungen Sohn.
6. Meine letzte Stelle als _____ Computerprogrammierer hat mir besser gefallen als jetzt _____ Systems Analyst zu sein.

7 _____ Manager hat keine fixen Arbeitszeiten. Dafür hat er aber _____ höheres Gehalt als _____ normaler Angestellter.

8 Er ist _____ Professor der anglikanischen Theologie, obwohl er selber _____ Atheist ist.

9 Er wollte _____ Soldat werden, aber als _____ Schwuler hat er Schwierigkeiten gehabt.

10 Der Schauspieler ist _____ Berliner. Das hört man an seiner Stimme.

11 Ich brauche _____ Anwalt.

12 Ich habe mit _____ Schweizer geredet, der drei Jahre lang _____ Übersetzer und _____ Dolmetscher war. Er sagte, das Übersetzen fiel ihm leicht, aber er war _____ sehr schlechter Dolmetscher, da er nicht schnell genug reden konnte.

FURTHER EXERCISES

2 Fill in the gaps with the DEFINITE article only where appropriate. Where present, use the contracted forms of the articles after prepositions, e.g. *am, im, zum, zur*:

1 Er isst immer ein gekochtes Ei zu _____ Frühstück.

2 In _____ Sommer wird es in _____ Griechenland bis zu _____ vierzig Grad.

3 Wir fahren in _____ Herbst in _____ USA.

4 Er wohnt in _____ Nordrhein-Westfalen.

5 „Ich suche _____ Gescherweg." „Fahren sie _____ Hammerstraße entlang bis zu _____ großen Kreisverkehr und nehmen Sie _____ dritte Straße links."

6 Jedes Jahr verbringt er _____ Urlaub an _____ Bodensee.

7 Er hat Probleme mit _____ Gesundheit.

8 Er liebt _____ Leben.

9 _____ Alter vor _____ Schönheit!

10 Ich interessiere mich sehr für _____ Musik und spiele _____ Gitarre und _____ Querflöte.

11 „Was hat dir in _____ Schule am besten gefallen?" „_____ Physik."

12 Ich studiere _____ Betriebswirtschaft an _____ Universität.

13 Wir werden es schon schaffen. Es ist nur eine Frage _____ Zeit.

14 „Kommt er aus _____ Polen?" „Nein, aus _____ ehemaligen Jugoslawien."

15 „Kommst du an _____ Montag?" „Nein, _____ Montag ist schwierig. _____ Dienstag wäre besser."

5 | Adjectives

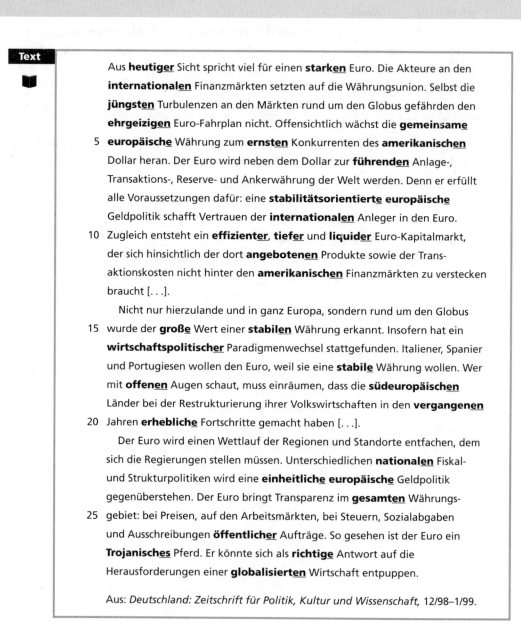

Aus **heutiger** Sicht spricht viel für einen **starken** Euro. Die Akteure an den **internationalen** Finanzmärkten setzten auf die Währungsunion. Selbst die **jüngsten** Turbulenzen an den Märkten rund um den Globus gefährden den **ehrgeizigen** Euro-Fahrplan nicht. Offensichtlich wächst die **gemeinsame**

5 **europäische** Währung zum **ernsten** Konkurrenten des **amerikanischen** Dollar heran. Der Euro wird neben dem Dollar zur **führenden** Anlage-, Transaktions-, Reserve- und Ankerwährung der Welt werden. Denn er erfüllt alle Voraussetzungen dafür: eine **stabilitätsorientierte europäische** Geldpolitik schafft Vertrauen der **internationalen** Anleger in den Euro.

10 Zugleich entsteht ein **effizienter, tiefer** und **liquider** Euro-Kapitalmarkt, der sich hinsichtlich der dort **angebotenen** Produkte sowie der Transaktionskosten nicht hinter den **amerikanischen** Finanzmärkten zu verstecken braucht [. . .].

Nicht nur hierzulande und in ganz Europa, sondern rund um den Globus

15 wurde der **große** Wert einer **stabilen** Währung erkannt. Insofern hat ein **wirtschaftspolitischer** Paradigmenwechsel stattgefunden. Italiener, Spanier und Portugiesen wollen den Euro, weil sie eine **stabile** Währung wollen. Wer mit **offenen** Augen schaut, muss einräumen, dass die **südeuropäischen** Länder bei der Restrukturierung ihrer Volkswirtschaften in den **vergangenen**

20 Jahren **erhebliche** Fortschritte gemacht haben [. . .].

Der Euro wird einen Wettlauf der Regionen und Standorte entfachen, dem sich die Regierungen stellen müssen. Unterschiedlichen **nationalen** Fiskal- und Strukturpolitiken wird eine **einheitliche europäische** Geldpolitik gegenüberstehen. Der Euro bringt Transparenz im **gesamten** Währungs-

25 gebiet: bei Preisen, auf den Arbeitsmärkten, bei Steuern, Sozialabgaben und Ausschreibungen **öffentlicher** Aufträge. So gesehen ist der Euro ein **Trojanisches** Pferd. Er könnte sich als **richtige** Antwort auf die Herausforderungen einer **globalisierten** Wirtschaft entpuppen.

Aus: *Deutschland: Zeitschrift für Politik, Kultur und Wissenschaft,* 12/98–1/99.

♀ Adjectives in the text

5.1 USE OF ADJECTIVE ENDINGS

In German, adjectives used **before** nouns require a special ending depending on the **gender** of the following noun (masculine, feminine or neuter), the **case** of the noun (nominative, accusative, genitive or dative), the **number** of the noun (singular or plural) and which type of element precedes the adjective (e.g. a definite or indefinite article, a pronoun with or without an ending): e.g. *der* **kleine** *Mann*, with an ending, versus *der Mann ist* **klein**, where the adjective is used predicatively (i.e. it follows the verb) and therefore has no ending. Consider the following examples taken from the text:

i) **Nominative**. Masculine is shown by -**er**, feminine and plurals by -**e**, neuter by -**es**. These are known as 'strong' endings.

Masc. sg.:   *ein effizienter, tiefer und liquider Euro-Kapitalmarkt* (10)
Fem. sg.:   *richtige Antwort* (27)
Neut. sg.:   *ein Trojanisches Pferd* (26–27)
All plurals: *erhebliche Fortschritte* (20)[29]

---

[29] This is accusative in the text, although the nominative would have the same form.

However, if these endings are contained in a preceding element which is not another adjective (e.g. articles *der, die, das*; pronouns *dieser, dieses, meine, viele* etc.), the 'default' adjective ending -**e** is used for all singulars and -**en** for all plurals. These are known as 'weak' endings.

Masc. sg.:   *der große Wert* (15)
Fem. sg.:   *die gemeinsame europäische Währung* (4–5)
Plurals: *die südeuropäischen Länder* (18–19)

Thus, a general principle operates whereby gender, case and number are shown either by the adjective or by the element preceding it, but not by both (except for feminine singulars), e.g. *ein großer Wert* vs. *der große Wert*, *ein Trojanisches Pferd* vs. *das Trojanische Pferd*.

ii) **Accusative**. Masculine singulars are always shown by -**en**. Otherwise the accusative adjective endings are identical to the nominative ones.

Masc. sg.: *einen starken Euro* (1), *den ehrgeizigen Euro-Fahrplan* (3–4).

iii) **Dative**. Masculine and neuter are shown by -**em**, feminine by -**er**, plurals by -**en**.

Fem. sg.:   *heutiger Sicht* (1)
Plural: *mit offenen Augen* (18)

When preceded by an element containing these endings (e.g. *dem, einem, der, dieser*), the 'default' or 'weak' adjective ending is -**en**:

Masc. sg.:	*zum ernst**en** Konkurrenten* (5)
Fem. sg.:	*zur führend**en** . . . Ankerwährung* (6–7)
Neut. sg.:	*im gesamt**en** Währungsgebiet* (24–25)
Plural:	*den vergangen**en** Jahren* (19–20)

iv) Genitive. Masculine and neuter are shown by -**en**, feminine and plurals by -**er**.

Plural:	*öffentlich**er** Aufträge* (26)

When preceded by an element containing the genitive endings *-es* and *-er* (e.g. *des, eines, der, einer*), the 'default' or 'weak' adjective ending is -**en**:

Masc. sg.:	*des amerikanisch**en** Dollar* (5–6)
Fem. sg.:	*einer stabil**en** Währung* (15), *einer globalisiert**en** Wirtschaft* (28)
Plural:	*der international**en** Anleger* (9)

In practice, genitive and dative endings with *-en* occur much more frequently than those with the 'strong' endings *-em* and *-er*, as demonstrated by the small number of examples with full/strong endings in the text versus the relatively large number of examples with *-en*.

Other points to note in the text

- Weak masculine noun: *Konkurrent**en*** (5) (see **3.3b**).
- Verbs taking dative object: *Unterschiedlich**en*** . . . *gegenüberstehen* (22–24), *dem* . . . *sich stellen* (21–22) (see **3.4a**).
- Present and past participles used as adjectives: *führ**end**en* (6), *stabilitätsorientierte* (8), *ang**e**boten**en* (11), *ver**gang**en**en* (19), *globalisierten* (28).
- Superlative: *jüng**st**en* (3) (see **6.2**).
- Passive: *wurde* . . . *erkannt* (15) (see **Ch. 18**).
- Abbreviated compounds: *Anlage-, Transaktions-, Reserve- und Ankerwährung* (6–7) (see **28.1c**, last point).

🔺 *Discover more about adjective endings*

5.2 **SUMMARY OF ADJECTIVE ENDINGS**

Below is a summary of adjective endings in German. It is advisable to learn these by heart together with an accompanying noun (and, where appropriate, article).[30]

---

[30] A full set of article and adjective endings within the context of a whole sentence is given in **Appendix 2**.

Table 7. 'Strong' endings

	Masc.	Fem.	Neut.	Plural
N	klein**ER** Mann	klein**E** Frau	klein**ES** Kind	klein**E** Kinder
A	klein**EN** Mann	"	"	"
D	klein**EM** Mann	klein**ER** Frau	klein**EM** Kind	klein**EN** Kindern
G	klein**EN** Mannes	klein**ER** Frau	klein**EN** Kindes	klein**ER** Kinder

The 'strong' endings in **Table 7** are used after elements without ending, e.g. **ein**, **kein**, **mein**, **viel, wenig**; and when **no article or pronoun** precedes the adjective: e.g. *kleine Kinder, zwei kleine Kinder*.

Table 8. 'Weak' (i.e. default) endings

	Masc.	Fem.	Neut.	Plural
N	der klein**E** Mann	die klein**E** Frau	das klein**E** Kind	die klein**EN** Kinder
A	den klein**EN** Mann	"	"	"
D	dem klein**EN** Mann	der klein**EN** Frau	dem klein**EN** Kind	den klein**EN** Kindern
G	des klein**EN** Mannes	der klein**EN** Frau	des klein**EN** Kindes	der klein**EN** Kinder

The 'weak' endings in **Table 8** are used after elements with ending, e.g. *der, die, das, dies-er/-em/-es, ein-er/-em/-es, kein-er/-em/-es, mein-er/-em/-es, alle, andere*.[31]

This means that when using the indefinite article *ein* (and similar forms like *kein* and the possessive pronouns *mein, dein, sein* etc.), both the strong and the weak/default endings are used, depending on whether the article has an ending (see **Table 9**).

[31] The plurals *einige* 'some', *mehrere* 'several', *viele* 'many' and *wenige* 'few' are exceptions to the above rules in that their following adjectives end in -e rather than the default -*en*: e.g. *viele kleine Kinder*.

Table 9. Endings after all forms of *ein*

	Masc.	Fem.	Neut.	Plural
N	ein klein**ER** Mann	eine klein**E** Frau	ein klein**ES** Kind	kein<u>e</u> klein**EN** Kinder
A	ein<u>en</u> klein**EN** Mann	"	"	"
D	ein<u>em</u> klein**EN** Mann	ein<u>er</u> klein**EN** Frau	ein<u>em</u> klein**EN** Kind	kein<u>en</u> klein**EN** Kindern
G	ein<u>es</u> klein**EN** Mannes	ein<u>er</u> klein**EN** Frau	ein<u>es</u> klein**EN** Kindes	kein<u>er</u> klein**EN** Kinder

A few examples of common exceptions to the above rules are:

- Adjectives ending in a vowel other than -e have no ending: e.g. *ein **lila** Rock, ein **sexy** Mann.*[32]
- Adjectives derived from names of towns and numerals always end in -er: e.g. *die **Berliner** Philharmonie, in den **sechziger** Jahren.*
- The first element of hyphenated adjectives has no ending: e.g. *die **österreichisch**-ungarische Monarchie.*

---

[32] Adjectives ending in -e drop the -e before adding the endings, e.g. *böse: ein böser Mann.*

5.3 ADJECTIVAL PHRASES BEFORE NOUNS

In written German it is common to place whole phrases which end in an adjective *before* the noun, particularly in quality newspapers and literary texts, e.g. *der **vor ihm stehende** Mann* 'the man standing in front of him' (literally 'the standing in front of him man'), where the adjective is derived from the present participle *stehend* and, like all adjectives before nouns, takes the necessary ending. These phrases are known as extended or expanded attributes and can sometimes be very long, particularly when used to create a particular effect in literary texts, e.g. *die **in dieser Landschaft und Natur und Architektur existierenden und sich von Jahr zu Jahr kopflos multiplizierenden** schwachsinnigen Bewohner* (Thomas Bernhard, *Die Ursache*). In the above text on the euro there is one (short) example of this: *hinsichtlich der **dort angebotenen** Produkte* (lines 11–12), where the adjective is derived from the past participle *angeboten*. Note that the final adjective(s) of the phrase(s) must take the usual ending: e.g. *ein klein**er** Tisch*, compare *ein **für meine Zwecke etwas zu klein**er Tisch*.

5.4 OMITTED NOUNS

Adjectives with endings are usually used before nouns but are also needed when the noun is omitted but understood, e.g. *Was für ein Auto hast du? Ein groß**es** oder ein klein**es**?, Ist es ein neu**er** Film? Nein, ein alt**er**.*

5.5 ADJECTIVAL NOUNS

It is common in German to use adjectives as nouns (adjectival nouns), particularly when referring to the appearance, characteristics or state of a person, e.g. *der **Alte** 'the old man', similarly der **Deutsche**, der **Arbeitslose**, der **Unglückliche**, all of which begin with capital letters. Sometimes the adjectival nouns may be derived from participles, *e.g. der **Geliebte*** ('the lover', literally 'the loved' from *geliebt*, past participle of *lieben*). In all these cases one must still use the appropriate adjective endings:

*Der Deutsch**e** kommt*   *Ich mag den Deutsch**en** nicht*
*Ein Deutsch**er** kommt*   *Die Frau des Deutsch**en** kommt*

When referring to unspecified *things* rather than people, *etwas* (or, in the negative, *nichts*) is used, followed by the neuter form of the adjective, e.g. *etwas **Gutes** 'something good', nichts **Schwieriges** 'nothing difficult':*

*Ich habe etwas Gut**es** gefunden*   *Er kam mit etwas Gut**em** nach Hause*

Similarly, expressions such as 'the nice thing', 'the bad thing' are is rendered by *das* + the adjectival noun in *-e*: e.g. **Das** *Schlimm**e** war, dass ich meinen Koffer verloren hat* 'The bad thing was that I lost my suitcase', *Das war für mich* **das** *Interessant**e** daran* 'That was the interesting thing for me'.

5.6 ADVERBS

German adverbs are usually identical to their related adjectives, e.g. *Er ist sehr* **langsam** (adjective 'slow'), *Er spricht sehr* **langsam** (adverb 'slow**ly**'). The difference appears when used before nouns, as adverbs, unlike adjectives, do not have an ending: e.g. (adjective) *eine schreckliche Familie* 'a terrible family' versus (adverb) *eine* **schrecklich** *nette Familie* 'a terri**bly** nice family'.

EXERCISES

Vocabulary topic: *Europa und ihre Produkte*

1 Fill in the gaps below with the appropriate adjective endings:

deutsch__ Bier	der englisch__ Tee	diese schwedisch__ Fleischklöße
holländisch__ Käse	ein schottisch__ Lachs	welcher österreichisch__ Wein?
spanisch__ Oliven	keine belgisch__ Pralinen	
das frisch__ französisch__ Brot	mein griechisch__ Schafskäse	

2 Fill in the gaps below with the appropriate adjective endings, paying particular attention to the CASE of the noun:

1 Frankreich ist für seinen gut__ Wein sehr bekannt.
2 Italien ist ein sehr schön__ Land und erwirtschaftet einen groß__ Teil seines heutig__ Bruttonationalprodukts durch Tourismus.
3 Schweden freut sich über den europaweit__ Erfolg seines riesig__ Möbelgeschäfts.
4 Deutschland produziert weltberühmt__ Autos von sehr hoh__ Qualität.[33]
5 Er kam mit einem sehr schick__ italienisch__ Anzug nach Hause.
6 Er gab ihr zwei klein__ Flaschen teuer__ französisch__ Parfums zum vierzigst__ Geburtstag.

[33] The adjective *hoch* changes to *hoh-* before adding an ending.

FURTHER EXERCISES

3 Put the underlined nouns into the plural and change the other words accordingly, paying particular attention to the adjective endings. Replace *ein* with *zwei*:

1 Mein schönes altes <u>Haus</u> hat *ein* besonders großes <u>Schlafzimmer</u>.
2 Das schwarze <u>Hemd</u> mit dem weißen <u>Streifen</u> hing im Kleiderschrank.
3 Guter <u>Wein</u> ist selten billig. Nimm diesen *einen* französischen, zum Beispiel.
4 Diese frischgepflückte <u>Blume</u> ist für meine neue <u>Freundin</u>.
5 Sie ist trotz des verspäteten <u>Zuges</u> relativ früh nach Hause gekommen.

4 Complete the following text by filling in the gaps using the appropriate adjective ending:

Als Gregor Samsa eines Morgens aus unruhig__ Träumen erwachte, fand er sich in seinem Bett zu einem ungeheuer__ Ungeziefer verwandelt. Er lag auf seinem panzerartig hart__ Rücken und sah, wenn er den Kopf ein wenig hob, seinen gewölbt__, braun__, von bogenförmig__ Versteifungen geteilt__ Bauch, auf dessen Höhe sich die Bettdecke, zum gänzlich__ Niedergleiten bereit, kaum noch erhalten konnte. Seine viel__, im Vergleich zu seinem sonstig__ Umfang kläglich dünn__ Beine flimmerten ihm hilflos vor den Augen.

»Was ist mit mir geschehen?«, dachte er. Es war kein Traum. Sein Zimmer, ein richtig__, nur etwas zu klein__ Menschenzimmer, lag ruhig zwischen den vier wohlbekannt__ Wänden. Über dem Tisch, auf dem eine auseinandergepackt__ Musterkollektion von Tuchwaren ausgebreitet war – Samsa war Reisender – hing das Bild, das er vor kurzem aus einer illustriert__ Zeitschrift ausgeschnitten und in einem hübsch__, vergoldet__ Rahmen untergebracht hatte. Es stellte eine Dame dar, die mit einem Pelzhut und einer Pelzboa versehen, aufrecht dasaß und einen schwer__ Pelzmuff, in dem ihr ganz__ Unterarm verschwunden war, dem Beschauer entgegenhob. Gregors Blick richtete sich dann zum Fenster, und das trüb__ Wetter – man hörte Regentropfen auf das Fensterblech aufschlagen – machte ihn melancholisch.

Aus: Franz Kafka, *Die Verwandlung*. Aufl. 1984. Fischer Taschenbuch Verlag.

5 a Take your answers to question 4 above and underline those adjectives which form the last element of an expanded attribute. Identify the whole attribute.

5 b Make expanded attributes out of the phrases following the comma, paying particular attention to the ending that they will take:

Example: Der Mann, der von der Hitze rot geworden ist.
Answer: Der von der Hitze rot geworden**e** Mann.

1 Seine Mutter, die vor zwei Tagen achtzig geworden ist.
2 Ein Schriftsteller, der von mehreren Akademikern viel gelobt wird.
3 Ein Gesetz, das von den Deutschen eingeführt wurde.
4 Sie bieten vier Arbeitsplätze an, die von der Gemeinde finanziert werden.
5 Sie haben keinen Kandidaten gefunden, der für die Stelle geeignet ist.

6 Replace the underlined words with the appropriate adjectival noun (inserting *etwas* where the object is a thing rather than a person):

Example: **a)** Der <u>Mann</u> lag im Bett [krank].   **b)** Ich habe ein <u>Kleid</u> gekauft [neu].
Answer: Der **Kranke** lag im Bett.   Ich habe **etwas Neues** gekauft.

1 Hier kommt die <u>Frau</u>. [unfreundlich]
2 Sie spielte mit dem <u>Kind</u>. [klein]
3 Der Chef feuerte den <u>Mann</u>. [angestellt]
4 Sie war die Freundin des <u>Mannes</u>. [gestorben]

5 Wir müssen für die <u>Menschen</u> mehr spenden. [arm]

6 Ich habe <u>ein Buch</u> gelesen. [interessant]

7 Ich muss dir leider <u>eine Sache</u> mitteilen. [traurig]

7 Translate the following sentences into German, paying particular attention to the adjectives and adverbs:

1 He has an unusually large nose.

2 What an incredibly dirty room!

3 She has a tastefully decorated flat.

4 It was an unpleasantly hot day.

☞ **For further exercises on adjective endings see Revision Text 1, Ex. 3 and for general exercises on article and adjective endings see Revision Texts 2 (Ex. 2), 3 (Ex. 1) and 4 (Ex. 3).**

6 | Comparatives and superlatives

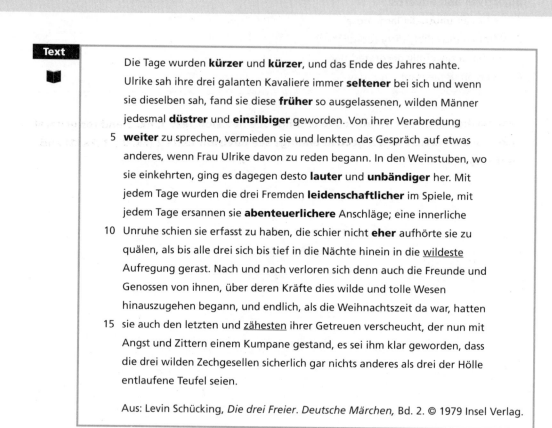

Text

Die Tage wurden **kürzer** und **kürzer**, und das Ende des Jahres nahte.
Ulrike sah ihre drei galanten Kavaliere immer **seltener** bei sich und wenn
sie dieselben sah, fand sie diese **früher** so ausgelassenen, wilden Männer
jedesmal **düstrer** und **einsilbiger** geworden. Von ihrer Verabredung
5 **weiter** zu sprechen, vermieden sie und lenkten das Gespräch auf etwas
anderes, wenn Frau Ulrike davon zu reden begann. In den Weinstuben, wo
sie einkehrten, ging es dagegen desto **lauter** und **unbändiger** her. Mit
jedem Tage wurden die drei Fremden **leidenschaftlicher** im Spiele, mit
jedem Tage ersannen sie **abenteuerlichere** Anschläge; eine innerliche
10 Unruhe schien sie erfasst zu haben, die schier nicht **eher** aufhörte sie zu
quälen, als bis alle drei sich bis tief in die Nächte hinein in die <u>wildeste</u>
Aufregung gerast. Nach und nach verloren sich denn auch die Freunde und
Genossen von ihnen, über deren Kräfte dies wilde und tolle Wesen
hinauszugehen begann, und endlich, als die Weihnachtszeit da war, hatten
15 sie auch den letzten und <u>zähesten</u> ihrer Getreuen verscheucht, der nun mit
Angst und Zittern einem Kumpane gestand, es sei ihm klar geworden, dass
die drei wilden Zechgesellen sicherlich gar nichts anderes als drei der Hölle
entlaufene Teufel seien.

Aus: Levin Schücking, *Die drei Freier. Deutsche Märchen*, Bd. 2. © 1979 Insel Verlag.

♀ Comparatives and superlatives in the text

6.1 COMPARATIVES

The comparative form of the adjective/adverb (given in bold print in our text) is used when comparing two or more things: e.g. *Er ist **kleiner** als ich* 'he's **smaller** than me'. In the text, the comparison is implicit rather than explicit: e.g. *Die Tage wurden **kürzer*** (line 1) 'the days were getting **shorter** (i.e. than they had been before)'. German comparatives are formed by adding *-er* (or *-r* after words ending in *-e*) to the adjective/adverb and, with certain words, umlauting the stressed vowel. Examples from the text are:

*selten-**er*** (2), *früh-**er*** (3), *einsilbig-**er*** (4), *weit-**er*** (5), *unbändig-**er*** (7), *leidenschaftlich-**er*** (8), *abenteuerlich-**er**-e* (9), *ehe-**r*** (10).

With umlautable vowels: *kurz – k**ü**rz-**er** (1) versus *laut – laut-**er** (7) (see **6.3**).

- Comparatives take the same endings as ordinary adjectives/adverbs: i.e. adjective endings when adjectives, e.g. *abenteuerlicher**e** Anschläge* (9); no adjective ending when adverbs, e.g. *seltener* (2).
- Adjectives/adverbs ending in *-el*, *-en*, *-er* may drop the *-e-* before adding the comparative ending: e.g. *düster – düst<u>r</u>**er*** (4). With those in *-en* and *-er* this is optional where no further adjective ending is used. Thus *düst**e**rer* would also be possible.

6.2 . SUPERLATIVES

The superlative (underlined in our text) is used to express the most extreme degree of the adjective/adverb: e.g. *der **höchste** Berg* 'the **highest** mountain', and, for adjectives, is formed by adding *-st* (or *-**e**st* after *-d*, *-t*, *-s*, *-ß*, *-sch*, *-z* and, optionally, after long vowels/diphthongs) to the adjective and, with some words, umlauting the stressed vowel: e.g. *wild-**est**-e* (11), *zäh-**est**-en* (15), which both have *-est* as one adjective ends in *-d* and the other in a long vowel (*h* is silent after a vowel).

Superlatives usually appear **before nouns** (or in place of a noun), which means that they always need additional adjective endings, as the examples from the text show. If they appear in place of a noun, they are written with a capital letter: e.g. *Er ist der Wildeste* 'he's the wildest (one)'. (For superlatives as adverbs see **6.4**.)

Other points to note in the text

- Extended attribute: *diese **früher so ausgelassenen, wilden** Männer* (3), *drei **der Hölle entlaufene** Teufel* (17–18) (see **5.3**).
- Genitive relative pronoun ('whose'): ***deren** Kräfte* (13) (see **9.3b**).
- Use of simple past in written narrative: e.g. *wurden* (1), *nahte* (1), *sah* (2), *fand* (3), *vermieden* (5) (see **Ch. 12**).
- Konjunktiv 1 in reported speech: *sei . . . geworden* (16), *seien* (18) (see **Ch. 17**).
- Missing finite verb for poetic effect: *bis alle drei sich . . . gerast* (missing *sind*) (11–12).
- Use of the older dative singular *-e*: *Tage* (8, 9), *Spiele* (8), *Kumpane* (16) (see footnote 18).

▲ *Discover more about comparatives and superlatives*

6.3 UMLAUT

Not all adjectives/adverbs with umlautable vowels have umlaut in the comparative and superlative: e.g. *groß – gr**ö**ßer- gr**ö**ßt* vs. *froh – froher- frohest*, but it is always the case that, if umlaut is present, it appears in **both** the comparative **and** the superlative. Here are some common examples that do have umlaut, many of which have the vowel *a*:

*alt – **ä**lter – **ä**ltest*	*lang – l**ä**nger – l**ä**ngst*	*jung – j**ü**nger – j**ü**ngst*
*arg – **ä**rger – **ä**rgst*	*scharf – sch**ä**rfer – sch**ä**rfst*	*klug – kl**ü**ger – kl**ü**gst*

arm – ärmer – ärmst	schwach – schwächer – schwächst	kurz – kürzer – kürzest
hart – härter – härtest	stark – stärker – stärkst	grob – gröber – gröbst
kalt – kälter – kältest	warm – wärmer – wärmst	
krank – kränker – kränkst	dumm – dümmer – dümmst	

Some adjectives have alternative forms with and without umlaut:

bang – banger – bangst	nass – nasser – nassest	krumm – krummer – krummst
bänger – bängst	nässer – nässest	krümmer – krümmst
blass – blasser – blassest	schmal – schmaler – schmalst	fromm – frommer – frommst
blässer – blässest	schmäler – schmälst	frömmer – frömmst
glatt – glatter – glattest	gesund – gesunder – gesundest	
glätter – glättest	gesünder – gesündest	

6.4   SUPERLATIVES WITH *AM ... -STEN*

When a superlative is used after a verb, i.e. as a predicative adjective or, more often, as an **adverb**, a special ending -**en** is added and the superlative is preceded by **am**. This is compulsory with adverbs (i.e. those superlatives occurring with verbs other than *sein* and *werden*), e.g.

Predicative adj.:   *Er ist schnell → Er ist **der Schnellste** or Er ist **am schnellsten**.*[34]

Adverb: *Er fährt schnell → Er fährt **am schnellsten** [NOT *Er fährt der Schnellste].*

> [34] The *am ... -sten* alternative is not possible if a qualifying statement follows: e.g. *Er ist **der Schnellste** der Rennfahrer*, NOT **Er ist am schnellsten der Rennfahrer*.

6.5   IRREGULAR FORMS

Some adjectives and adverbs (which, incidentally, are very frequently used in the comparative and superlative) are irregular. Consider the following examples:

groß	größer	grö**ßt** [after verb: *am grö**ßt**en*]
gut	**bess**er	**bes**t [after verb: *am **bes**ten*]
hoch	hö**h**er	höchst [after verb: *am höchsten*]
nah	näher	nä**ch**st [after verb: *am nä**ch**sten*]
viel	**meh**r	**mei**st [after verb: *am **mei**sten*]
gern	**lieb**er	*am **lieb**sten* [adverb only]

Note that *mehr* 'more' (and *weniger* 'fewer', the comparative of *wenig* 'few') never take adjective endings: e.g. *Hier gibt es mehr/weniger Leute*.

6.6   COMMON CONSTRUCTIONS WITH COMPARATIVES AND SUPERLATIVES

i)   **'-er than'**. 'Than' is translated as *als* in German and is usually followed by a noun/pronoun in the **nominative** case:[35] e.g. *Ich bin ruhiger als der Nachbar; Du bist schneller als ich* (literally: 'you are quicker than **I**'). By contrast, a sentence such as 'I am just as clever as you' is rendered as *Ich bin **ebenso** klug **wie** du*.[36]

³⁵ Unless the **verb** requires use of another case: e.g. *Ich helfe ihm lieber als seinem Bruder.*

³⁶ In colloquial German, particularly in the South and in Austria, *als* and *wie* are often confused: e.g. *Er ist kleiner **wie** sein Sohn.*

ii) '-er **and** -er'. This can be directly translated as two comparatives joined by *und*, e.g. *kürzer und kürzer* 'shorter and shorter' (line 1 of our text), or, perhaps more commonly, by *immer* + comparative, e.g. *Er wird **immer** schwieriger* 'he's getting more and more difficult'.

iii) '<u>the</u> -er . . . <u>the</u> -er'. Expressions such as '<u>the</u> sooner you come, <u>the</u> better' are rendered by *je* + comparative . . . ***desto*** + comparative: e.g. *Je früher du kommst **desto besser***, and with two full clauses, *Je mehr Zeit ich mit ihm verbringe, **desto mehr** mag ich ihn.*

iv) '**the -est of all**'. The superlative can be stressed by prefixing it with *aller-* to render the meaning 'of all': e.g. *Er ist der **aller**beste, der **aller**liebste.* Otherwise 'of' is translated using the genitive or *von*: e.g. *Sie ist die fleißigste **der** (or **von** den) Studenten.*

✎ EXERCISES

Vocabulary topic: *Maße*

1 Put the following adjectives into a) the comparative, b) the superlative:

niedrig	breit	dick	schmal
hoch	schlank	fett	flach

2 Put the adjectives in bold into a) the comparative, b) the superlative:

1 Er trägt den **langen** Mantel.
2 Gefällt dir der **kurze** Rock?
3 Hast du das **kleine** Kind gesehen?
4 Welche Weintrauben nimmst du? Die **großen** schmecken am besten.
5 Ich möchte die **dünne** Scheibe, bitte.

✎ FURTHER EXERCISES

3 Put the following adjectives into EITHER the comparative OR the superlative depending on the context of the sentence:

1 Mein Bruder ist **jung** als ich.
2 Ich bin der **Alte** in der Familie.
3 Man merkt, dass Klaus **alt** wird. Er wird immer **langsam**.
4 Er ist der **gute** Fußballspieler in Deutschland.
5 Je **reich** er wird, desto **arrogant** er wird.
6 Normalerweise ist Deutschland im Sommer **warm** und im Winter **kalt** als England.
7 Er hält sich für den **klugen** Burschen in der Klasse.
8 Ich liebe dich. Du bist der **Gute**!
9 Welchen Wein möchten Sie? Den **billigen**, bitte.
10 Der Geruch wird immer **stark**.

**4 Put the following adjectives into the superlative and decide whether to use the -*st*
or the *am . . . -sten* form. Sometimes both are possible:**

Example: Diese Blumen sind **schön**.

Answers: a) Diese Blumen sind **die schönsten**; b) Diese Blumen sind **am schönsten**.

1   Dieses Warenhaus ist **teuer**.
2   Klaus spielt nicht schlecht, aber Hermann spielt **gut**.
3   Wo verbringst du **gern** deinen Urlaub?
4   Wer kann **laut** singen?
5   Das war der **nasse** Tag des Jahres.

7 | Personal pronouns and possessives

Herberts Flirtkurs für Männer

Sie begegnen einer attraktiven Frau – jetzt müssen **Sie** schnell handeln.
Nicht einfach nur den Mund aufsperren – ein kurzer Flirtspruch muss „**sie**"
mitten ins Herz treffen. Frauen reden ständig davon, dass die alte
Rollenverteilung nicht mehr gilt, dass **sie** selbst die Männer anreden

5 würden, die **ihnen** gefallen – Unsinn! In einem mehrmonatigen
Selbstversuch habe **ich** mich in Straßencafés, Bars und Biergärten in die
Nähe von attraktiven Frauen gesetzt – **ich** wurde kein einziges Mal
eingeladen oder angemacht! Nein, liebe Mit-Männer, ob **wir** wollen oder
nicht – die Initiative bleibt momentan noch immer **uns** überlassen. Aber

10 wie fängt **man** an? Bitte, nicht mit den ewigen langweiligen „Kennen **wir**
uns nicht?", „Oft hier?" oder „So alleine?" Seien **Sie** originell!

Sprüche für Romantiker:

● Wenn **sie** gerade das Lokal verlassen will: „Hast **du** nicht etwas vergessen?"
Sie: „Was?" „**Mich**!"

15 ● Mit den Händen auf <u>ihren</u> Schultern: „Oh – das sind Schulterblätter.
Ich dachte, es wären Flügel."

● „**Ich** bin neu in der Stadt. Könntest **du** mir den Weg zu <u>deiner</u>
Wohnung zeigen?"

● „Wenn **ich** dir nach Hause folgen würde, würdest du **mich** behalten?"

20 ● „War <u>dein</u> Vater ein Außerirdischer? Weil so etwas wie **dich** gibt es
nicht auf der Erde."

● „**Ich** habe <u>meine</u> Telefonnummer verlegt. Könnte **ich** mir <u>Ihre</u> leihen?"

● „**Ich** frage mich, wie <u>unsere</u> Kinder aussehen würden."

Aus: *Herberts Männerseiten* [www.maennerseiten.de]

♀ Personal pronouns and possessives in the text

7.1 **PERSONAL PRONOUNS**

7.1a Personal pronouns and case

Personal pronouns are the pronouns used to refer to persons and things: e.g. 'I', 'you', 'he', 'she', 'it'.
In English, some of these pronouns have different forms depending on whether they appear as

the subject or the object of the sentence: e.g. subj. '**I** love John' vs. obj. 'John loves **me**'. The same principle applies in German, yet here there is an additional difference between the direct object pronoun, which is in the **accusative**, and the indirect object pronoun, which is in the **dative** (see **Table 10**). These accusative and dative forms are also used after prepositions and other elements which require a particular case. Examples of personal pronouns in the text appear in bold print.

Table 10. Personal pronouns

Subject (nom.)		Object (acc.)	Indirect Object (dat.)
ich	'I'	*er liebt* **mich**	*er sagt* **mir**
*du**	'you'	*er liebt* **dich**	*er sagt* **dir**
er	'he'	*er liebt* **ihn**	*er sagt* **ihm**
sie	'she'	*er liebt* **sie**	*er sagt* **ihr**
es	'it'	*er liebt* **es**	*er sagt* **ihm**
wir	'we'	*er liebt* **uns**	*er sagt* **uns**
*ihr**	'you'	*er liebt* **euch**	*er sagt* **euch**
sie	'they'	*er liebt* **sie**	*er sagt* **ihnen**
*Sie**	'you'	*er liebt* **Sie**	*er sagt* **Ihnen**

*German has three different words for 'you' depending on the number of people addressed and the speaker's relationship to them. **Du** (*dich, dir*) is the informal singular form – it is used: i) to address a person who the speaker is on friendly terms with;[37] ii) to address children (up to about 14–15); iii) among young adults (e.g. students) who wish to be informal. **Ihr** (*euch*) is the plural form of **du**, which is used to address two or more people who would each normally be addressed as *du*. **Sie** (*Ihnen*), which is always written with a capital letter, is the polite form used to address (adult) strangers and people who are acquaintances but not on familiar terms with the speaker (e.g. work colleagues). It is used for singular and plural addressees.

Examples of personal pronouns used in the text are: *ich* (6, 7, 16, 17, 19, 22, 23) vs. *mich* (14, 19) vs. *mir* (17); *du* (13, 17) vs. *dich* (20) vs. *dir* (19); *sie* 'she' (13, 14), *sie* 'her' (2); *wir* (8, 10) vs. *uns* (9); *sie* 'they' (4) vs. *ihnen* (5); *Sie* 'you' (1, 11).

Note that, in the text, 'Herbert' uses the polite *Sie* to address his readers, as they are strangers to him, yet most of the chat-up lines use *du*, since the man's aim is to become familiar with the woman.

[37] But it can also be used to show contempt, if it is used with a stranger or someoné who would normally be addressed more politely.

7.1b *man*

In addition, German has a general 'impersonal' pronoun, *man* (accusative *einen*, dative *einem*), which corresponds to English 'one': e.g. *wie fängt* **man** *an?* (10) 'how does one begin?'. However, as English 'one' is considered rather formal, it is usually avoided in the spoken language and 'you', 'they', 'people', 'someone' or a passive construction are used to translate *man*: 'How do you begin?'. This means that when English 'you' is used to mean 'people in general', it must be translated by *man* (*einen, einem*) and not *du*.[38] The possessive form of *man* is *sein*, even when referring to women: e.g. *Man erlebt* **seine** *Schwangerschaft jedesmal anders*.[39]

> [38] In more formal English, a passive construction is often preferred to 'you', 'people', 'they' etc.: e.g. *Man sagt oft, dass . . .* 'It is often said that . . .'.
>
> [39] This has often been criticised by feminist linguists (see Senta Trömel-Plötz, *Frauensprache – Sprache der Veränderung*, Fischer Taschenbuch-Verlag, 1982).

7.2 POSSESSIVES

Possessives (see **Table 11**) are used to indicate possession in constructions such as '**my** friend', '**your** bike'. As with personal pronouns, there are three forms for 'your' in German, depending on whether the addressee would be *du*, *ihr* or *Sie*. All possessives take the **same endings as the indefinite article** (see **Table 12**; compare with **Table 5**).

Table 11. Possessives

Singular		Plural	
mein	'my'	*unser*	'our'
dein	'your' (informal sg.)	*euer**	'your' (informal pl.)
sein	'his'	*ihr*	'their'
ihr	'her'	*Ihr*	'your' (polite sg. and pl.)
sein	'its'		

* This tends to become *eur-* when an ending is added: e.g. *eure Wohnung*.

Table 12. Forms of the possessives

	Masc.	Fem.	Neut.	Pl.
N	*mein Mann*	*meine Frau*	*mein Kind*	*meine Kinder*
A	*meinen Mann*	*meine Frau*	*mein Kind*	*meine Kinder*
D	*meinem Mann*	*meiner Frau*	*meinem Kind*	*meinen Kindern*
G	*meines Mannes*	*meiner Frau*	*meines Kindes*	*meiner Kinder*

Examples of possessives in the text are (underlined): *auf ihren Schultern* (15), *zu deiner Wohnung* (17–18), *meine Telefonnummer* (22), *unsere Kinder* (23), *Ihre* (22)[40].

This last example, *Ihre*, meaning 'yours', shows that the noun may be omitted but is understood from the context: i.e. *Ihre Telefonnummer*. The possessive takes the form it would normally take if the noun were present. This is the case for all possessives except the masc. nom. sg. and the neuter nom./acc. sg. which take *-er* and *-(e)s* respectively when no noun follows:

> [40] Note that, on this occasion the speaker is using the polite form *Ihr* instead of the informal *dein* which is used in line 17.

Ist das **dein** *Schlüssel? Ja es ist* **meiner***.*

Du hast **dein** *Bier ausgetrunken. Willst du auch* **meines** *haben?*[41]

---

[41] *Meines, deines, seines* etc. are usually pronounced (and often written) *meins, deins, seins* etc.

Other points to note in the text

- Genitive possessive: *Herberts* (Title) (see footnote 13).
- Verbs with dative object: *begegnen* (1), *gefallen* (5), *überlassen bleiben* (9), *folgen* (19), and with a dative reflexive pronoun: *leihen* (22) (see **3.4a**).
- Imperative in *Sie*-form: *Seien Sie* (11) (see **11.3**).
- Conditional: *anreden* **würden** (4–5), *folgen* **würde, würdest** . . . *behalten* (19), *aussehen* **würden** (23) (see **Ch. 16**).
- Konjunktiv II for conditional: *könnte* (22); used to express something unreal: *wären* (16) (see **16.3**).
- Indicative instead of subjunctive in reported speech: *gilt* (4), a feature of informal German (see **17.4b–c**).
- Passive in past tense: **wurde** . . . *eingeladen oder angemacht* (7–8) (see **Ch. 18**).

▲ *Discover more about personal pronouns and possessives*

7.3 GENITIVE FORMS

Personal pronouns also have genitive forms, e.g. *meiner, deiner, seiner*, but these are considered archaic and only very rarely used. The only genitive forms which are still in general use are taken from the demonstrative pronoun: *dessen* (plural *deren*) and usually render English 'of it' ('of them'): e.g. *Mädchen sei dir* **dessen** *stets bewusst* 'girl, always be aware of it' (line 12 of text in Chapter **11**).

7.4 PRONOUNS FOR NON-HUMAN NOUNS

In English, non-human nouns are usually given the pronoun 'it' (possessive 'its'): e.g. 'Did you read the book?' 'Yes, **it** was good, but **its** characters were a bit unrealistic.' In German, however, every noun has a gender, which means that the **choice of pronoun depends on the gender of the word**: e.g. *der Film* takes the masculine singular pronoun (and its different case forms, depending on the context) while *die Musik* takes the feminine singular pronoun. (The plural pronoun is the same for all genders.) Consider the following examples:

Hast du den Film gesehen? – Ja, **er** *war sehr gut, aber ich fand* **ihn** *ein bisschen lang.*
Das war eine Wespe. Has du **sie** *gesehen? – Gesehen? Ja,* **sie** *hat mich gestochen!*

Thus, 'it' is only translated as *es* with neuter nouns, e.g. *Das Buch hat mir gefallen.* **Es** *war sehr interessant,* and when the pronoun does not refer to a specific noun but is used more generally: **Es** *ist sehr schön heute.*[42]

---

[42] It can also be used when the noun (or something standing in for the noun) is mentioned later, after the verb: e.g. **Es** *war ein sehr guter* *Film*; *Ja es war* *ein guter;* **Der Ring** *– es ist* *meiner*.

7.5 PREPOSITIONS WITH NON-HUMAN PRONOUNS

If a preposition occurs with a personal pronoun meaning 'it' or 'they/them' referring to a non-human noun, **da-** (*dar-* before a vowel) + preposition may be used as an alternative to the usual personal pronouns. In fact, it is used very frequently:

Kennst du den Film? Was hältst du von ihm

or **davon**?   '... What do you think of **it**?'

Die Ohrringe? Ich habe DM30 für sie bezahlt

or **dafür**[43]   '... I paid 30 marks for **them**'

Da(r)- + preposition is **obligatory** i) when the alternative pronoun would be *es*, as with neuter nouns, e.g. *Das Buch – Was hast du **dafür*** (not **für es*) *bezahlt?*; ii) when 'it' refers to a general idea or abstract entity rather than to a specific concrete noun, e.g. *Ich muss heute Überstunden machen – ich bin **damit** nicht zufrieden* 'I have to work overtime today – I'm not happy **about it**' (i.e. with the situation in general).

---

[43] With animals, particularly pets, the same personal pronouns are used as for humans (as is the case in English): e.g. *Das ist mein Hund. Ich gehe jetzt mit **ihm** spazieren*, not **damit** 'with **it**'.

7.6 DEMONSTRATIVES (*DER, DIE, DAS* ETC.) USED AS PERSONAL PRONOUNS

In colloquial spoken German it is very common to use demonstrative pronouns (see **8.2**) instead of the third person forms of the personal pronouns (i.e. instead of *er, sie, es* and plural *sie*, whether referring to people or things). In this case they often appear at the beginning of the clause: e.g.

Klaus? Ja, der gefällt mir ganz gut.	Klaus? Yes, I quite like him.
Ute? Die kann ich überhaupt nicht leiden.	Ute? I can't stand her at all.
*Datteln? Von **denen** kriege ich Durchfall.*	Dates? They give me diarrhoea.

7.7 *DESSEN* AND *DEREN* AS POSSESSIVES

The genitive forms of the demonstrative pronouns, *dessen* (masc./neut. sg.) and *deren* (fem. sg. and all pl.) may be used instead of the ordinary possessives *sein* and *ihr* in cases where ambiguity is possible. For instance, if two or more nouns are mentioned which could be connected to the possessive, the use of *dessen/deren* makes it clear that it is **the last noun mentioned** that the possessive refers to, e.g.

Klaus kam mit Fritz und seiner Frau.	'Klaus came with Fritz and his wife' [*seiner* probably refers to Fritz but, theoretically, could refer to Klaus].
*Klaus kam mit Fritz und **dessen** Frau.*	[This makes it clear that it is Fritz's wife].

7.8 THE POSSESSIVE DATIVE

In some constructions, particularly when referring to parts of the body, it is more common to use a dative to express possession rather than an ordinary possessive. For instance, when used reflexively, *Ich wasche* **mir** *die Haare, Du putzt* **dir** *die Zähne, Er hat* **sich** *das Bein gebrochen*, with a dative reflexive pronoun and a definite article before the noun (see **20.2** for dative reflexive pronouns), are more commonly used than *Ich wasche* **meine** *Haare* etc. Similarly with other objects: e.g. *Ich wasche* **ihm** *das Gesicht, Ich trockne* **dem** *Kind die Haare* are more common than *Ich wasche* **sein** *Gesicht, Ich trockne die Haare* **des** *Kindes* (see **3.1a(iv)** for the genitive possessive).

✎ **EXERCISES**

Vocabulary topic: *Ausgehen*

1 Fill in the appropriate personal pronouns:

1 Hast _____(*you*) Lust mit _____(*me*) ins Kino zu gehen?

2 Was wollt _____(*you, plural*) mit Klaus machen? _____(*we*) gehen mit _____(*him*) ins Theater.

3 _____(*I*) gehe in die Kneipe. Möchten _____(*you, polite*) mitkommen?

4 _____(*they*) haben _____(*him*) in der Disco gesehen. _____(*he*) tanzt wie ein Affe.

5 Hat _____ (*you, informal sg.*) Kerstin zum Abendessen eingeladen? _____(*she*) ist verrückt nach _____(*you*).

6 _____(*we*) treffen _____(*you, informal pl.*) um acht Uhr im Café.

7 Brigitte? Kennst _____(*you*) _____(*her*)? Ja, _____(*I*) war gestern mit _____(*her*) auf einer Studentenfete.

8 Vielen Dank, dass_____(*you, polite*) _____(*me*) eingeladen haben. Es war sehr schön, mit _____(*you*) zu unterhalten.

2 Fill in the appropriate personal pronouns and possessives:

1 Kommt _____(*your, informal sg.*) Bruder zu _____(*your*) Geburtstagsfeier?

2 Seht _____(*you, informal plural*) _____(*your*) Eltern oft? Ja. _____(*we*) waren gestern mit_____(*them*) im Restaurant.

3 Der film hat _____(*me*) besser gefallen als _____(*my*) Freundin.

4 Wo ist _____(*your, informal sg.*) Schwester? _____(*she*) ist mit _____(*her*) Freund auf einem Rockkonzert.

5 _____(*my*) Wein schmeckt mir nicht. Kann ich _____(*yours, informal sg.*) probieren?

6 Der Tanz wird ziemlich vornehm sein. _____(*I*) muss mich schön anziehen und _____(*my*) Haare waschen.

7 Robert hat _____(*us*) auf _____(*his*) Verlobungsfest eingeladen.

8 _____(*he*) hat ein schönes Haus, aber ich finde _____(*ours*) gemütlicher.

9 Marion spielt heute Abend Karten mit _____(*her*) Freundin und _____(*her*) Mann.

10 War Karl mit _____(*you, informal pl.*) im Nachtlokal? Ja, es hat _____(*him*) Spaß gemacht.

✎ **FURTHER EXERCISES**

3 Form possessive phrases using the following nouns, first using the possessive + noun, then using the possessive as a pronoun:

Example: Die Limonade – ich.

Answers: i) Das ist **meine Limonade**; ii) Das ist **meine**.

1 Der Lippenstift – ich.

2 Das Zimmer – du.

3 Die Schuhe – er.

4 Der Wagen – wir.

5 Die Bücher – ihr.

6 Die Ohrringe – sie ('she').

7 Das Baby – sie ('they').

8 Der Kaffee – Sie.

4 Replace the nouns in bold print with the appropriate German word for 'it' (or 'they/them' in the plural):

1 Die Tür steht offen. – Ja, er hat **die Tür** nicht zumachen wollen.

2 Wo sind deine Handschuhe? – Ich habe **die Handschuhe** verloren.

3 Schmeckt dir der Tee nicht? – Nein, **der Tee** ist kalt geworden.

4 Der Kuchen ist lecker. – Danke, ich habe **den Kuchen** selbst gebacken.

5 **Der Rock** war ein teurer Rock.

6 **Der Wagen** ist meiner.

7 Ich habe das Auto von meinem Bekannten gekauft. Er hat nur DM2000 für **das Auto** verlangt.

8 Hier sind deine Pommes. Möchtest du Ketchup auf **die Pommes** haben?

9 Er ist nicht sehr begeistert von **der Idee**.

10 Ich habe meinen Schlüssel verloren. – Hast du **den Schlüssel** irgendwo gesehen?

5 Translate the following sentences into English, paying particular attention to the translation of *man* (acc. *einen,* dat. *einem*):

1 Man darf hier nicht rauchen.

2 Man hat eben eine neue Brücke gebaut.

3 Das kann einem wirklich auf die Nerven gehen.

4 Man hält die Deutschen für sehr fleißig.

5 Das Wetter hier kann einen ziemlich deprimieren.

☞ **For further exercises on personal pronouns/possessives see Revision Text 5, Ex. 3 and for exercises on demonstratives used as personal pronouns see Ch. 8, Ex. 4.**

8 | Demonstratives

Text

Ill: Schön, dass du gekommen bist.

Claire Zachanassian: **Das** habe ich mir immer vorgenommen. Mein Leben
lang, seit ich Güllen verlassen habe.

Ill: **Das** ist lieb von dir.

5 Claire Z.: Auch du hast an mich gedacht?

Ill: Immer, *das* weißt du doch, Klara.

Claire Z.: Es war wunderbar, all **die** Tage, da wir zusammen waren.

Ill (*stolz*): Eben. (*Zum Lehrer*): Sehen Sie, Herr Lehrer, *die* habe ich im Sack.

Claire Z.: Nenne mich, wie du mich immer genannt hast.

10 Ill: Mein Wildkätzchen.

Claire Z. (*schnurrt wie eine alte Katze*): Wie noch?

Ill: Mein Zauberhexchen.

Claire Z.: Ich nannte dich ‚mein schwarzer Panther'.

Ill: **Der** bin ich noch.

15 Claire Z.: Unsinn, du bist fett geworden. Und grau und versoffen.

Ill: Doch *du* bist die gleiche geblieben. Zauberhexchen.

Claire Z.: Ach, was. Auch ich bin alt geworden und fett. Dazu ist mein linkes
Bein dahin. Ein Autounfall. Ich fahre nur noch Schnellzüge. Doch **die** Prothese
ist vortrefflich, findest du nicht? (*Sie hebt ihren Rock in die Höhe und*

20 *zeigt ihr linkes Bein*): Lässt sich gut bewegen.

Ill (*wischt sich den Schweiß ab*): Wäre nie daraufgekommen, Wildkätzchen.

Claire Z.: Darf ich dir meinen siebenten Gatten vorstellen, Alfred? Besitzt
Tabakplantagen. Führen eine glückliche Ehe.

Ill: Aber bitte.

25 Claire Z.: Komm, Moby, verneig dich. Eigentlich heißt er Pedro, doch macht
sich Moby schöner. Es passt auch besser zu Boby, wie der Kammerdiener
heißt. **Den** hat man schließlich fürs Leben, da müssen sich dann eben die
Gatten nach seinem Namen richten.

Aus: Friedrich Dürrenmatt, *Der Besuch der alten Dame*. © 1985 Diogenes
Verlag AG Zürich.

⌕ Demonstratives in the text

8.1 DEMONSTRATIVES BEFORE NOUNS

Demonstratives are used to point out a specific person or thing, differentiating it from other similar members of its class: e.g. **this** man', **that** table'. In German, the most commonly used demonstrative has the same form as the definite article (see **Table 4**): e.g. *der* Mann 'that man', *die* Frau 'that woman', *das* Kind 'that child'. It is usually used to mean 'that', but can also be used in contexts where English would use 'this': e.g. *Mmm, der Wein ist lecker* 'Mmm, this wine is lovely'.[44]

Since demonstratives have the same form as the definite article they are often difficult to regognise in a written text. For instance, in line 18–19, *Doch die Prothese ist vortrefflich*, *die* could be an article, 'the prosthesis', yet when taken within the whole context (i.e. Clara lifts up her skirt to show her artificial leg) it is more likely to be a demonstrative '**this** prosthesis'. Similarly, *all die Tage* (7) is probably best rendered as 'all **those** days.'[45]

[44] *Jener* is also a demonstrative meaning 'that' and takes the same endings as *dieser* (see **8.4**). However, it is much less commonly used than *der*.

[45] One indication of demonstrative rather than article status is the use of the full form rather than the contracted form: e.g. *zur Zeit* 'at the time/moment' vs. *zu der Zeit* 'at **that** time/moment'.

8.2 DEMONSTRATIVE PRONOUNS

8.2a With omitted nouns

Sometimes demonstratives can be used in place of a noun which is omitted but understood. In this case the demonstrative has the same gender and number as the omitted noun (and also the appropriate case): e.g. *Welchen Saft möchten Sie? – Ich möchte den, bitte.* 'Which juice would you like? – I'd like **this one/that one**, please' [< *ich möchte den Saft*] (see **Table 13**).[46] There is one example of this in the text: *Der bin ich noch* (14) [i.e. *ein schwarzer Panther*]. Note that in the **genitive** case and in the **dative plural**, the forms of the demonstrative differ from those of the definite article. The genitive forms, **dessen** (masc./neut. sg.), **deren** (fem. sg.) and **derer** (all plural) are less commonly used and are mainly restricted to the written language: e.g. *Die Anzahl derer, die in den letzten zwei Jahren nach Deutschland gekommen sind* 'the number **of those** who have come to Germany in the last two years'.

[46] English 'the one who/that . . .' is usually translated by *derjenige, der . . .*, which behaves like a definite article + adjective as far as endings are concerned, but is written as one word, *derjenige, der; diejenige, die; dasjenige, das; mit demjenigen, der* etc.: e.g. *Klaus? Ist das derjenige, der jetzt in Afrika wohnt?* 'Klaus? Is he the one who now lives in Africa?'

Table 13. The demonstrative pronouns

	Masc.	Fem.	Neut.	Plural
N	*der schmeckt gut*	*die schmeckt gut*	*das schmeckt gut*	*die schmecken gut*
A	*ich möchte den*	*ich möchte die*	*ich möchte das*	*ich möchte die*
D	*ein Stück von dem*	*ein Stück von der*	*ein Stück von dem*	*zwei von denen*

8.2b Replacing personal pronouns

In **spoken** German it is very common to use demonstrative pronouns instead of ordinary personal pronouns (without meaning 'this' or 'that'). In this case, the demonstratives usually come at the beginning of the clause and are often stressed: *die* habe ich im Sack (8) 'I've got round **her**', *Den* hat man schließlich fürs Leben (27) 'after all, you've got **him** for life'.[47]

[47] They can also be used without stress: e.g. *Wo ist mein Schlüssel? – Ich weiß es nicht. Den habe ich nicht gesehen.*

8.3 DAS

When 'this' and 'that' refer not to particular nouns but to whole ideas, *das* is used. In fact, because of this function, it is the most frequently used demonstrative of all: *das* habe ich mir immer vorgenommen (2), *Das* ist lieb von dir (4), *das* weißt du doch (6).

Similarly, *das* is used when the noun (or something standing in for the noun) is mentioned later: e.g. (not in text) *Das* ist mein Freund, Karl 'This is my friend, Karl', *Das* ist er 'That's him'.

Other points to note in the text

- Personal pronouns: *ich* (2, 3, 13, 14, 17, 18, 22), *mich* (5, 9); *du* (1, 5, 6, 9, 15, 16, 19), *dich* (13), *dir* (4, 22); *er* (25); *sie* (19), *es* (7, 26); *wir* (7); *Sie* (8); *man* (27) (see **7.1**).
- Personal pronouns omitted for stylistic effect in speech: [*Es*] *Lässt sich* (20), [*Er*] *Besitzt* (22), [*Wir*] *Führen* (23).
- Possessives: *mein* (2, 10, 12, 13, 17), *meinen* (22), *ihren* (19), *ihr* (20) (see **7.2**).
- Reflexive pronouns: *sich* (20, 21, 26, 29), *dich* (25); dative: *mir* (2) (see **Ch. 20**).
- Conditional perfect: *wäre . . . daraufgekommen* (21) (see **16.2b**).
- Subordinating conjunctions: *dass* (1), *seit* (3), *da* (7), *wie* (9, 26) (see **25.1**).
- *Alle* drops -e before definite article (7), also before demonstratives and possessives.

▲ Discover more about demonstratives

8.4 DIESER, DIES

Sometimes, 'this' is expressed using *dieser*, which takes similar endings to the definite article (see **Table 14**).

Table 14. Forms of *dieser*

	Masc.	Fem.	Neut.	Pl.
N	dieser	diese	dieses	diese
A	diesen	diese	dieses	diese
D	diesem	dieser	diesem	diesen
G	dieses	dieser	dieses	dieser

One should note, however, that *dieser* may also be used when English would use 'that': e.g. *Ich war zu* **dieser** *Zeit sehr glücklich* 'I was very happy at that time'. It is used quite often, but is much less common than *der*, particularly when used as a demonstrative **pronoun** (e.g. *Ich möchte* **den** is more common than *Ich möchte* **diesen**). When referring to a particular **idea** (rather than to a single noun) that has just been mentioned in the previous sentence, **dies** is sometimes used: e.g. **Dies** *führe zu einem miesepetrigen Gesichtsausdruck* (in line 6 of the text in Chapter **3**, where *dies* refers to the position of the mouth when pronouncing German umlauts). On the whole, however, *das* is used more frequently than *dies* to refer to an idea (see **8.3** above).

8.5   *DA+ PREPOSITION*

When demonstrative pronouns occur with prepositions, *da-* + preposition (*dar-* before vowels) is often used as an alternative to the ordinary pronoun, as long as it is referring to things and not to people: e.g.

Von dem weiß ich überhaupt nichts / **Davon** *weiß ich überhaupt nichts*	I don't know anything about that
Nein, mit dem bin ich nicht zufrieden / *Nein,* **damit** *bin ich nicht zufrieden*	No, I'm not happy about that

As the examples suggest, *da-* tends to be used when referring to general ideas rather than concrete objects which are stressed: e.g. *Mit welchem Messer kann man am besten Fleisch schneiden? Mit* **dem** *oder mit* **dem**? vs. *Was halten Sie von der Situation? – Ich bin* **damit** *überhaupt nicht zufrieden.*

Less commonly, *dies* with a preposition becomes *hier-*. This is primarily used in formal styles of German: e.g. **Hiermit** *bestätige ich* . . . 'I hereby confirm . . .'. Mostly, a preposition + 'this' is translated as *da(r)* + preposition: e.g. 'Do you know anything about this?' *Weißt du etwas* **davon**?

✎ **EXERCISES**

Vocabulary topic: *Kleidung*

1 Fill in the gaps with the appropriate form of the demonstrative, first using *der* and then using *dieser*:

Example: Ich muss d___ Hemd bügeln.
Answers: i) Ich muss **das** Hemd bügeln; ii) Ich muss **dieses** Hemd bügeln.

1 D___ Rock darfst du nicht anziehen. Er ist viel zu kurz.
2 Die Schuhe passen sehr gut zu d___ Hose.
3 D___ schwarze Mantel ist sehr schön.
4 Kannst du mit d___ hohen Schuhen überhaupt gehen?
5 Die Farbe d___ Pullis gefällt mir nicht.
6 Die Löcher in d___ Socken werden immer größer!

2 Answer the following questions using the appropriate form of the demonstrative pronoun, first using *der* and then using *dieser*:

Example: Welches Kleid gefällt dir am besten?
Answers: i) **Das** da; ii) **Dieses** da.

1   Welche Jacke willst du anziehen?
2   Welcher Schal ist wärmer?
3   Zu welchen Handschuhen passt mein Mantel am besten?
4   Welchen Hut hat er getragen?
5   Von welcher Weste hat sie gesprochen?
6   Von welchen Stiefeln sind die Absätze zu hoch?
7   Welcher Schuh hat ein Loch drin?
8   Welche Krawatte soll ich anziehen?

✎ FURTHER EXERCISES

3 Fill in the gaps with the appropriate form of the demonstrative *der*:

1   D_____ Kaffee trinke ich am liebsten.
2   Gehen wir ins Kino? – Ja, d_____ ist eine gute Idee.
3   D_____ ist mein Freund Robert.
4   Robert ist d_____, der früher bei Siemens gearbeitet hat.
5   Was ist mit d_____ passiert, der nach Australien ausgewandert ist?
6   Er wollte mir mir über die politische Situation in Uganda reden, aber ich verstehe nichts von d_____.
7   Es ist höchster Zeit, dass er eine richtige Arbeit sucht, aber an d_____ denkt er nie.

4 Replace the personal pronouns in bold print with demonstrative pronouns and move them to the beginning of the clause, as is common in colloquial spoken German:

Example: Was hältst du von Katrin? – Ich finde **sie** sehr sympathisch.
Answers: Was hältst du von Katrin? – **Die** finde ich sehr sympathisch.

1   Wie geht's Klaus? – Ich weiß es nicht. Ich habe **ihn** seit langem nicht gesehen.
2   Wo ist Oskar? – **Er** ist im Urlaub.
3   Hast du auch ein Geschenk von deinen Eltern bekommen? – Ja, ich habe **von ihnen** diese Uhr gekriegt.
4   Was hast du Astrid zum Geburtstag geschenkt? – Ich habe **ihr** eine CD gegeben.
5   Warum will Tobias nicht ins Fischrestaurant gehen? – Fisch und Meeresfrüchte schmecken **ihm** überhaupt nicht.

9 | Relative pronouns

Der Prüfungstraum

Jeder, **der** mit der Maturitätsprüfung seine Gymnasialstudien abgeschlossen hat, klagt über die Hartnäckigkeit, mit **welcher** der Angsttraum, dass er durchgefallen sei, die Klasse wiederholen müsse u. dgl., ihn verfolgt. Für den Besitzer eines akademischen Grades ersetzt sich dieser typische Traum durch einen
5 anderen, **der** ihm vorhält, dass er beim Rigorosum nicht bestanden habe, und gegen **den** er vergeblich noch im Schlaf einwendet, dass er ja schon seit Jahren praktiziere, Privatdozent sei oder Kanzleileiter. Es sind die unauslöslichen Erinnerungen an die Strafen, **die** wir in der Kindheit für verübte Untaten erlitten haben, **die** sich so an den beiden Knotenpunkten unserer Studien, an
10 dem »*dies irae, dies illa*« der strengen Prüfungen in unserem Inneren wieder geregt haben. [. . .]
    Eine weitere Erklärung der Prüfungsträume danke ich einer Bemerkung von Seite eines kundigen Kollegen, **der** einmal in einer wissenschaftlichen Unterhaltung hervorhob, dass seines Wissens der Maturatraum nur bei Personen
15 vorkomme, **die** diese Prüfung bestanden haben, niemals bei solchen, **die** an ihr gescheitert sind. Der ängstliche Prüfungstraum, **der**, wie sich immer mehr bestätigt, dann auftritt, wenn man vom nächsten Tage eine verantwortliche Leistung und die Möglichkeit einer Blamage erwartet, würde also eine Gelegenheit aus der Vergangenheit herausgesucht haben, bei **welcher** sich die große Angst als
20 unberechtigt erwies und durch den Ausgang widerlegt wurde. Es wäre dies ein sehr auffälliges Beispiel von Missverständnis des Trauminhalts durch die wache Instanz. Die als Empörung gegen den Traum aufgefasste Einrede: Aber ich bin ja schon Doktor u. dgl., wäre in Wirklichkeit der Trost, **den** der Traum spendet und **der** also lauten würde: Fürchte dich doch nicht vor morgen; denke daran, welche Angst
25 du vor der Maturitätsprüfung gehabt hast, und es ist dir doch nichts geschehen.

Aus: Sigmund Freud, *Die Traumdeutung*. © 1991 Fischer Taschenbuch Verlag.

♀ Relative pronouns in the text

9.1 **THE FORM OF RELATIVE PRONOUNS**

9.1a The relatives *der, die, das*

Relative pronouns in German correspond to the use of English 'who', 'which' and 'that' after a noun: e.g. 'the man who lives next door', 'the car which/that[48] I just bought'. In German, the relative pronoun is often identical to the **definite article**, agreeing in gender and number with the preceding noun that it is referring to: e.g. *der Mann,* **der** *auf den Bus wartet.* It can also appear in all four cases depending on the context, but the nominative is the most common. **Table 15** lists all forms of the relative pronoun, underlining those that differ from the definite article. Note that relative pronouns are identical to demonstrative pronouns (see **8.2a**).

> [48] English learners of German are often tempted to use the conjunction *dass* instead of a relative pronoun, as it also means 'that'. However, if English 'that' could also mean 'which' or 'who', then it must be translated using a relative pronoun in German: e.g. *das Auto,* **das** (not* *dass*) *ich kaufte.*

Table 15. Relative pronouns

	Masc.	Fem.	Neut.	Plural
N	der Mann, **der**	die Frau, **die**	das Kind, **das**	die Kinder, **die**
A	der Mann, **den**	die Frau, **die**	das Kind, **das**	die Kinder, **die**
D	der Mann, **dem**	die Frau, **der**	das Kind, **dem**	die Kinder, **denen**
G	der Mann, **dessen**	der Frau, **deren**	das Kind, **dessen**	die Kinder, **deren**

Examples from the text are in the nominative and accusative (see **9.3** for the dative and genitive):

Nom.: *der ängstliche Prüfungstraum,* **der** . . . *auftritt* (16–17)
 nur bei Personen vorkomme, **die** . . . *bestanden haben* (14–15)
Acc.: *der Trost,* **den** *der Traum spendet* (23)
 Strafen, **die** *wir in der Kindheit . . . erlitten haben* (8–9)

We can see from these examples that the relative pronouns are always preceded by a comma and send the following finite verb to the end of the clause.

9.1b Further notes on relative pronouns

i) Relative pronouns can also refer back to other pronouns: *Jeder,* **der** . . . *abgeschlossen hat* (1–2); *bei solchen,* **die** . . . *gescheitert sind* (15–16).

ii) Where a preposition is used, it always precedes the relative pronoun, as in formal English 'the man **with** whom she lived', 'the story **about** which I know very little', and the relative pronoun appears in the case required by the preposition: *einen anderen . . .,* **gegen** **den** *er vergeblich . . . einwendet* (4–6).

iii) Unlike English, German relative pronouns are never omitted: *der Trost,* **den** *der Traum spendet* = 'the consolation (that) the dream gives', where 'that' (or 'which') can be omitted in less formal styles of English.[49]

> [49] Similarly, English constructions of the type 'the man **waiting** for the bus', where the relative pronoun 'who' and the finite verb 'is' are omitted, must be translated using a relative pronoun in German: *der Mann,* **der** *auf den Bus wartet.*

9.2   WELCHER

A more formal alternative to the relative pronouns given above is *welcher*, which is often found in written German. It has basically the same endings as the relatives *der, die, das* etc., except that it does not occur in the genitive (see **Table 16**).

Table 16. Forms of *welcher*

	Masc.	Fem.	Neut.	Plural
N	welch**er**	welch**e**	welch**es**	welch**e**
A	welch**en**	welch**e**	welch**es**	welch**e**
D	welch**em**	welch**er**	welch**em**	welch**en**

It is often used as an alternative to *der* etc. to avoid repetition: *die Hartnäckigkeit, mit* **welcher** *der Angsttraum . . .* (2) [instead of *mit* **der** *der Angsttraum . . .*], although *der der* etc. would not be incorrect. Often it is simply used as a more formal variant of *der* etc.: *eine Gelegenheit . . ., bei* **welcher** *sich die große Angst als unberechtigt erwies* (18–20). In the Sigmund Freud text, *welcher* appears to be used particularly after prepositions.

Other points to note in the text

- Weak masculine noun: *eines kundigen* **Kollegen** (13) (see **3.3b**).
- Extended attribute: *Die* **als Empörung gegen den Traum aufgefasste** *Einrede* (22) (see **5.3**).
- Imperative: **Fürchte** *dich doch nicht* (24), **denke** *daran* (24) (see **Ch. 11**).
- *Konjunktiv 1* in reported speech: *durchgefallen* **sei** (3), *wiederholen* **müsse** (3), *bestanden* **habe** (5), *praktiziere* (7), *sei* (7), *vorkomme* (15) (see **Ch. 17**).
- *Konjunktiv II* in reported speech: **würde** *. . . herausgesucht haben* (18–19), *wäre* (20, 23), *lauten* **würde** (24). (see **17.4**).
- Use of reflexive instead of passive: *ersetzt* **sich** (4).
- Use of the older dative singular -e: *vom nächsten* **Tage** (17) (see footnote 18).

▲ Discover more about relative pronouns

9.3 RELATIVE PRONOUNS IN THE DATIVE AND GENITIVE

9.3a Dative

If the relative pronoun is an indirect object or occurs with a preposition or verb taking the dative, it appears in the dative (**dem** for masculines and neuter singulars, **der** for feminine singulars and **denen** for all plurals):

*Das ist der Polizist, **dem** ich alles erklärt habe.*
*Hier kommt die alte Frau, **der** du geholfen hast.*
*Das sind die Computer, mit **denen** er arbeitet.*

9.3b Genitive ('whose')

Genitive relative pronouns are the German equivalent of English 'whose' (or, with inanimate objects, 'of which'). If the preceding noun referred to is masculine or neuter singular, **dessen** is used, and if it is feminine or plural, **deren** is used:

*Ich suche den Mann, **dessen** Auto vor der Tür steht.*
*Wo ist das Haus, **dessen** Fenster eingeschlagen worden sind?*
*Hier kommt die Frau, **deren** Sohn eben geheiratet hat.*
*Das sind die Nachbarn, auf **deren** Hund ich aufgepasst habe.*

9.4 USE OF WAS

The relative pronoun *was* is used when no particular noun precedes it, i.e. it refers back to indefinite expressions such as *das, etwas, nichts, vieles* etc. (see (i)) or to a whole clause (see (ii)):

i) *Das, **was** ich immer sage.*
   *Ich habe etwas gefunden, **was** dich interessieren wird.*
ii) *Er gibt sein Studium auf, **was** meiner Meinung nach ein Fehler ist.*

9.5 USE OF WO(R)- WITH PREPOSITIONS

If a construction with **was** needs a preposition, *was* becomes *wo-* (*wor-* before a vowel) and the preposition is added to the end: e.g. *Er gibt sein Studium auf, **womit** ich nicht einverstanden bin, Das ist etwas, **woran** ich immer denke.*

✎ EXERCISES

Vocabulary topic: *Arbeit*

1 Fill in the gaps with the appropriate relative pronouns:

1   Er arbeitet bei einer Firma, ___ fünftausend Angestellte hat.
2   Ich habe einen Chef, ___ ständig zu spät in die Arbeit kommt.
3   Das ist der Trainingskurs, ___ ich letztes Jahr gemacht habe.
4   Das Büro, ___ gegenüber von meinem liegt, ist seit einem Monat leer.

5   Das war die Sitzung, bei ___ die Entlassungen besprochen wurden.

6   Sie stellen fünfzig neue Arbeiter ein, ___ natürlich sehr gut ist.

7   Die Sekretärin, ___ ich die Unterlagen gegeben habe, hat sich heute krank gemeldet.

8   Der Umsatz, ___ wir in den letzten drei Monaten erzielt haben, war sehr hoch.

9   Im ersten Jahr habe ich vieles gelernt, ___ ich für meinen Lebenslauf gebrauchen kann.

10 Der Kollege, ___ ich immer geholfen habe, will jetzt kündigen.

2   Make the underlined noun phrases the subject of the sentence by placing them at the beginning (in the nominative case) and using relative pronouns:

Example: Ich arbeite seit 20 Jahren mit <u>meinem Geschäftspartner</u> zusammen.

Answer: **Mein Geschäftspartner, mit dem** ich seit 20 Jahren zusammen arbeite.

1   Ich habe eine Gehaltserhöhung von <u>meinem Chef</u> bekommen.

2   Ich kann mich auf <u>die Assistentin</u> verlassen.

3   Er wartet seit einer halben Stunde auf <u>den Kunden</u>.

4   Die Papiere <u>des Abteilungsleiters</u> liegen auf dem Tisch.

5   Der Computer <u>der Sekretärin</u> funktioniert nicht.

6   Ich bin an <u>dem Vorstellungsgespräch</u> gescheitert.

7   Du arbeitest mit <u>dem Computer</u>.

8   Er hat auf <u>den neuen</u> <u>Drucker</u> gewartet.

9   Ich weiß nicht viel über <u>die neuen</u> <u>Arbeitsbedingungen</u>.

10 Der Manager hat von <u>den flexiblen Arbeitszeiten</u> geredet.

3   Join the phrases together using either *was* or *wo(r)* + preposition where appropriate:

Example: Er hat eine Beförderung bekommen. Das ist natürlich super.

Answer: Er hat eine Beförderung bekommen, **was** natürlich super ist.

1   Wir haben nur zehn Minuten Kaffeepause. Das ist viel zu wenig.

2   Ich muss heute Abend lange arbeiten. Ich freue mich nicht darauf.

3   Mein Kollege ist heute auf Abruf. Er ist nicht sehr glücklich damit.

4   Ich kriege keine Überstunden mehr bezahlt. Das finde ich nicht richtig.

5   Wir können morgens früher anfangen und abends früher nach Hause gehen. Ich habe nichts dagegen.

✎ FURTHER EXERCISES

4   Underline the relative pronouns in the following text and explain their form:

Ein jetzt 35jähriger Mann erzählt einen gut erinnerten Traum, den er mit vier Jahren gehabt haben will: *Der Notar, bei dem das Testament des Vaters hinterlegt war [. . .], brachte zwei große Kaiserbirnen, von denen er eine zum Essen bekam. Die andere lag auf dem Fensterbrett des Wohnzimmers.* [. . .]. Er erwachte mit der Überzeugung von der Realität des Geträumten und verlangte hartnäckig von der Mutter die zweite Birne [. . .].

Analyse: Der Notar war ein jovialer alter Herr, der, wie er sich zu erinnern glaubt, wirklich einmal Birnen mitbrachte. Das Fensterbrett war so, wie er es im Traume sah. Anderes will ihm dazu nicht einfallen; etwa noch, dass die Mutter kürzlich ihm einen Traum erzählt. Sie hat zwei Vögel auf ihrem Kopfe sitzen, fragt sich, wann sie fortfliegen werden, aber sie fliegen nicht fort, sondern der eine fliegt zu ihrem Munde und saugt aus ihm.

Das Versagen der Einfälle des Träumers gibt uns das Recht, die Deutung durch Symbolersetzung zu versuchen. Die beiden Birnen [. . .] sind die Brüste der Mutter, die ihn genährt hat; das Fensterbrett der Vorsprung des Busens [. . .]. Sein Wirklichkeitsgefühl nach dem Erwachen hat recht, denn die Mutter hat ihn wirklich gesäugt, sogar weit über die gebräuchliche Zeit hinaus, und die Mutterbrust wäre noch immer zu haben. Der Traum ist zu übersetzten: Mutter, gib [. . .] mir die Brust wieder, an der ich früher einmal getrunken habe.

Aus: Sigmund Freud, *Die Traumdeutung*. © 1991 Fischer Taschenbuch Verlag.

10 | Present tense

Anglizismen – ein Problem für die deutsche Sprache?

Noch **sprechen** 100 Millionen Menschen auf der Erde Deutsch. Aber viele, vielleicht sogar die meisten, nur recht widerwillig. Der moderne Modell-Germane **joggt, jumpt, trekkt, walkt, skatet** oder **biket, hat** fun und feelings, moods und moments, sorrows und emotions, und **scheint** vor nichts auf

5 Erden solche Angst zu haben, als seine eigene Sprache zu benutzen – Deutsch zu sprechen **ist** vielen Deutschen ganz offensichtlich lästig oder peinlich. Dass Musik, sofern gesungen, im deutschen Radio fast nur noch auf English **stattfindet, ist** schon so normal geworden, dass es niemandem mehr **auffällt**. Und andere Kommunikationskanäle **holen** mit großem Tempo **auf**.

10 Was **sagt** der ZDF-Reporter bei der Übertragung der letzten Sonnenfinsternis, als der Mond zum ersten Mal die Sonne **berührt**: first contact. Eben hat der first contact stattgefunden. [. . .].

    Diese indirekte Bitte an das Ausland, Deutsch erst gar nicht zu erlernen, **hat** ihren Gegenpart in der perversen Lust der Deutschen selber, das

15 Deutsch, das sie noch **können**, möglichst gründlich wieder zu vergessen. Wie selbstverständlich **scheinen** viele Menschen, die Deutsch als Muttersprache **haben**, heute das Englische als ihre Leit- und Kommandosprache aufzufassen. Das **fängt** mit einem angel-shop im Erzgebirge (Laden für Weihnachtszubehör) oder einer alten Dame **an**, die auf dem Bahnhof nach dem Eis-Zug **fragt** (so

20 gesehen auf dem Hauptbahnhof in München), und **hört** bei Jugendlichen **auf**, die den deutschen Ausdruck turteln ohne nachzudenken auf die Gehweise von Schildkröten **beziehen**.

    Der Gipfel dieser Anbiederung an den angelsächsischen Kulturkreis **ist** erreicht, wenn deutsche Politiker deutsche Wähler mit englischen

25 Werbesprüchen zu gewinnen **suchen**: „Vote Yellow" (so die FDP bei der Kommunalwahl NRW), „Law and order is a Labour issue" (SPD-Plakat bei der Wahl zur Bürgerschaft in Hamburg), „Welcome today, welcome tomorrow" (Wahlkampflied der CDU in Niedersachsen) usw. Hier **scheint** die bekannte Einschätzung von Churchill, dass man die Deutschen entweder an der Gurgel

30 oder an den Füßen habe, eine weitere Bestätigung zu finden.

Aus einem Artikel von Prof. Dr. Walter Krämer. © *Forschung und Lehre*, Oktober 2000.

◌ **The present tense in the text**

10.1 USAGE

As in English, the present tense in German is primarily used to refer to present time, e.g. *sprechen* (line 1 of text), habitual actions, e.g. *joggt, jumpt, trekt* (3), or in general statements which are not linked to any particular time, e.g. *fängt . . . an, hört . . . auf* (18–20). One particular narrative technique is to use the present tense to refer to past events, which can create a feeling of immediacy, excitement or humour, e.g. *sagt* (10), *berührt* (11). There is no special progressive form of the present in German. Thus, 'they speak' and 'they are speaking' are both rendered by *sie sprechen.*[50]

> [50] If, however, a speaker/writer of German feels that it is important to emphasise the progressive aspect in a particular context, the following alternatives may be used: e.g. 'I'm writing an essay' *Ich schreibe* **eben** *(or* **gerade***) einen Aufsatz* OR *Ich bin* **eben/gerade dabei***, einen Aufsatz zu schreiben.* In addition, where no object is present, *beim* + infinitival noun is possible: e.g. *Ich bin* **beim Schreiben***.* These constructions can also be used in tenses other than the present: e.g. *Ich telefonierte gerade; Ich war beim Lesen, Ich* **bin** *eben dabei* **gewesen***, meine Mutter anzurufen.*

10.2 FORMATION

10.2a Regular verbs

The present tense is formed using the **present tense stem** (the infinitive minus *-en*) with the following endings:

		e.g. *sagen*:	*ich* **sage**[51]	*wir* **sagen**
-e	*-en*	(Stem: *sag-*)	*du* **sagst**	*ihr* **sagt**
-st	*-t*		*er/sie/es* **sagt** (10)	*sie/Sie* **sagen**
-t	*-en*			

This chapter's text uses the third person singular (i.e. the *er/sie/es*-form), e.g. *joggt, jumpt* (3), *scheint* (4, 28), *berührt* (11), and the third person plural (*sie*-form), e.g. *sprechen* (1), *können* (15), *scheinen* (16), *haben* (17), *suchen* (25).

Points to note:

- For ease of pronunciation, if the stem of the verb ends in *-d, -t* or a consonant + *n* or *m*, **-e-** is added before the endings *-st* and *-t*, e.g. *stattfinden* becomes *stattfind-**e**-t* (line 8).
- The *du*-form ending *-st* becomes *-t* after *s, ß, z* and *x*, e.g. *reisen – du reis-**t***.
- *-en* appears as *-n* when the infinitive of the verb has *-n*, e.g. *tu**n**, klingel**n***.

> [51] In spoken German (and in writing imitating dialogue), *-e* is often dropped, especially in more colloquial speech, e.g. *ich sag', ich denk', ich find'*.

10.2b Separable verbs

Separable prefixes are sent to the end of the clause when the verb is in the present tense. Examples in the text are *aufholen* (9), *anfangen* (18–19), *aufhören* (20). The separable verbs *stattfinden* (8) and *auffallen* (9) appear with their prefixes attached because the verbs themselves have been sent to the end of the clause following *dass*. (See Chapter **19** for more information on separable verbs.)

10.2c Irregular verbs

Some of the verbs which are irregular in the past tense are also irregular in the present, particularly in the *du-* and *er/sie/es*-forms (see **10.4**). Examples from the text are *fängt . . . an* from *anfangen* (18–19), *auffällt* from *auffallen* (9). *Haben* and *sein* are also irregular: *hat* (3, 14), *ist* (6, 8, 23).

Other points to note in the text

- Perfect tense: *ist . . . geworden* (8), *hat . . . stattgefunden* (11–12) (see **Ch. 13**).
- *Konjunktiv I*: *habe* (30) (see **Ch. 17**).
- *Sein*-passive: *ist . . . erreicht* (23–24) (see **18.9**).
- Prepositions with different usage from English equivalents: *auf* (1, 4, 19, 21) *in* (7), *mit* (9), *bei* (10, 25, 26), *zu* (11, 27), *an* (13, 23, 29, 30), *nach* (19) (see **24.5**).

▲ Discover more about the present tense

10.3 USAGE

In some cases, German uses a present tense where English would not:

i) To refer to the **future**, particularly where it is clear from the context that the future is meant and no ambiguity with the present can arise: e.g. *Ich **komme** um 2 Uhr* 'I'll come at 2 o'clock', *Wir **treffen** uns vor dem Kino* 'We'll meet in front of the cinema.'

ii) To refer to an action or event **beginning in the past** which is still **continuing into the present**. This would be expressed using a perfect tense in English: e.g. *Ich **wohne** hier seit vier Jahren* 'I've been living here for four years (and still am)'. These constructions are usually used with *seit* (or *seitdem* followed by a clause) 'since' and *schon* 'already': e.g. *Ich **bin** seit Januar verheiratet* 'I've been married since January', *Seitdem er die neue Arbeit **hat**, geht er sehr selten aus* 'Since he's had the new job he rarely goes out'.

iii) To indicate present relevance, even when speaking in the **past** (or perfect) tense. For instance, in English the past tense tends to be used after another past to keep the tenses consistent. Thus 'I <u>knew</u> that he **was** over forty' can be used to refer to the present (i.e. he is over forty now), as it would be ungrammatical to say *'I knew that he **is** over forty'. In German, however, a present is used here: *Ich <u>wusste</u>, dass er über vierzig **ist**.*

10.4 IRREGULAR PRESENT FORMS

Verbs with a vowel change in the *du-* and *er/sie/es*-forms of the present are:[52]

e – i	*brechen* – **brichst, bricht**, *(fr)essen* – **(fr)isst, (fr)isst**, *gelten* – **gilt**, *helfen* – **hilfst, hilft**, *messen* – **misst, misst**, *sprechen* – **sprichst, spricht**, and (with long e) *geben* – **gibst, gibt**, *nehmen* – **nimmst, nimmt**, *treten* – **trittst, tritt**.
e – ie	*lesen* – **liest, liest**, *stehlen* – **stiehlst, stiehlt**.
a(u) – ä(u)	Most verbs in -*a*- and -*au*- with an irregular past tense. Some examples are: *fallen* – **fällst, fällt**, *fangen* – **fängst, fängt**, *halten* – **hältst, hält**, *schlafen* – **schläfst, schläft**, *wachsen* – **wächst, wächst**, *laufen* – **läufst, läuft**.

---

[52] For more information, see **Appendix 1** for a full list of common irregular verbs.

Table 17 lists some other irregular present tense forms.

Table 17. Other common irregular verbs

	ich	du	er/sie/es	wir	ihr	sie/Sie
haben	habe	hast	hat	haben	habt	haben
sein	bin	bist	ist	sind	seid	sind
werden	werde	wirst	wird	werden	werdet	werden
dürfen	darf	darfst	darf	dürfen	dürft	dürfen
können	kann	kannst	kann	können	könnt	können
mögen	mag	magst	mag	mögen	mögt	mögen
müssen	muss	musst	muss	müssen	müsst	müssen
sollen	soll	sollst	soll	sollen	sollt	sollen
wollen	will	willst	will	wollen	wollt	wollen
wissen	weiß	weißt	weiß	wissen	wisst	wissen

10.5 DERIVED VERBS

Verbs with prefixes follow the same pattern as the verbs from which they are derived: i.e. if the basic verb is irregular, the derived verb will also be irregular: e.g. *fallen – fällt* gives *auffallen – auffällt, einfallen – einfällt, umfallen – umfällt* etc.

10.6 PRESENT PARTICIPLES

Present participles in German are formed by taking the infinitive of the verb and adding *-d*: e.g. *lachend, weinend,* and are mainly used as adjectives, e.g. *der **kommende** Montag, ein **rauchender** Jugendlicher* (particularly in extended attributes, see **5.3**), and adverbs, e.g. *Er saß **schweigend**.* By contrast, English present participles are used in many verbal constructions: e.g. 'I was working', 'He's the man reading a newspaper', 'He left the house, saying that he'd be late', where German would have a simple finite verb (see footnote 50, footnote 49 and **25.5**, respectively).

✎ EXERCISES

Vocabulary topic: *Sprache*

1 Put the verbs in square brackets into the present tense:

a 1 Du [können] gut Englisch.
   2 Stefan [finden] Russisch sehr schwierig, aber es [gefallen] ihm trotzdem.
   3 Wie [aussprechen] man „Chrysantheme"?
   4 Bettina [lesen] einen französischen Roman.
   5 Ich [denken], die Grammatik und der Wortschatz [sein] relativ einfach, aber die Aussprache [sein] sehr schwer.

b Anglizismen – ein Problem für die deutsche Sprache (*contd. from above*).

Es [sein] vor allem diese „linguistic submissiveness" (so die Londoner *Times*), die die in Deutschland grassierende Anglizitis über ihre Gefahr für die Sprache als solche zu einer so peinlichen und würdelosen Affäre [machen] – man [sich fühlen] angeschleimt und ausländischen Gästen gegenüber oft beschämt. („[Sein] ich hier in Chicago oder wo?" – Kommentar eines polnischen Gastwissenschaftlers auf dem „airport" Düsseldorf). Denn anders als die Englisch-Englisch-über-alles Lobby hierzulande gerne [glauben] und immer wieder als Begründung für das Fliehen aus der Muttersprache [anführen], [werden] ebendiese sprachliche Selbstaufgabe andernorts keineswegs als das Zeichnen weltoffenen Kosmopolitentums verstanden, als das viele Deutsche es so gerne sähen. Man [denken] ganz im Gegenteil an Churchill und [sich aufwappnen] für den Moment, wo man die Deutschen wieder an der Gurgel [haben]. Nicht umsonst [heißen] ein altes Sprichwort unter Reisenden: Trau nur dem, der sich selbst [vertrauen], und mit diesem peinlichen Anbiedern an das Englische [setzen] wir ein für alle Welt unübersehbares Misstrauensvotum gegen unsere eigene Sprache und Kultur.

2 Complete these German tongue-twisters (*Zungenbrecher*) by filling in the gaps using the present tense of the given verbs. Read your answers out loud:

1 Fischers Fritz _____ [fischen] frische Fische.
2 Hinter Hermann Hannes Haus _____ [raushängen] hundert Hemden.
3 Welch schlecht berechtigtes Vermächtnis _____ [entwachsen] dem schwächlichen Gedächtnis.
4 Max, wenn du Wachsmasken _____ [mögen], dann mach Wachsmasken!
5 Wenn der Benz _____ [bremsen], _____ [brennen] das Benz-Bremslicht.
6 Tuten _____ [tun] der Nachtwächter. Und wenn er genug getutet hat, _____ [reintun] er seine Tute wieder in den Tutkasten.
7 Wer gegen Aluminium minimal immun _____ [sein], _____ [besitzen] Aluminiumminimalimmunität.
8 Der Schweizer Schweißer _____ [schwitzen] und _____ [schweißen].

✎ **FURTHER EXERCISES**

3 Complete these German jokes by putting the verbs into the present:

1 Ein älteres Ehepaar _____ [gehen] zum ersten Mal in die Oper. Neben einer kleinen Mahlzeit _____ [mitbringen] es auch zwei Flaschen Apfelsaft. Am Eingang _____ [fragen] die Platzanweiserin: „_____ [wollen] Sie ein Opernglas?" _____ [antworten] der Mann: „Nein, danke, wir _____ [trinken] aus der Flasche."
2 Susanne _____ [sitzen] mit ihrer Freundin bei leckerer Torte im Café und _____ [meinen]: „_____ [wissen] du was, Beate? Ich habe in der letzten Woche 82 Kilo verloren." – „Quatsch, das _____ [glauben] du doch selber nicht! Wie _____ [sollen] das denn gehen?" – „Ganz einfach: Ich habe meinen Mann vor die Tür gesetzt!"

3 _____ [fragen] der Arzt seinen Patienten: „_____ [sprechen] Sie im Schlaf?" – „Nein, ich _____ [sprechen], wenn andere _____ [schlafen]" – „Wieso das denn?" Antwort: „Ich _____ [sein] Lehrer!"

4 „So, dann _____ [müssen] Sie mich begleiten", _____ [befehlen] der Polizist. Darauf der Straßenmusikant: „Aber gerne, Herr Wachtmeister! Was _____ [singen] Sie denn?"

5 „Mutti", _____ [sagen] der kleine Erwin, „hier _____ [stehen], dass das Theater Statisten sucht. Was _____ [sein] denn das?" – „Statisten _____ [sein] Leute, die nur _____ [herumstehen] und nichts zu sagen _____ [haben]." – „Aber Mutti, das wäre doch etwas für Papi!"

6 Bei einem Klassentreffen _____ [fragen] der Lehrer einen seiner ehemaligen Schüler: „Na, du _____ [sein] doch der Karl? Wie _____ [gehen] es dir, _____ [sein] du verheiratet?" „Ja, ich _____ [haben] acht Kinder". – „So, du warst schon immer sehr fleißig, aber aufgepasst hast du nie!"

7 Die kleine Veronika _____ [laufen] zum Infostand im Kaufhaus: „Sie, wenn eine aufgeregte Frau _____ [kommen], die ihr Kind verloren hat, dann richten Sie aus, ich _____ [sein] in der Spielzeugabteilung."

4 Change the perfect tense forms in bold into the present only where appropriate (i.e. if the sentence is ungrammatical):

1 Ich **habe** sehr gern bei der Firma **gearbeitet**.

2 Er **hat** seit Februar in Berlin **gewohnt**.

3 Sie **sind** um drei Uhr in die Stadt **gefahren**.

4 Wir **sind** seit vier Jahren zusammen **gewesen**.

5 Seitdem ich meine neue Wohnung **gehabt habe**, bin ich viel glücklicher.

5 Complete the following crossword by filling in the gaps in the clues (umlauts are indicated by placing e after the vowel in question, e.g. *für* = fuer):

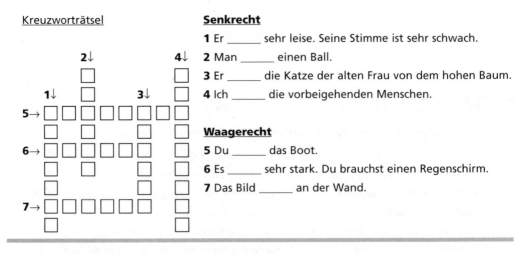

Kreuzworträtsel

Senkrecht

1 Er _____ sehr leise. Seine Stimme ist sehr schwach.

2 Man _____ einen Ball.

3 Er _____ die Katze der alten Frau von dem hohen Baum.

4 Ich _____ die vorbeigehenden Menschen.

Waagerecht

5 Du _____ das Boot.

6 Es _____ sehr stark. Du brauchst einen Regenschirm.

7 Das Bild _____ an der Wand.

☞ **For further exercises on the present tense see Revision Text 3, Ex. 2.9**

11 | Imperative

Männer sind Schweine

Hallo mein Schatz, ich liebe dich, du bist die Einzige für mich
Die anderen find' ich alle doof, deswegen mach' ich dir den Hof.
Du bist so anders, ganz speziell, ich merke sowas immer schnell,
Jetzt **zieh** dich **aus** und **leg** dich **hin**, weil ich so verliebt in dich bin . . .

5 Gleich wird es dunkel, bald ist es Nacht – da ist ein Wort der Warnung angebracht:
Männer sind Schweine, **traue** ihnen nicht, mein Kind
Sie wollen alle das Eine, weil Männer nunmal so sind
Ein Mann fühlt sich erst dann als Mann, wenn er es dir besorgen kann
Er lügt, dass sich die Balken biegen, nur um dich ins Bett zu kriegen

10 Und dann, am nächsten Morgen, weiß er nicht einmal mehr, wie du heißt
Rücksichtslos und ungehemmt, Gefühle sind ihm völlig fremd
Für ihn ist Liebe gleich Samenverlust – Mädchen **sei** dir dessen stets bewusst:
Männer sind Schweine, **frage** nicht nach Sonnenschein
Ausnahmen gibt's leider keine, in jedem Mann steckt auch immer ein Schwein

15 Männer sind Säue, **glaube** ihnen nicht ein Wort,
Sie schwören dir ewige Treue, und dann am nächsten Morgen sind sie fort . . .
Und wenn du doch den Fehler machst und dir 'nen Ehemann anlachst
Dann wird dein Rosenkavalier kurz nach der Hochzeit auch zum Tier
Da zeigt er dann sein wahres Ich, ganz unrasiert und widerlich

20 Trinkt Bier, sieht fern und wird schnell fett, und rülpst und furzt im Ehebett
Dann hast du King Kong zum Ehemann – darum sag' ich dir, **denk** bitte
stets daran:
Männer sind Schweine, **traue** ihnen nicht, mein Kind
Sie wollen alle nur das Eine, für wahre Liebe sind sie blind.

© Die Ärzte, 1999, Hot Action Records.

♀ The imperative in the text

11.1 USAGE

The imperative mood is used to express a command: e.g. '**Come** here!', '**Put** that down!', '**Take** a seat!'. In German, there are three different forms of the imperative depending on whom the speaker is addressing: i) the informal singular form for a person who would be addressed as _du_;

ii) the informal plural form for people addressed as *ihr*; iii) the polite form for people (singular and plural) who would be addressed as *Sie*.[53] The former category is the most commonly used and it is this type of imperative which appears in our text.

11.2 FORMATION OF THE *DU*-IMPERATIVE

The form of the imperative used in the text is the informal singular (*du*) form which is made up from the present tense stem of the verb (the infinitive minus *-en*; see **10.2a**) plus the ending *-e*, e.g. *trau-e* (6, 23), *frag-e* (13), *glaub-e* (15). Note, however, the following:

- The *-e* is often dropped in spoken German and less formal written German. This text has a mixture of forms with and without *-e*: e.g. *denk* (21) versus *frag-e* (13), although *frag, glaub, trau* would also be acceptable.[54] *Sei* (12) never has *-e*.
- As in the present tense, separable prefixes are sent to the end of the clause in the imperative: e.g. *Jetzt zieh dich **aus** und leg dich **hin*** (4). These examples also show the use of the reflexive pronoun *dich* with reflexive verbs (see **Ch. 20** for reflexives).
- Verbs which change their stem vowel from *-e-* to *-i-* or *-ie-* in the present tense show the same change in the imperative. Examples (not in text) are: *g**i**b, n**i**mm, **i**ss, h**i**lf, l**ie**s* (see **10.4**). The ending *-e* is never added to verbs with a vowel change.

11.3 OTHER IMPERATIVES

The **informal plural** (*ihr*) and **polite** (*Sie*) imperatives are less problematic than the *du*-imperative as they simply use their present tense forms (see **10.2**), with a following pronoun in the case of *Sie*:

informal pl. (*ihr*):		formal sg. and pl. (*Sie*):	
	*komm**t***		*komm**en** Sie*[55]
	*nehm**t***		*nehm**en** Sie*
	*arbeite**t***		*arbeit**en** Sie*
	*setz**t** euch*		*setz**en** Sie sich*

Other points to note in the text

- Features of spoken German: i) dropping of *-e* in the present tense: *find' ich* (2), *mach' ich* (2), *sag' ich* (21); ii) reduction of articles and pronouns: *gibt's* (14), *'nen Ehemann* (17).
- Expressions taking dative: *jemandem den Hof machen* (2), *jemandem trauen* (6, 23), *es*

jemandem besorgen (8), *jemandem fremd sein* (11), *sich* (dat.) *einer Sache* (gen.) *bewusst sein* (12), *jemandem etwas schwören* (16), *sich* (dat.) *jemanden anlachen* (17), *jemandem etwas sagen* (21) (see **3.4a**).

- Genitive pronoun: *sei dir **dessen** . . . bewusst* 'be aware **of it**' (12) (see **7.3**).
- Negation: *nicht* (6, 13), *nicht einmal* (10), *keine* (14), *nicht ein* (15) (see **Ch. 22**).

✎ **EXERCISES**

Change the following questions into imperatives, using the correct form of address:

Example: Kannst du dein Bier austrinken?

Answer: **Trink** dein Bier aus!

1 Kannst du heute Abend mitkommen?	9 Willst du deinen Regenschirm mitnehmen?
2 Willst du mir einen Kuss geben?	10 Willst du dir die Hände waschen?
3 Könnt ihr brav zu Hause bleiben?	11 Willst du dich ausruhen?
4 Können Sie mir Bescheid sagen?	12 Kannst du dir die Situation vorstellen?
5 Könnt ihr euer Zimmer aufräumen?	13 Wollen wir ins Kino gehen?
6 Würden Sie mich entschuldigen, bitte?	14 Wollen wir uns setzen?
7 Willst du dein Gemüse essen?	15 Darf man den Rasen nicht betreten?
8 Kannst du das noch einmal sagen?	

☞ **For further exercises on the imperative see Revision Text 5, Ex. 2.**

12 | Past tense

Nackte Übermacht – Allein unter Deutschen

Neue Runde im Handtuchkrieg: Die britische Boulevardpresse hat ihre
Lieblingsfeinde wiederentdeckt – die deutschen Touristen. Bayerische
Volksmusik, Schnitzel zum Abendessen und rundherum nur nackte
Deutsche. Für zwei Briten **entwickelte** sich der Kanarenurlaub zum
5 Alptraum. Jetzt wollen die beiden ihr Geld zurück.
London – Lange hatten sich die beiden Briten Dick und Angie Emery, beide
40, auf ihre Sommerferien gefreut – und dann das: Ihr Hotel **war** voller
Deutscher. Ein gefundenes Fressen für die Boulevardpresse auf der Insel.
„Urlaub in der Hölle", **titelte** das Massenblatt „The Sun" am Donnerstag
10 „exklusiv" und in großer Aufmachung. Zu ihrem Schrecken **mussten** die
beiden Briten feststellen, dass in dem Hotel auf Fuerteventura nur deutsch
gesprochen **wurde**. Vor der Speisekarte **rätselten** sie, was mit „Schnitzel"
gemeint sein könnte. Der Fernseher auf ihrem Zimmer **war** nur auf
deutsche Sender programmiert. Und abends **gab** es bayerische
15 Volksmusik.
    Doch das Schlimmste: „Viele Gäste **sonnten** sich nackt – und das **war**
nicht gerade ein schöner Anblick." Mit Schrecken **erinnerte** sich Angie:
„Wir **waren** geradezu umzingelt. Sie **waren** einfach überall." Schon im
Morgengrauen hatten sich die Deutschen die besten Liegen mit ihren
20 Handtüchern gesichert. Für Dick, inzwischen wieder zurück in Birmingham,
ist die Sache klar: „Wir wollen unser Geld zurück."

Aus: *Spiegel Online,* 17. August 2000.

⌕ The past tense in the text

12.1 USAGE

In German, the past tense, also known as the 'simple past', 'imperfect' or 'preterite', is usually used
to refer to events in the past, particularly when narrating a story, and is mostly associated with
the **written language**, e.g. novels and newspaper reports[56] referring to past events. On the other
hand, in spoken German it is more common to use the perfect tense to refer to past events (see
Ch. 13).

As there are no special progressive forms of tenses in German, a sentence such as *Viele Gäste* **sonnten** *sich nackt* could mean 'many guests sunbathed naked' or 'many guests **were sunbathing** naked' (see footnote 50). Usually it is apparent from the whole context which version is required. Similarly, English expressions such as 'used to' and 'would', as in 'I would visit him every day', which refer to repeated or habitual actions, are often rendered by simply using the past tense in German: e.g. *Sie sonnten sich nackt* could mean 'they used to sunbathe naked' or 'they would sunbathe naked'.[57]

---

[56] Although in newspaper reports it is usual to have the first sentence in the perfect tense and the rest in the past (see lines 1–2 of text).

[57] Habitual 'would' should not be confused with conditional 'would', as in 'I would go if I could' (German *Ich* **würde** *gehen, wenn ich könnte*, see **Ch. 16**).

12.2 FORMATION

12.2a Regular verbs

The past tense of regular verbs is formed using the present tense stem (infinitive minus *-en*; see **10.2a**) plus the past tense ending *-te*. This gives the **past tense stem**. In the plurals and the *du* and *Sie* forms, further personal endings are added to the past tense stem:

-te	*-te-n*	e.g. *sagen:*	*ich* **sagte**[58]	*wir* **sagten**
-te-st	*-te-t*	(Past stem: *sagte*)	*du* **sagtest**	*ihr* **sagtet**
-te	*-te-n*		*er/sie/es* **sagte**	*sie/Sie* **sagten**

This text uses the third person singular (*er/sie/es*-form), e.g. *entwickel***te** (4), *titel***te** (9), *erinner***te** (17), and the third person plural (*sie*-form), e.g. *rätsel***ten** (12), *sonn***ten** (16).

---

[58] For ease of pronunciation, if the stem of the verb ends in *-d, -t* or a consonant + *n* or *m*, *-e-* is added before the past tense ending, e.g. *arb..en – arbeit-e-te*.

12.2b Irregular verbs

Most commonly used verbs in German are irregular, which means that they have a past tense stem different from that of regular verbs. Examples from the text are **war**, **waren** from *sein* (7, 13, 16, 18), **mussten** from *müssen* (10), **gab** from *geben* (14) and **wurde** from *werden* (12) which, here, forms a past passive construction (see Ch. **18**).

The irregular past tense stems take the following endings:

–	*-en*	e.g. *war:*	*ich* **war**	*wir* **waren**
-st	*-t*		*du* **warst**	*ihr* **wart**
–	*-en*		*er/sie/es* **war**	*sie/Sie* **waren**

Other points to note in the text

- Genitive plural ending: *voll***er** *Deutscher* (7–8) (see **5.1(iv)**).
- Perfect tense in first sentence: *hat . . . wiederentdeckt* (1–2) (see footnote 56).
- Pluperfect: *hatten sich . . . gefreut* (6–7), *hatten sich . . . gesichert* (19–20) (see **Ch. 14**).
- *Konjunktiv II* as conditional: *könnte* 'could' (13) (see **16.3**).

- Reflexive verbs: *entwickelte sich* (4), *hatten sich ... gefreut* (6–7), *sonnten sich* (16), *erinnerte sich* (17), *hatten sich ... gesichert* (19–20) (see **Ch. 20**)

▲ Discover more about the past tense

12.3 IRREGULAR VERBS

12.3a Irregular past tense stems

Some of the most commonly used German verbs are irregular in the past tense, which means that their irregular stems have to be learned as exceptions to the general past tense rule. In addition to these, there are other verbs whose irregularities are more systematic in that the vowel change pattern used to mark the past tense is shared by certain other verbs. This second type of verb is often referred to as 'strong' and these are best learnt in groups according to their vowel changes.

Learn the past tense stems in bold print in **Table 18** and **Table 19**. These serve as the *ich-* and *er/sie/es* forms. For the other personal forms, add the endings given in **12.2b** (e.g. *du ging**st**, wir ging**en***). **Table 18** contains frequently used irregular verbs (and strong verbs which do not follow a systematic pattern common to many other verbs). **Table 19** contains relatively systematic strong verbs. Note that the corresponding past participles are also listed here, as they usually (but not always) follow the same pattern as the past tense forms and are therefore best learnt together with the past tense. Note that a subset of strong verbs have a vowel change in their simple past form only, with the past participle following the form of the infinitive – see the last three groups in **Table 19**. (For a comprehensive alphabetical list of common irregular and strong verbs, see **Appendix 1**.)

Table 18. Frequently occurring irregular verbs

bringen	–	**brachte**	–	gebracht	lügen	–	**log**	–	gelogen
denken	–	**dachte**	–	gedacht	mögen	–	**mochte**	–	gemocht
dürfen	–	**durfte**	–	gedurft	müssen	–	**musste**	–	gemusst
fangen	–	**fing**	–	gefangen	nennen	–	**nannte**	–	genannt
gehen	–	**ging**	–	gegangen	rennen	–	**rannte**	–	gerannt
haben	–	**hatte**	–	gehabt	rufen	–	**rief**	–	gerufen
hängen	–	**hing***	–	gehangen	sein	–	**war**	–	gewesen
heißen	–	**hieß**	–	geheißen	sitzen	–	**saß**	–	gesessen
kennen	–	**kannte**	–	gekannt	stehen	–	**stand**	–	gestanden
kommen	–	**kam**	–	gekommen	tun	–	**tat**	–	getan
können	–	**konnte**	–	gekonnt	werden	–	**wurde**	–	geworden
laufen	–	**lief**	–	gelaufen	wissen	–	**wusste**	–	gewusst

* Only when intransitive: e.g. *Das Bild **hing** an der Wand*. When used transitively (i.e. with a direct object), *hängen* is regular: e.g. *Ich **hängte** das Bild an die Wand*.

Table 19. Frequently occurring strong verb patterns

ei – ie – ie	bleiben – **blieb** – geblieben	schreien – **schrie** – geschrie(e)n
	leihen – **lieh** – geliehen	schweigen – **schwieg** – geschwiegen
	reiben – **rieb** – gerieben	steigen – **stieg** – gestiegen
	scheiden – **schied** – geschieden	treiben – **trieb** – getrieben
	scheinen – **schien** – geschienen	vermeiden – **vermied** – vermieden
	schreiben – **schrieb** –geschrieben	weisen – **wies** – gewiesen
ei – i – i	beißen – **biss** – gebissen	schleichen – **schlich** – geschlichen
	gleiten – **glitt** – geglitten	schmeißen – **schmiss** – geschmissen
	leiden – **litt** – gelitten	schneiden – **schnitt** – geschnitten
	reißen – **riss** – gerissen	schreiten – **schritt** – geschritten
	reiten – **ritt** – geritten	streichen – **strich** –gestrichen
	scheißen – **schiss** – geschissen	streiten – **stritt** – gestritten
e – a – o	befehlen – **befahl** – befohlen	sprechen – **sprach** – gesprochen
	brechen – **brach** – gebrochen	stehlen – **stahl** – gestohlen
	erschrecken – **erschrak** – erschrocken	sterben – **starb** -gestorben
	helfen – **half** – geholfen	treffen – **traf** – getroffen
	nehmen – **nahm** – genommen	verderben – **verdarb** – verdorben
		werfen – **warf** – geworfen
i – a – u	binden – **band** – gebunden	sinken – **sank** – gesunken
	dringen – **drang** – gedrungen	springen – **sprang** – gesprungen
	finden – **fand** – gefunden	stinken – **stank** – gestunken
	gelingen – **gelang** – gelungen	trinken – **trank** – getrunken
	klingen – **klang** – geklungen	zwingen – **zwang** – gezwungen
	singen – **sang** – gesungen	
i – a – o	beginnen – **begann** – begonnen	schwimmen – **schwamm** – geschwommen
	gewinnen – **gewann** – gewonnen	spinnen – **spann** – gesponnen
ie – o – o	biegen – **bog** – gebogen	riechen – **roch** gerochen
	fliegen – **flog** – geflogen	schieben – **schob** – geschoben
	fliehen – **floh** – geflohen	schießen – **schoss** – geschossen
	fließen – **floss** – geflossen	schließen – **schloss** – geschlossen
	genießen – **genoss** – genossen	verlieren – **verlor** – verloren
	gießen – **goss** – gegossen	wiegen – **wog** – gewogen
	kriechen – **kroch** – gekrochen	ziehen – **zog** – gezogen
e – a – e	geben – **gab** – gegeben	essen – **aß** – gegessen
	lesen – **las** – gelesen	fressen – **fraß** – gefressen
	sehen – **sah** – gesehen	messen – **maß** – gemessen
	treten – **trat** – getreten	
a – ie – a	blasen – **blies** – geblasen	fallen – **fiel** – gefallen
	braten – **briet** – gebraten	halten – **hielt** – gehalten
	schlafen – **schlief** – geschlafen	lassen – **ließ** – gelassen
a – u – a	fahren – **fuhr** – gefahren	tragen – **trug** – getragen
	schlagen – **schlug** – geschlagen	wachsen – **wuchs** – gewachsen

12.3b Derived verbs

Verbs with prefixes (separable and inseparable) which are derived from irregular verbs follow the same past tense patterns as the original irregular verb. Some common examples are:

from **kommen**: *ankommen, bekommen, auskommen, mitkommen, umkommen*
from **fallen**: *auffallen, ausfallen, einfallen, gefallen, umfallen*
from **sprechen**: *aussprechen, besprechen, entsprechen, versprechen*
from **stehen**: *aufstehen, bestehen, entstehen, gestehen, verstehen*

12.3c Separable verbs

As is the case in the present tense, separable prefixes are sent to the end of the clause when the verb is in the past tense: e.g. *ankommen: Er **kam** heute morgen **an*** (see **Ch. 19**). This applies to both regular and irregular verbs.

✎ EXERCISES

Vocabulary topic: *Urlaub*

1 The following sentences are in the present tense. Put them into the simple past:

1 Andreas und Ute buchen ihren Urlaub.
2 Wir reservieren ein Hotelzimmer.
3 Er übernachtet in einer billigen Pension.
4 Du willst ein Zimmer mit Bad und Dusche.
5 Ihr amüsiert euch auf dem Campingplatz.
6 Ich kaufe mehr als 50 Ansichtskarten.
7 Die Kinder spielen gern am Strand.
8 Der Urlaub dauert zwei Wochen.
9 Wir wandern auf die Alm.
10 Wir frühstücken auf dem Balkon.

2 Put the bracketed infinitives into the simple past. Note that many of these are irregular verbs, and some have separable prefixes which must be moved:

1 Er [haben] nicht viel Geld übrig.
2 Die Kinder [schwimmen] im Meer.
3 Meine Eltern [fliegen] nach Griechenland.
4 Wir [ankommen] um halb elf am Flughafen.
5 Wir [essen] lieber im Restaurant als im Hotel.
6 Die Jugendherberge [kosten] viel weniger als das Hotel.
7 Der Tourist [aufnehmen] alles mit der Videokamera.
8 Die Reiseleiter [sein] alle sehr freundlich.
9 Der Bus [abreisen] um 16 Uhr.
10 Wir [ansehen] uns die schönsten Städte.

☞ **For further exercises on the use of the simple past versus the perfect, see Ch. 13, Ex. 4.**

✎ **FURTHER EXERCISES**

3 **Complete the following crossword. All answers are in the past tense and are near synonyms of the clues:**

Kreuzworträtsel

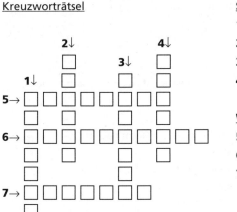

Senkrecht

1 soffen

2 sprach

3 guckte

4 entdeckten

Waagerecht

5 rügten

6 erwiderte

7 kamen zum Ende

4 **Complete the following text by putting the bracketed infinitives into the appropriate form of the past tense:**

Das salomonische Urteil

Damals [kommen] zwei Dirnen und [treten] vor den König. Die eine [sagen]: Bitte, Herr, ich und diese Frau wohnen im gleichen Haus, und ich habe dort in ihrem Beisein geboren. Am dritten Tag nach meiner Niederkunft [gebären] auch diese Frau. Wir [sein] beisammen; kein Fremder [sein] bei uns im Haus, nur wir beide [sein] dort. Nun [sterben] der Sohn dieser Frau während der Nacht; denn sie hatte ihn im Schlaf erdrückt. Sie [aufstehen] mitten in der Nacht, [wegnehmen] mir mein Kind, während deine Magd [schlafen], und [legen] es an ihre Seite. Ihr totes Kind aber [legen] sie an meine Seite. Als ich am Morgen [aufstehen], um mein Kind zu stillen, [sein] es tot. Als ich es aber am Morgen genau [ansehen], [sein] das nicht mein Kind, das ich geboren hatte. Da [rufen] die andere Frau: Nein, mein Kind lebt, und dein Kind ist tot. Doch die erste [entgegnen]: Nein, dein Kind ist tot, und mein Kind lebt. So [streiten] sie vor dem König. Da [beginnen] der König: Diese sagt: Mein Kind lebt, und dien Kind ist tot! und jene sagt: Nein, dein Kind ist tot und mein Kind lebt. Und der König [fortfahren]: Holt mir ein Schwert! Man [bringen] es vor den König. Nun [entscheiden] er: Schneidet das lebende Kind entzwei, und gebt eine Hälfte der einen und eine Hälfte der anderen! Doch nun [bitten] die Mutter des lebenden Kindes den König – es [regen] sich nämlich in ihr die mütterliche Liebe zu ihrem Kind: Bitte, Herr, gebt ihr das lebende Kind, und tötet es nicht! Doch die andere [rufen]: Es soll weder mir noch dir gehören. Zerteilt es! Da [befehlen] der König: Gebt jener das lebende Kind, und tötet es nicht; denn sie ist seine Mutter. Ganz Israel [hören] von dem Urteil, das der König gefällt hatte, und sie [aufschauen] mit Ehrfurcht zu ihm; denn sie [erkennen], dass die Weisheit Gottes in ihm [sein], wenn er Recht [sprechen].

Aus der Bibel: *1 Könige 3, 16–28*. Einheitsübersetzung der Heiligen Schrift. © 1980 Katholische Bibelanstalt, Stuttgart.

5 **Write a paragraph describing what you did yesterday, using the simple past.**

13 | Perfect tense

Kommissar Kress: Hat er Sie eigentlich noch **angerufen** gestern Nacht – der
Florian Balsam?

Weigelt: Nein, warum sollte er?

Kress: **Sind** Sie, nachdem Sie mit Ihrer Frau gestern Nacht nach Hause

5 **gekommen sind**, nochmal **weggefahren**?

Weigelt: Ist Ihnen diese Art der Routine nicht langweilig, Herr Kress?

Kress: **Sind** Sie nochmal **weggefahren**?

Weigelt: Nein, **bin** ich nicht.

Kress: **Habe** ich Ihnen schon **gesagt**, dass wir die hunderttausend bei

10 Balsams Eltern **gefunden haben**? Das Geld von Richard Lotke aus dem
Einbruch.

Weigelt: Nein, das **haben** Sie mir nicht **gesagt**.

Kress: Und was fangen Sie jetzt an . . . mit der Unschuld von Florian Balsam?
Sie wussten, dass er schuldig ist. Seit wann wissen Sie es, Herr Weigelt?

15 Weigelt: Jetzt ist es ein Verhör, nicht wahr?

Kress: Ja, das ist es.

Weigelt: Dann **sind** Sie taktisch sehr schlecht **vorgegangen**, Herr Kress.

Kress: Was **ist** gestern Nacht **passiert**, Herr Weigelt?

Weigelt: Ihre Fragen werden dadurch nicht besser, dass Sie sie wiederholen.

20 Kress: Was **ist** gestern Abend, als Sie den Freispruch **gefeiert haben** – Sie,
ihre Frau, Florian Balsam und Hubert Schatz – was **ist** da **vorgefallen**?

Weigelt: Nichts. Absolut nichts.

Kress: Herr Weigelt, **hat** Florian Balsam Sie in der Nacht noch **angerufen**?

Weigelt: Nein. Ich sagte Ihnen das bereits.

25 Kress: Ich frage Sie noch mal. **Sind** Sie noch **weggefahren** in der Nacht?

Weigelt: Nein.

Kress: Herr Weigelt, **sind** Sie von Florian Balsam in der Nacht noch **angerufen
worden**?

Weigelt: Nein.

30 Kress: Sie lügen. Und ich kann Ihnen das beweisen.

Weigelt: Der Telefoncomputer im Hotel Einberger, nicht wahr?

Frau Weigelt (*kommt herein*): Guten Abend.

Kress: Guten abend, Frau Weigelt. Stimmt das, dass Ihr Mann gestern Nacht
nochmal **weggefahren ist**?

35 Frau Weigelt: Ja.

Aus: *Der Alte* [Deutscher TV-Krimi]. © 1988 Volker Vogeler (Drehbuch). Folge:
Der Freispruch.

♀ The perfect tense in the text

13.1 USAGE

The perfect tense in German is usually used to refer to events in the past. Some of these may have relevance to the present, e.g. *Schau! Ich **habe** diesen Wein **gekauft*** 'Look, I've bought this wine' (and it's still here to be drunk), others may be completed actions in the past which would be expressed using the past tense rather than the perfect in English, e.g. *Was **ist** gestern Nacht **passiert**?* (line 18) 'What <u>happened</u> last night?', NOT *'What <u>has happened</u> last night?' This means that events in the past can be expressed in German either by using the simple past (see **Ch. 12**) or the perfect. The main difference in usage is that **the perfect is mainly used in spoken German** (and forms of writing which imitate speech: e.g. dialogues, hence the extensive use of the perfect in the chosen text), while the simple past is usually used in written narratives (see the news report in the previous chapter).[59]

> [59] The preference of the perfect over the past is most striking in southern Germany, Austria and Switzerland, where the past is rarely used in speech (apart from with very common verbs (see Further notes: i), and even these often appear in the perfect. In northern and central Germany the past can be used in speech, yet it is much less frequent than the perfect. One example of the past being used in northern/central German speech is in the narration of a series of events, e.g. *Ich **stand** auf, **ging** in die Küche und **machte** mir einen Kaffee* (although the perfect would not be incorrect here either).

Further notes:

i) Very common verbs such as *haben, sein, sagen, wissen* and the modal verbs *dürfen, können, mögen, müssen, sollen, wollen*[60] often appear in the **simple past** rather than the perfect, even in the spoken language: *Nein, warum **sollte** er?* (line 3), *Sie **wussten**, dass er schuldig ist* (14), *Ich **sagte** Ihnen das bereits* (24).

ii) In expressions with *seit/seitdem* 'for, since' German uses a **present** tense where English would use a perfect: *Seit wann **wissen** Sie es, Herr Weigelt?* (14) 'since when **have** you **known**, Herr Weigelt?' (see **10.3(ii)**).

> [60] When modal verbs (and *lassen* 'to let') occur in the perfect tense with another verb, two infinitives are used instead of a past participle: e.g. *Ich bin weg**ge**fahren* 'I left', vs. *Ich habe **wegfahren wollen*** 'I wanted to leave', *Ich habe es ihn **machen lassen*** 'I let him do it'. *Haben* is used with all modals, · irrespective of the verb with which they co-occur (for modal verbs see **21.4**).

13.2 FORMATION

13.2a Parts of verbs used

The perfect tense is formed using the present tense of the auxiliary verbs **haben** or **sein** plus the **past participle** of the main verb:[61]

*ich **habe gesagt*** (9)	*ich **bin gekommen***
*du **hast gesagt***	*du **bist gekommen***
*er/sei/es **hat gesagt***	*er/sie/es **ist gekommen***
*wir **haben gesagt***	*wir **sind gekommen***

ihr **habt gesagt**   *ihr* **seid gekommen**

sie/Sie **haben gesagt** (12)   *sie/Sie* **sind gekommen** (5)

From the text we see that the past participle usually appears at the end of the clause: *weggefahren* (5, 7), *gesagt* (9, 12), *vorgegangen* (17), *passiert* (18), *vorgefallen* (21), *angerufen* (23), *worden* (28), unless the auxiliary verb has been sent to the end because of a subordinating conjunction or relative pronoun: e.g. *gefunden* **haben** (10), or some other element has been moved to the end for special emphasis: e.g. *gestern Nacht* (1) (see 'Other points to note in the text').[62] It can also sometimes be omitted to avoid repetition: *Nein, bin ich nicht* (8) instead of *ich bin nicht weggefahren*.[63]

> [61] For the future perfect, e.g. *Er* **wird** *es* **gesagt haben**, and the conditional perfect, *Er* **hätte** *es* **gesagt**, see **15.4** and **16.2b** respectively.
>
> [62] Further occurrences of *haben/sein* following the past participle can be found in the future perfect, e.g. *Er* **wird** *es gemacht* **haben** (see **15.4**), and with modals, e.g. *Er* **muss** *es gemacht* <u>haben</u> (see **21.5a**).
>
> [63] This is an abbreviated version of *Nein, das bin ich nicht*, which is used in colloquial speech.

13.2b Formation of regular past participles

Regular past participles are formed by adding *ge-* and *-t*[64] to the present tense stem (the infinitive minus *-en*; see **10.2a**): e.g. *sagen* → **ge**-*sag*-**t** (9, 12), *feiern* → **ge**-*feier*-**t** (20). If the stem is not stressed on the first syllable (i.e. if it begins with an inseparable prefix, e.g. *be-, ent- er-, ge-, ver-,* or ends in *-ier*), *ge-* is dropped: e.g. *passieren* → *passiert* (18), NOT **gepassiert*.

> [64] or *-et* after *t, d* or a consonant + *n* or *m*: e.g. *landen* – **ge**land**et**, *öffnen* – **ge**öffn**et**.

13.2c Irregular past participles

As is the case in the simple past tense, most commonly used verbs have irregular past participles,[65] hence their relatively high rate of occurrence in the text. Most irregular past participles end in *-en* and many have a vowel change in the stem: *gekomm***en** (5), *gefund***en** (10) from *finden*. The past participle of *werden* is *geworden*, yet it appears in this text as *worden* (28) as it is used in a passive construction (see **18.5**). Irregular participles are best learnt together with their corresponding simple past forms, as they are often (but not always) very similar. See **12.3a** for the past participles of common irregular and strong verbs.

> [65] Note, however, that *haben* has a regular participle: *gehabt*.

13.2d Past participles of separable verbs

Separable prefixes **precede** *ge-* in past participles. Many of the irregular participles in this text are from separable verbs: <u>weg</u>*gefahr***en** (5, 7, 25, 34), <u>an</u>*geruf***en** (1, 23, 28), <u>vor</u>*gegang***en** (17) from *vorgehen*, <u>vor</u>*gefall***en** (21) (see **Ch. 19**).

13.2e Choice of auxiliary: *haben* or *sein*?

Most verbs take *haben* in the perfect tense, which means that those which take *sein* must be learned as exceptions, although the group is quite large. Verbs taking *sein* are **intransitive** (i.e.

they do not occur with an accusative object), and the factors that determine which intransitive verbs take *sein* are set out in **13.3** below. In the text we have three common intransitive verbs taking *sein*: **kommen** (5), **passieren** (18), **werden** (28) and three verbs which are derived from common intransitives taking *sein*: **wegfahren** (5, 7, 25, 34) from *fahren*, **vorgehen** (17) from *gehen*, **vorfallen** (21) from *fallen*.

Other points to note in the text

- Present tense used i) after *seit*: <u>Seit</u> wann **wissen** Sie es? (14); ii) after a past tense: Sie <u>wussten</u>, dass er schuldig **ist** (14) (see **10.3(ii)**, **10.3(iii)**).
- Questions with i) subject–verb inversion, e.g. **hat** er (1), **ist** Ihnen diese Art (6), **sind** Sie (4, 7, 25, 27), **habe** ich (9), **hat** Florian Balsam (23), **stimmt** das (33); ii) interrogatives, e.g. warum (3), was (13, 18, 20, 21), seit wann (14) (see **Ch. 23**).
- Subordinating conjunctions sending the finite verb to the end of the clause: **nachdem** . . . gekommen sind (4–5), **dass** . . . gefunden haben (9–10), **dass** . . . ist (14), **dass** . . . wiederholen (19), **als** . . . gefeiert haben (20), **dass** . . . weggefahren ist (33–34), (see **25.1**).
- Expressions of time placed at the end of the clause (after the past participle) for emphasis: gestern Nacht (1), in der Nacht (25) (see **26.7**). This emphasis can be understood within the context: i.e. something happened on the previous night (a murder).

▲ *Discover more about the perfect tense*

13.3 VERBS TAKING *SEIN*

13.3a Verbs which always take *sein*

All verbs taking *sein* in the perfect tense are **intransitive** (i.e. do not occur with a direct object) and can roughly be divided into two main categories. The first category consists of verbs denoting **movement** from A to B: e.g. *Er **ist** nach Hause **gegangen***. Other examples are: *ist* **gefahren**, *ist* **geflogen**, *ist* **gerannt**, *ist* **gelaufen**, *ist* **geklettert**, *ist* **gekrabbelt**, *ist* **gefallen**, *ist* **gestürzt**, *ist* **gerast**, *ist* **gekommen**.

The second category consists of verbs denoting a **change of state:** e.g. *Er **ist** alt **geworden***. Other examples are: *ist* **geboren**, *ist* **gestorben**, *ist* **gewachsen**, *ist* **geschrumpft**, *ist* **verwelkt**, *ist* **gebrochen**, *ist* **aufgewacht**, *ist* **eingeschlafen**, *ist* **aufgestanden**, *ist* **erschienen**, *ist* **verschwunden**.

In addition, there are some common verbs taking *sein* which are difficult to classify, among them the verb *sein* itself:[66] *ist* **gewesen**, *ist* **geblieben**, *ist* **passiert/geschehen**, *ist* **gelungen** etc.

[66] In southern varieties of German (including Swiss and Austrian), verbs denoting position occur with *sein*: e.g. *Er ist gestanden/gesessen/gelegen*.

13.3b Verbs that take *sein* or *haben* depending on the following object

If a verb which would usually take *sein* is used **transitively** (i.e. with a direct object in the accusative), *haben* will be used in the perfect, as this is the case with all transitive verbs. Similarly, **reflexive** verbs always take *haben*. Consider the following examples with the accusative objects underlined:

Er **ist** nach Frankreich gefahren	He went/drove/travelled to France
Er **hat** <u>den neuen Wagen</u> gefahren	He drove the new car
Er **ist** vom Dach gestürzt	He fell/plunged from the roof
Er **hat** <u>sich</u> in die Arbeit gestürzt	He threw/plunged himself into his work
Er **ist** seinem Bruder gefolgt	He followed his brother (with dative)
Er **hat** <u>seinem Lehrer</u> gefolgt	He followed (i.e. obeyed) his teacher

13.3c Derived verbs

Intransitive verbs derived (usually by the addition of prefixes) from verbs taking *sein* usually take *sein* themselves:[67]

e.g. *ist gekommen:*   *ist <u>an</u>gekommen, ist <u>ent</u>kommen, ist <u>ver</u>kommen, ist <u>vor</u>gekommen;*
  ist gefallen: *ist <u>auf</u>gefallen, ist <u>ein</u>gefallen; ist gegangen, ist <u>mit</u>gegangen.*

---

[67] A verb taking *haben* may occasionally have a corresponding prefixed form which expresses movement or a change of state. In this case, the prefixed verb takes *sein*: e.g. *Er **hat** vor dem Haus **gestanden*** 'He stood in front of the house' vs. *Er **ist** früh <u>**aufgestanden**</u>* 'He got up early'.

✎ **EXERCISES**

Vocabulary topic: *Reisen und Verkehrsmittel*

1 The following sentences are in the present tense. Put them into the perfect:

1 Wir warten auf den Bus.
2 Der Zug hat Verspätung.
3 Ich brauche eine Rückfahrkarte.
4 Kauft ihr ein neues Auto?
5 Wir verkaufen unser altes Motorrad.
6 Sie treffen sich am Bahnhof.
7 Wir sitzen im Nichtrauchercoupé.
8 Siehst du die Straßenbahn?

2 Fill in the gaps with the appropriate forms of *haben* or *sein*:

1 Wir _____ um 8 Uhr am Flughafen angekommen.
2 Ich _____ Erste Klasse gefahren.
3 Der Taxifahrer _____ plötzlich gebremst.
4 Der Bus _____ noch nicht da gewesen.
5 Ich _____ bei der Bushaltestelle gestanden.
6 _____ du dein Fahrrad verloren?
7 Ich _____ heute mein neues Auto gefahren.
8 Das Flugzeug _____ schon abgeflogen.
9 Sein Bruder _____ eine Harley-Davidson gefahren.
10 Meine Eltern _____ gestern mit dem Boot abgereist.

11 Das Kind _____ seinen Opa in seinem alten Wohnwagen besucht.

12 Wie _____ du dorthin gekommen? Ich _____ zu Fuß gegangen.

✎ **FURTHER EXERCISES**

3 Put the following past tense forms into the perfect:

1 Der Junge **lief** nach Hause.

2 Die Teekanne **fiel** zu Boden und **brach**.

3 Es tut mir leid, ich **zerbrach** das Weinglas.

4 Die Kinder **blieben** in ihrem Zimmer und **spielten**.

5 Wir **flogen** mit KLM nach Amsterdam.

6 Er **flog** heute zum ersten Mal sein Modellflugzeug, aber leider **stürzte** es **ab**.

7 Der Schüler **trat** einen Mitschüler in den Bauch.

8 Der Lehrer **trat** ins Zimmer.

9 Pass auf! Du **tratst** mir auf den Fuß!

10 Der Dieb **brach** in das Haus **ein**.

4 The following text is an extract from a novel. Decide which past tenses, i.e. simple past or perfect, would be appropriate to use with the bracketed verbs, bearing in mind that some of it is narrative and some is dialogue. Where you decide to use the perfect, take care where to place the past participle:

«Du kennst doch die Geschichte, die vor vier Jahren im Institute [stattfinden]?»

«Welche Geschichte?»

«Nun, die gewisse!»

«Nur beiläufig. Ich weiß bloß, dass es damals wegen irgendwelcher Schweinereien einen großen Skandal [geben] und dass eine ganze Anzahl deswegen strafweise entlassen werden [müssen].»

«Ja, das meine ich. Ich [erfahren] Näheres darüber einmal auf Urlaub von einem aus jener Klasse. Sie [haben] einen hübschen Burschen unter sich, in den viele von ihnen verliebt [sein]. Das kennst du ja, denn das kommt alle Jahre vor. Die aber [treiben] damals die Sache zu weit.»

«Wieso?»

«Nun, . . . wie. . .?! Frag doch nicht so dumm! Und dasselbe tut Reiting mit Bassini!»

Törleß [verstehen], worum es sich zwischen den beiden [handeln], und er [fühlen] in seiner Kehle ein Würgen, als ob Sand darinnen wäre.

«Das hätte ich nicht von Reiting gedacht.» Er [wissen] nichts Besseres zu sagen. Beineberg [zucken] die Achseln.

«Er glaubt, uns betrügen zu können.»

«Ist er verliebt?»

«Gar keine Spur. so ein Narr ist er nicht. Es unterhält ihn, höchstens reizt es ihn sinnlich.»

«Und Basini?»

«Der . . .? [Auffallen] dir nicht, wie frech er in der letzten Zeit [werden]? Von mir [lassen] er kaum mehr etwas sagen. Immer [hießen] es nur Reiting und wieder Reiting, – als ob der sein persönlicher Schutzheiliger wäre. Es ist besser, [denken] er sich wahrscheinlich, von dem einen sich alles gefallen zu lassen als von jedem etwas. Und Reiting wird ihm [versprechen], ihn zu schützen, wenn er ihm in allem zu Willen ist. Aber sie sollen sich [irren], und ich werde es Basini noch austreiben!»

«Wie [kommen] du darauf?»

«Ich [nachgehen] ihnen einmal.»

Aus: Robert Musil, *Die Verwirrungen des Zöglings Törleß.* ©1978 Rowohlt Verlag.

14 | Pluperfect tense

⌕ The pluperfect in the text

14.1 USAGE

The pluperfect in German is used in much the same way as the pluperfect in English: to indicate
that a particular event is one step further into the past than the past events related to it, i.e. it
had (already) happened: e.g. *Der Mann, der mich **eingeladen hatte**, begrüßte mich sehr herzlich*
'the man who **had invited** me greeted me heartily'. The chosen text from the Bible contains a
mixture of verbs in the past tense, which is commonly used in written narratives, and in the
pluperfect, the latter indicating that these events occurred prior to those denoted by the past: e.g.

Von allen Tieren **waren** *Männchen und Weibchen* **gekommen,** *wie Gott ihm* **aufgetragen hatte.**
Dann schloss der Herr hinter ihm zu (lines 6–8).' And male and female of all flesh **had gone** in, as
God **had commanded** him: and the Lord shut him in.'[68]

> [68] In English, the pluperfect progressive (e.g. 'I **had been** doing my homework when he arrived') is often
> used to refer to an action in the past which had not been completed (contrast the completed action in
> the ordinary pluperfect 'I **had done** my homework'). As German does not have progressive forms and
> the German pluperfect is only used to refer to completed actions in the past, English progressive
> pluperfects cannot be translated by the pluperfect in German. Instead, the **simple past** is used: e.g. 'I
> **had been cooking** when he arrived' → *Ich* **kochte** *(gerade) als er ankam* (see footnote 50). Similarly:
> 'I **had been living** there for five years → *Ich* **wohnte** *dort seit fünf Jahren.*

14.2 FORMATION

The pluperfect tense is formed using the **past tense** of the auxiliary verbs *haben* or *sein*[69] plus the
past participle of the main verb. (Details on the formation of past participles are given in
13.2(b–d)):

ich **hatte gesagt**	*ich* **war gekommen**
du **hattest gesagt**	*du* **warst gekommen**
er/sei/es **hatte gesagt**	*er/sie/es* **war gekommen**
wir **hatten gesagt**	*wir* **waren gekommen**
ihr **hattet gesagt**	*ihr* **wart gekommen**
sie/Sie **hatten gesagt**	*sie/Sie* **waren gekommen** (5, 7)

From the text we see that the past participle usually appears at the end of the clause, as it does in
the perfect: *waren . . . gegangen* (1–3), *waren . . . gekommen* (5, 7), *war . . . angeschwollen* (12,
13–14), *hatte . . . zugedeckt* (14), unless the auxiliary verb appears at the end because of a
subordinating conjuction or relative pronoun: *aufgetragen hatte* (8), *geregt hatten* (15),
gewimmelt hatte (16).

> [69] Verbs that take *sein* in the perfect also do so in the pluperfect: e.g. **waren** *. . . gegangen* (1–3), **waren**
> *. . . gekommen* (5, 7), *war . . . angeschwollen* (12, 13–14). These are dealt with in **13.3**.

Other points to note in the text

- Genitives: *Noachs* (1), *seiner Söhne* (2), *alle Arten* **der** *Tiere . . .* **des** *Viehs . . .* **der** *Kriechtiere*
  (3–4), *alle Arten* **der** *Vögel . . .* **des** *fliegenden Getiers* (4–5) (see **3.1a(iv)**).
- Relative pronouns: **die** *. . . regen* (4), *in* **denen** *. . . ist* (6), **die** *es . . . gibt* (13), **die** *. . . geregt*
  hatten (15), **wovon** *. . . gewimmelt hatte* (16), **was** *. . . atmete* (17–18) (see **Ch. 9**).
- Present tense used after past and pluperfect: *regen* (4), *ist* (6), *gibt* (13) (see **10.3(iii)**).
- Past passive: **wurden** *. . . vertilgt* (19–20) (see **Ch. 18**).

✎ **EXERCISES**

Vocabulary topic: *Wetter und Natur*

1 Put the bracketed verbs into the pluperfect:

1 Der Rasen stand unter Wasser, da es vier Tage lang [regnen].

2 Am vorigen Tag [schneien] es und die Felder waren alle weiß.

3 Die Sonne [untergehen] und es wurde kühler.

4 Es [geben] einen Sturm und zwei Bäume [umfallen] und blockierten die Straße.

5 Es [sein] in letzter Zeit am Meer sehr windig, deshalb wollte ich dort nicht Fahrrad fahren.

6 Man sah von den Beulen auf dem Autodach, dass es in der Nacht sehr stark [hageln].

2 Put the sentences in Chapter 13, Exercises 2 and 3 into the pluperfect.

3 Translate the following sentences into German, paying particular attention to whether the pluperfect or the past tense is needed:

1 I had driven home in the fog.

2 I had been driving home from work when the thunderstorm started.

3 It had been quite warm and the ice had melted.

4 I had been sunbathing in the garden when the telephone rang.

5 It had been cloudy all day.

15 | Future

Text

Wie **wird** es im Jahre 2010 in Deutschland **aussehen**? Eine Frage, über die so genannte Zukunftsforscher trefflich streiten können. Nur in einem Punkt scheinen sie sich einig: Der Osten **wird** auch in zehn Jahren noch **hinterherhinken**.

5 Berlin – Die Zukunft ist auch nicht mehr das, was sie mal war. Dieser Satz von Karl Valentin trifft auch heute noch zu. Das sagt Klaus Burmeister, Zukunftsforscher aus Essen. Vor zehn Jahren malte der damalige Kanzler Helmut Kohl (CDU) die Zukunft in den schönsten Farben, in politischen Programmen wurden Reformperspektiven entworfen. Nach zehn Jahren

10 deutscher Einheit sind alle schlauer, und die Kritik an der Vergangenheit ist billig zu haben. Viel schwerer zu beantworten ist die Frage: Wie sehen die nächsten zehn Jahre aus, wo **wird** die Bundesrepublik in zehn Jahren **stehen**? Und wer könnte dies besser beantworten als Zukunftsforscher?

„Der Angleichungsprozess **wird** die Unterschiede im Lebensstil weiter
15 **verwischen**, aber in der Wirtschaft **wird** das Ungleichgewicht zwischen West und Ost im Wesentlichen ungelöst **sein**. "Diese Prognose geben viele Zukunftsforscher. [. . .] „Egal, welche Regierung in zehn Jahren an der Macht ist, sie **wird** reagieren **müssen**", sagt Karlheinz Steinmüller von Sekretariat für Zukunftsforschung in Gelsenkirchen. Nach seiner Analyse **wird** keine

20 Regierung um eine offensive Einwanderungspolitik, verstärkte Klimaschutzmaßnahmen und weitere Rentenabsenkungen **herumkommen**. „Auch 2010 **wird** das alles ungelöst **sein**, "meint er. „Es gibt keine Alternative zum Energiesparen", hebt auch Burmeister hervor. [. . .]

„Deutschland **wird** von der Osterweiterung der EU **profitieren**", so viel ist
25 Steinmüller zu entlocken. Insbesondere die neuen Bundesländer, die teilweise noch über die alten Kontakte verfügen. Und: „Russisch **wird** wichtiger **werden**." Welche Parteien in zehn Jahren **regieren werden**, kann auch Burmeister nicht sagen, doch eines steht für ihn ziemlich fest: „Wir **werden** in Deutschland mit Wahlbeteiligungen um 50 Prozent leben **müssen**." Das sei

30 kein Beinbruch, in den USA und der Schweiz sei die Beteiligung ähnlich gering, und das seien doch stabile Demokratien.

Aus einem Artikel von Gerald Mackenthun (dpa). *Spiegel (Online) – Wissenschaft*, 19. September 2000.

♀ The future tense in the text

15.1 USAGE

The future tense is primarily used to refer to future time, particularly when making promises or predictions, hence the abundant use of future forms in the chosen text: e.g. *Wie* **wird** *es im Jahre 2010 in Deutschland* **aussehen**? (1), *Auch 2010* **wird** *das alles ungelöst* **sein** (22), *Russisch* **wird** *wichtiger* **werden** (26–27).

15.2 FORMATION

The future tense is formed using the present tense of the auxiliary verb **werden** plus the **infinitive** of the main verb:

ich **werde stehen**	*wir* **werden stehen**
du **wirst stehen**	*ihr* **werdet stehen**
er/sei/es **wird stehen** (13–14)	*sie/Sie* **werden stehen**

From the text we see that the infinitive goes to the end of the clause: *aussehen* (1), *hinterhinken* (4), *stehen* (13), *verwischen* (15), *sein* (16, 22), *herumkommen* (21), *profitieren* (24), unless the auxiliary verb has been sent to the end: *regieren* **werden** (27). The future may be used with modal verbs: *wird reagieren* **müssen** (18), *werden leben* **müssen** (28–29) and with *werden* itself, meaning 'will become': *wird wichtiger* **werden** (26–27).

Other points to note in the text

- Comparatives: *schlauer* (10), *schwerer* (11), *wichtiger* (26). Superlative: *schönsten* (8), (see **Ch. 6**)
- Subjunctive in reported speech: *sei* (29), *seien* (31) (see **Ch. 17**).
- Passive: *werden*-passive: **wurden** . . . *entworfen* (9); *sein*-passive: *ungelöst* **sein** *(22)* (see **18.1–18.3, 18.9**).
- Interrogatives: *wie* (1, 11), *wo* (12), *wer* (13) (see **23.3–23.4**); used as conjunctions: *welche* (17, 27) (see **23.5**).
- Subject–verb word order after subordinate clause instead of 'correct' verb–subject order (see **26.1b(ii)**): *Egal, welche Regierung . . . an der Macht ist, sie* **wird** *reagieren* (17–18). This may occur where a pause between the two clauses is implied (e.g. for emphasis).

⚒ Discover more about the future tense

15.3 USAGE

15.3a Expressing probability

As in English, the future tense in German is often used to express a supposition or probability which is not necessarily associated with future time: e.g. *Er ist nicht zu Hause – er* **wird** *noch in* *der Arbeit **sein*** 'He's not at home – he'**ll** still **be** at work'. Here it is clear from the context that we are dealing with the present (i.e. he **is** probably still at work).

15.3b Use of present to express future

German uses the future tense much less often than English to refer to future time, unless the speaker/writer is making a promise or prediction (see text). Wherever possible, the present is used instead: e.g. *Ich **komme** morgen um vier Uhr* 'I'll come/I'm coming tomorrow at four', although the future would not be grammatically incorrect here. There is also an example of present tense usage in our text: *Egal, welche Regierung in zehn Jahren an der Macht **ist*** (17–18). Only if the use of the present would create ambiguity (i.e. if it was not clear from the context whether present or future time was meant) would it be replaced by the future.

15.4 FUTURE PERFECT

To refer to completed actions in the future, German has a future perfect tense similar to that of English: e.g. *Ich **werde** es bis nächste Woche **gelesen haben*** 'I **will have read** it by next week'. The future perfect is formed using the future tense of *haben* or *sein* plus the past participle of the main verb:

*ich werde **gearbeitet haben***	*ich werde **gegangen sein***
*du wirst **gearbeitet haben***	*du wirst **gegangen sein***
*er/sei/es wird **gearbeitet haben***	*er/sie/es wird **gegangen sein***
*wir werden **gearbeitet haben***	*wir werden **gegangen sein***
*ihr werdet **gearbeitet haben***	*ihr werdet **gegangen sein***
*sie/Sie werden **gearbeitet haben***	*sie/Sie werden **gegangen sein***

As with the simple future tense, the future perfect may also be used to express an assumption: e.g. *Er **wird** sie gestern **angerufen haben*** 'He will have phoned her yesterday.'

EXERCISES

Vocabulary topic: *Politik*

1 Put the following present tense forms into the future:

1 Welche Partei **ist** nächstes Jahr an der Macht?
2 Es **gibt** wahrscheinlich eine Koalition.
3 Welchen Kandidaten **wählst** du?
4 Die nächste Wahl **findet** im Juni dieses Jahres **statt**.
5 Alle Parteien **unterstützen** das Verhältniswahlrecht.
6 In welchem Wahlkreis **seid** ihr nächstes Jahr?
7 Ich **schreibe** dem Innenminister.
8 Er **wird** wahrscheinlich Außenminister.
9 Der Abgeordnete **vertritt** seine Wähler.
10 Die Politiker, die an die Macht **kommen**, sind die, die dem Publikum **zuhören**.

2 Put the following verbs into the future perfect:

1 Die Regierung **reduziert** ihre Ausgaben.
2 Die Linken **investieren** mehr in das Schulwesen.
3 Der Bundeskanzler **tritt zurück**.
4 Die Rechten **lösen sich auf**.
5 Er **ist** Mitglied des Europaparlaments.

✎ FURTHER EXERCISES

3 The present tense is commonly used to refer to future time. Determine which of the bracketed verbs can be put into the present (referring to the future) and which need to be in the future tense. Explain the reasons for your choice:

1 Wir [treffen] uns morgen um drei Uhr.
2 Wann [fahren] ihr nach Spanien?
3 Wir wollen heute Nachmittag im Wald spazierengehen. Ich glaube, es [sein] schön.
4 Schau! Es kommen graue Wolken. Es [regnen].
5 Der Zug [ankommen] um 18 Uhr.
6 Morgen [schneien] es.
7 Was [machen] du morgen Abend?
8 Was [machen] er?

4 The future tense is often used to express a supposition. Change the following sentences into suppositions by putting them into the future (or future perfect where appropriate) and adding *wahrscheinlich* after the finite verb (and accusative object):

Example: Johannes **ist** zu Hause
Answer: Johannes **wird wahrscheinlich** zu Hause **sein**.

1 Klaus **arbeitet** noch.
2 Ruf ihn nicht zu früh an. Er **schläft** noch.
3 Peter **hat** es schon **gemacht**.
4 Die Nachbarn **sind** schon **abgereist**.
5 Er **hat** es seiner Frau **erzählt**.

16 | Conditional

Marienkäfer: Diese Maus ist immer noch nicht da. Dann müssen wir ihn
aufgeben. Es ist schon über eine Woche. Wenn er noch **leben würde**,
hätten wir von ihm **gehört**.

Flip: Dieser Wasserfall ist ihm zum Verhängnis geworden.

5 Willi: Und es ist meine Schuld. Es war meine Idee, die Flasche den Hügel
hinunterzurollen. Ich bin kein Genie. Nein, ich bin ein ganz großer
Dummkopf. Nein, nein. Warum wollte ich mich da einmischen […].
Ach, Alexander!

Maja: Lass gut sein, Willi.

10 Holzwurm: Bilde dir nicht sowas ein, Willi. In Wirklichkeit bin doch ich schuld.
Jawohl, ich habe ihn in den Wasserfall stürzen lassen. **Hätte** ich nicht so viel
gegessen und **hätte** den Zweig **durchgebissen**, **hätten** wir ihn vielleicht
retten können.

Flip: **Hätte**, **hätte** . . ., lass gut sein. Du hast ja dein Bestes versucht.

15 Holzwurm: Nein, nein, nein. Ich **hätte** vorher auch nicht so viel **fressen dürfen**.
Was bin ich für ein Vielfraß. Abscheulich!

Aus: *Die Biene Maja* [deutsche TV-Kinderserie], © ENTV.
Folge: *Die Maus in der Flasche*.

♀ The conditional in the text

16.1 USAGE

The conditional is primarily used to refer to hypothetical situations and to indicate that something does not correspond to reality. Consequently, it often co-occurs in a sentence with words such as *wenn* 'if', *als ob* 'as if' and *aber* 'but': e.g. *Ich* **würde** *dich besuchen, aber ich habe keine Zeit* 'I **would** visit you but I don't have time'.[70] In the text there are two types of conditional used:

i)   the **simple conditional**, which corresponds to English 'would + verb': *Wenn er noch* **leben** **würde** (2) literally 'If he **would** still be alive' (although English uses a past tense form for conditionals after 'if' (i.e. 'If he was[71] still alive').

ii) the **conditional perfect**, which corresponds to English **would have**: **hätten** *wir ... gehört* (3) 'we **would have heard**'.[72] Sometimes German dispenses with the word *wenn* and expresses the concept of 'if' by moving the finite verb to the beginning of the sentence or clause: *Hätte ich nicht so viel gegessen und hätte den Zweig durchgebissen* (11–12) 'If I hadn't eaten so much and had bitten through the twig'. Again, English uses a past form (in this case pluperfect) after 'if', but the conditional perfect is needed in German.[73]

> [70] And, like the English conditional, it can also be used in polite requests: e.g. *Würden Sie mich begleiten? Könnten Sie das wiederholen?*
>
> [71] Or even an old subjunctive with the verb 'to be': 'if he **were** still alive'.
>
> [72] The finite verb *hätten* precedes the subject as it follows a subordinate clause (see **26.1b(ii)** on word order).
>
> [73] It is interesting that one of the speakers makes a play on the conditional meaning of *hätte* in line 14 in order to express the idea that there's no point in talking about what **could have** happened.

16.2 FORMATION

16.2a Conditional

The conditional tense is formed by taking the past tense form of the auxiliary verb *werden* and adding an umlaut (*wurde* → **würde**, otherwise known as the *Konjunktiv II* form, see **16.3**) plus the **infinitive** of the main verb:

ich **würde leben** 'I would live'	*wir* **würden leben**
du **würdest leben**	*ihr* **würdet leben**
er/sei/es **würde leben** (2)	*sie/Sie* **würden leben**

16.2b Conditional perfect

The conditional perfect tense is formed using the *Konjunktiv II* form of the auxiliary verbs *haben* or *sein* plus the past participle of the main verb. The distribution of *haben* and *sein* is the same as for the ordinary perfect tense:

ich **hätte gehört** 'I would have heard'	*ich* **wäre gekommen** 'I would have come'
du **hättest gehört**	*du* **wärst gekommen**
er/sie/es **hätte gehört**	*er/sie/es* **wäre gekommen**
wir **hätten gehört** (3)	*wir* **wären gekommen**
ihr **hättet gehört**	*ihr* **wäret gekommen**
sie/Sie **hätten gehört**	*sie/Sie* **wären gekommen**

Note that it is quite common to have a **modal** verb (*dürfen, können, mögen, müssen, sollen, wollen*) used with another verb in the conditional perfect to express meanings such as 'could have', 'should have' etc. Where this occurs, **two infinitives** are used instead of past participles, as is the case with the ordinary perfect (see footnote 60). All modals take *haben*, irrespective of the verb with which they co-occur. Examples from the text are:

Wir **hätten** *ihn* **retten können** (12–13)	We could have rescued him.
Ich **hätte** *nicht so viel* **fressen dürfen** (15)	I shouldn't have eaten so much.

If *hätte* is sent to the end by a subordinating conjunction or relative pronoun it must **precede** the two infinitives: e.g. *Ich dachte, <u>dass</u> wir ihn vielleicht* **hätten retten können**.

Other points to note in the text

- Present tense used with *schon* 'already' where English would use perfect: *Es **ist** schon über eine Woche* (2) 'It has already been more than a week' (see **10.3(ii)**).
- Imperatives: *lass* (9, 14), *bilde . . . ein* (10) (see **Ch. 11**).
- Double infinitive in the perfect: *habe . . . stürzen lassen* (11) (see footnote 60).

▲ Discover more about the conditional

16.3 CONDITIONALS EXPRESSED USING THE *KONJUNKTIV II*

16.3a Formation of the *Konjunktiv II*

As mentioned in **16.2a** above, simple conditionals are formed using *würde(-st, -t, -en)* plus the infinitive: e.g. *Ich würde schlafen*. However, for regular verbs and some common irregular verbs there is an alternative form of the conditional, known as the *Konjunktiv II*, which is formed as follows:

- For regular verbs, the *Konjunktiv II* is identical to the **past tense** indicative (see **12.2a**): e.g. *ich mach**te**, du mach**test*** etc.
- For irregular verbs, take the past tense stem (**12.2b**) of the verb, which is used in the *ich* and *er/sie/es* forms, **add -e** (if the stem does not already end in *-e*) and **umlaut** the vowel where possible: e.g. *ich war → wär-**e**, ich kam → käm-**e**, ich ging → ging-**e**, ich hatte → hätte*. This *Konjunktiv II* stem then needs the following personal endings (which are the same as the personal endings in the ordinary simple past tense indicative):

–	**-n**
-st	**-t**
–	**-n**

e.g. *sein*:
(Konj. II stem: *wäre*)

*ich **wäre***   *wir **wären***
*du **wärest**[74]*   *ihr **wäret***
*er/sie/es **wäre***   *sie/Sie **wären***

In practice, only very common verbs have a frequently used *Konjunktiv II* form (see Table 20).

[74] In spoken German the *-e-* is often dropped before *-st* and *-t*.

Table 20. The *Konjunktiv II* form of common verbs

	ich	du	er/sie/es	wir	ihr	sie/Sie
haben	*hätte*	*hättest*	*hätte*	*hätten*	*hättet*	*hätten*
sein	*wäre*	*wärest*	*wäre*	*wären*	*wäret*	*wären*
werden	*würde*	*würdest*	*würde*	*würden*	*würdet*	*würden*
dürfen	*dürfte*	*dürftest*	*dürfte*	*dürften*	*dürftet*	*dürften*
können	*könnte*	*könntest*	*könnte*	*könnten*	*könntet*	*könnten*
mögen	*möchte*	*möchtest*	*möchte*	*möchten*	*möchtet*	*möchten*
müssen	*müsste*	*müsstest*	*müsste*	*müssten*	*müsstet*	*müssten*
wissen	*wüsste*	*wüsstest*	*wüsste*	*wüssten*	*wüsstet*	*wüssten*

16.3b Use of the *Konjunktiv II*

In **written German**, particularly in more formal styles of writing, the *Konjunktiv II* forms are used quite often in the conditional, particularly with **regular** verbs and with the **common** verbs listed in **Table 20** (plus *sollen* and *wollen*).[75] There are also some other irregular verbs which can be used in their *Konjunktiv II* form in the written language: *geben* (*gäbe*), *gehen* (*ginge*), *kommen* (*käme*), *tun* (*täte*) and, less commonly *fahren* (*führe*), *lassen* (*liesse*), *halten* (*hielte*), *sitzen* (*säße*), *stehen* (*stünde*). Consider the following example from Robert Musil's *Die Verwirrungen des Zöglings Törleß*:

*Du machst ja gerade so, als ob der Schwefelregen schon vor der Tür **stünde**, um uns alle zu vernichten, wenn wir Basini noch länger unter uns **behielten**.*

These verb forms are clearly characteristic of a higher register, and some writers who prefer a less formal style would probably replace them with *werden* + infinitive: e.g. *als ob der Schwefelregen schon vor der Tür **stehen würde**.*

In **spoken German** the ***werden* + infinitive** construction is preferred for all regular verbs and most irregular verbs, except for the very common ones given in **Table 20** (plus *wollen* and *sollen*). In addition, the verbs *kommen* (*käme*), *tun* (*täte*) and *gehen* (*ginge*[76]) may be used in the *Konjunktiv II* but less frequently than the *werden* + infinitive alternative: e.g. *Es wäre schön, wenn du **kämest*** (more commonly: *Es wäre schön, wenn du **kommen würdest***).[77]

---

[75] The verbs *sollen* and *wollen* never have an umlaut. Thus their *Konjunktiv II* form is identical to the past tense: *wollte, wolltest,* etc.

[76] Especially in the phrase *Wenn es nach mir ginge* 'If it were up to me'.

[77] In colloquial German one may hear a *Konjunktiv II* form of *brauchen,* **bräuchte**, which is becoming increasingly acceptable.

16.4 FURTHER EXAMPLES OF CONDITIONALS IN 'IF' CLAUSES

One problematic aspect of 'if' clauses for speakers of English is that 'if' is followed not by a conditional in English but a past tense form, even though the *meaning* is conditional: e.g. 'If I **had** more time'. This is not possible in German, as the verb must be in the conditional: *Wenn ich mehr Zeit **hätte**.* Below are some examples of 'if' clauses, both in the conditional and conditional perfect, as used in everyday spoken German. Students are advised to learn these patterns by heart:

<u>Conditional</u>

- *Wenn wir das Geld **gewinnen würden**, **würden** wir in den Urlaub **fahren***
  If we **won** the money, we **would go** on holiday
- *Wenn er richtig krank **wäre**, **würde** er ins Bett **gehen***
  If he **was/were** really ill, he **would go** to bed
- *Wenn du Lust **hättest**, **könntest** du mich anrufen*
  If you **wanted** to, you **could** ring me

- *Wenn ich samstags arbeiten **müsste**,*   If I **had to** work on Saturdays I
  würde** ich meine Stelle **aufgeben   **would give up** my job

Conditional perfect

- *Wenn[78] wir das Geld **gewonnen hätten**,*   If we **had won** the money
  wären** wir in Urlaub **gefahren   we **would've gone** on holiday
- *Wenn er richtig krank **gewesen wäre**,*   If he **had been** really ill, he
  wäre** er ins Bett **gegangen   **would've gone** to bed
- *Wenn du Lust **gehabt hättest**,*   If you **had wanted** to, you **could've**
  hättest** du mich **anrufen können   **phoned** me
- *Wenn ich samstags **hätte arbeiten müssen**,[79]*   If I **had had to** work on Saturdays I
  hätte** ich meine Stelle **aufgegeben   **would've given up** my job

---

[78] Alternatives without *wenn*: **Hätten** *wir das Geld gewonnen;* **Wäre** *er richtig krank gewesen;* **Hättest** *du Lust gehabt;* **Hätte** *ich samstags arbeiten müssen* (see **16.1(ii)**).

[79] See **16.2b** for the position of *hätte* after a subordinating conjunction like *wenn*.

✎ EXERCISES

Vocabulary topic: *Im Garten*

1 Put the bracketed verbs into the simple conditional ('would . . .'), using either *würde* + infinitive or the *Konjunktiv II* as appropriate:

Examples: i) Jörg [mähen] den Rasen; ii) Jörg [haben] einen Rasenmäher.

Answers: i) Jörg **würde** den Rasen **mähen**; ii) Jörg **hätte** einen Rasenmäher.

   1 Ich [gießen] die Blumen.

   2 Er [eingraben] die neuen Pflanzen.

   3 Wir [mögen] auf der Terasse frühstücken.

   4 Es [sein] schön beim Brunnen zu sitzen.

   5 Ich [finden] es schwierig, den großen Busch zurückzuschneiden.

   6 Wir [müssen] eigentlich den Rosenstrauch düngen.

   7 Der Baum [verlieren] im Winter seine Blätter.

   8 [Können] du Unkraut jäten? Ich [haben] eine Schaufel.

   9 Ich [sollen] einen richtigen Komposthaufen machen.

 10 [Wissen] du zufällig, wo der Rechen sein [können]?

2 The following sentences are in the simple past. Put them into the conditional perfect ('would have . . .'):

Example: Jörg **mähte** den Rasen.

Answer: Jörg **hätte** den Rasen **gemäht**.

   1 Der Gärtner **machte** es besser.

   2 Ich **kaufte** eine Regentonne, aber sie war zu groß zu transportieren.

3 Ein guter Spaten **war** zu teuer. Deshalb habe ich die Schaufel genommen.

4 Ich **sollte** den Gartenzaun streichen, aber es war zu viel Arbeit.

5 Rhododendrons haben eigentlich sehr kleine Wurzeln. Du **konntest** sie in einen Topf pflanzen.

6 Eine schöne Elster **flog** in den Garten, aber die Katze hat sie weggescheucht.

3 Make 'wenn clauses' out of the following sentences, using the simple conditional (or Konjunktiv II where appropriate) and translate your answers into English:

Example: Jörg mäht den Rasen. Sein Garten sieht schöner aus.

Answer: **Wenn** Jörg den Rasen **mähen würde**, **würde** sein Garten schöner **aussehen**.
'If Jörg mowed the lawn, his garden would look nicer.'

1 Es regnet nicht. Die Erde ist sehr trocken.

2 Sie haben Geld. Sie kaufen einen Wintergarten.

3 Ich habe ein Glashaus. Ich kann Tomaten ziehen.

4 Das Wetter ist besser. Die Kletterpflanzen wachsen höher.

5 Du gibst mir den Gartenschlauch. Ich spritze den Rasen.

6 Wir pflanzen jetzt die Zwiebeln. Die Krokusse und Narzissen kommen im Frühling.

7 Der Blumenstock verwelkt. Ich muss ihn umtopfen.

8 Du willst mir helfen. Du kannst den Gartenschuppen aufbauen.

4 Take your answers to 3 above and put them into the conditional perfect. Then translate them into English:

Example: Wenn Jörg den Rasen mähen würde, würde sein Garten schöner aussehen.

Answer: Wenn Jörg den Rasen **gemäht hätte**, **hätte** sein Garten schöner **ausgesehen**.
'If Jörg **had** mowed the lawn, his garden would **have looked** nicer.'

☞ **For further exercises on the conditional see Revision Text 5, Ex. 4 and for modal verbs in the conditional perfect ('could have', should have' etc.) see Ch. 21, Ex. 4.**

17 | Subjunctive in reported speech

Text

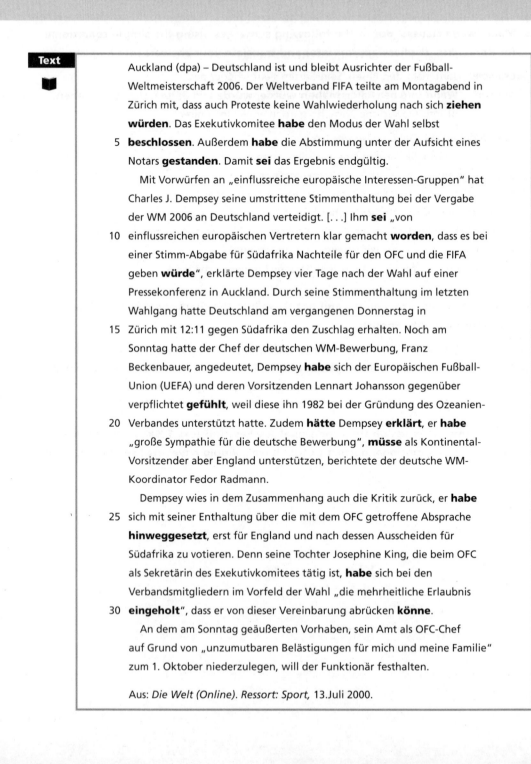

Auckland (dpa) – Deutschland ist und bleibt Ausrichter der Fußball-Weltmeisterschaft 2006. Der Weltverband FIFA teilte am Montagabend in Zürich mit, dass auch Proteste keine Wahlwiederholung nach sich **ziehen würden**. Das Exekutivkomitee **habe** den Modus der Wahl selbst
5 **beschlossen**. Außerdem **habe** die Abstimmung unter der Aufsicht eines Notars **gestanden**. Damit **sei** das Ergebnis endgültig.

Mit Vorwürfen an „einflussreiche europäische Interessen-Gruppen" hat Charles J. Dempsey seine umstrittene Stimmenthaltung bei der Vergabe der WM 2006 an Deutschland verteidigt. [. . .] Ihm **sei** „von
10 einflussreichen europäischen Vertretern klar gemacht **worden**, dass es bei einer Stimm-Abgabe für Südafrika Nachteile für den OFC und die FIFA geben **würde**", erklärte Dempsey vier Tage nach der Wahl auf einer Pressekonferenz in Auckland. Durch seine Stimmenthaltung im letzten Wahlgang hatte Deutschland am vergangenen Donnerstag in
15 Zürich mit 12:11 gegen Südafrika den Zuschlag erhalten. Noch am Sonntag hatte der Chef der deutschen WM-Bewerbung, Franz Beckenbauer, angedeutet, Dempsey **habe** sich der Europäischen Fußball-Union (UEFA) und deren Vorsitzenden Lennart Johansson gegenüber verpflichtet **gefühlt**, weil diese ihn 1982 bei der Gründung des Ozeanien-
20 Verbandes unterstützt hatte. Zudem **hätte** Dempsey **erklärt**, er **habe** „große Sympathie für die deutsche Bewerbung", **müsse** als Kontinental-Vorsitzender aber England unterstützen, berichtete der deutsche WM-Koordinator Fedor Radmann.

Dempsey wies in dem Zusammenhang auch die Kritik zurück, er **habe**
25 sich mit seiner Enthaltung über die mit dem OFC getroffene Absprache **hinweggesetzt**, erst für England und nach dessen Ausscheiden für Südafrika zu votieren. Denn seine Tochter Josephine King, die beim OFC als Sekretärin des Exekutivkomitees tätig ist, **habe** sich bei den Verbandsmitgliedern im Vorfeld der Wahl „die mehrheitliche Erlaubnis
30 **eingeholt**", dass er von dieser Vereinbarung abrücken **könne**.

An dem am Sonntag geäußerten Vorhaben, sein Amt als OFC-Chef auf Grund von „unzumutbaren Belästigungen für mich und meine Familie" zum 1. Oktober niederzulegen, will der Funktionär festhalten.

Aus: *Die Welt (Online). Ressort: Sport,* 13.Juli 2000.

⌕ The subjunctive in the text

17.1 USAGE

The subjunctive mood, particularly the form of the subjunctive in German known as the *Konjunktiv I*, is used to indicate reported speech: it signals that someone other than the writer of the text has made a particular statement, e.g. the use of the subjunctive in *Damit **sei** das Ergebnis endgültig* (line 6) makes it clear that FIFA made this statement, not the writer of the report. The subjunctive is primarily a feature of the **written language** – it is used extensively in newspaper reports and in literary texts – and tends to be avoided in spoken German, e.g. *Er sagt, das Ergebnis **ist** endgültig*, where simply the indicative is used. The subjunctive can be used in the present tense: e.g. *Es **sei** endgültig*, the perfect tense: *Dempsey **habe** sich . . . verpflichtet **gefühlt*** (17–19) and, less commonly, in the future tense (e.g. ***werde** plus infinitive*). As can be seen from the above text, the perfect subjunctive is particularly common in newspaper reports.

17.2 FORMATION

The *Konjunktiv I* is formed using the present tense stem (**10.2a**) e.g. *mach-, komm-, woll-, müss-,*[80] plus the personal endings given in the box below. Unlike the indicative present tense, there are no irregularities in the *Konjunktiv I*: e.g. indicative *ich gebe, du gibst* vs. subjunctive *ich gebe, du gebest.*

-e	*-en*
-est	*-et*
-e	*-en*

e.g. *können*:
[present tense stem: *könn-*]

ich **könne**	wir **können**
(*du **könnest***)	(*ihr **könnet***)[81]
er/sie/es **könne** (30)	*sie/Sie* **können**

One can change a **perfect** indicative into its subjunctive equivalent by using the *Konjunktiv I* forms of the appropriate auxiliary verbs: *haben* or *sein*. Note that *sein* does not have *-e* in the singular:

beschließen:	*ich* **habe** *beschlossen*	*wir* **haben** *beschlossen*
(4–5)	(*du* **habest** *beschlossen*)	(*ihr* **habet** *beschlossen*)
	er/sie/es **habe** *beschlossen*	*sie/Sie* **haben** *beschlossen*

werden:[82]	*ich* **sei** *geworden*	*wir* **seien** *geworden*
(9–10)	*du* **sei(e)st** *geworden*	*ihr* **seiet** *geworden*
	er/sie/es **sei** *geworden*	*sie/Sie* **seien** *geworden*

Similarly, the **future** (and **passive**) auxiliary *werden* also has a regular *Konjunktiv I* form:

ich **werde** *gehen*	*wir* **werden** *gehen*
du **werdest** *gehen*	*ihr* **werdet** *gehen*
er **werde** *gehen*	*sie* **werden** *gehen*

---

[80] Infinitives ending in *-eln* drop e and n: e.g. *lächeln → er lächl-e.*

[81] In practice, the *du* and *ihr* forms of the *Konj. I* are rarely used with verbs other than *sein*, as they are felt to be rather stilted.

[82] In this text the verb *werden* is used to indicate a passive. Thus, *ihm ist klar gemacht worden* 'it was made clear to him' (hence the use of the dative) is put into the subjunctive *ihm **sei** klar gemacht worden* to indicate that the writer is reporting what was said (see **Ch. 18** for details on the passive).

17.3 USE OF PARTICULAR TENSE FORMS IN WRITTEN GERMAN

It is customary when reporting an utterance to keep to the same tense as originally used by the speaker. For instance, if someone says *Ich **brauche** viel Geld*, the **present** subjunctive is used when reporting the utterance, even if the preceding verb, e.g. *sagen, berichten* etc., is in the past: *Er sagte, er **brauche** viel Geld* (or *er sagte, **dass** er viel Geld brauche*). By contrast, English uses the past tense after verbs in the past: 'He said (that) he **needed** a lot of money'. Examples of present subjunctives in the text are given below, with the original utterance in square brackets:

- *Damit **sei** das Ergebnis endgültig* (6)   [*„Damit **ist** das Ergebnis endgültig"*]
- *er **habe** große Sympathie* (20–21)   [*„ich **habe** große Sympathie"*]
- *[er] **müsse** als Kontinental-Vorsitzender* (21–22)   [*„ich **muss** als Kontinental-Vorsitzender"*]
- *dass er . . . abrücken **könne*** (30)   [*„dass ich . . . abrücken **kann"***]

When the original utterance refers to the **past** (i.e. when the past, perfect or pluperfect tense is used), the reported speech is given in the **perfect subjunctive**, e.g. *Ich **brauchte** damals nicht viel Geld* → (*Er sagte*), *er **habe** damals nicht viel Geld **gebraucht***. Examples of perfect subjunctives in the text are:

- *Das Exekutivkomitee **habe** den Modus der Wahl selbst **beschlossen*** (4–5)
- *Außerdem **habe** die Abstimmung . . . **gestanden*** (5–6)
- *Ihm **sei** . . . klar gemacht **worden*** (9–10)
- *Dempsey **habe** sich . . . verpflichtet **gefühlt*** (17–19)
- *er **habe** sich mit seiner Enthaltung über . . . **hinweggesetzt*** (24–26)
- *seine Tochter . . . **habe** sich . . . die mehrheitliche Erlaubnis **eingeholt*** (27–30)

These uses of the perfect subjunctive suggest that the original speaker used some sort of past tense:

- *„Das Exekutivkomitee **hat** . . . **beschlossen"*** or *„Das Exekutivkomitee **beschloss"***
- *„Außerdem **hat** . . . **gestanden"*** or *„Außerdem **stand** . . ."*
- *„Mir **ist** . . . klar gemacht **worden"*** or *„Mir **wurde** klar gemacht . . . ."* etc.

For the use of ***würde**(**n**)* and ***hätte*** in the text, see **17.4** below.

Other points to note in the text

- Extended attributes: *die **mit dem OFC getroffene** Absprache* (25), *an dem **am Sonntag geäußerten** Vorhaben* (31) (see **5.3**).
- *Dessen* and *deren* used as possessives: *[UEFA] und **deren** Vorsitzenden* (18), *für England und nach **dessen** Ausscheiden* (26) (see **7.7**).
- Separable verbs: ***mit**teilen* (2–3), ***an**deuten* (17), ***zurück**weisen* (24), *sich **hinweg**setzen* (25–26), *sich **ein**holen* (28–30), ***ab**rücken* (30), ***nieder**legen* (33), ***fest**halten* (33) (see **Ch. 19**).

🔺 *Discover more about the subjunctive*

17.4 **USE OF THE *KONJUNKTIV II***

17.4a Written German

When replacing an original verb by its subjunctive equivalent in reported speech there is a danger that the subjunctive form may be identical to the original indicative, particularly in the case of plurals ending in *–en*, e.g. *Sie **haben** große Sympathie für die deutsche Bewerbung*, where *haben* could be indicative or subjunctive. In order to make it clear that a subjunctive is being used for the reported speech it is necessary to take a different form of the subjunctive, commonly known as the *Konjunktiv II*, which is formed by taking the **past tense** stem of the verb (e.g. *mach**te***) and, for most irregular verbs, adding umlaut (e.g. *h**ä**tte*) (see **16.3a** for the formation of the *Konjunktiv II*).

Thus, *haben* in a sentence like *Sie haben große Sympathie für die deutsche Bewerbung* would be replaced by ***hätten*** in reported speech. Contrast:

„Ich habe große Sympathie" → *Er sagte, er **habe** große Sympathie*[83]
„Wir haben große Sympathie" → *Sie sagten, sie **hätten** große Sympathie*

Similarly, in line 4 of the text the *Konjunktiv II* of *werden* is used:

*. . . dass auch Proteste keine Wahlwiederholung nach sich ziehen **würden***
(originally: *„auch Proteste **werden** keine Wahlwiederholung nach sich ziehen"*)

Other examples are:

- *„Wir können es machen"* → *sie sagten, sie **könnten** es machen*
- *„Wir werden es machen"* → *sie sagten, sie **würden** es machen*
- *„Wir wissen nichts davon"* → *sie sagten, sie **wüssten** nichts davon*

And with regular verbs:

- *„Wir arbeiten jetzt daran"* → *sie sagten, sie **arbeiteten** jetzt daran*
- *„Wir machen große Verluste"* → *sie sagten, sie **machten** große Verluste*

The use of *Konjunktiv II* in writing is restricted to regular verbs and very common irregular ones (i.e. those discussed in **16.3**). Other irregular verbs have *würde* (pl. *würden*) plus the infinitive as their *Konjunktiv II* equivalent:

- *„Wir sprechen nie darüber"* → *sie sagten, sie **würden** nie darüber **sprechen***
- *„Wir stehen zu unserer Meinung"* → *sie sagten, sie **würden** zu ihrer Meinung **stehen***[84]

When the original utterance refers to the **past** and, according to the rules in **17.3** above, is replaced by a perfect subjunctive, the auxiliary *haben* may need to be replaced by *hätten* to avoid ambiguity with the indicative:

- *„Ich sprach nie darüber"* → *er sagte, er **habe** nie darüber gesprochen*
- *„Wir sprachen nie darüber"* → *sie sagten, sie **hätten** nie darüber gesprochen*

[83] Such sentences are possible with or without *dass*. If *dass* is used, the finite verb is sent to the end of the clause, e.g. *Er sagte, dass er große Sympathie **habe*** (see **26.1b** for word order).

[84] *stünden* is also possible, but many speakers find it rather old-fashioned and stilted.

17.4b Spoken German

As mentioned in **17.1** above, the *Konjunktiv I* tends to be avoided in the spoken language unless a more formal register is required. In everyday colloquial German, the original indicative is simply used in reported speech, e.g. *Er sagte, er **ist** krank*. If, however, the speaker wants to use the subjunctive to indicate reported speech, particularly if s/he does not agree with or doubts the validity of the original statement, the ***Konjunktiv II*** is used instead:

i) It is used with **very common verbs** such as the modals *dürfen, können, mögen, müssen, sollen, wollen* and also *haben, sein, werden*, when used either as main verbs or auxiliaries:

- „*Ich **bin** krank*" →   *Er sagte, er ist krank* (Indicative)
       *Er sagte, er **wäre** krank* (Subjunctive)

- „*Ich **muss** gehen*" →   *Er sagte, er muss gehen* (Ind.)
       *Er sagte, er **müsste** gehen* (Subj.)

- „*Es **wird** regnen*" →   *Er sagte, es wird regnen* (Ind.)
       *Er sagte, es **würde** regnen* (Subj.)

- „*Ich **habe** es gemacht*" →   *Er sagte, er hat es gemacht* (Ind.)
       *Er sagte, er **hätte** es gemacht* (Subj.)

- „*Wir **blieben** zu Hause*" →   *Sie sagten, sie blieben zu Hause* (Ind.)
       *Sie sagten, sie **wären** zu Hause geblieben* (Subj.)

- „*Ich **war** sehr zufrieden*" →   *Er sagte, er war sehr zufrieden* (Ind.)
       *Er sagte, er **wäre** sehr zufrieden gewesen.* (Subj).[85]

ii) With other verbs, i.e. all regular verbs and those irregular ones not belonging to the very common group discussed in **17.4b(i)** above, ***würde**(-st, -t, -n)* plus the infinitive is used (when the original utterance is in the present):[86]

- „*Ich arbeite morgen*" →   *Er sagte, er arbeitet morgen* (Ind.)
       *Er sagte, er **würde** morgen **arbeiten*** (Subj.)

- „*Wir bleiben zu Hause*" →   *Sie sagten, sie bleiben zu Hause* (Ind.)
       *Sie sagten, sie **würden** zu Hause **bleiben*** (Subj.)

There is also an example of this in the text: *dass es bei einer Stimm-Abgabe für Südafrika Nachteile für den OFC und die FIFA **geben würde*** (10–12).

[85] The formal *Konjunktiv I* forms of the last three examples are *er **habe** es gemacht, sie **seien** zu Hause geblieben* and *er **sei** zufrieden gewesen* as the original statements are in the perfect or past tense, which requires a perfect subjunctive equivalent. Thus, it is the auxiliaries *haben* and *sein* that are put into the *Konjunktiv II* in less formal German, not the main verbs themselves, e.g. *machen, bleiben*.

[86] The *Konjunktiv II* of the verbs *kommen, tun* and, particularly, *wissen* (*käme, täte, wüsste*) are sometimes heard in spoken German, alongside their alternatives with *würde*, e.g. *Er sagte, er **wüsste** nichts davon.*

17.4c Degree of formality

Although a generalisation can be made that, to indicate reported speech, the *Konjunktiv I* is used in written German and the *Konjunktiv II* is used in the spoken language (except when the *Konjunktiv II* is used to disambiguate a form, as described in **17.4a**), less formal written texts may use more instances of the *Konjunktiv II* and, conversely, speakers in a formal situation may use the *Konjunktiv I*. Indeed, in some texts they may be used interchangeably. For instance, in our text from *Die Welt*, *Konjunktiv I* is preferred, as this is a quality newspaper. However, there is one occurrence of *Konjunktiv II* which cannot be explained by the traditional rules: *Zudem **hätte** Dempsey erklärt, er habe „große Sympathie für die deutsche Bewerbung . . . "* (20–21). The use of the less formal **hätte** could be explained by the fact that this is a sports report rather than a more 'serious' news item or a finance, politics or current affairs report. Furthermore, *hätte* may have been chosen by the writer to avoid repetition of *habe*: *Zudem **habe** Dempsey erklärt, er **habe** „große Sympathie für die deutsche Bewerbung . . . "*, although this is not strictly necessary.

✎ EXERCISES

Vocabulary topic: *Sport*

1 Imagine you are writing a sports report for a quality newspaper.

a) Put the following quotations into reported speech, using the appropriate form of the *Konjunktiv I*. (Remember to change the punctuation and pronouns where necessary.)

> *Example:* Der Stürmer sagte: „Ich habe besonders schlecht gespielt."[87]
>
> *Answer:* Der Stürmer sagte, <u>er</u> **habe** besonders schlecht gespielt.

1 Das Formel 1 Team teilte mit: „Eddie Irvine kann voraussichtlich aus dem Krankenhaus entlassen werden." „Kein medizinischer Eingriff ist nötig", stellten die Ärzte nach eingehenden Untersuchungen fest.

2 Der jüngere der beiden Klitschko-Brüder sagte: „Ich will diesen Kampf unbedingt und ich hoffe, dass ich bald diese Chance bekomme." Klitschko sagte: „Ich warte auf große Kämpfe. Zu 70 Prozent bin ich zufrieden, 30 Prozent muss ich mir noch erarbeiten."

3 „Wenn der Vertrag unter Dach und Fach ist", ergänzte Schaaf, „kommt Verlaat bereits in der nächsten Woche mit ins Trainingslager nach Österreich."

4 „Es kann nicht sein", betonte Völler, „dass es nur als Pflichtübung gilt, in der Nationalmannschaft zu spielen. Jeder muss es wollen. Es muss eine Ehre sein."

5 Die dreimalige Olympiasiegerin sagte: „Ich bin froh, das ich es versucht habe. Ich werde nichts in Zweifel ziehen, jetzt liegt alles hinter mir."

6 „Als ich über die Ziellinie lief, kamen jahrelang angestaute Gefühle auf", jubelte Anna Jones. „Seit ich neun bin, träumte ich davon, im Olympia-Team zu stehen. Jetzt ist der Traum wahr."

7 „Eigentlich hatte ich gar nicht so recht mit diesem Sieg gerechnet, weil ich diese Rallye nicht kannte", erklärte der 32 Jahre alte Finne. „Daher freue ich mich umsomehr darüber."

---

[87] In German a colon is placed before the direct speech when the preceding verb is a verb of saying.

b) Put the following sentences into reported speech, using *Konjunktiv I*, or *Konjunktiv II* when necessary:

Example: Der Stürmer sagte: „Wir haben besonders schlecht gespielt."

Answer: Der Stürmer sagte, sie **hätten** besonders schlecht gespielt.

1 Werder-Trainer Thomas Schaaf sagte am Sonntag: „Wir haben uns am Wochenende mit Verlaat und Ajax so weit geeinigt, dass man davon ausgehen kann, er kommt zu uns."

2 Baumanns Anwalt Michael Lehner kommentierte: „Dieter Baumann soll sich erst einmal in Ruhe auf Sydney vorbereiten, dann sehen wir weiter."

3 Rüdiger Nickel, Vorsitzender des DLV-Bundesausschusses Leistungssport, sagte: „Natürlich fehlen die großen Reißer. Aber wir haben eine sehr ausgeglichene Mannschaft, wobei die Frauen gegenüber dem letzten Jahr deutlich im Aufwind sind. Bei den Männern muss man sehen. Der erste Tag war nie der Tag der Deutschen. Die big points werden sicher morgen kommen."

4 Völler fügte hinzu: „Nach einer EM oder großen Turnieren gab es immer einen Schnitt. Einige hören aus Altersgründen auf, andere fallen durch das Sieb. Wenn ein neuer Trainer kommt, hat man andere Vorstellungen."

5 „Die Australier rechnen zu 90 Prozent damit, dass sie zum Endspiel nach Spanien reisen müssen und nicht gegen die USA im heimischen National Tennis Centre in Melbourne antreten können", berichtete die dpa.

6 Der Coach meinte: „Die MetroStars werden die Entscheidung treffen. Lothar hat da nur noch wenig zu sagen [. . .] Ich glaube, dass er die falsche Einstellung hat. Es dreht sich hier nicht alles um Lothar Matthäus, das hat es nie getan." Der Coach erklärte: „Wir hatten einige Fragen an Lothar zu seiner Verletzung und seiner Einstellung zur Mannschaft. Alle haben ihre Meinung gesagt."

Sentences adapted from *Die Welt (Online), Ressort Sport, News-Ticker,* 17 July 2000.

2 Imagine that you are telling a friend what someone has said. Use the less formal *Konjunktiv II* to indicate reported speech:

Example: Klaus sagte: „Ich bin mit dem neuen Kapitän nicht zufrieden."

Answer: Klaus sagte, er **wäre** mit dem neuen Kapitän nicht zufrieden.

1 Paul sagte: „Ich spiele lieber Squash als Tennis."

2 Mein Bruder sagte: „Matthäus hat zwei Tore innerhalb fünf Minuten geschossen."

3 Meine Freundin meinte: „Ich interessiere mich überhaupt nicht für Autorennen."

4 Benno sagte: „Der Schiedsrichter zeigte ihm die gelbe Karte."

5 Unsere Gegner drohten uns: „Wir werden euch mit fünf zu null schlagen."

6 Anton sagte: „Ich muss mich beeilen. Ich gehe gleich ins Fußballstadion."

7 Sabine sagte: „Ich weiß nicht, ob er gewonnen hat."

8 Mein Schilehrer sagte: „Man muss beim Schifahren immer auf der Piste bleiben, sonst kann ein Unfall passieren."

9 Mein Vater sagte: „Es gibt nichts schöneres als Pferderennen!"

10 Ulrike sagte: „Ich wollte mit ihm Badminton spielen, aber er hatte keine Zeit."

✎ **FURTHER EXERCISES**

3 Put the highlighted indicatives into the corresponding tense and appropriate form of the subjunctive to indicate reported speech in a written text:

In diesem Augenblick erst zog Katharina die beiden Ausgaben der ZEITUNG aus der Tasche und fragte, ob der Staat – so drückte sie es aus – nichts tun **kann**, um sie gegen diesen Schmutz zu schützen und ihre verlorene Ehre wiederherzustellen. Sie **weiß** inzwischen sehr wohl, dass ihre Vernehmung durchaus gerechtfertigt **ist**, wenn ihr auch dieses »Bis-ins-letzte-Lebensdetail-Gehen« nicht **einleuchtet**, aber es **ist** ihr unbegreiflich, wie Einzelheiten aus der Vernehmung – etwa der Herrenbesuch – **haben** zur Kenntnis der ZEITUNG gelangen können. Hier griff Staatsanwalt Hach ein und sagte, . . . [b]eleidigende und möglicherweise verleumderische Details der Berichterstattung **kann** sie zum Gegenstand einer Privatklage machen, und – falls sich **herausstellt**, dass es »undichte Stellen« innerhalb der untersuchenden Behörde **gibt**, so **wird** diese, darauf **kann** sie sich verlassen, Anzeige gegen Unbekannt erheben und ihr zu ihrem Recht verhelfen [. . .]

[Blorna] teilte Hach mit, dass Katharinas Mutter wahrscheinlich infolge eines Besuchs von Tötges von der ZEITUNG unerwartet **starb**. Hach war milder als am Morgen, bat Katharina, die ihm gewiss nicht **grollt**, wozu sie auch keinen Grund **hat**, sein persönliches Beileid auszusprechen. Im Übrigen **steht** er jederzeit zur Verfügung. Er **ist** zwar jetzt sehr beschäftigt mit den Vernehmungen von Götten, **wird** sich aber freimachen; im Übrigen **ergab** sich aus den Vernehmungen Göttens bisher nichts Belastendes für Katharina. Er **sprach** mit großer Zuneigung und fair von ihr und über sie. Eine Besuchserlaubnis **ist** allerdings nicht zu erwarten, da keine Verwandtschaft **vorliegt** und die Definition »Verlobte« sich bestimmt als zu vage herausstellen und nicht stichhaltig sein würde [. . .].

Natürlich konfrontierte Katharina Dr. Heinen mit der Ausgabe der ZEITUNG, in der das Tötges-Interview erwähnt und ihre Mutter zitiert wurde, sie teilte aber keineswegs Dr. Heinens Empörung über das Interview, sondern meinte, diese Leute **sind** Mörder und Rufmörder, sie **verachtet** das natürlich, aber offfenbar **ist** es doch geradezu die Pflicht dieser Art Zeitungsleute, unschuldige Menschen um Ehre, Ruf und Gesundheit zu bringen.

Aus: Heinrich Böll, *Die verlorene Ehre der Katharina Blum*. ©1974 Verlag Kiepenheuer & Witsch, Köln.

4 Write a quality newspaper report putting the direct speech into reported speech by changing the verb forms in bold print and dropping the inverted commas:

Jede zweite Frau fühlt sich zu fett

Berlin – In einer Umfrage des Forsa-Instituts im Auftrag der Zeitschrift *Brigitte* und des Bundesgesundheitsministeriums sollten die Ernährungsgewohnheiten der Frauen erfragt werden. Die Ergebnisse der Umfrage präsentierte die stellvertretende Chefredakteurin Tania Miglietti in Berlin.

Was gilt überhaupt als Diät? „Jede zweite Frau in Deutschland möchte weniger wiegen. 44 Prozent der Frauen zwischen 20 und 60 Jahren **wollen** kalorienbewusst essen. Fast die Hälfte der befragten Frauen **hat angegeben**, schon einmal eine Diät gemacht zu haben", sagte

Miglietti. „Allerdings **werden** 88 Prozent so genannte *Formula-Diäten*, also das Ersetzen einer Mahlzeit durch einen Drink, nicht als Diät angesehen. Auch eine Mahlzeit ausfallen zu lassen, **wird** von 80 Prozent nicht als Abmagerungskur empfunden."

Der Griff zur Tüte: Miglietti erklärte, dass „jede siebte Frau zur Gruppe der *unkritischen Pflichtesserinnen* **gehört**. Diese *Trash-Fress-Frauen* **greifen** häufig zu Fertiggerichten oder **beschäftigen** sich neben dem Essen noch mit anderen Dingen. Vor allem junge Singles im Alter von 20 bis 30 Jahren **gehören** zu dieser Gruppe".

„43 Prozent der Frauen **essen** beim Fernsehen, 42 Prozent **lassen** sich vom leckeren Anblick der Speisen verleiten", erklärte die Journalistin. „80 Prozent der Frauen **haben angegeben**, gesundheitsbewusst zu kochen. Demgegenüber **haben** allerdings 54 Prozent **erklärt**, sie **benutzen** auch Halbfertig- oder Fertigprodukte wie Soßenpulver. 62 Prozent **müssen** immer Salziges oder Süßes zum Knabbern zu Hause haben. Ein entspanntes Verhältnis zum Essen **haben** nur 40 Prozent der 20- bis 60-Jährigen. Sie **sind** auch eher mit ihrem Gewicht zufrieden."

Adapted from *Der Spiegel (Online)*. 4. September 2000.

18 | Passive

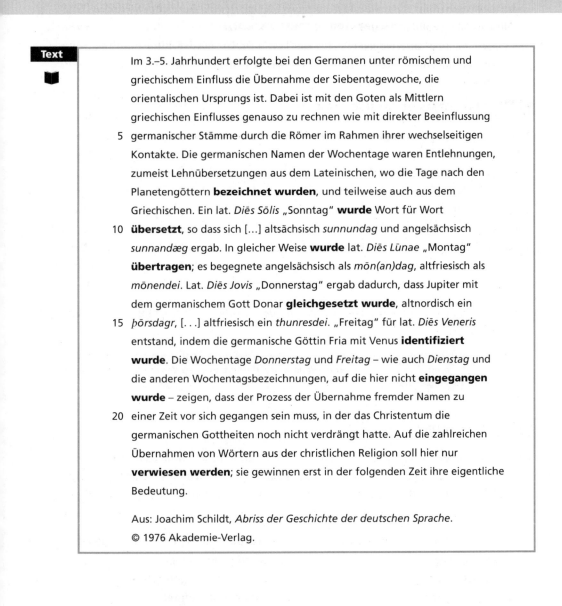
Im 3.–5. Jahrhundert erfolgte bei den Germanen unter römischem und griechischem Einfluss die Übernahme der Siebentagewoche, die orientalischen Ursprungs ist. Dabei ist mit den Goten als Mittlern griechischen Einflusses genauso zu rechnen wie mit direkter Beeinflussung
5 germanischer Stämme durch die Römer im Rahmen ihrer wechselseitigen Kontakte. Die germanischen Namen der Wochentage waren Entlehnungen, zumeist Lehnübersetzungen aus dem Lateinischen, wo die Tage nach den Planetengöttern **bezeichnet wurden**, und teilweise auch aus dem Griechischen. Ein lat. *Diēs Sōlis* „Sonntag" **wurde** Wort für Wort
10 **übersetzt**, so dass sich [...] altsächsisch *sunnundag* und angelsächsisch *sunnandæg* ergab. In gleicher Weise **wurde** lat. *Diēs Lūnae* „Montag" **übertragen**; es begegnete angelsächsisch als *mōn(an)dag*, altfriesisch als *mōnendei*. Lat. *Diēs Jovis* „Donnerstag" ergab dadurch, dass Jupiter mit dem germanischem Gott Donar **gleichgesetzt wurde**, altnordisch ein
15 *þōrsdagr*, [...] altfriesisch ein *thunresdei*. „Freitag" für lat. *Diēs Veneris* entstand, indem die germanische Göttin Fria mit Venus **identifiziert wurde**. Die Wochentage *Donnerstag* und *Freitag* – wie auch *Dienstag* und die anderen Wochentagsbezeichnungen, auf die hier nicht **eingegangen wurde** – zeigen, dass der Prozess der Übernahme fremder Namen zu
20 einer Zeit vor sich gegangen sein muss, in der das Christentum die germanischen Gottheiten noch nicht verdrängt hatte. Auf die zahlreichen Übernahmen von Wörtern aus der christlichen Religion soll hier nur **verwiesen werden**; sie gewinnen erst in der folgenden Zeit ihre eigentliche Bedeutung.

Aus: Joachim Schildt, *Abriss der Geschichte der deutschen Sprache.*
© 1976 Akademie-Verlag.

♀ The passive in the text

18.1 USAGE

The passive voice is used to shift the emphasis away from the agent (i.e. the 'doer') of the action described by the verb to the **recipient** of the action. Thus, an ordinary 'active' sentence like *Clara* *und Lisa fragte den Lehrer* 'Clara and Lisa asked the teacher' becomes *Der Lehrer* **wurde** *(von Clara und Lisa)* **gefragt** 'The teacher **was asked** (by Clara and Lisa)' in the passive.

Passives are often used when a speaker/writer does not want to specify the agent. For instance, in our chosen text the main aim of the writer is to inform us how the days of the week originally got their names. The emphasis is not on **who** did the naming but on what the names are and where they came from: e.g. *wo die Tage nach den Planetengöttern* **bezeichnet wurden** (lines 7–8), *Ein lat. Diēs Sōlis „Sonntag"* **wurde** *Wort für Wort* **übersetzt** (9–10), *In gleicher Weise* **wurde** *lat. Diēs Lūnae „Montag"* **übertragen** (11–12) etc. This 'agentless passive' is the most frequently used passive in German and is more common in the **written** language than in speech.

18.2   CASE FORMS OF PASSIVE SUBJECTS

We can see by the first example given in **18.1** above, *Clara und Lisa fragten den Lehrer* → *Der Lehrer wurde von Clara und Lisa gefragt*, that the recipient of the action (*den Lehrer* in the accusative) becomes the **subject** of the passive sentence, which is shown by making it nominative in German: ***Der*** *Lehrer wurde . . .*, and the finite verb (in this case *werden*) agrees with the new subject: it is now singular. If, on the other hand, the recipient of the action is in the **dative** or **genitive** or is preceded by a **preposition** it does not become nominative in the passive but **stays the same**, and the verb is in the third person singular: e.g. *Clara und Lisa antworteten* **dem** *Lehrer* → ***Dem*** *Lehrer wurde (von Clara und Lisa) geantwortet.*[88] Similarly, there is an example in our text of a recipient (shown here by underlining) being preceded by a preposition in the passive:

Auf die zahlreichen Übernahmen von Wörtern aus der christlichen Religion soll hier nur **verwiesen werden** (21–23).

> [88] If, however, there is another noun or pronoun in the passive sentence that functions as the subject (and is not preceded by *von* or any other preposition), the verb must agree with that: e.g. *Dem Lehrer* **wurden** *viele Fragen gestellt.*

18.3   FORMATION

The passive can be used in all the main tenses (although some are more common than others). It is formed using the appropriate tense of the auxiliary verb **werden** plus the **past participle** of the main verb (see **13.2b–c**). Below are examples of the present and simple past passive, the latter of which is used extensively in our text:

ich **werde** *oft* **gefragt** 'I am often asked'	*ich* **wurde** *oft* **gefragt** 'I was often asked'
du **wirst** *oft* **gefragt**	*du* **wurdest** *oft* **gefragt**
er/sie/es **wird** *oft* **gefragt**	*er/sie/es* **wurde** *oft* **gefragt**
wir **werden** *oft* **gefragt**	*wir* **wurden** *oft* **gefragt**
ihr **werdet** *oft* **gefragt**	*ihr* **wurdet** *oft* **gefragt**
sie/Sie **werden** *oft* **gefragt**	*sie/Sie* **wurden** *oft* **gefragt**

The text mainly uses the third person singular (*er/sie/es*) form in the past: **wurde** *übersetzt* (9–10), **wurde** *übertragen* (11–12), *gleichgesetzt* **wurde** (14), *identifiziert* **wurde** (16–17), *eingegangen* **wurde** (18–19) and one third person plural (*sie*-form): *bezeichnet* **wurden** (8). The passive can also be used with modals, in which case *werden* is in the infinitive (e.g. *Es muss gemacht werden* 'it must **be done**'). There is an example of this in the text: *soll* . . . *verwiesen werden* (23).

<h3>18.4   *ZU* + INFINITIVE WITH A PASSIVE MEANING</h3>

When *zu* plus an infinitive occurs with the verbs *sein* and *bleiben* it often has a passive meaning: *Dabei **ist** mit den Goten als Mittlern griechischen Einflusses genauso **zu rechnen** wie* . . . (3–4) 'As mediators of Greek influence the Goths are just as much to **be reckoned** with as . . .'. Other examples (not from the text) are:

*Diese Kriterien <u>sind</u> **zu erfüllen**.*	These criteria are to be fulfilled.
*Das Problem <u>bleibt</u> noch **zu besprechen**.*	The problem remains to be discussed.
*Der Aufsatz <u>ist</u> bis nächste Woche **abzugeben**.*	The essay is to be handed in by next week.

Other points to note in the text

- Extensive use of genitive: ***der*** *Siebentagewoche* (2), *orientalisch**en** Ursprung**s*** (3), *griechisch**en** Einflusse**s*** (4), *germanisch**er** Stämme* (5), *ihr**er** wechselseitig**en** Kontakte* (5–6), ***der*** *Wochentage* (6), ***der*** *Übernahme fremd**er** Namen* (19) (see **3.1a(iv)**).
- Pluperfect: *verdrängt hatte* (21) (see **Ch. 14**).
- *Müssen* used with a perfect tense to express probability: *vor sich **gegangen sein muss*** (20) (see **21.5a**).
- Compound words: i) nouns *Jahrhundert* (1), *Siebentagewoche* (2), *Wochentage*, (6, 17), *Lehnübersetzungen* (7), *Planetengöttern* (8), *Wochentagsbezeichnungen* (18); ii) adjectives *wechselseitig* (5), *altsächsich* (10), *angelsächsisch* (10, 12), *altfriesisch* (12, 15), *altnordisch* (14), *zahlreich* (21); iii) verbs: *gleichgesetzt* (14) (see **27.4**).
- Full stops after ordinal numbers: *3.–5.* (1) (see **28.1c**).

▲ *Discover more about the passive*

<h3>18.5   OTHER TENSES OF THE PASSIVE</h3>

The perfect and pluperfect tenses also have passive equivalents,[89] which are formed using the **perfect** and **pluperfect** tenses of *werden* respectively, plus the past participle of the main verb. Note that *geworden* is shortened to *worden* to avoid having to pronounce two participles beginning with *ge-*:

---

[89] The future passive (e.g. *Ich **werde** gefragt **werden*** 'I will be asked') is rarely used, as the present is preferred when referring to the future. Future perfect, conditional and conditional perfect passives also exist (e.g. *Ich werde gefragt **worden sein*** 'I will have been asked', *Ich **würde** gefragt werden* 'I would be asked'; *Ich **wäre** gefragt **worden*** 'I would've been asked') though, in practice, they are not frequently used.

Perfect: 'I have been asked'   *Ich **bin** (du bist/er ist/wir sind/ihr seid/sie sind)*
                                 gefragt worden

Pluperfect: 'I had been asked'   *Ich **war** (du warst/er war/wir waren/ihr wart/sie waren)*
                                 gefragt worden

The tenses are used in the passive in the same way as in the active: e.g. the perfect passive is used mainly in **spoken** German to refer to the past while the simple past passive is used mainly in **written** German, hence its frequency of occurrence in our text.

18.6   THE AGENT

Some passive sentences may specify an agent: e.g. 'He was asked <u>by the girl</u>'. In German, the direct agent of the action is usually introduced by *von* (+dat.): *Er wurde **von** dem Mädchen gefragt*. This usually refers to **people**, although inanimate objects can also be preceded by *von* if they are seen as being the direct agent:

- *Das Fenster wurde **von** den Kindern*   The window was broken by the children.
  kaputt gemacht.
- *Sie ist **von** ihrem Chef gefeuert worden.*   She was fired by her boss.
- *Die Katze wurde **von** einem Auto überfahren.*   The cat was run over by a car.

When 'by' means 'by means of' or 'through', and is not referring to the *direct* agent of the action, *durch* is used. This is more commonly used with **things** rather than with people:[90]

- *Die Katze wurde **durch** fahrlässiges*   The cat was killed through careless
  Fahren getötet.   driving.
- *Die Wirtschaft wird **durch** die Inflation*   The economy is weakened by/through
  geschwächt.   inflation.

[90] Although it can be used with people when it means 'through': *Sie wurde von ihrem Chef **durch** seine Sekretärin gefeuert* 'She was fired by her boss through his secretary'.

18.7   THE USE OF *ES* WITH A PASSIVE

If the passive is used in a general statement not referring to any specific person or thing, the sentence can appear without a proper subject: e.g. 'There was a lot of smoking going on', where the emphasis is on the action of the verb and not on who was actually doing the smoking or what was being smoked. In English, such sentences often begin with 'there', which has a very general meaning. In German, the equivalent is *es*: *Es wurde viel geraucht*, and the verb is in the third person singular. If other words appear at the beginning of the sentence, however, *es* is omitted: e.g. *Auf der Fete wurde viel geraucht* 'There was a lot of smoking (going on) at the party'.

   Es can also occur when there **is** a proper subject in the sentence, but only when the subject **follows** the verb, thereby allowing *es* to appear at the beginning of the sentence: e.g. *Es wurden viele Zigaretten geraucht* is an alternative to *Viele Zigaretten wurden geraucht*. We can see by the plural verb form that the verb agrees with the subject where present, not with *es*.

18.8 THE PASSIVE IN SPOKEN GERMAN

The passive is used much less frequently in spoken German than in the written language. This may cause problems for English learners of German, as the passive is used extensively both in written and in spoken English. Often an English passive is best translated as an ordinary active sentence in German, particularly where an agent is present: e.g. 'I was treated badly by my boss' → *Mein Chef hat mich schlecht behandelt.* If the agent is not present, speakers will either use the passive ('I was treated badly' → *Ich wurde schlecht behandelt*) or, very often, an active construction with *man* 'one' as the subject: **Man** *hat mich schlecht behandelt* (see **7.1b**).

18.9 THE *SEIN*-PASSIVE

Usually, when one talks of 'the passive' in German one is referring to the *werden* + past participle constructions outlined above. There is, however, another type of passive which is formed using the auxiliary verb **sein** plus the past participle and, consequently, is known as the 'sein-passive'. The difference between the *werden*-passive and the *sein*-passive is that the former indicates an **action**, which is often indicated using 'being' in English, while the latter describes a **state**:

Das Brot **wird** geschnitten.	The bread is being cut (i.e. at this moment).
Das Brot **ist** geschnitten.[91]	The bread is cut (i.e. has already been cut).
Das Auto **wurde** repariert.	The car was being repaired.
Das Auto **war** repariert.	The car was repaired.

---

[91] In the *sein*-passive, the past participle functions like an **adjective**. Thus *Das Brot ist geschnitten* is grammatically equivalent to *Das Brot ist frisch.*

✎ **EXERCISES**

Vocabulary topic: *Schule*

1 Put the bracketed verbs into the present passive using the correct word order:

1 Musik oft als Wahlfach [nehmen].
2 Die Hausarbeit muss bis Montag [abgeben].
3 Fragen können während der Gruppenarbeit [stellen].
4 Das Klassenzimmer [aufräumen].
5 Wie viele Fächer hier [unterrichten]?

2 Put the bracketed verbs into the appropriate tense of the passive:

1 Der Unterricht [stören, *past*].
2 Die Prüfungen [verschieben, *perfect*].
3 Dieses Thema schon dreimal [besprechen, *pluperfect*], aber trotzdem fanden es die Schüler sehr schwierig zu verstehen.

4 Die Übungen nicht [machen, *perfect*].

5 Keine Taschenrechner dürfen [benutzen, *present*].

6 Die Schüler nächsten Monat in diesem Fach [prüfen, *future*].

3 Put the active sentences below into the passive and pay attention to the following: i) Do not change the TENSE of the original sentence; ii) Decide whether the AGENT should be preceded by *von* or *durch*. If the agent is *man*, it should be omitted:

Example: Der Schüler fragte den Lehrer, wer Bismarck war.

Answer: Der Lehrer **wurde von** dem Schüler **gefragt**, wer Bismarck war.

1 Die Schüler beleidigten den Lehrer.

2 Der Klassensprecher hat das Problem erwähnt.

3 Der Sportlehrer hatte Klaus für die Fußballmannschaft der Schule ausgewählt.

4 Das schlechte Wetter ruinierte das Hockeyturnier.

5 Das Geräusch des Rasenmähers hat die Konzentration der Prüfungskandidaten gestört.

6 Der Direktor wird den Unruhestifter aus der Schule herausschmeißen.

7 Die Lehrer zwangen Peter wegen seiner schlechten Noten sitzenzubleiben.

8 Die Prüfer haben sechs Auszeichnungen erteilt.

9 Die Organisatoren hatten den Schüleraustausch wegen Mangel an Interesse gestrichen.

10 Man kann ihn wegen Schwänzerei der Schule verweisen.

✎ **FURTHER EXERCISES**

4 Put the active sentences below into the passive, moving the underlined nouns/pronouns to the beginning of the passive sentence with their accompanying articles, pronouns, prepositions etc. Bear in mind that SOME of these must be put into the nominative while others must stay unchanged. Omit the agent:

Example: Er rechnete nicht mit der <u>Frage</u>.

Answer: <u>Mit der Frage</u> **wurde** nicht **gerechnet**.

1 Man hat meinem <u>Sohn</u> geholfen.

2 Jemand hat mitten in der Nacht meinen <u>Mann</u> angerufen.

3 Bei uns in der Firma nehmen sie auf <u>keinen</u> Rücksicht.

4 Man redet oft über <u>Geld</u>, aber es gibt wichtigere Dinge im Leben.

5 Jemand folgte meiner <u>Freundin</u> nach Hause.

6 Sie hatten die <u>Nachbarn</u> nicht eingeladen.

7 Sie haben den <u>Angestellten</u> nichts gesagt.

8 Man spielt nicht mit <u>Elektrizität</u> herum!

9 Schau, man hat <u>mir</u> diese leckeren Pralinen geschenkt!

10 Man hatte den <u>Brief</u> noch nicht weggeschickt.

5 a Rewrite your answers to question 2 above using *man* instead of the passive.

5 b Translate the following sentences into German using *man*:

Example: He was seen → **Man** *sah ihn* (OR **Man** *hat ihn gesehen*).

1 My handbag has been stolen!
2 What can be done?
3 I was given a cheque.
4 He is often described as arrogant.

6 Put the following sentences into the *Sein*-passive (present tense) to express a state. Where this is not grammatically possible (i.e. where the verb cannot describe a state), use a *Werden*-passive in the perfect. Translate your answers into English:

Example: Jemand hat den Tisch gedeckt.
Answer: Der Tisch **ist gedeckt**. 'The table is set'.

1 Jemand hat die Tasse gebrochen.
2 Jemand hat den Nagel gebogen.
3 Jemand hat meinen Bruder gesehen.
4 Jemand hat Maria eben geküsst.
5 Jemand hat das Kind angezogen.
6 Jemand hat die Zeitung gelesen.

7 Identify the passives (and other constructions with a passive meaning) in the following text and explain their use:

Der Religionsunterricht ist in den öffentlichen Schulen mit Ausnahme der bekenntnisfreien Schulen ordentliches Lehrfach. Unbeschadet des staatlichen Aufsichtsrechtes wird der Religionsunterricht in Übereinstimmung mit den Grundsätzen der Religionsgemeinschaften erteilt. Kein Lehrer darf gegen seinen Willen verpflichtet werden, Religionsunterricht zu erteilen.

Das Recht zur Errichtung von privaten Schulen wird gewährleistet. Private Schulen als Ersatz für öffentliche Schulen bedürfen der Genehmigung des Staates und unterstehen den Landesgesetzen. Die Genehmigung ist zu erteilen, wenn die privaten Schulen in ihren Lehrzielen und Einrichtungen sowie in der wissenschaftlichen Ausbildung ihrer Lehrkräfte nicht hinter den öffentlichen Schulen zurückstehen und eine Sonderung der Schüler nach den Besitzverhältnissen der Eltern nicht gefördert wird. Die Genehmigung ist zu versagen, wenn die wirtschaftliche und rechtliche Stellung der Lehrkräfte nicht genügend gesichert ist.

Eine private Volksschule ist nur zuzulassen, wenn die Unterrichtsverwaltung ein besonderes pädagogisches Interesse anerkennt oder, auf Antrag von Erziehungsberechtigten, wenn sie als Gemeinschaftsschule, als Bekenntnis- oder Weltanschauungsschule errichtet werden soll und eine öffentliche Volksschule dieser Art in der Gemeinde nicht besteht.

Aus dem Grundgesetz für die Bundesrepublik Deutschland, 1993. Artikel 7. Schulwesen [§3–5].

19 | Separable verbs

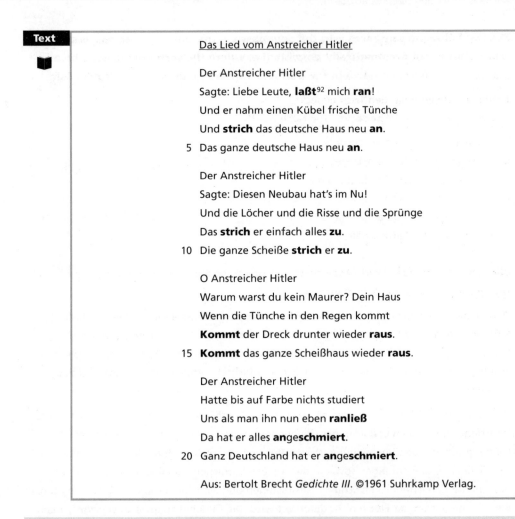

Das Lied vom Anstreicher Hitler

Der Anstreicher Hitler
Sagte: Liebe Leute, **laßt**[92] mich **ran**!
Und er nahm einen Kübel frische Tünche
Und **strich** das deutsche Haus neu **an**.
5 Das ganze deutsche Haus neu **an**.

Der Anstreicher Hitler
Sagte: Diesen Neubau hat's im Nu!
Und die Löcher und die Risse und die Sprünge
Das **strich** er einfach alles **zu**.
10 Die ganze Scheiße **strich** er **zu**.

O Anstreicher Hitler
Warum warst du kein Maurer? Dein Haus
Wenn die Tünche in den Regen kommt
Kommt der Dreck drunter wieder **raus**.
15 **Kommt** das ganze Scheißhaus wieder **raus**.

Der Anstreicher Hitler
Hatte bis auf Farbe nichts studiert
Uns als man ihn nun eben **ranließ**
Da hat er alles **an**ge**schmiert**.
20 Ganz Deutschland hat er **an**ge**schmiert**.

Aus: Bertolt Brecht *Gedichte III*. ©1961 Suhrkamp Verlag.

---

[92] Now spelt *lasst*.

⌕ Separable verbs in the text

19.1   POSITION OF PREFIX

German has a special class of verbs known as **separable**, as their prefixes are separated from the verb in certain grammatical constructions. For instance, when the verb is finite (i.e. when it indicates a certain tense, person and number) its prefix is sent to the end of the clause. Thus, the infinitive **ran***lassen* becomes *lasst . . . ran* when it is finite (2). Similarly: *anstreichen → strich . . . an* (4, 5), *zustreichen → strich . . . zu* (9, 10), **raus***kommen → kommt . . . raus* (14, 15).[93] If the finite verb has itself been sent to the end, due to the presence of a subordinating conjunction, for example, the prefix and verb come together again: *als . . .* **ran***ließ* (18). In the past participle, *ge-* appears between the separable prefix and the verb stem: *an**ge**schmiert* (19, 20). Similarly, in a '*zu* + infinitive' construction the *zu* is placed between prefix and verb: e.g. *raus**zu**kommen, an**zu**schmieren* (not in text).

[93] Note that, in longer sentences containing two or more clauses, the prefix goes to the end of its clause, not to the end of the sentence: e.g. *Ich strich das Zimmer an und putzte die Fenster.*

Other points to note in the text

- Imperative in *ihr*-form: *lasst* (2) (see **11.3**).
- Use of *wenn* and *als*: *wenn* with present tense (13), *als* with past (18) (see **25.3a**).
- Colloquial usage: *heranlassen →* **ran***lassen* (2), *herauskommen →* **raus***kommen* (14, 15), *hat es → hat's* (7), *darunter → drunter* (14).

▲ *Discover more about separable verbs*

19.2 SEPARABLE VERSUS INSEPARABLE

19.2a Separable verbs

Separable verbs are recognised by the fact that their prefixes are usually identical to **prepositions**, e.g. *an, aus, mit, um, vor,* zu, or variants thereof. Variants can be formed by prefixing prepositions with *her-*, e.g. *heran, heraus* (which in the text are shortened to the more colloquial *ran* and *raus*); *hin-*, e.g. *hinein*,[94] *hinaus, hinüber*;[95] and *da(r)-*, e.g. *davon-, dazu-, daraus-* (see **24.3**). Often, the meaning of the preposition is recognisable within the verb, e.g. *ausgehen* 'to go out', *aufschauen* 'to look up', *mitkommen* 'to come with (someone)', but this is not always the case: e.g. *umkommen* does not mean 'to come around' but 'to die'. In speech, separable prefixes are always stressed (indicated here by underlining): e.g. *ankommen, mitmachen*.

There are also several separable verbs whose prefixes are not prepositional: e.g. **fern***sehen*, **kennen***lernen*, **teil***nehmen*, **statt***finden*, **voll***stopfen*.

[94] Note that *ein-* = 'in', not **in-*.

[95] Often *her* is used to indicate movement towards the speaker while *hin* indicates movement away from the speaker: e.g. *Er kam in mein Zimmer* **her***ein* vs. *Er ging aus dem Zimmer* **hin***aus. Her-* and *hin-* can also be used on their own as separable prefixes: e.g. *hinlegen, herkommen*.

19.2b Inseparable verbs

By contrast, inseparable prefixes are not usually prepositional (but see **19.2c** below). They are: *be-, ent-, er-, ge-, ver-, zer-* and are unstressed: e.g. **be***sprechen*, **ent***sprechen*, **er***kennen*, **ge***stehen*, **ver***stehen*, **zer***stören*. They are never separated from the verb, e.g. *Ich* **ver***stehe das*, and do not admit *ge-* in the past participle, e.g. *Ich habe es* **be***sprochen/***er***kannt/***ver***standen/***zer***stört* (see **27.3**a for their meanings).

19.2c Prefixes which may be separable or inseparable

Less commonly, a prefix can be separable or inseparable depending on the verb to which it attaches: e.g. **_durch_**_kommen_ 'to get through' (_Ich komme durch_) vs. _durch<u>denk</u>en_ 'to think through' (_Ich durchdenke es_); _sich_ **_um_**_drehen_ 'to turn around' (_Ich drehe mich um_) vs. _um<u>arm</u>en_ 'to hug' (_Ich umarme dich_). Sometimes the verbs may look identical and differ only in meaning (indicated by the placing of stress): e.g. **_über_**_ziehen_ 'to put on' (_Ich ziehe mir einen warmen Pulli über_) vs. _über<u>zieh</u>en_ 'to cover' (_Ich **überziehe** das Bett mit einer frischen Decke_).

19.3 COMMON SEPARABLE PREFIXES

Below is a list of the most frequently used separable prefixes and some of the meanings usually associated with them:

ab-	'away/off':	_Ich fahre_ **ab** 'I'm setting off'
an-	'on':	_Ich ziehe einen Mantel_ **an** 'I put on a coat'
auf-	'up'; 'open':	_Ich stehe_ **auf** 'I get up', _Ich mache die Tür_ **auf** 'I open the door'
aus-	'out/off':	_Ich gehe_ **aus** 'I go out', _Ich ziehe den Mantel_ **aus** 'I take the coat off'
ein-	'in':	_Er bricht_ **ein** 'He's breaking in'
mit-	'with/along/too':	_Komm_ **mit**! 'Come along', _Er spielt_ **mit** 'He's playing with (us)/too'
nach-	'after':	_Er läuft ihr_ **nach** 'He's running after her'
vor-	'in front/ahead':	_Er drängelt ständig_ **vor** 'He's always pushing ahead'
weg-	'away':	_Geh_ **weg**! 'Go away!', _Er lief_ **weg** 'He ran away'
zu-	'towards'; 'shut':	_Er kam auf mich_ **zu** 'He came towards me',
		Ich machte die Tür **zu** 'I shut the door'

✎ EXERCISES

Vocabulary topic: _Wohnen_

1 **Complete the following sentences by inserting the correct form of the bracketed separable verbs in the correct place. All sentences are in the present tense:**

1 Wir [einziehen] am Samstag in unser neues Haus.
2 Ich [umziehen] heute.
3 Wann [ausziehen] du?
4 Die Männer [anstreichen] gerade die Wand.
5 Die Gäste [sich hinsetzen].
6 Ich versuche durch das Küchenfenster zu [hinausschauen], aber es ist zu schmutzig.
7 Wir [vorhaben] die neuen Gardinen zu [aufhängen].
8 [Aufdrehen] du den Wasserhahn?

2 **Put your answers to question 1 above into the perfect tense, paying particular attention to the form of the past participle.**

3 **Complete the following sentences by inserting the correct form of the bracketed verbs in the correct place, using the tenses given. Note that some of the bracketed verbs are separable and others are inseparable:**

  1 Er war müde und [sich hinlegen, *past*] aufs Sofa.

  2 Als er ins Badezimmer [hereinkommen, *past*], saß sie schon im Bad.

  3 Ich [ersetzen, *present*] diesen alten Teppich.

  4 Wir [einrichten, *present*] eine neue Küche.

  5 [Wegreißen, *perfect*] du die alte Tapete im Wohnzimmer?

  6 Die Katze [zerreißen, *perfect*] meine neue Bettdecke.

  7 Wenn du das Fenster [aufmachen, *present*], können wir das Schlafzimmer ein bisschen lüften.

  8 Der Maurer versucht die Wand zu [verputzen].

  9 Ich habe keine Zeit dieses Geschirr zu [abtrocknen].

10 Man [herrichten, *perfect*] das Zimmer noch nicht.

11 [Ausschalten, *imperative: 'du'-form*] den Fernseher!

12 Er [überziehen, *present*] den Esstisch mit einer bunten Tischdecke.

20 | Reflexive verbs

Newton: Darf ich Ihnen ein Geheimnis anvertrauen, Herr Inspektor?

Inspektor: Selbstverständlich.

Newton: Ich bin nicht Sir Isaak. Ich gebe **mich** nur als Newton aus.

Inspektor: Und weshalb?

5 Newton: Um Ernesti nicht zu verwirren.

Inspektor: Kapiere ich nicht.

Newton: Im Gegensatz zu mir ist doch Ernesti wirklich krank. Er bildet **sich**
ein, Albert Einstein zu sein.

Inspektor: Was hat das mit Ihnen zu tun?

10 Newton: Wenn Ernesti nun erführe, dass ich in Wirklichkeit Albert Einstein
bin, wäre der Teufel los.

Inspektor: Sie wollen damit sagen …

Newton: Jawohl. Der berühmte Physiker und Begründer der Relativitätstheorie
bin ich. Geboren am 14. März 1879 in Ulm.

15 Inspektor (*erhebt **sich** etwas verwirrt*): Sehr erfreut.

Newton (*erhebt **sich** ebenfalls*): Nennen Sie mich einfach Albert.

Inspektor: Und Sie mich Richard.

(*Sie schütteln **sich** die Hände.*)

Newton: Ich darf Ihnen versichern, dass ich die Kreutzersonate bei weitem
20   schwungvoller hinunterfiedeln würde als Ernst Heinrich Ernesti eben. Das
Andante spielt er doch einfach barbarisch.

Inspektor: Ich verstehe nichts von Musik.

Newton: Setzen wir **uns**.

(*Er zieht ihn aufs Sofa. Newton legt den Arm um die Schulter des Inspektors*).
25   Richard.

Inspektor: Albert?

Newton: Nicht wahr, Sie ärgern **sich**, mich nicht verhaften zu dürfen.

Inspektor: Aber Albert.

Newton: Möchten Sie mich verhaften, weil ich die Krankenschwester
30   erdrosselt oder weil ich die Atombombe ermöglicht habe?

Aus: Friedrich Dürrenmatt, *Die Physiker*. © 1985 Diogenes Verlag AG Zürich.

◊ Reflexive verbs in the text

20.1 **REFLEXIVE PRONOUNS**

A reflexive verb is a verb whose direct object is a **reflexive pronoun**: e.g. *Ich wasche* **mich** 'I wash **myself**'. A reflexive pronoun always refers to the same person/thing as the subject (i.e. 'I' and 'myself' are the same person). The reflexive pronouns in German are as follows:

e.g. infinitive: *sich ärgern*	*ich ärgere* **mich**	*wir ärgern* **uns**
	du ärgerst **dich**	*ihr ärgert* **euch**
	er/sie/es ärgert **sich**	*sie/Sie ärgern* **sich** (27)

Reflexive pronouns usually follow the same word order as direct objects: i.e. they most commonly occur immediately after the subject and verb: *Ich gebe* **mich** . . . *aus* (3), *erhebt* **sich** (15, 16), *Sie ärgern* **sich** (27), *Setzen wir* **uns** (23).

The plural reflexive pronouns, in addition to meaning '-selves', e.g. *Sie setzen* **sich** 'They sit (themselves) down', can also mean 'each other' depending on the context. Thus, in line 18, *Sie schütteln* **sich** *die Hände* means 'They shake each other's hand'.

Other points to note in the text

- Imperative: *nennen Sie mich* (16), *setzen wir uns* (23). (see **11.3**).
- *Konjunktiv II* as conditional: *erführe* (10). The use of this verb form is uncommon (see **16.3b**).
- Omission of auxiliary *habe* in the first part of a subordinate clause (30) (see **25.4**).
- Placing of elements at beginning of sentence for emphasis: *Der berühmte Physiker* . . . (13–14) (see **26.6**).

▲ *Discover more about reflexive verbs*

20.2 **DIFFICULTIES WITH REFLEXIVES**

For English learners one of the most difficult aspects of reflexive verbs in German is that they often do not correspond to English reflexives. Thus, while *Ich wasche mich* corresponds to the English reflexive 'I wash myself',[96] *Ich erinnere mich* 'I remember' is not reflexive in English. This means that reflexive verbs in German must simply be learnt as such. A selection of common verbs which are often used reflexively is given in **Table 21** below as a starting point. Note that those verbs marked with an asterisk are 'true reflexives' which can only be used with a reflexive pronoun. The others, although very often used reflexively, can also be used with other objects, e.g.:

---

[96] The option of omitting the reflexive pronoun with some verbs in English is not available in German: e.g. 'I wash myself' or 'I wash' is always *Ich wasche* **mich** with the pronoun.

Ich wasche **mich** *– wasche* **mein Auto**	I wash (myself) – wash my car
Ich ziehe **mich** *an – ziehe* **mein Baby** *an*	I dress (myself) – dress my baby
Ich ärgere **mich** *– ärgere* **meine Mutter**	I'm annoyed – annoy my mother
Ich amüsiere **mich** *– amüsiere* **meine Freunde**	I enjoy myself – entertain my friends

A further complication arises from the fact that some reflexive verbs take a **dative** reflexive pronoun instead of the more common accusative reflexive given above. The dative pronouns differ from the accusatives only in the *ich-* and *du-*form:

e.g. *sich vorstellen:*	*ich stelle* **mir** *vor*[97]	*wir stellen uns vor*
'to picture, imagine'	*du stellst* **dir** *vor*	*ihr stellt euch vor*
	er stellt sich vor	*sie/Sie stellen sich vor*

There is an example of a dative reflexive in the text: *Er bildet* **sich** *ein* (7), although this is not obvious at first sight, as *sich* is identical in the accusative and dative. The equivalents for *ich* and *du* would be *Ich bilde* **mir** *ein, Du bildest* **dir** *ein*. In **Table 21** the difference between the accusative and dative reflexives is made explicit by using the first person *ich*-form in the examples.[98]

---

[97] Contrast the accusative *Ich stelle mich vor* etc. 'I introduce myself'.

[98] A major difference between accusative and dative reflexive pronouns is that the former cannot co-occur with an accusative object while the latter can: e.g. *Du bildest* **dir** <u>den Hass deines Chefs bloß ein</u>.

Table 21. Verbs commonly used reflexively

ACCUSATIVE

ich amüsiere mich	'I enjoy myself'	*ich fühle mich*	'I feel'
ich ärgere mich	'I get annoyed'	*ich interessiere mich für*	'I'm interested in'
*ich bedanke mich**	'I thank'	*ich irre mich**	'I am wrong'
*ich beeile mich**	'I rush/hurry'	*ich langweile mich*	'I am bored'
*ich benehme mich**	'I behave (myself)'	*ich lege mich hin*	'I lie down'
ich bewege mich	'I move'	*ich rasiere mich*	'I shave'
ich drehe mich um	'I turn around'	*ich schäme mich**	'I'm ashamed'
ich dusche mich	'I have a shower'	*ich setze mich*	'I sit down'
ich erinnere mich	'I remember'	*ich verstecke mich*	'I hide'
ich frage mich	'I wonder'	*ich wasche mich*[†]	'I wash (myself)'
*ich freue mich**	'I am pleased'	*ich ziehe mich an/ aus/um*	'I get dressed/ undressed/changed'
*ich freue mich auf**	'I look forward to'		

DATIVE

*ich bilde mir ein**	'I imagine (wrongly)'	*ich stelle mir vor**	'I imagine'
*ich nehme mir vor**	'I plan/intend to'	*ich widerspreche mir*	'I contradict myself'
*ich überlege mir (etw)**	'I think (sth.) over'	*ich tue mir weh*	'I hurt myself'

* 'True' reflexive

† But if a body part is mentioned, the possessive dative is used: e.g. *Ich wasche **mir** die Hände/die Haare.* Similarly: *Ich putze **mir** die Zähne, Ich habe **mir** das Bein gebrochen* (see **7.8**).

20.3 REFLEXIVE PRONOUNS USED WITH OTHER VERBS

Reflexive pronouns can also be used with verbs which are not usually reflexive if the meaning '-self' is required: i) after **prepositions** (and sometimes *selbst* or *selber* '-self' is added for emphasis), e.g. *Sie spricht nie über **sich** selbst/selber* 'She never talks about herself';[99] ii) with dative reflexive pronouns in constructions such as *Ich kaufe **mir** ein neues Kleid* 'I'm buying myself a new dress'.

---

[99] Contrast a sentence like 'I'll do it myself' → *Ich tue es selbst/selber*, where there is no preposition and '-self' is rendered by *selbst/selber* rather than by a reflexive pronoun.

✎ EXERCISES

Vocabulary topic: *Körper und Gesundheit*

1 Replace the subjects in bold print with those given in brackets, changing the reflexive pronouns and verb forms where necessary. All reflexive pronouns are in the accusative:

Example: **Andreas** fühlt sich nicht gut. [ich]

Answer: **Ich fühle mich** nicht gut.

1 **Ich** bemühe mich sehr das Rauchen aufzugeben. [er]
2 **Die Kinder** haben sich erkältet. [du]
3 **Dein Freund** hat sich mit dem Whiskeytrinken krank gemacht. [wir]
4 Als **sie** schwanger war hat **sie** sich jeden Morgen übergeben. [ich]
5 **Ich** hatte vor zwei Wochen eine Grippe, aber jetzt habe **ich** mich erholt. [die Kinder]
6 **Du** musst dich warm anziehen, sonst bekommst **du** einen Schnupfen. [ihr]

2 The verbs in bold are all used reflexively below but the reflexive pronouns are missing. Insert the correct reflexive pronoun (either accusative or dative depending on the construction) in the correct place:

1 Habt ihr die Zähne **geputzt**?
2 Ich werde **duschen** und die Haare **waschen**.
3 Du hast einen Unfall gehabt? Hast du **wehgetan**?
4 Du bist ganz schmutzig. Hast du heute nicht **gewaschen**?

5 Ich habe das Bein **gebrochen**.

6 Ich muss **beeilen**. Ich habe einen Arzttermin.

7 Sie müssen ärztlich **untersuchen** lassen.

8 Er hat aufgehört zu **rasieren**. Der Stoppelbart passt ihm sehr gut.

9 Wir **schämen** beide wegen unseres Gewichts.

10 Hast du das Handgelenk **verstaucht**?

✎ **FURTHER EXERCISES**

3 **Some (but not all!) of the sentences below are ungrammatical due to missing reflexive pronouns. Add the appropriate pronouns in the correct place only where necessary:**

1 Interessierst du für Fußball?

2 Er arbeitet für eine andere Firma.

3 Ich freue sehr auf die Sommerferien.

4 Erinnert ihr an letzten Silvester?

5 Ich habe vergessen, wieviel ich für das Auto bezahlt habe.

6 Nein, das stimmt nicht. Sie müssen geirrt haben.

7 Er langweilt zu Hause.

8 Kannst du vorstellen, wie ich gefühlt habe?

9 Er hat erzählt, dass ihn seine Frau verlassen habe.

10 Wir wollten irgendwo hinsetzen, aber es gab keinen Platz.

21 | Infinitives and modal verbs

Vielleicht haben triviale Gespräche vor allem die Funktion, dass man von sich selbst **reden** <u>kann</u>; daher auch die nicht **enden** <u>wollenden</u> Themen wie Krankheit, Kinder, Reisen, Erfolg, wie auch die unzähligen, einem wichtig erscheinenden täglichen Begebenheiten. Da man ja nicht beständig
5 über sich selbst **reden** <u>kann</u>, ohne in den Verdacht **zu geraten**, langweilig **zu sein**, <u>muss</u> man – **um** nur über sich selbst reden **zu können** – auch bereit **sein**, anderen **zuzuhören**, wenn sie nur über sich selbst reden. Private Treffen und oftmals auch Treffen von Vereinigungen und Gruppen sind kleine Märkte, wo man sein Bedürfnis, über sich **zu reden** und den
10 Wunsch, angehört **zu werden**, gegen das gleiche Bedürfnis anderer austauscht. Die meisten respektieren dieses gegenseitige Arrangement. Die, die dies nicht tun und mehr über sich selbst **reden** <u>wollen</u>, als sie bereit sind, anderen **zuzuhören** sind „Spielverderber"; sie sind unbeliebt und <u>müssen</u> sich, **um** toleriert **zu werden**, minderwertige Gesellschaft
15 **aussuchen**.

    Man <u>kann</u> das Bedürfnis vieler Menschen, über sich selbst **zu reden** und auch angehört **zu werden**, kaum **überschätzen**. Wäre dieses Bedürfnis nur bei sehr narzisstischen, ganz von sich absorbierten Personen vorhanden, so <u>könnte</u> man es leicht **verstehen**. Aber wir finden
20 es auch beim Durchschnittsmenschen, und die Gründe dafür wurzeln in unserer Kultur. Der moderne Mensch ist ein Massenmensch, er ist in hohem Maße „sozialisiert", aber er ist sehr vereinsamt [. . .]. Der Mensch hat sich von den anderen entfremdet und befindet sich in einem Dilemma: Er hat vor nahem Kontakt mit anderen Angst, und er hat genauso Angst,
25 allein **zu sein** und keinen Kontakt **zu haben**. Es ist die Aufgabe der trivialen Unterhaltung, die Frage **zu beantworten**: Wie <u>kann</u> ich alleine bleiben, ohne einsam **zu sein**? Das Reden wird zur Sucht. Während ich rede, weiß ich, dass ich existiere, dass ich kein Niemand bin, dass ich eine Vergangenheit, einen Beruf, eine Familie habe. Indem ich über all das
30 rede, bestätige ich mich selbst. Ich brauche aber jemanden, der mir zuhört. Hätte ich nur mich, würde ich verrückt **werden**; der Zuhörer verhilft mir zur Illusion eines Dialogs, wo es sich in Wirklichkeit um einen Monolog handelt.

Aus: Erich Fromm, *Vom Haben zum Sein: Wege und Irrwege der Selbsterfahrung*. Hrsg. von Rainer Funk. ©1989 Rainer Funk.

♀ Infinitives in the text

21.1 INFINITIVES WITH *ZU*

The infinitive is the form of the verb, usually ending in -*en*, which is always given in dictionaries: e.g. *machen, kommen, gehen*. It most commonly occurs in a clause with *zu* (known as an 'infinitive clause') which is dependent on a preceding (or, less frequently, following) clause with a finite verb: e.g. *Ich habe heute keine Zeit <u>mit dir ins Kino</u> **zu gehen** '*I don't have time **to go** to the cinema with you today'. As can be seen from this example, *zu* immediately precedes the infinitive, which comes at the end of the clause.[100] If there are two infinitives, *zu* precedes the last one: e.g. *Ich habe Lust schwimmen **zu** gehen*. Separable verbs have *zu* between the prefix and main verb: e.g. . . . *mit dir mitzukommen*, written as one word. Examples of *zu* + infinitive from the text are:

- *bereit sein, anderen **zuzuhören*** (7)   to be prepared **to listen** to others
- *sein Bedürfnis, über sich **zu reden*** (9)   his need **to talk** about himself
- *den Wunsch angehört **zu werden*** (10)   the wish **to be** listened to
- *Es ist die Aufgabe der trivialen Unterhaltung, die Frage **zu beantworten*** (25–26)   It is the task of trivial conversation **to answer** the question

As can be seen from the above examples, *zu* + infinitive usually corresponds to English 'to + verb'. However, after **ohne** 'without' and certain nouns, *zu* + infinitive corresponds to an '-ing' form in English:[101]

- *ohne in den Verdacht **zu geraten**, langweilig **zu sein*** (5–6)   without arous**ing** suspicion of be**ing** boring
- *ohne einsam **zu sein*** (27)   without be**ing** lonely
- *Angst, allein **zu sein** und keinen Kontakt **zu haben*** (24–25)   fear **of being** alone and **having** no contact

[100] In older texts such as this, a comma is always used before an infinitive clause with *zu*. This is no longer compulsory and is now a matter of the writer's preference.

[101] *Zu* + infinitive can only be used for English 'to' and '-ing' when the subject of the infinitive clause is the **same** as the preceding subject, otherwise a different clause with a finite verb must be used. Contrast 'I tried to ring her' *Ich versuchte sie anzurufen* vs. 'I asked <u>him</u> to ring her' *Ich fragte ihn, ob er sie anrufen könnte* (lit. 'I asked him if he could ring her'; 'he' being the subject of the second clause). Similarly with modals: 'I wanted to come' *Ich wollte kommen* vs. 'I wanted <u>you</u> to come' *Ich wollte, dass du kommst*.

21.2 INFINITIVES WITH *UM . . . ZU*

When *zu* + infinitive expresses a **purpose** (i.e. if it can be rendered by 'in order to . . .' in English) the infinitive clause begins with **um**:[102]

- **um** *nur über sich selbst reden **zu können*** (6)   **(in order) to be able to** just talk about oneself
- **um** *toleriert **zu werden*** (14)   **(in order) to be** tolerated

[102] *Um . . . zu* is also used after adjectives qualified by *zu* or *genug*: e.g. *Ich bin zu müde um auszugehen* 'I'm too tired to go out' (although *um* is sometimes omitted in the spoken language).

21.3 INFINITIVES WITH MODAL VERBS

Modal verbs are unusual in that when they occur with another verb it is always a **bare infinitive** (i.e. without *zu*): e.g. *Ich **will** es <u>machen</u>* 'I want to do it' (not **Ich will es zu machen*).[103] There are six modal verbs in German: *dürfen* 'to be allowed to/may', *können* 'to be able to/can', *mögen* 'to like to', *müssen* 'to have to/must', *sollen* 'to be supposed to/should' and *wollen* 'to want to', three of which appear in this text (underlined):

• *dass man von sich selbst **reden** <u>kann</u>* (2, 5)	that one <u>can</u> **talk** about oneself
• *die nicht **enden** <u>wollenden</u> Themen* (2)	the subjects that don't <u>want to</u> **end**
• *Man <u>kann</u> das Bedürfnis [. . .] kaum* **überschätzen** (16–17)	One <u>can</u> hardly **overestimate** the need
• *so <u>könnte</u> man es leicht **verstehen*** (19)	then one <u>could</u> easily **understand** it
• *<u>muss</u> man [. . .] auch bereit **sein*** (6–7)	one <u>must</u> also **be** prepared
• *Die, die [. . .] mehr über sich selbst **reden** <u>wollen</u>* (12)	Those who <u>want to</u> **talk** more about themselves

The 'bare' infinitive *werden* in line 31 is not dependent on a modal verb but is used as part of a conditional construction: *würde ich verrückt werden* 'I would become mad' (see **16.2a**).

> [103] A few other verbs can also occur with a bare infinitive: verbs of perception such as *sehen, hören, fühlen*, some verbs of motion such as *fahren, gehen, kommen* and the verbs *lassen* and *bleiben*: e.g. *Ich hörte ihn **kommen**, Er geht **spazieren**, Sie **lassen** ihn warten.*

Other points to note in the text

- Use of genitive: *ander**er*** (10), *viel**er** Menschen* (16), *d**er** trivial**en** Unterhaltung* (25–26), *ein**es** Dialog**s*** (32) (see **3.1a(iv)**).
- Verbs taking a dative object: *ein**em** wichtig erscheinenden* (3–4), *ander**en** zuzuhören* (7, 13), *verhilft **mir*** (31) (see **3.4a**).
- Extended attributes: *die **nicht enden wollenden** Themen* (2), *die unzähligen, **einem wichtig erscheinenden** täglichen Begebenheiten* (3–4), *bei . . . **ganz von sich absorbierten** Personen* (18–19) (see **5.3**).
- Use of *man*: (1, 4, 6, 9, 16) and in the dative: *einem* (3) (see **7.1b**).
- Relative pronouns: *jemanden, **der*** (30); and with scope over two verbs, *Die, **die** dies nicht <u>tun</u> und mehr über sich selbst reden <u>wollen</u>* (12) (see **Ch. 9**).
- Conditional clauses with *wenn* omitted: *Wäre . . . so könnte . . .* (17–19), *Hätte . . . , würde . . .* (31) (see **16.4**).
- Reflexive pronouns: *sich* (9, 14, 18, 23, 32), *sich* emphasised by adding *selbst* (2, 5, 6, 7, 12, 16), *mich* (31), *mich selbst* (30) (see **Ch. 20**).
- Clauses beginning with subordinating conjunctions: *dass . . . kann* (1–2), *da . . . kann* (4–5), *wenn . . . reden* (7), *wo . . . austauscht* (9–11), *während . . . rede* (27–28), *dass . . . bin* (28), *dass . . . habe* (28–29), *indem . . . rede* (29–30), *wo . . . handelt* (32) (see **25.1**).

🔺 *Discover more about modal verbs*

21.4 **THE FORMS OF THE MODALS**

21.4a Formation of modal verbs

As modal verbs are very frequently used, students are advised to learn all their forms, many of which are irregular (indicated in bold print in **Table 22**).

Table 22: Modal verbs

	Present		Past stem*	Past participle†	*Konjunktiv II* stem
dürfen	ich **darf**	wir dürfen	*durfte*	*gedurft*	*dürfte*
'may/be	du **darfst**	ihr dürft			
allowed'	er **darf**	sie dürfen			
können	ich **kann**	wir können	*ko**nnte*	*geko**nnt*	*könnte*
'be able/	du **kannst**	ihr könnt			
can'	er **kann**	sie können			
mögen	ich **mag**	wir mögen	**mochte**	**gemocht**	**möchte**
'like'	du **magst**	ihr mögt			
	er **mag**	sie mögen			
müssen	ich **muss**	wir müssen	*mu**sste*	*gemu**sst*	*müsste*
'have to/	du **musst**	ihr müsst			
must'	er **muss**	sie müssen			
sollen	ich **soll**	wir sollen	*sollte*	*gesollt*	*sollte*
'supposed	du **sollst**	ihr sollt			(no *umlaut*)
to/should'	er **soll**	sie sollen			
wollen	ich **will**	wir wollen	*wollte*	*gewollt*	*wo**llte*
'want'	du **willst**	ihr wollt			(no *umlaut*)
	er **will**	sie wollen			

* The personal endings must then be added to the past and *Konjunktiv II* stems: e.g. *ich durfte, du durfte**st,** er/sie/es durfte, wir durft**en,** ihr durft**et,** sie/Sie durft**en;** ich könnte, du könnt**est** etc. (see **12.2b**).
† All modal verbs take *haben* as their perfect and pluperfect auxiliary.

21.4b Double infinitives with modals

In all perfect, pluperfect and future tenses, the modal verb appears in its **infinitive** form <u>after</u> the infinitive of the co-occurring verb:[104]

*Er wird wahrscheinlich <u>mitkommen</u> **wollen.***	He'll probably want to come too.
*Ich habe es nicht <u>machen</u> **können.***	I haven't been able to do it.
*Wir hätten zu Hause <u>bleiben</u> **sollen.***	We should have stayed at home.

This is particularly striking in the perfect, pluperfect and conditional perfect, as we would normally expect a past participle here (e.g. **Ich habe es nicht machen gekonnt*, which is completely ungrammatical). The past participles of modal verbs are only used when there is no co-occurring verb: e.g. *Ich habe es nicht* **gemocht** 'I didn't like it'; and as modals are much more often used together with another verb than they are on their own, the past participles of modals are relatively infrequent.

When a double infinitive construction appears in a **subordinate** clause (see **26.1b**), the finite auxiliary verbs are sent not to the end of the clause, as would normally be the case, but to the position **immediately before the two infinitives**: e.g.

Ich meine, <u>dass</u> er wahrscheinlich **wird** *mitkommen wollen.*
<u>Obwohl</u> *ich es nicht* **habe** *machen können.*
Ich wusste, <u>dass</u> wir zu Hause **hätten** *bleiben sollen.*

> [104] This also applies to *lassen* and verbs of perception such as *sehen* and *hören* when used together with another verb: e.g. *Ich habe mein Auto <u>reparieren</u>* **lassen** 'I have had my car repaired', *Er hat mich <u>kommen</u>* **sehen** 'He saw me coming' (but not to *gehen, fahren, bleiben* etc.).

21.5 OTHER TENSES FREQUENTLY USED WITH MODALS

In addition to ordinary present and past constructions, e.g. *Ich* **will** *kommen, ich* **wollte** *kommen,* and the future and perfect constructions mentioned in **21.4b** above, e.g. *Er* **wird** *nicht kommen* **wollen**, *er* **hat** *nicht kommen* **wollen**, modals are commonly used in the following ways:

21.5a With a verb in the perfect tense (infinitive of *haben*/*sein* + past participle)
This is often used to express a **supposition**:

Er **kann** *es nicht <u>gemacht haben</u>.*	He can't have done it.
Er **könnte** *der Mörder <u>gewesen sein</u>.*	He could have been the murderer.
Sie **müssen** *schon <u>weggefahren sein</u>.*	They must have already left.

21.5b In the conditional perfect
Here, it is the modal verb that is in the conditional perfect, which means that *haben* is always used as the auxiliary, irrespective of the co-occurring verb. This type of construction is used extremely frequently, so students are advised to learn these patterns by heart:

Das **hättest** *du nicht <u>machen</u>* **sollen**!	You shouldn't have done that!
Wir **hätten** *früher <u>kommen</u>* **können**.	We could have come earlier.

Note that 'could have' expresses a supposition when translated as *könnte* + perfect tense (see **21.5a**) while in the conditional perfect example above it means 'would have been able to'. This is also true of the other modals when used in this way: e.g. *Er* **müsste** *es schon gemacht haben* 'He should have done it already' (i.e. 'I'm assuming that he has done it') vs. *Er* **hätte** *es machen* **müssen** 'He should have done it' (i.e. 'He had to do it but didn't').

21.6 SEMANTIC DIFFICULTIES WITH MODALS

In particular contexts, modal verbs may have meanings that differ from the basic meanings given in **21.4a**. Some of these are particularly problematic for English learners of German:

- In English, 'can' is often used instead of 'may' when asking for permission: e.g. *Can I use your car?* This is usually translated not by *können* but by *dürfen*: **Darf** *ich dein Auto benutzen?* Similarly 'can't' is translated by *nicht dürfen* when refusing permission: *Hier* **darfst** *du nicht parken* 'You can't park here' (i.e. 'you're not allowed').[105]

- 'Must/have to' is usually translated by *müssen*: e.g. *Ich muss gehen*, yet when it is negative (i.e. 'must not'), *dürfen* is used: e.g. *Das* **darfst** *du nicht machen* 'You mustn't do that'. If *müssen* is used negatively, e.g. *Das* **musst** *du nicht machen*, it means 'don't **have to**': 'You don't have to do that'.

- *Sollen* usually means 'to be supposed/meant to': e.g. *Es* **soll** *eine Überraschung sein* 'It's supposed to be a surprise'. When used in the past/*Konjunktiv II*, *sollte* means 'should/ought to' and is very similar in meaning to *müssen*: e.g. *Ich* **sollte** *gehen* 'I should/ought to go'.

- *Wollen* usually means 'to want to', but when used with *eben* or *gerade* it has the meaning 'to be about to': e.g. *Ich* **wollte** *dich* **eben/gerade** *anrufen* 'I was just about to phone you'.

- The *Konjunktiv II* forms *könnte* and *dürfte* are often used to express possibility and probabability respectively: i.e. *könnte* means 'could/may/might' and *dürfte* means 'is likely': e.g. *Klaus* **könnte** *jetzt zu Hause sein* 'Klaus could/may/might be at home now' vs. *Klaus* **dürfte** *jetzt zu Hause sein* 'Klaus is probably/likely to be at home now'. Similarly, *müßte* is used to mean 'ought to' when expressing probability: *Ja, Klaus* **müsste** *jetzt zu Hause sein* 'Yes, Klaus should be at home now.'

- The English expression 'can't help + -ing' (e.g. 'I couldn't help laughing') is commonly translated using *einfach müssen*: e.g. *Ich* **musste einfach** *lachen*. However, when the -ing form is absent, e.g. 'I can't help it', *können* is used: *Ich* **kann** *nichts dafür*.

- *Mögen* usually means 'to like' but it is sometimes used to mean 'may' in contexts where the speaker then goes on to qualify what was said, usually putting the other side of the argument: e.g. *Das* **mag** *wohl sein, aber . . .* 'That may well be, but . . .'.

- *Lassen* (*ich lasse, du/er/sie/es lässt, wir lassen, ihr lasst, sie/Sie lassen*) is not technically a modal verb but it behaves like one in that it often occurs together with the infinitive form of other verbs. It usually means 'to let' *Er* **ließ** *den Hund auf dem Rasen spielen* 'He let the dog play on the lawn'; but it can also mean 'to have/get something done' *Ich* **lasse** *mir die Haare schneiden* 'I'm having my hair cut'; or 'to make' (= 'to cause to'): *Es* **lässt** *mich denken* 'It makes me think'.

---

[105] If 'can' is used with a passive meaning, e.g. 'It **can** be done', German often renders this using *sich lassen* + infinitive: *Das lässt sich machen*. Similarly, *Diese Kartoffeln lassen sich gut schälen* 'These potatoes are easy to peel' (= 'These potatoes can be peeled easily').

✎ **EXERCISES**

Vocabulary topic: *Alltägliche Aktivitäten*

1 Where needed, insert *zu* or *um . . . zu* in the correct position in the sentence. Where an infinitive clause is not possible (in two cases), rewrite it as a proper finite clause:

1 Es ist zu spät essen. Ich gehe bald schlafen.
2 Ich habe heute keine Zeit einkaufen gehen.

3   Ich habe die Absicht morgen um 6 Uhr aufstehen.

4   Du musst heute früher ins Bett gehen.

5   Hast du Lust heute Abend ausgehen?

6   Willst du bei mir zu Abend essen? Oder willst du wir in ein Café gehen?

7   Ich habe versucht meine Zeitung lesen, aber ich war zu müde.

8   „Was möchtest zum Frühstück trinken?" „Kannst du mir einen Kaffee machen?"

9   Wie lange brauchst du das Mittagessen vorbereiten?

10 Er möchte jetzt teilzeit arbeiten mehr Zeit zu Hause mit seinen Kindern verbringen können.

11 Ich freue mich darauf mich heute Abend vor dem Fernseher entspannen.

12 Ich freue mich darauf du heute Abend kochen.

13 Sie ist zu krank zur Arbeit gehen.

14 Er hat vorgeschlagen einen Spaziergang machen.

15 Ich brauche nur 15 Minuten mich duschen und mir die Haare waschen.

16 Ich habe nichts mehr anziehen. Alles muss gewaschen werden.

17 Es ist sehr nett von dir uns einladen. Um wieviel Uhr sollten wir kommen?

2 Put the bracketed verbs into the form required:

1   Wir (wollen, *past*) Musik hören.

2   Ich (müssen, *past*) mich zuerst waschen und mir die Haare bürsten.

3   (Können, *conditional*) du das Abendbrot herrichten?

4   (Müssen, *present*) du heute tanken?

5   (Dürfen, *present*) er dein Fahrrad benutzen?

6   Er (wollen, *present*) den Rasen mähen.

7   Die Kinder wussten, dass sie keine Computerspiele spielen (dürfen, *past*).

8   Er (lassen, *past*) sein Auto reparieren.

3 Go back to question 2 above and put the bracketed verbs into the PERFECT tense.

✎ FURTHER EXERCISES

4 Translate the following sentences into German:

1   I would like four bread rolls.

2   Can I smoke here?

3   Do you have to work today?

4   You mustn't forget your keys.

5   You don't have to wait for me.

6   He's supposed to be quite rich. (= 'it is said that')

7   I was supposed to ring him but I forgot.

8   Where's Peter? He could be at his girlfriend's.

9   He would have to come at five thirty.

10 I was just about to make a cup of tea.

11 You should have phoned me yesterday.

12 He could have stayed longer but he didn't want to.

13 Who has drunk my beer? It could have been Peter.

14 I wouldn't have been able to go.

15 They wouldn't have wanted to come anyway.

16 Normally I wouldn't have had to work on a Saturday, but my colleague was ill.

22 | Negation

Auch schrieb Frau Mangold Amanda Briefe, die ich manchmal sah, wenn
ich die Post aus dem Hausbriefkasten holte. Sie trugen **keine** Briefmarke,
waren also **nicht** von der Post befördert, **sondern** persönlich in den Kasten
gesteckt worden. Damals fand ich diese Form des schriftlichen Verkehrs

5 normal, später sah ich das Konspirative daran.

Auch wenn mich die Gespräche der beiden **nicht** interessierten, wurde ich
mit der Zeit doch neugierig auf Amandas sogenannten Roman. Da sie **nie**
darüber sprach, ich aber **keine** Lust hatte, ihr deshalb Vorwürfe zu machen
und so für neuen Unfrieden zu sorgen, verschaffte ich mir auf andere

10 Weise Kenntnis: Zweimal ging ich, als ich allein in der Wohnung war,
in ihr Zimmer und las. Ich wusste, wo sie war und wann sie frühestens
nach Hause kommen würde, brauchte mich also vor Entdeckung **nicht** zu
fürchten. Abgesehen davon, dass auch eine Entdeckung **kein** Einbruch
gewesen wäre. Um es Ihnen gleich zu sagen – ich wurde enttäuscht. Meine

15 Erwartung war **nicht** übertrieben hoch, ich wusste schon vorher, dass ich
nicht in das Zauberreich einer bedeutenden Schriftstellerin eindringen
würde; aber ich wusste zugleich, dass sie eine aufregende Person und
witzig ist. Auch wenn ich es mir **nicht** eingestand – ich hätte für mein Leben
gern etwas Großartiges entdeckt.

Aus: Jureck Becker *Amanda Herzlos*. © 1992 Suhrkamp Verlag.

♀ Negation in the text

There are various ways of negating a sentence in German, the most common being the use of
nicht and **kein**.

22.1 *NICHT 'NOT'*

22.1a The position of *nicht*

Most sentences in German are made negative by the use of *nicht*. The position of *nicht* can cause
problems for English learners, as it very much depends on the nature of the other elements in the
sentence. The following rules are given as a rough guide, although they are often broken when a
shift of emphasis is required (see **22.3b**).

Nicht usually appears at the **end** of a clause: e.g. *Ich liebe dich* **nicht**, *Ich kenne den Mann* **nicht.** This end-of-clause rule does not apply, however, with the verbs *sein* and *werden*, where *nicht* **precedes** the main noun or pronoun: contrast *Ich kenne den Mann nicht* with *Das* *ist* **nicht** *der Mann.*

If a **past** participle or (*zu* +) **infinitive** is present, *nicht* appears immediately **before** it: *brauchte mich also vor Entdeckung* **nicht** *zu fürchten* (12–13). Likewise, if a verb or separable prefix has been **sent to the end** of the clause, *nicht* appears immediately **before** it, *Auch wenn mich die Gespräche der beiden* **nicht** *interessierten* (6), *Auch wenn ich es mir* **nicht** *eingestand* (18).

If the main verb has an object beginning with a **preposition**, *nicht* usually precedes it, e.g. **nicht** *in das Zauberreich . . . eindringen* (16).[106]

If the sentence contains an **adjective**, *nicht* usually precedes it: e.g. *Meine Erwartung war* **nicht** *übertrieben hoch* (14–15). Likewise, if the sentence contains an expression of **manner** (i.e. *how* something is done), *nicht* usually precedes it: e.g. *waren also* **nicht** *von der Post befördert* (3).

If a sentence contains **both** a main verb with an object beginning with a preposition **and** *either* an adjective *or* an expression of manner, *nicht* usually precedes the adjective or expression of manner.

There are a number of words which follow similar rules to those for *nicht*. Among these are *nie* 'never' (e.g., *Da sie* **nie** *darüber* sprach (7–8) where *nie* precedes a prepositional object), *nicht mehr* 'no more/no longer', *noch nicht* 'not yet', *auch nicht* 'not … either' (and *auch* on its own, meaning 'also'), *kaum* 'hardly', *bloß* 'merely' and *schon* 'already'.[107]

---

[106] As opposed to constructions like *Ich kann es vor Freitag* **nicht** *machen*, where the prepositional phrase *vor Freitag* is not the object of the verb *machen* (in this case, *es* is the object).

[107] *Nichts* 'nothing' acts like an ordinary direct object: e.g. *Ich weiß* **nichts**, *Ich habe ihm* **nichts** *gesagt.*

22.1b Nicht . . ., sondern

In sentences of the type '**not** X **but** Y', 'but' is rendered not by the usual word *aber* but by **sondern**: e.g. **nicht** *von der Post . . .,* **sondern** *persönlich* (3). *Sondern* is usually preceded by a comma.

22.2 KEIN 'NOT A', 'NO'

Kein is used, instead of *nicht*, to negate an **indefinite noun** (i.e. a noun which appears with an indefinite article or with no article at all) and takes the place of the indefinite article. Thus, a sentence such as 'That's not a good reason' would not be **Das ist nicht ein guter Grund* but *Das ist* **kein** *guter Grund.* Similarly, *Ich habe* **keine** *Milch* 'I have no milk' (NOT **Ich habe Milch nicht*) and, in the plural, *Ich mag* **keine** *Oliven* 'I don't like olives' (contrast: *Ich mag die Oliven nicht* 'I don't like those olives' where *die* is definite).

Kein takes the same endings as possessives such as *mein* (see **7.2**, **Table 12**). Examples from the text are: *keine Briefmarke* (2), *keine Lust* (8), *kein Einbruch* (13).

Other points to note in the text

- Adjectival nouns: *das Konspirative* (5), *etwas Großartiges* (19) (see **5.5**).
- Conditional perfect: *gewesen wäre* (14), *hätte entdeckt* (18–19) (see **16.2b**).
- Pluperfect passive: [*waren*] *. . . gesteckt worden* (3–4), where *waren* is omitted but understood (see **18.5**).
- Interrogatives used indirectly: *wo* (11), *wann* (11) (see **23.5**).
- Subordinating conjunction affecting two verbs: *da . . . <u>sprach</u>, ich . . . <u>hatte</u>* (7–8) (see **25.4**).
- *Wenn* used with the past tense, meaning 'whenever' (1) (see **25.3a**).

◢ *Discover more about negation*

22.3 *NICHT*

22.3a With indefinite nouns

In some contexts, *nicht* can appear with an indefinite noun, instead of *kein*:

- When a **preposition** precedes the article and noun: e.g. *Ich will <u>mit</u> einem Computer* **nicht** *arbeiten.*
- When *nicht* is negating a **verb** rather than a noun: e.g. *Hier darf man* **nicht** *Rad <u>fahren</u>* (where *Rad* is seen as part of the verb *Rad fahren*).
- When **emphasis** is required: e.g. *Das ist* **nicht** *eine Maus, sondern eine Ratte!*

22.3b Placing of *nicht* for emphasis

If the speaker wishes to emphasise the negation of a particular element in the sentence, *nicht* is placed in front of that element, even though under normal circumstances it would usually follow it. Some examples are:

Er ist gestern nicht gekommen. *Er ist* **nicht** *gestern gekommen, sondern vorgestern.*
Ich habe den Professor nicht gesehen. *Ich habe* **nicht** *den Professor gesehen, sondern seinen Assistenten.*

22.4 *KEIN-* AS A PRONOUN

When the noun is omitted but understood, *kein-* can stand in for the noun, in which case it takes the same endings as it would have done if the noun had been present, e.g. *Wo sind die Brötchen?* *– Ich habe keine gekauft*, except in the **masc. nom. sg.** and the **neut. nom./acc. sg.**, which take *-er* and *-(e)s* respectively (compare *einer*, **3.2b(ii)**), e.g. **Keiner** *ist gekommen* [< *Kein Mensch* 'no one']; *Hast du ein Taschentuch? – Nein, ich habe* **keines** *mit* [usually pronounced (and sometimes written) *kein**s***].

✎ **EXERCISES**

Vocabulary topic: *Freizeit und Hobbys*

1 Make the following sentences negative by inserting *nicht* in the correct place:

1 Wolfgang tanzt.

2 Er geht in die Disco.

3 Jutta hat das neueste Buch von Martin Walser gelesen.

4 Mein Vater liest oft Zeitung, weil er viel Freizeit hat.

5 Ich habe diese Schmuckschachtel für dich gebastelt.

6 Meine Eltern sehen fern.

7 Meine Mutter will mir den selbstgebackenen Marmorkuchen geben.

8 Mit dieser alten Nähmaschine kannst du nähen.

9 Ich will, dass du in einer Band spielst.

10 Er ist der beste Sänger im Chor.

2 Make the following sentences negative by using *nicht* or *kein* (+ necessary endings) where appropriate:

1 Er treibt Sport.

2 Hast du die Briefmarkensammlung mit?

3 Er hat die zwei Modellschiffe selber gebaut.

4 Es kommt eine neue Folge von „Tatort" im Fernsehen.

5 Natürlich habe ich den neuen Film von Heiner Lauterbach gesehen. Du weißt doch, dass ich ins Kino gegangen bin.

6 Wir sammeln Schmetterlinge.

7 Ich male mit Ölfarben.

3 EMPHASIS/CONTRAST: Answer the following questions negatively using *nicht . . ., sondern* (or *kein . . ., sondern*) + the words underlined. Where present, place *nicht* in front of the element to be emphasised:

Example: Hast du meinen Mann auf der Fete gesehen? – Nein, <u>seinen Freund</u>.

Answer: Nein, ich habe **nicht** deinen Mann auf der Fete gesehen, **sondern** seinen Freund.

1 Hast du meinen Mann im Fitnesszentrum gesehen? – Nein, <u>in der Kneipe</u>.

2 Hast du mit Bernhard Tennis gespielt? – Nein, <u>mit Fredi</u>.

3 Warst du mit Klaus im Theater? – Nein, <u>in der Oper</u>.

4 Hast du einen CD-Spieler gekauft? Nein, <u>einen Mini-Disc-Spieler</u>.

5 Zeichnest du die Landschaft? Nein, <u>die Pferde in dem Feld da</u>.

6 Möchte er Bücher zum Geburtstag? Nein, <u>Computerspiele</u>.

4 Answer the following questions negatively using the appropriate form of the PRONOUN *kein* in place of the words underlined:

Example: Hast du <u>Schlittschuhe</u>?

Answer: Nein, ich habe **keine**.

1 Hast du <u>ein Skateboard</u>?
2 Hat er <u>einen Trainingsanzug</u>?
3 Sind sie mit <u>zwei</u> von ihren Freunden joggen gegangen?
4 <u>Welcher Squashschläger</u> gefällt dir?
5 Brauchst du <u>Federbälle</u>?

23 | Questions

Rheinwiederhall

Wie heißt der Bürgermeister von Wesel**?** – Esel!
Wer sind seine Räte und Schreiber**?** – Räuber!

Die Herrn sind alle weltbekannt,
An allen Orten viel genannt
5   Im Land, im Land.
Das Echo hat sich Maul verbrannt,
Das Echo hat sich Maul verbrannt.

Was tun sie in Zünften und Zechen**?** – Zechen!
Was werden sie niemals vergessen**?** – Essen!
10   Die Herrn sind alle weltbekannt ....

Was sind die gelahrten Doktoren**?** – Toren!
Ist ihnen die Weisheit beschwerlich**?** – Schwerlich!
Die Herrn sind alle weltbekannt ....

Was haben die Väter geschaffen**?** – Affen!
15   **Wie** werden die jungen Geschlechter**?** – Schlechter!
Die Herrn sind alle weltbekannt ....

Man munkelt von ihren Talenten**?** – Enten!
Doch die sich durch Tugend empfehlen**?** – Fehlen!
Sie sind ja alle weltbekannt,
20   An allen Orten laut genannt . . .

Deutsches Volkslied von W. von Zuccalmaglio (1803–1869)

♀ Questions in the text

There are three ways of forming a question in German, all of which are present in the above text.

23.1   SUBJECT–VERB INVERSION

Simple 'yes/no' questions (i.e. those that can be answered with a 'yes' or 'no', e.g. 'Are you going out tonight?') are formed by inverting the order of the subject and the verb: **Ist** ihnen (line 12).

23.2 INTONATION OR QUESTION MARK

Alternatively, but less commonly, the sentence can be left as it is and, in the written language, a question mark is added: *Man munkelt . . .?* (17), *Doch die . . .?* (18). In the spoken language, a rising intonation is used.

23.3 INTERROGATIVES

In addition, specific interrogatives can be used, such as 'who?', 'what?', 'where?', 'why?' etc., which are immediately followed by the verb: *wie* (1, 15), *wer* (2), *was* (8, 9, 11, 14). A list of commonly used interrogatives in German is given in **Table 23**.

Table 23. Interrogatives

wann?	'when?'	**Wann** *fängt die Vorlesung an?*
warum?*	'why?'	**Warum** *kann er nicht kommen?*
was?	'what?'	**Was** *hast du gesagt?*
[*wo-* (*wor-* before vowel) with preposition]		**Womit** *kann ich Ihnen helfen?*
was für? + noun	'what sort of?'	**Was für** <u>ein</u> *Hund ist das?*
[*für* does not require the accusative here]		*In* **was für** *ein<u>em</u> Haus wohnt er?*
welcher?	'which?/which one?'	**Welch<u>es</u>** *Brot/***welch<u>en</u>** *Wein möchten Sie?*
[with same endings as *dieser*, see **8.4**]		**Welchen** *trinken Sie am liebsten?*
wer? [acc. **wen**, dat. **wem**] 'who(m)?'		**Wer** *bist du?* **Wen** *kennst du?*
[gen. **wessen** 'whose?']		**Wessen** *Mantel ist das?* †
wie?	'how?'	**Wie** *sagt man 'how' auf Deutsch?*
[**wie lange** 'how long', **wie oft** 'how often'		**Wieviel** *Milch und* **wie viele** *Eier?*
wieviel 'how much', **wie viele** 'how many']		**Wie** *heißt du?* [literally: How are you called?]
wo?	'where?'	**Wo** *wohnst du?*
[**woher** 'where from', **wohin** 'where to']		**Woher** *kommst du?*

* Other words for 'why' are *wieso* (colloquial), *weshalb* (formal) and *wozu* (= 'what for').
† A more commonly used alternative to *wessen* is *von wem*: e.g. *Von wem sind diese Schuhe?* 'Whose shoes are these?'

Other points to note in the text

- Noun plurals: ⸚e, *Räte* (2); -(e)n, *Zechen* (8), *Doktoren* (11), *Toren* (11), *Affen* (14), *Enten* (17), *Herrn* (3, 10, 16) [more usually: *Herren*]; -er, *Geschlechter* (15), -, *Schreiber* (2), *Räuber* (2); ⸚, *Väter* (14). **Dative** plurals in -n: *Orte-n* (4), *Zünfte-n* (8), *Talente-n* (17). (see **Ch. 2**).
- Possessives: *seine* (2), *ihren* (17) (see **7.2**).
- *Sein*-passive: [*sind*] . . . *genannt* (4, 20). *Sind* is omitted but understood (see **18.9**).
- Older form: *gelahrten* (11) for modern German *gelehrten*.
- Pronoun omitted: *Doch die sich* (18) instead of *Doch* **die**, *die sich*. (This was permissible in older forms of German but is now considered ungrammatical.)

▲ *Discover more about interrogatives*

23.4 INTERROGATIVES USED WITH PREPOSITIONS

When used with **prepositions**, the interrogatives immediately follow (except for *was* → *wo(r)-* + prep.), which means that there is no splitting of interrogative and preposition, unlike in English: e.g.

Bis wann *muss ich es machen?*	**When** do I have to do it **by**?
Seit wann *arbeiten Sie hier?*	**How long** have you worked here (**for**)?
Auf wen *wartest du?*	**Who** are you waiting **for**?

23.5 INTERROGATIVES IN INDIRECT QUESTIONS

As is the case in English, interrogatives in German can be used in indirect questions of the type 'He asked me **what** I was doing and **who**(m) I was doing it with'. In this case, the interrogative is similar to a subordinating conjunction in that, in German, it sends the finite verb to the end of the clause (and is preceded by a comma in writing): e.g. *Er fragte mich,* **was** *ich* <u>*machte*</u> *und mit* **wem** *ich es* <u>*machte*</u>. Other examples are:

Ich weiß nicht, **wann** *er kommt.*[108]	I don't know **when** he's coming.
Ich verstehe nicht, **warum** *du das tust.*	I don't understand **why** you do that.
Ich fragte ihn, in **welchem** *Haus er wohnt.*	I asked him **which** house he lived in.

> [108] Not to be confused with the conjunction *wenn* 'if/when': e.g. *Sag es mir,* **wenn** *du fertig bist* 'Tell me **when** you're ready/finished'.

✎ **EXERCISES**

Vocabulary topic: *Nach dem Weg fragen*

1 Write questions to the following answers using interrogatives for the words and phrases underlined:

Example: Man muss <u>bei der Verkehrsampel</u> links abbiegen.
Answer: **Wo** muss man links abbiegen?

1   Das Krankenhaus liegt <u>gegenüber vom Park</u>.
2   <u>Das</u> ist der kürzeste Weg zum Postamt.
3   Man muss <u>mit dem Bus</u> fahren.
4   Zu Fuß dauert es <u>ungefähr eine halbe Stunde</u>.
5   Zum Bahnhof muss man <u>ziemlich weit</u> gehen.
6   Man muss <u>um vier Uhr</u> losfahren um am Flughafen rechtzeitig anzukommen.

2 Fill in the gaps with an appropriate interrogative:

1   Entschuldigen Sie, bitte. _____ komme ich am besten zum Markt?
2   „_____ darf man hier nicht rechts abbiegen?" – „Weil das eine Einbahnstraße ist."

3 _____ Richtung muss ich jetzt nehmen?

4 In _____ Straße hat er sein Geschäft?

5 _____ kann mir am besten den Weg zum Fußballstadion erklären?

6 Von _____ hast du den Straßenplan bekommen? Von Peter?

3 Make yes/no questions out of the following statements:

Example: Das ist eine Einbahnstraße.

Answer: **Ist** das eine Einbahnstraße?

1 Man muss geradeaus fahren um in die Stadtmitte zu kommen.

2 Ich kann einfach auf der Straße bis zum großen Kreisverkehr bleiben.

3 Der Taxifahrer ist in die dritte Straße rechts abgebogen.

4 Du nimmst die zweite Straße links nach dem Zebrastreifen.

5 Nur beim Fußgängerübergang darf man über die Straße gehen.

6 Wir sind auf dem falschen Weg. Wir müssen umdrehen.

4 Take your answers to questions 1 and 2 above and make them into indirect questions by preceding them with *Ich weiß*:

Example: **Wo** muss man links abbiegen?

Answer: Ich weiß, **wo** man links abbiegen <u>muss</u>.

For question **2**(1) omit 'Entschuldigen Sie, bitte'.

☞ **For further exercises on 'yes/no' questions see Revision Text 5, Ex. 1.**

Text

<u>Studieren **in** England</u>

„Die Lehre ist hier studentengerechter", glaubt Kathrin Brost, 27, die gerade einen Master-Kurs **in** Umweltmanagement **an** der Uni Durham **in** Englands Nordosten abschließt. Ein deutscher Dozent **an** einer britischen Elite-Uni sagt es noch deutlicher: „Die Unis gehören **zu** den wenigen
5   Dingen, die dieses Land vernünftig hingekriegt hat. Im Vergleich **zu** hier sind die deutschen Hochschulen verkommen."

Der Bachelor-Abschluss **nach** drei bis vier Jahren sowie Master-Kurse **von** einem oder zwei Jahren sind zwar mittlerweile auch **an** deutschen Unis zu haben. Doch das zusätzliche Plus, **in** der Weltsprache Englisch zu
10   studieren, lockt immer mehr Lernwillige **auf** die Insel. Viele kommen schon **nach** dem Abitur. Dar**an** hat auch die Einführung **von** Studiengebühren **für** Bachelor-Studenten (derzeit: 1050 Pfund/3400 Mark) nichts geändert. **Auf** „fast 5000" schätzt Sebastian Fohrbeck, **bis vor** kurzem Leiter des Londoner Büros des Deutschen Akademischen Austauschdienstes
15   (DAAD), die Zahl jener, die ihr ganzes Studium **auf** der Insel absolvieren.

Curt Schmitt, 25, ist so einer. **Nach** dem Abitur kam der Westfale 1995 **zum** Geschichtsstudium **an** die London School of Economics (LSE) und erlebte dort, wo**von** seine Kommilitonen **in** Deutschland meist nur träumen: „**Mit** meinem Tutor hatte ich intensive Gespräche. Aber auch die anderen
20   Professoren waren **für** jeden Anfänger ansprechbar." [. . .]

Die oft gelobte Verschulung und die strukturierten Kurse haben aber auch Nachteile. „Ich habe einen sehr guten Überblick **über** alle Strömungen **in** meinem Fachgebiet bekommen", berichtet Sabine Grenz, 32, die **nach** Studienabschluss **in** Köln und vier Berufsjahren gerade **an**
25   der LSE einen Master **in** Gender Studies absolviert hat. „**Am** Tiefgang hat es aber gelegentlich gefehlt."

Auch diesen Satz hören die DAAD-Betreuer immer wieder. Wor**an** das liegt? „**Von** den Bachelor-Studenten wird ohnehin weniger Wissenschaftlichkeit erwartet als **in** Deutschland," glaubt Grieshop. [. . .]
30   Besonders **in** den ersten beiden Studienjahren müssen die angelsächsischen Studenten viel Grundwissen aufholen. Die deutschen Studenten glänzen **in** der Regel **durch** eine breitere Allgemeinbildung als viele Studenten **aus** Übersee, zumal **aus** den USA, hat Christopher Coker beobachtet, der **an** der LSE Internationale Beziehungen lehrt. „Die
35   Deutschen wollen immer gründlich sein."

Aus einem Artikel von Sebastian Borger, *Uni-Spiegel (Online)*. 23.Oktober 2000.

⚲ Prepositions in the text

24.1 USE OF CASE WITH PREPOSITIONS

A major difficulty for English learners of German is the fact that prepositions always require the following noun or pronoun to be in the accusative, genitive or dative, which is evident when an article, pronoun and/or adjective is used. This is indicated in our text with underlining: e.g. *mit* + dative, *Er kam **mit** dem Hund/**mit** seiner Frau/**mit** guten Freunden*.

24.1a Prepositions taking one case

Acc.: *durch* (32), *für* (20), *bis* (13, see **24.4 (note iii)**).
Dat.: *aus* (33), *mit* (19), *nach* (7, 11, 16), *von* (8, 11, 28), *zu* (4, 17).[109]
Gen.: Less common, hence no examples in text (see **Table 24** for examples).

[109] *Zum* (17), and later *am* (25), are contracted forms of the preposition + *dem* (see **24.4 (note i)**).

24.1b Prepositions taking two alternative cases

Some prepositions may take the **accusative** or **dative** depending on the construction that they are in. Examples from the text are ***an, auf, in, über, unter, vor***. Generally speaking, if the meaning of the preposition implies **movement towards** the following noun, the **accusative** is used, otherwise the dative is the norm.[110] Contrast the following:

*Ich fahre nicht gern **in** die Stadt.*   I don't like driving into town.
*Ich fahre nicht gern **in** der Stadt.*   I don't like driving in town.

Even though both sentences express movement, only the first one implies movement *towards* the following noun, which is suggested by the use of '-to' in English. Examples from the text are: ***an*** + **dat**. (2, 3, 8, 24–25, 34) 'at the University etc.' vs. ***an*** + **acc**. (17) 'to the London School of Economics'; ***auf*** + **dat**. (15) 'on the island' vs. ***auf*** + **acc**. (10) 'onto the island'. Other examples have the dative: ***in*** + **dat**. (9, 23, 32), ***vor*** + **dat**.(13). ***Über*** 'above' follows the same rules (i.e. + dative unless movement is involved), yet when it means 'about' it takes the accusative (see line 22).

[110] Unless the preposition is linked with a particular verb (see **24.6**).

24.1c Scope of preposition + case

Case is not simply assigned to the element which immediately follows the preposition but to the **whole noun phrase**, i.e. to the noun and any articles, pronouns and adectives preceding it: e.g. *in den ersten beiden Studienjahren* (30). Even if another element, e.g. a numeral or a proper name, appears between preposition and noun phrase, case is still assigned: e.g. ***nach** drei bis vier Jahren* (7). Similarly, if the preposition refers to two or more noun phrases, they all have to be in the appropriate case: e.g. (not in text) *Er kam **mit** seiner Frau, seinem Bruder und seinen Kindern*; *Er arbeitet **bei** der VOEST, einer sehr großen Stahlfabrik in Linz*.

24.2 DIFFERENT MEANINGS OF PREPOSITIONS

A further difficulty for English learners of German lies in the fact that many German prepositions do not correspond directly to English ones, i.e. they may have different meanings depending on the context in which they are used. For instance, the preposition **an** usually means 'on', yet it has a number of different meanings in the text: **an** *der Uni* (2) 'at the University', *kam* ... **an** *die LSE* (17) 'came ... **to** the LSE', and when linked with particular verbs, **am** *Tiefgang hat es ... gefehlt* (25–26) 'it was ... lacking **in** depth', *Wor**an** das liegt?* (27–28) 'What's the reason **for** this? etc. The different meanings of the most common prepositions in German are discussed in **24.5**.

The meanings of other prepositions in the text are:

auf = 'on' (15), 'onto' (9), 'at' (12) with *schätzen* 'to estimate <u>at</u>'.
aus = 'from' (33).
bis = 'up to/until' (13).
durch = 'through' (32).
für = 'for' (11, 20).
in = 'in' (title, 2, 9, 18, 23, 24, 25, 29, 30), 'as' (32) in set phrase '<u>as</u> a rule'.
mit = 'with' (19).
nach = 'after' (7, 11, 16, 24).
über = 'about' (22), yet here corresponds to English 'of' in 'I have a good overview <u>of</u> ...'.
vor = 'ago', when used with expressions of time. Here *vor kurzem* (13) = 'recently'.
von = 'of' (8, 11, 18, 28).
zu = 'to' (4, 5, 17).

24.3 DA- AND WO- + PREPOSITION

If a preposition occurs with pronouns meaning 'it', 'them', 'that' and 'those' referring not to persons but to **things**, da- (or dar- before a vowel) is used and the preposition is added on the end: **Daran** *hat die Einführung von Studiengebühren ... nichts geändert* (11–12), literally: 'the introduction of student fees hasn't changed anything <u>about that</u>'. If it occurs in a question with *was?* or with a relative pronoun referring to things, not people, then wo- (wor- before a vowel) + preposition is used: **Woran** *das liegt?* (27) [NOT *an was] '<u>what</u>'s the reason <u>for</u> this?', **wovon** *seine Kommilitonen... nur träumen* (18) [NOT *von was] '<u>about which</u> his fellow students ... only dream'.[111]

[111] For further details and examples see **7.5** for preposition + 'it', **8.5** for preposition + 'this/that', **9.5** for preposition + 'which/that' and **23.4** for preposition + interrogatives.

Other points to note in the text

- Comparative constructions: *studentengerecht**er*** (1), *deutlich**er*** (4), *weniger ... als* (28–29), *breiter-... als* (32) (see **6.1, 6.6(i)**).
- Demonstratives: ***dieses*** *Land* (5), ***diesen*** *Satz* (27); as pronoun *die Zahl **jener*** (15); with preposition ***daran*** (11) (see **8.4–8.5** and footnote 44).

- Relative pronouns: *die . . . abschließt* (1–3), *die . . . hingekriegt hat* (5), *die . . . absolvieren* (15), *die . . . absolviert hat* (24–25), *der . . . lehrt* (34); and with preposition **wo**von . . . *träumen* (18), **wor**an (27) (see **Ch. 9**).
- Passive: *wird . . . erwartet* (28–29) (see **Ch. 18**).
- Elements (other than subject) placed at beginning of clause, causing the verb to follow immediately: *Im Vergleich zu hier* **sind** (5–6), *Daran* **hat** (11), *Auf „fast 5000"* **schätzt** (12–13), *Nach dem Abitur* **kam** (16), *Mit meinem Tutor* **hatte** (19), *Am Tiefgang* **hat** (25), *Auch diesen Satz* **hören** (27), *Von den Bachelor-Studenten* **wird** (28), *Besonders in den ersten beiden Studienjahren* **müssen** (30). Contrast *Aber auch . . .* followed by normal word order (19–20) (see **26.1a(ii)**, **26.6**).

▲ *Discover more about prepositions*

24.4 CASE

Tables 24 and 25 set out the most common prepositions in German and the cases they take. Students are advised to learn the prepositions together with an article and noun (in **Table 24**) and in whole sentences (in **Table 25**), since this makes it easier to remember which case is needed.

Table 24. Prepositions taking one case

Accusative only		Genitive only		Dative only	
durch den Wald	'through'	**außerhalb** des Dorfes	'outside'	**ab** dem 1. Mai ✐	'from'
für den Chef	'for'	**innerhalb** eines Monats/des Bezirks	'inside/within'	**aus** dem Fenster	'from, out of'
gegen den Baum	'against'	**statt** des Essens	'instead of'	**außer** dem Kind	'except for'
ohne den Vater	'without'	**trotz** des Regens	'in spite of'	**bei** (de)m Bäcker	'at'
um den Park	'round'	**während** des Tages	'during'	**mit** dem Auto	'with/by'
		wegen des Verkehrs[122]	'because of'	**gegenüber** dem Haus	'opposite'
				nach dem Krieg	'after'
				seit dem Tag	'since'
				von (de)m Chef	'from, of'
				zu (de)m Geschäft	'to'

* *Wegen* is often used with the dative in spoken German, e.g. *wegen* **dem** *Verkehr*.

Table 25. Prepositions taking accusative OR dative

Dative	Accusative	English
Der Spiegel hängt **an** _der_ Wand	Er hängt den Spiegel **an** _die_ Wand	on/onto
Er sitzt **auf** _dem_ Stuhl	Er setzt sich **auf** _den_ Stuhl	on/onto
Büsche wachsen **entlang** _der_ Straße	Er fährt _die_ Straße **entlang**	along
Er steht **hinter** _dem_ Baum	Er geht **hinter** _das_ Haus	behind
Er arbeitet **in** _der_ Stadt	Er fährt **in** _die_ Stadt	in/into
Er wohnt **neben** _dem_ Krankenhaus	Er stellt das Glas **neben** _die_ Flasche	next to
Das Bild hängt **über** _dem_ Kamin	Er hängt das Bild **über** _den_ Kamin	over/above
Er sucht seine Schuhe **unter** _dem_ Bett	Die Maus läuft **unter** _das_ Bett	under
Er wartet **vor** _dem_ Haus	Er stellt sein Fahrrad **vor** _das_ Haus	in front of
Er sitzt **zwischen** _der_ Chefin und _der_ Sekretärin	Er setzt sich **zwischen** _die_ Chefin und _die_ Sekretärin	(in) between

As outlined in **24.1(b)**, the accusative is usually used to indicate movement towards a noun/pronoun, as the examples in **Table 25** illustrate. Thus, taking the last sentence as an example: _Er sitzt zwischen **der** Chefin und **der** Sekretärin_ denotes position (i.e. he is already sitting down between them), while _Er setzt sich zwischen **die** Chefin und **die** Sekretärin_ denotes movement (i.e. he is in the process of sitting down between them).

Further notes on prepositions

i) Contracted forms. _An, bei, in, von_ and _zu_ + _dem_ = **am, beim, im, vom, zum**; _an, in_ + _das_ = **ans, ins**; _zu_ + _der_ = **zur**, e.g. _ich war am Strand/beim Bäcker/im Wasser_ etc. These are used in speech and writing when the articles _dem, das_ etc. do not need to be stressed. Other contractions such as **aufs** (_auf_ + _das_), **fürs** (_für_ + _das_), **ums** (_um_ + _das_) are common in speech but only used in less formal styles of writing, or in some set phrases, e.g. **ums** _Leben kommen_.

ii) Prepositions **after** the noun. _Gegenüber_, when meaning 'opposite', may precede or follow the noun, depending on the type of noun used. It always follows **pronouns**, e.g. _Er wohnt mir_ **gegenüber**, and tends to follow nouns referring to people, e.g. _Ich saß meinem Chef_ **gegenüber**. Otherwise it usually precedes the noun. **Entlang**, when meaning 'along', usually precedes a noun in the dative and follows a noun in the accusative (see **Table 25**).

iii) Use of **two** prepositions. Some prepositions require a second preposition in some circumstances, e.g. _vorbei_ 'past' occurs with _an_ (+ dat.): e.g. _Ich fuhr **an** dem Haus **vorbei**_, _bis_ 'until', 'up to' requires _zu_ (+dat.) or _an_ (+ acc.) **before an article**: e.g. _bis Frankfurt_ versus **bis** _zum Schloss/**bis ans** Meer_. **Bis auf** means 'except' (see **24.5b** below).

24.5 ALTERNATIVE MEANINGS

Below is a list of common prepositions with more than one meaning. Only the frequently used meanings are given as a rough guide:

Accusative

- **bis** until, up to: *Ich fuhr **bis** Frankfurt, **bis zum** Schloss; Ich wartete **bis** vier Uhr.*

  (with *auf*) except: *Alle kamen **bis auf** den Chef.*

  by (with time): *Können Sie es **bis** nächsten Dienstag liefern?*

- **durch** through: *Ich ging **durch** die Tür.*

  by (in passive): *Es wurde **durch** fleißige Arbeit geschafft.*[112]

- **gegen** against: *Der Besen steht **gegen** den Zaun; Ich bin **gegen** die Todesstrafe.*

  around (time): *Sie kommt **gegen** halb drei.*

- **um** round: *Sie saßen **um** das Feuer; Er fuhr zu schnell **um** die Kurve.*

  at (time): *Sie kommt **um** halb fünf.*

  around/approximately (with ages): *Sie ist **um** die dreißig* (note use of article).

Dative

- **aus** out of: *Er kam **aus** dem Büro.*

  from (place): *Sie kommt **aus** Hamburg/**aus** der Türkei.*

- **bei** at (house, business): *Er wohnt noch **bei** den Eltern; Ich habe es **bei** Aldi gekauft.*

  near (place): *Sie wohnt **bei** München/ **bei** der Brücke.*

  in (weather): ***Bei** schlechtem Wetter ist die Straße gesperrt.*

- **gegenüber** opposite: *Er saß **gegenüber** seiner Frau.*

  towards: *Seiner Frau **gegenüber** ist er sehr zärtlich (**gegenüber** usually follows the noun when it has this meaning).*

- **mit** with: *Ich war **mit** meinem Freund zu Hause.*

  by (transport): *Ich fahre lieber **mit** dem Auto als mit **dem** Bus.*

  at (age, speed): ***Mit** 16 darf man heiraten; Er fuhr **mit** 120 km/h.*

- **nach** to (places): *Er fährt nach Amsterdam/nach Frankreich* (with proper nouns).

  after: *Wir sehen uns **nach** der Arbeit.*

- **seit** since: ***Seit** letztem Juli arbeite ich an diesem Projekt.*

  for (='since'): *Ich wohne **seit** einem Jahr in England.*

- **von** from: *Ich warte auf einen Anruf **von** meinem Chef.*

  by (in passive): *Er wurde **von** dem neuen Chef entlassen.*[112]

  of: *Er ist ein Freund **von** meinem Bruder; Das ist sehr nett **von** dir.*

- **zu** to: *Ich fahre **zum** Supermarkt/**zu** meiner Freundin.*

  Sie ist immer sehr nett zu mir (used when expressing an attitude).

  at/on: *Er kommt zu Weihnachten/zu Ostern/zu meiner Geburtstag* (used for festive occasions).

---

[112] See **18.6** for the use of *von* versus *durch* in the passive.

Accusative or dative

- **an**   on (the side of):   *Das Bild hängt **an** der Wand; Ich hänge es **an** die Wand.*
  - (dat.)   on (days and dates):   *Wir kommen **am** Montag/**am** vierten Mai.*
  - (dat.)   at (the side of):   *Wir saßen **am** Tisch; Er klopft **an** der Tür.*
  - (acc.)   to (the side of):   *Alle gingen **an** den Tisch/**ans** Fenster; Ich gehe **an** die Tür.*
- **auf**   on (top of):   *Er saß **auf** dem Bett; Er setzte sich **auf** das Bett.*
  - (dat.)   at (some events):   *Ich war **auf** dem Markt/**auf** einem Konzert/**auf** einer Fete.*
  - (acc.)   to (some events):   *Ich ging **auf** den Markt/**auf** ein Konzert/**auf** eine Fete.*
  - (acc.)   in (languages):   *Hat er es **auf** Deutsch oder **auf** Englisch gesagt?*
- **in**   in: *Er sitzt **im** Haus; Er geht **ins** Haus; Ich gehe **in** drei Tagen.*
  - (dat.)   at (with buildings):   *Sie ist **im** Geschäft/**in** der Schule/**in** der Arbeit.*
  - (acc.)   to (with buildings):   *Sie geht **ins** Geschäft/**in** die Schule/**in** die Arbeit.*
  - (dat.)   on (TV, radio etc.):   *Es kommt ein guter Film **im** Fernsehen/**im** Kino.*
- **über**   above/over: *Das Bild hängt **über** dem Kamin; Ich hänge es **über** den Kamin.*
  -    (with ages):   *Er ist **über** sechzig.*
  - (acc.)   about: *Er redet immer **über** seine Arbeit; Es ist ein Film **über** den Tod.*
- **unter**   under/below: *Der Hund liegt **unter** dem Tisch; Der Hund läuft **unter** den Tisch.*
  -    (with ages):   *Er ist **unter** zwanzig.*
  - (dat.)   among(st):   *Sie ist die klugste **unter** den Schülern.*
- **vor**   in front of: *Er steht **vor** dem Haus; Er stellt sein Fahrrad **vor** das Haus.*
  - (dat.)   before: *Kannst du **vor** Montag dem zwanzigsten kommen?.*
  - (dat.)   ago: *Ich habe ihn **vor** zwei Tagen gesehen; Das war **vor** langer Zeit.*

Notes:

- **für**, when denoting time, is often omitted, e.g. 'I'm going to Italy for 2 weeks' = *Ich fahre **für** 2 Wochen nach Italien* or *Ich fahre 2 Wochen nach Italien*, 'I was in the office for 4 hours' = *Ich war **für** vier Stunden im Büro* or *Ich war 4 Stunden im Büro* or *Ich war 4 Stunden lang im Büro* (*lang* is often used when referring to the past).
- **in** is omitted before **dates**: e.g. *Ich bin 1935 geboren* (or *Ich bin **im Jahre** 1935 geboren*).
- **ohne** is usually used without the indefinite article *ein(-e, -en)*: e.g. *Ich bin **ohne** Regenschirm ausgegangen*. **Ohne zu + infinitive** renders 'without -ing': e.g. *Er kam herein **ohne zu** klopfen* 'He came in without knocking'.
- Common phrases with unpredictable prepositions are: **nach** Hause 'home' (e.g. *Ich fahre jetzt nach Hause*), **zu** Hause 'at home' (e.g. *Ich will heute zu Hause bleiben*), **im** Urlaub 'on holiday' (e.g. *Er ist **im** Urlaub/Er fährt **in** den Urlaub*), or, colloquially, **auf** Urlaub, **in** dem Alter 'at that age', **auf** dem Niveau 'at that level'.

24.6   COMMON VERBS AND ADJECTIVES TAKING A PREPOSITION

24.6a   Choice of preposition and case

A number of verbs and adjectives co-occur with a set preposition, the most problematic being those whose prepositions differ from the English equivalents: e.g. 'to wait for' = *warten **auf*** (not **für*). In these constructions, prepositions which can take an accusative **or** dative usually take an

accusative (particularly if the verb is simple, i.e. is not prefixed or part of a compound): e.g. *Ich warte auf **den** Mann.*[113] Tables 26 and 27 list common verbs and adjectives taking a set preposition which is often different from the English equivalent. Students are advised to learn these in phrases which make the case of the preposition explicit.

[113] This is a tendency rather than a hard and fast rule: e.g. *fehlen an* 'to lack' takes the dative, as can be seen in our text (25–26).

Table 26. Verbs + preposition

ACCUSATIVE

an	Ich **denke** <u>an</u> dich.	think of
	Er **erinnert** mich <u>an</u> meinen Vater.	remind of
	Ich **erinnere mich** <u>an</u> die Geschichte.	remember
auf	Ich **freue mich** <u>auf</u> das Wochenende.	look forward to
	Ich **konzentriere mich** <u>auf</u> die Arbeit.	concentrate on
	Ich **passe** <u>auf</u> das Baby **auf**.	look after
	Ich **verlasse mich** <u>auf</u> dich.	rely on
	Ich **warte** <u>auf</u> dich.	wait for
für	Ich **danke** dir <u>für</u> das Geschenk.	thank for
	Ich **interessiere mich** <u>für</u> die Literatur.	be interested in
in	Ich **verliebte mich** <u>in</u> meinen Chef.	fall in love with
über	Ich **denke** <u>über</u> die Situation **nach**.	think about/consider
	Ich möchte <u>über</u> meine Gehaltserhöhung **sprechen**.	talk about
	Ich **freue/ärgere mich** <u>über</u> seine Entscheidung.	be happy/angry about
um	Ich **bitte** dich <u>um</u> Entschuldigung.	ask for
	Der Film **handelt sich** <u>um</u> einen alten Rockstar.	deal with/be about
	Ich **mache mir Sorgen** <u>um</u> dich	worry about

DATIVE

an	Ich **arbeite** <u>an</u> einem Projekt	work on
	Er **leidet** <u>an</u> einer Ohrenentzündung	suffer from
	Er **starb** <u>an</u> einem Herzinfarkt	die of
	Ich **nehme** <u>an</u> einem Wettbewerb **teil**.	take part in
mit	Ich **fange** <u>mit</u> meiner neuen Arbeit **an**.	begin
	Kannst du da<u>mit</u> **aufhören**?*	stop
	Kann ich <u>mit</u> dir **sprechen**?	speak/talk to

nach	Ich **fragte** <u>nach</u> einem Kaffee.	ask for
	Es **schmeckt/riecht** <u>nach</u> Knoblauch.	taste/smell of
von	Er **erzählt** mir <u>von</u> seinem Jugend.	tell/talk about
	Es **hängt** <u>von</u> der Situation **ab**.	depend on
	Ich **träume** jede Nacht <u>von</u> dir.	dream of
vor	Ich **habe Angst/fürchte mich** <u>vor</u> Mäusen.	be afraid of
	Ich will es <u>vor</u> ihm **verbergen**.	hide from
zu	Er **gratuliert** mir <u>zu</u> meinem Geburtstag.	congratulate on

* For the use of *da*+preposition see **24.3**.

Table 27. Adjectives + preposition

ACCUSATIVE

an	Ich bin <u>an</u> dieses Wetter **gewöhnt**.	accustomed/used to
auf	Ich bin **böse/wütend** <u>auf</u> dich.	angry/furious with
	Sie ist **eifersüchtig/neidisch** <u>auf</u> ihre Schwester.	jealous/envious of
	Ich bin sehr **neugierig** <u>auf</u> deinen neuen Freund.	curious about
	Ich bin **gespannt** <u>auf</u> den Urlaub.	excited about
	Sie ist sehr **stolz** <u>auf</u> ihren Sohn.	proud of
um	Er ist **besorgt** <u>um</u> seine Tochter	worried about

DATIVE

an	Ich bin <u>an</u> der Geschichte **interessiert**.	interested in
	Ich bin **schuld** <u>an</u> dem Missverständnis.	to blame for
mit	Sie ist <u>mit</u> einem Arzt **verheiratet**.	married to

Often adjectives take the same preposition as their related verbs: e.g. *abhängig* **von** 'dependent on' (< *abhängen von*), *besorgt* **um** (< *sich Sorgen machen um*), *dankbar* **für** (< *jemandem danken für*), *verliebt* **in** 'in love with' (< *sich verlieben in*). Similarly, **nouns** usually (but not always!) take the same prepositions as their related adjectives and/or verbs: e.g. *der Gedanke* **an**, *die Erinnerung* **an**, *die Bitte* **um**, *das Interesse* **an**, *die Wut* **auf**, *der Eifersucht* **auf**, *die Schuld* **an**.

24.6b *Da-* plus preposition before whole clause

When the verb, adjective etc. + preposition is not followed by a noun/pronoun object but by a whole clause, *da-* (*dar-* before vowels) + preposition is used. Contrast the following pairs:

Object	Clause
Ich denke **an** <u>dich</u>.	Ich denke **daran**, <u>was ich machen würde</u>.
Ich warte **auf** <u>dich</u>.	Ich warte **darauf**, <u>dass du einen Fehler machst</u>.

*Ich dachte **über** die Situation nach.*   *Ich dachte **darüber** nach, was eben passiert war.*
*Ich bin **auf** den Urlaub gespannt.*   *Ich bin **darauf** gespannt, was passieren wird.*

These forms with *da(r)-* are often omitted in the spoken language and in some less formal styles of writing, e.g. *Ich bin gespannt, was passieren wird.* They tend to be omitted with adjectives and nouns rather than with verbs, yet there are some verbs which also allow omission, e.g. *Sie fragte ihn (**danach**), was er jetzt machen würde.*

✎ EXERCISES

Vocabulary topic: *Studium*

1 Put the bracketed words into the correct case which is determined by the preposition in bold print:

1 Ich studiere **an** [eine deutsche] Universität.
2 Welche Kurse zählen **für** [der] Abschluss?
3 **Nach** [das erste] Semester muss ich einen Deutschkurs ablegen.
4 **Über** [die] Sprachwissenschaft weiß ich sehr wenig.
5 Er ist **während** [die] Vorlesung eingeschlafen.
6 Die Assistentin kam **in** [der] Seminarraum und schrieb etwas Unverständliches **an** [die] Tafel.
7 Er war **vor** [sein] Vortrag sehr nervös.
8 Über zweihundert Studenten saßen **in** [der] Hörsaal.

2 Fill in the gaps by choosing an appropriate preposition for the context and put the bracketed words into the correct case. Some contexts may permit two or more possible prepositions:

1 Der heutige Student kann sehr leicht ____ [Computer] umgehen.
2 Das ist der Lehrer, ____ [der] ich Spanisch gelernt habe.
3 Er ist ____ [die mündliche] Prüfung durchgefallen.
4 Ich wartete ____ [die] Universitätsbibliothek ____ [mein Kommilitone].
5 Die nächste Vorlesung handelt ____ [das] Ende der Weimarer Republik.
6 Ich freue mich überhaupt nicht ____ [die] Klausuren.
7 Ich muss ____ [die] nächsten vier Wochen lernen.
8 Der neue Doktorand arbeitet sehr eifrig ____ [seine] Doktorarbeit.
9 Ich habe ____ [die] Studenten gehört, dass der Leistungsdruck dieses Jahr sehr hoch ist.
10 Sie war ____ [ihre] ausgezeichneten Noten sehr zufrieden.
11 „Fahren wir ____ [der] Bus oder ____ [das] Auto ____ [die] Uni?" „____ [der] Bus. ____ [der] Uniparkplatz ist es immer voll".
12 Ich muss ____ vier [Hauptseminare] und zwei [Proseminare] teilnehmen.

3 Complete the following text by filling in the gaps with appropriate prepositions and decide which following elements need to change their case endings:

Die meisten Studenten zieht es noch immer ____ ('into') die Metropole London. ____ ('for') die Provinzstädte spricht freilich, dass dort die Lebenshaltungskosten deutlich niederiger sind.

Curt Schmitt etwa ging ____ ('after') Bachelor und Master ____ ('at') die LSE zur Promotion nicht nur wegen des Renommees ____ ('to') Cambridge. Er floh auch ____ ('from') die Preise ____ ('in') die fünfteuerste Stadt der Welt: "Cambridge ist teuer genug, aber deutlich günstiger als London."

Dort schätzt etwa die LSE die durchschnittlichen Kosten ____ ('for') ein Student ____ ('at') 670 Pfund (rund 2200 Mark) monatlich. ____ ('because of') der Kursverlust der Mark reichen nun selbst die großzügig bemessenen DAAD-Stipendien [. . .] nicht mehr aus. Die LSE-Studentin Sabine Gremz musste ____ ('for') das Leben in London ungefähr 500 Mark pro Monat zusätzlich ____ ('to') das DAAD-Geld aufwenden.

Adapted from: *Uni-Spiegel* (Continued from main text).

FURTHER EXERCISES

4 Insert the correct prepositions and put the articles and pronouns in brackets into the correct case. Use the contracted forms of the articles where appropriate:

Example: Er war gestern __ (das) Theater. (at)
Answer: Er war gestern **im** Theater.

1   Ich möchte kurz schauen, was heute ____ (das) Fernsehen ist. (on)
2   Er geht morgen ____ (seine) Freundin ____ (ein) Rockkonzert. (with, to)
3   Ich gehe lieber ____ (das) Kino. (to)
4   Heute gibt es ein Sommerfest ____ (das) großen Zelt und vorne ____ (der) Rasen ist die Kinderunterhaltung. (in, on)
5   Der Chef hat uns ____ (eine) Fete ____ (er) zu Hause eingeladen. (to, at)
6   Er sprach ____ (seine) Lieblingsfernsehserie. (about)
7   Wir wollen heute abend ____ (der) Garten grillen. Hast du Lust, ____ (wir) zu kommen? (in, to)
8   Wollen wir heute ____ (die) Disco gehen? Wir können ____ (das) Taxi fahren. (to, by)
9   Wann warst du das letzte Mal ____ (die) Oper? Ach, ____ (viele) Jahren. (at, ago)
10 Was machen wir ____ (unser) Hochzeitstag? Gehen wir ____ (das) Restaurant. (on, to)

5 Complete the following story by filling in the gaps with any prepositions you feel are appropriate. Remember to make any necessary changes to articles (using contractions where possible), pronouns, adjectives etc.:

Norbert hat wieder Liebeskummer

Ich bin gestern abend ____ der Bus ____ die Stadt gefahren. Ein hübsches Mädchen saß alleine ____ der Bus. Sie erinnerte mich ____ meine Ex-Freundin und ich verliebte mich sofort ____ sie. Ich setzte mich ____ sie und fing an, ____ sie ____ eine halbe Stunde ____ Fußball zu reden. (Ich komme nämlich ____ Dortmund und bin ein Fan ____ Borussia.) Sie interessierte sich aber nicht ____ Fußball. Sie wusste nichts ____ Fußball und nahm ____ unser Gespräch wenig teil. ____ eine Weile merkte ich, dass sie sich langweilte und ich wechselte das Thema __ das Eishockey. Ich informierte sie ____ die verschiedenen Positionen ____ das Spiel, nannte ein paar Mannschaften, ____ die ich mich erinnern konnte, aber sie gähnte nur. „Ich bin ____

Sport gar nicht interessiert," sagte sie, und ich merkte Ärger ____ ihre Stimme. OK, dachte ich, ich werde mich ____ etwas Neutrales konzentrieren. Ich dachte ____ ein neues Thema: Fernsehen. „Hast du gestern das Snooker ____ Fernsehen gesehen?," fragte ich und gab ihr Informationen ____ die verschiedenen Kreidesorten, die man ____ der Billardstock tun kann. Warum rollte sie die Augen? Ich wollte doch nur freundlich ____ sie sein. Schließlich fragte ich sie, „Willst du ____ ich ____ das Bett gehen?" Sie verpasste mir einen Schlag ____ der Kopf ____ ihr Regenschirm. Frauen: ich verstehe sie einfach nicht!

6 **Insert the correct prepositions, preceded by *da(r)*- where appropriate, and put the bracketed articles, pronouns and adjectives into the correct form. Use contracted articles where appropriate:**

Example: Er sprach oft __, wie er das Leben __ [die ehermalige DDR] sehr schwierig gefunden hat.

Answer: Er sprach oft **darüber**, wie er das Leben **in der ehemaligen** DDR sehr schwierig gefunden hat.

1 „Ich freue mich sehr __ [dein] Besuch." „Ja, ich freue mich auch __, dich wiederzusehen."

2 „Kommst du heute Abend __ [das] Essen?" „Es hängt __ ab, ob ich länger arbeiten muss oder nicht."

3 Er ist sehr stolz __, dass seine Frau einen Bestseller geschrieben hat.

4 Du bist selber __ schuld, dass du dich __ [deine] Freunden gestritten hast.

5 Ich bin __ gewöhnt, meinen eigenen Weg zu gehen, aber jetzt muss ich mich __ [andere] Leute verlassen.

6 Kannst du mich __ erinnern, die Telefonrechnung zu bezahlen, bevor wir __ [der] Urlaub fahren?

7 „Was ist das Problem?" „Es handelt sich __, dass zwei Jugendliche __ [eine alte] Frau eingebrochen sind und viertausend Mark __ [ihre] Ersparnissen gestohlen haben, die __ [ihre] Matratze versteckt waren."

8 Der Gedanke __, dass er __ [ein] Jahr seine Frau betrügt, gefällt mir überhaupt nicht.

25 | Conjunctions

Text

Bärbel: Was ist los mit deinem Mann?

Marion: Er ist ein Dreckschwein. Nein, er . . . ich weiß nicht . . . ich kann mich mit ihm nirgendwo sehen lassen, **weil** er <u>ist</u> mir oft auch peinlich. Erstens: er putzt sich zweimal im Jahr die Zähne.

5 Teddy: Reicht das doch nicht aus?

Marion: Ja, für dich würde das reichen, genau.

Bärbel: Küsst du ihn noch?

Marion: **Wenn** es unbedingt sein <u>muss</u>, aber nur so ganz kurz [. . .].

Teddy: Liebst du deinen Mann? Du sagst, dein Mann ist ein Dreckschwein

10 . . . er . . . ich meine, es kommt mir nicht so vor, **als ob** du ihn überhaupt <u>liebst</u>.

Alex: **Und**, ich <u>meine</u>, deine Zähne kommen mir nicht gerade gepflegt vor, muss ich ganz ehrlich sagen.

Marion: Moment, ich putz' sie mir aber! **Und** ich <u>weiß</u>, wie man sich wäscht,

15 ich weiß, was ein Stück Seife ist, was ein Waschlappen ist, was ein Handtuch ist.

Bärbel: Also, er putzt sich nicht die Zähne. Duscht er?

Marion: Jetzt, **seitdem** er eine Arbeit <u>hat</u>, ja [. . .].

Bärbel: In welchem Abstand hat er dann vorher geduscht? [. . .]

20 Marion: **Je nachdem** wie sehr ich gedrängelt <u>hab</u>'.

Bärbel: Wechselt er die Klamotten?

Marion: **Wenn** ich super danach <u>guck</u>', dann ja. **Aber** heute <u>hab</u>' ich's ihn alleine machen lassen und . . ., guck ihn dir an! [. . .]

Bärbel: **Aber** du <u>hast</u> ihn ja trotzdem . . ., ich meine, ihr kennt euch schon

25 relativ lange. Du hast ihn vor einem Jahr geheiratet.

Marion: Ich hab' nicht gesagt, **dass** ich ihn nicht <u>liebe</u>.

Alex: Du erzählst, du liebst ihn **und** <u>erzählst</u> gleichzeitig, der Mann ist ein Schwein. **Entweder** ich <u>liebe</u> auch einen, **oder** ich <u>behaupte</u>, er ist ein Schwein.

30 Marion: Moment, **als** wir uns kennengelernt <u>haben</u>, war ja auch alles in Ordnung [. . .].

Bärbel: OK, ich würde sagen, wir holen deinen Mann mal 'rein. Er heißt Karl **und** wir <u>werden</u> sehen, **ob** er stellvertretend für viele Männer in Deutschland <u>ist</u>, **oder ob** er eine Ausnahme <u>ist</u>. Herzlich willkommen, Karl!

Bärbel Schäfer Talkshow, RTL. 10.November 2000.

⌕ Conjunctions in the text

25.1 WORD ORDER AFTER CONJUNCTIONS

A conjunction is a word used to link two clauses together and appears either between the clauses, e.g. 'I saw him **as** I got off the bus', or at the beginning of the whole sentence, e.g. '**As** I got off the bus I saw him'. This is also the case in German, but here there is an added complication. In German there are two main categories of conjuction with regard to their influence on the position of the **following finite verb**: co-ordinating conjunctions which do not affect word order; and subordinating conjunctions which send the following finite verb to the end of the clause (see the underlined verbs in the text for their position after the conjunction). The latter group is much larger than the former and, because of the change in word order involved, needs particular attention. A list of the most commonly used conjunctions is given in **Tables 28** and **29**.

Table 28. Common co-ordinating conjunctions

aber	but	**oder**	or
(after negative: **sondern**, see **22.1b**)		(or **beziehungsweise**, often abbreviated to **bzw.** in writing)	
denn	as/because	**und**	and
entweder ... oder	either ... or	**weder ... noch**	neither ... nor

Examples of co-ordinating conjunctions in the text are *und* (14, 27, 32), *aber* (22, 24), *oder* (34), *entweder . . . oder* (28).[114]

[114] As in English, the subject of the sentence can be omitted after the conjunction if it has already appeared beforehand: e.g. *Du liebst ihn* **und (du** omitted) *erzählst* . . . (27) 'you love him and say . . .'.

Table 29. Common subordinating conjunctions

als	when (in past)	**obwohl**	although
als ob	as if/as though	**ohne dass**[see 116]	without
angenommen, dass	assuming that	**seit(dem)**	since (re: time)
bevor/ehe	before	**sobald**	as soon as
bis	until/by the time	**so dass**	so (that)
da	as/since (= because)	**solange**	as long as
damit	so (that)	**soweit**	as far as
dass	that	**vorausgesetzt, dass**	provided that
es sei denn, dass	unless	**während**	while
je nachdem	depending on/according to	**weil**	because
nachdem	after	**wenn**	if/when/whenever
ob	whether/if	**wie**	as/like

Examples of subordinating conjunctions in the text are *wenn* (8, 22), *als ob* (10), *seitdem* (18), *je nachdem* (20), *dass* (26)[115] *als* meaning 'when', (30), *ob* (33, 34). As *weil* is also a subordinating conjunction it usually sends the verb to the end, although in colloquial spoken German it may be followed by normal word order, which is the case in this text (3). This may be due to confusion between *weil* and the co-ordinating conjunction *denn*, which also means 'because' but is much less commonly used.

[115] As in English, *dass* can optionally be omitted after the verbs *sagen*, *erzählen* and *meinen* (see lines 27–28, where *dass* is omitted before *du liebst ihn* and *der Mann ist ein Schwein*).

25.2 INTERROGATIVES BEHAVING LIKE CONJUNCTIONS

In addition to the 'proper' conjunctions listed in **25.1**, some other elements may behave like conjunctions in that they send the finite verb to the end of the clause when linking two clauses together. This is very often the case with interrogatives such as *was* 'what', *wer* 'who', and *wie* 'how' when used in indirect questions (see **23.5**). Examples from the text are: **wie** *man sich* wäscht (14), **was** *ein Stück Seife* ist, **was** *ein Waschlappen* ist, **was** *ein Handtuch* ist (15–16).

These interrogatives can also be used with *auch* (following the subject) to render the meanings 'what**ever**', 'who**ever**', 'how**ever**' etc. In this case, they often appear at the beginning of the sentence: e.g. (not in text): **Was** *du* **auch** *denkst, ich finde ihn in Ordnung* '**Whatever** you (may) think, I find him alright'; **Wie** *fleißig er* **auch** *arbeitet, wird er nie richtig geschätzt* '**However** hard he works he's never really appreciated'.

Other points to note in the text

- Features of spoken German: i) pauses (2, 10, 23, 24); ii) filler words and phrases: *ich meine* (10, 12, 24), *auch* (3, 28, 30), *ja* (30), *OK* (32); iii) dropping of -e in the first person singular present: *putz'* (14), *hab'* (20, 22, 26), *guck'* (22); iv) abbreviated forms: *es* → *'s* (22), *herein* → *'rein* (32); v) use of indicative instead of subjunctive in reported speech: *Du sagst, dein Mann* **ist** (9), *Du erzählst, du* **liebst** . . . *der Mann* **ist** (27).
- Reflexive pronouns: accusative: *mich* (2), *sich* (14); dative: *sich* (3, 17), *mir* (10, 12, 14), *dir* (23). Reciprocal 'each other': *euch* (24), *uns* (30) (see **Ch. 20**).
- Questions: *Was* . .? (1), *Reicht* . . .? (5), *Küsst* . . .? (7), *Liebst* . . .? (9), *Duscht* . . .? (17), *In welchem* . . .? (19), *Wechselt* . . .? (21) (see **Ch. 23**).
- Relative order of objects: i) pronouns – acc. + dat.: *ich putz'* **sie mir** (14), *guck* **ihn dir** *an* (23), *ich kann* **mich** *mit* **ihm** (2); 2 accusatives.: *hab'* **ich's ihn** (22); ii) pronoun + noun: *er putzt* **sich** . . . **die Zähne** (3–4, 17) (see **26.9b**).

▲ *Discover more about conjunctions*

25.3 NOTES ON INDIVIDUAL CONJUNCTIONS

25.3a Differences in meaning

Some of the conjunctions listed in **25.1** can be problematic in that they may have different meanings depending on the context in which they are used. Some common difficulties are discussed below:

- *Als/wenn* both mean 'when', yet *als* is used when referring to the **past** (simple past, perfect, pluperfect) and *wenn* refers to the present and future: e.g. *Als* wir uns <u>kennengelernt haben</u> (line 30 of text) '**When** we met each other' vs. *Wenn* wir uns am Wochenende <u>sehen</u> '**When** (or **whenever**) we see each other at the weekend'. If *wenn* is used to refer to the past it means 'whenever': e.g. *Wenn* wir uns <u>gesehen haben</u> '**Whenever** we saw each other'.

- *Wenn* means both 'if' and 'when'. It is sometimes evident from the context which meaning is required (e.g. if used with a subjunctive or conditional it means 'if'), but this is often not the case: e.g. *Wenn* es unbedingt sein muss (line 8 of text) could mean '**If** it's really necessary' or '**When**(ever) it's really necessary'. When a speaker wants to make it absolutely clear that s/he means 'if' and not 'when', s/he can use *falls*: e.g. *Falls* ich bis 8 Uhr nicht fertig bin 'If (it's the case that) I'm not ready by 8 o'clock'. When 'if' also means 'whether', *ob* is used: e.g. *Ich weiß nicht, **ob** er heute kommt* 'I don't know if/whether he's coming today'.

- *Damit/so dass* both mean 'so (that)', but *damit* expresses purpose (i.e. 'in order that/in order to'[116]) while *so dass* expresses result (i.e. 'with the result that'): e.g. *Der Chef gab mir einen Laptop, **damit** ich zu Hause arbeiten konnte* 'The boss gave me a laptop **so that** (= in order that) I could work at home' vs. *Der Laptop war kaputt, **so dass** ich zu Hause nicht arbeiten konnte* 'The laptop didn't work, **so** (**that**) I couldn't work at home'.

- When *als ob* 'as if' is used with a verb in a tense other than the present, the conditional (or conditional perfect, see **16.2b**) tends to be used, as this introduces an idea which does not correspond to reality: e.g. *Er tat, **als ob** er mich nicht gesehen <u>hätte</u>* 'He acted **as if** he hadn't seen me'.

---

[116] When the subject of both clauses is the same, *um . . . zu* + infinitive usually renders 'in order to': e.g. *Ich stand heute früher auf, **um** den Bus nicht **zu verpassen*** (rather than *damit ich den Buss nicht verpassen würde*). This is also the case with *ohne . . . dass/ohne . . . zu*: e.g. *<u>Er ging</u>, **ohne dass** <u>ich</u> ihm etwas sagen konnte* vs. *Er ging **ohne** etwas **zu sagen***.

25.3b Commas

Most conjunctions (except *und*, when not followed by another conjunction, and, in some contexts, *oder*, when the following subject is omitted, see **28.1b(ii)**) are preceded by a **comma**. In addition, some (but not all, see **Table 29**) conjunctions with *dass* require a comma before *dass*: e.g. *Ich komme um fünf Uhr nach Hause, **es sei denn, dass** ich länger arbeiten muss*. Commas tend to be used before *dass* when the preceding element contains a verb (or part of a verb such as a past participle, e.g. an**genommen**, dass; voraus**gesetzt**, dass).

25.4 THE SCOPE OF CONJUNCTIONS

Sometimes a conjunction can refer to a whole sentence rather than just one clause. In this case, if the sentence consists of two or more clauses and the conjunction is a subordinating one, **every verb in the sentence** must go to the end of its respective clause: e.g. *Als er mit seinem essen fertig <u>war</u>, es aber noch nicht weggeräumt <u>hatte</u> . . .*; *Ich wusste, **dass** ich ihn schon gesehen <u>hatte</u>, mit ihm gesprochen <u>hatte</u> und ihm sogar meine Telefonnummer gegeben <u>hatte</u>* (alternatively, to avoid repetition, the first two instances of *hatte* can be omitted: *Ich wusste, **dass** ich ihn schon gesehen, mit ihm gesprochen und ihm sogar meine Telefonnummer gegeben <u>hatte</u>*).

25.5 **USE OF ENGLISH '-ING'**

It is often the case in English that constructions with '-ing' are used instead of conjunctions: e.g.
'**Walking** down the street I noticed . . .', 'He left the house **saying** that he would be late back'.
These constructions must be translated into German using an appropriate conjunction and an
ordinary finite verb. Some examples are:

- *Als ich in die Stadt <u>fuhr</u>, bemerkte ich . . .*   Driv**ing** into town I noticed . . .
- *Er saß im Garten **und** <u>beobachtete</u> die Vögel.*   He sat in the garden watch**ing** the birds.
- *Da ich ihn nicht beleidigen <u>wollte</u>, nahm*   Not want**ing** to offend him, I accepted his
  ich seine Einladung an.   invitation.

Similarly '**by** + -ing' is often translated using ***indem***, which acts like a subordinating conjunction
in that it sends the finite verb to the end of the clause: e.g.

- *Man bekommt gute Noten, **indem** man*   You get good marks **by** work**ing** hard.
  fleißig <u>arbeitet</u>.
- *Ich habe ihn beleidigt, **indem** ich ihm*   I insulted him **by** not offer**ing** him any coffee.
  keinen Kaffee angeboten <u>habe</u>.

✎ EXERCISES

Vocabulary topic: *Haushalt*

1 Join the following clauses using the conjunctions given in brackets and change the word order where necessary:

Example: Ich weiß nicht. Er hat sein Zimmer schon aufgeräumt. [ob]
Answer: Ich weiß nicht, **ob** er sein Zimmer schon aufgeräumt <u>hat</u>.

  1 Ich habe staubgesaugt. Ich habe den Boden gewischt. [und]
  2 Du kochst. Du musst abwaschen. [entweder . . . oder]
  3 Ich muss einkaufen gehen. Ich habe kein Brot und keine Milch. [weil]
  4 Kannst du die Kerze anzünden. Du hast den Tisch gedeckt? [nachdem]
  5 Er hatte die Fenster geputzt. Sie sahen immer noch ziemlich dreckig aus. [aber]
  6 Kannst du deine Wäsche aufhängen. Du gehst weg? [bevor]
  7 Ich wusste nicht. Du hast eine Mikrowelle. [dass]
  8 Du kannst den Kaffee machen. Ich bereite das Frühstück vor. [während]
  9 Er versucht die Waschmaschine zu reparieren. Er hat das richtige Werkzeug nicht. [obwohl]
10 Dieses Fleisch darf man nicht einfrieren. Man muss es innerhalb von zwei Tagen kochen.
    [sondern]

2 Subordinate clauses (i.e. those beginning with a subordinating conjunction) may often BEGIN a sentence. Take your answers to question 1 above and place the subordinate clause (where present) at the beginning:

Example: Ich weiß nicht, ob er sein Zimmer schon aufgeräumt hat.
Answer: **Ob er sein Zimmer schon aufgeräumt hat**, weiß ich nicht.

3 Translate the bracketed conjunctions into German and join the clauses together, changing word order where necessary:

Example: [*After*] ich hatte mich angezogen. Ich machte das Bett.

Answer: **Nachdem** ich mich angezogen <u>hatte</u>, <u>machte</u> ich das Bett.

1 [*Until*] der Ofen wird repariert. Ich kann keinen Rostbraten machen.
2 Abwaschen ist die reine Hölle. [*Unless*] man hat einen Geschirrspüler.
3 [*When*] wir haben unser Haus gekauft. Wir haben uns kein Möbel leisten können.
4 [*When*] ich wische Staub. Ich benutze immer einen nassen Fetzen.
5 [*If*] du mehr hättest mehr Zeit. Du könntest ein paar Regale aufstellen.
6 Ich weiß nicht. [*If*] er kann mit einer Bohrmaschine umgehen.
7 Man muss die Wand zweimal streichen. [*So that*] Die ursprüngliche Farbe scheint nicht durch.
8 Er hatte die Tassen nicht richtig gespült. [*So*] Mein Kaffee schmeckte nach Seife.
9 Ich hasse es. [*When*] er lümmelt auf dem Sofa und legt seine Füße auf den Tisch.
10 Ich habe bemerkt. [*That*] mein Putzmann hat das Klo nicht gründlich geputzt und hat eine Zigarettenkippe im Waschbecken gelassen.

4 Translate the following sentences into German using an appropriate conjunction for the context, and using the simple past tense rather than the perfect for questions 2–4:

1 She's sitting at the table cutting bread.
2 Knowing that he couldn't cook very well, I suggested a good restaurant.
3 I cut my finger preparing dinner last night.
4 I made him ill by putting too much chilli in his meal.

☞ **For further exercises on conjunctions see Revision Text 5, Ex. 5 and for exercises on interrogatives functioning as subordinating conjunctions see Ch. 23, Ex. 4.**

26 | Word order

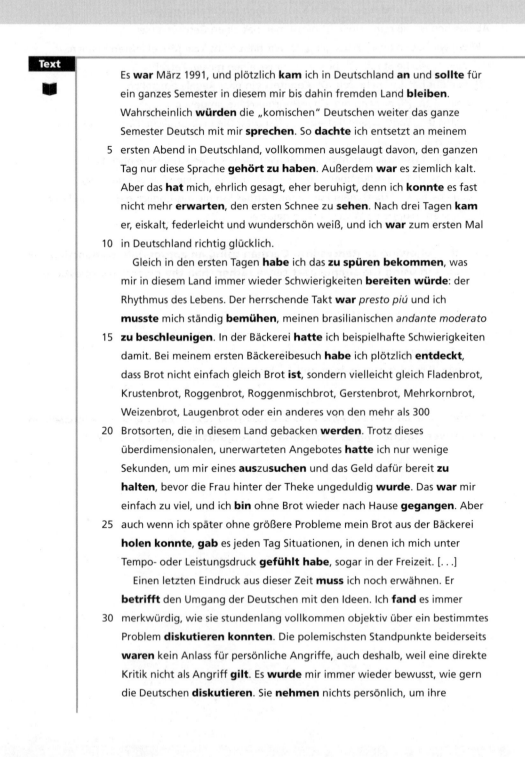

Es **war** März 1991, und plötzlich **kam** ich in Deutschland **an** und **sollte** für ein ganzes Semester in diesem mir bis dahin fremden Land **bleiben**. Wahrscheinlich **würden** die „komischen" Deutschen weiter das ganze Semester Deutsch mit mir **sprechen**. So **dachte** ich entsetzt an meinem
5 ersten Abend in Deutschland, vollkommen ausgelaugt davon, den ganzen Tag nur diese Sprache **gehört zu haben**. Außerdem **war** es ziemlich kalt. Aber das **hat** mich, ehrlich gesagt, eher beruhigt, denn ich **konnte** es fast nicht mehr **erwarten**, den ersten Schnee zu **sehen**. Nach drei Tagen **kam** er, eiskalt, federleicht und wunderschön weiß, und ich **war** zum ersten Mal
10 in Deutschland richtig glücklich.

Gleich in den ersten Tagen **habe** ich das **zu spüren bekommen**, was mir in diesem Land immer wieder Schwierigkeiten **bereiten würde**: der Rhythmus des Lebens. Der herrschende Takt **war** *presto più* und ich **musste** mich ständig **bemühen**, meinen brasilianischen *andante moderato*
15 **zu beschleunigen**. In der Bäckerei **hatte** ich beispielhafte Schwierigkeiten damit. Bei meinem ersten Bäckereibesuch **habe** ich plötzlich **entdeckt**, dass Brot nicht einfach gleich Brot **ist**, sondern vielleicht gleich Fladenbrot, Krustenbrot, Roggenbrot, Roggenmischbrot, Gerstenbrot, Mehrkornbrot, Weizenbrot, Laugenbrot oder ein anderes von den mehr als 300
20 Brotsorten, die in diesem Land gebacken **werden**. Trotz dieses überdimensionalen, unerwarteten Angebotes **hatte** ich nur wenige Sekunden, um mir eines **aus**zu**suchen** und das Geld dafür bereit **zu halten**, bevor die Frau hinter der Theke ungeduldig **wurde**. Das **war** mir einfach zu viel, und ich **bin** ohne Brot wieder nach Hause **gegangen**. Aber
25 auch wenn ich später ohne größere Probleme mein Brot aus der Bäckerei **holen konnte**, **gab** es jeden Tag Situationen, in denen ich mich unter Tempo- oder Leistungsdruck **gefühlt habe**, sogar in der Freizeit. [. . .]

Einen letzten Eindruck aus dieser Zeit **muss** ich noch erwähnen. Er **betrifft** den Umgang der Deutschen mit den Ideen. Ich **fand** es immer
30 merkwürdig, wie sie stundenlang vollkommen objektiv über ein bestimmtes Problem **diskutieren konnten**. Die polemischsten Standpunkte beiderseits **waren** kein Anlass für persönliche Angriffe, auch deshalb, weil eine direkte Kritik nicht als Angriff **gilt**. Es **wurde** mir immer wieder bewusst, wie gern die Deutschen **diskutieren**. Sie **nehmen** nichts persönlich, um ihre

> 35 Gesprächspartner nicht **zu verletzen** und auch nicht **zu verlieren**. So **können**
>
> sie nach einem heftigen Wortwechsel zusammen einen gemütlichen
>
> Spaziergang **machen**.
>
> Aus einem Artikel von Luciana Dabdab Waquil, einer ehemaligen
>
> Germanistikstudentin aus Brasilien. *DAAD. Letter*, 12/2000.

⌕ Word order in the text

26.1 ORDER OF VERBS

26.1a In main clauses

i) In an ordinary German main clause, the finite[117] verb is always the **second** 'idea', while infinitives, past participles and separable prefixes appear at the **end**. The following examples show the finite verbs in bold print and the infinitives/participles underlined:[118]

- *Der herrschende Takt* **war** *presto più und ich* **musste** *mich ständig* <u>bemühen</u> . . . (13–14)
- *Das* **war** *mir einfach zu viel, und ich* **bin** *ohne Brot wieder nach Hause* <u>gegangen</u> (23–24)
- *. . . und* **sollte** *für ein ganzes Semester . . .* <u>bleiben</u> (1–2)

This last example shows that the subject can sometimes be omitted (in this case, *ich*). Further examples with finite verbs are: *Es* **war** (1), *Das* **war** (23), *Er* **betrifft** (28–29), *Ich* **fand** (29), *Es* **wurde** (33), *Sie* **nehmen** (34), *Die polemischen Standpunkte beiderseits* **waren** (31–32). The last example shows that the first 'idea' in the stentence can be quite long; the verb does not necessarily have to be the second *word*.

ii) If an expression of time or some other element appears at the beginning of the clause, the finite verb must still be in second position, which means that the subject (underlined here) has to **follow** the verb. As you can see from our text, this is extremely common: e.g.

- *. . . plötzlich* **kam** <u>ich</u> *in Deutschland an*[119] (1)
- *Wahrscheinlich* **würden** <u>die „komischen" Deutschen</u> . . . (3)
- *So* **dachte** <u>ich</u> . . . (4)
- *Außerdem* **war** <u>es</u> *ziemlich kalt* (6)

If the subject and verb are directly preceded by a co-ordinating conjunction such as *und, aber, oder, denn* etc. (see **Table 25**), their word order is not affected:[120] e.g.

---

[117] The *finite* verb carries information on person (e.g. *ich, du, er*), number (singular, plural) and tense (e.g. present, past), e.g. *ich mache, wir singen, du warst*. Infinitives and participles are **not** finite verbs.

[118] For the order of verbs in questions see **23.1**.

[119] The separable prefix appears at the end of the clause (see **Ch. 19** for separable verbs).

[120] This also applies to interjections (e.g. *ach!, mein Gott!*), to *ja* and *nein* and other words which are 'cut off' from the following clause, usually with a comma: e.g. *Ja/Zum Beispiel/Im Gegenteil,* <u>er</u> **kommt** *jeden Tag*.

- *Aber <u>das</u> **hat** mich . . .* (7)
- *Denn <u>ich</u> **konnte** . . .* (7)
- *Und <u>ich</u> **war*** (9)

Other examples of the subject following the verb due to the presence of a sentence-initial element are: *Nach drei Tagen **kam** <u>er</u>* (8–9), *Gleich in den ersten Tagen **habe** <u>ich</u>* (11), *In der Bäckerei **hatte** <u>ich</u>* (15), *Bei meinem ersten Bäckereibesuch **habe** <u>ich</u>* (16), *Trotz dieses überdimensionalen, unerwarteten Angebotes **hatte** <u>ich</u>* (20–21), *Einen letzten Eindruck aus dieser Zeit **muss** <u>ich</u>* (28), *So **können** <u>sie</u>* (35–36).

26.1b In subordinate clauses

i) The finite verb appears at the **end** of subordinate clauses: i.e. those clauses preceded by a **subordinating conjunction** such as *dass, wenn, weil, da, obwohl* (see **Table 26**), a **relative pronoun** such as *der Mann, **der** die Karten verkauft* (see **Ch. 9**) and **interrogatives used indirectly** such as *ich weiß, **wer** du wirklich bist* (see **23.5**): e.g.

- *. . ., <u>was</u> mir in diesem Land immer wieder Schwierigkeiten bereiten **würde*** (12)
- *. . ., <u>dass</u> Brot nicht einfach gleich Brot **ist*** (17)
- *Brotsorten, <u>die</u> in diesem Land gebacken **werden*** (20)

Other examples of subordinate clauses are: *<u>bevor</u> die Frau . . . ungeduldig **wurde*** (23), *Situationen, <u>in denen</u> ich mich . . . gefühlt **habe*** (26–27), *<u>wie</u> sie . . . diskutieren **konnten*** (30–31), *<u>weil</u> eine direkte Kritik nicht als Angriff **gilt*** (32–33), *<u>wie</u> gern die Deutschen **diskutieren*** (33–34).[121]

Note that, in sentences consisting of more than one clause, the finite verb goes to the end of its **clause** and not to the end of the whole sentence:

*Aber auch wenn ich später ohne größere Probleme mein Brot aus der Bäckerei holen **konnte**, gab es jeden Tag Situationen, in denen ich mich unter Tempo- oder Leistungsdruck gefühlt **habe*** (25–27) [where *konnte* does NOT follow *habe*].[122]

ii) If, within a sentence, a main clause follows a subordinate clause, the finite verb of the main clause must come **first**: e.g. (subordinate clause underlined):

*Aber auch wenn <u>ich später ohne größere Probleme mein Brot aus der Bäckerei holen konnte</u>, **gab** es jeden Tag Situationen, in denen ich mich unter Tempo- oder Leistungsdruck gefühlt habe.* (25–27)

---

[121] With **double infinitive** constructions, used with modals and some other verbs, the finite auxiliaries **precede** the two infinitives in subordinate clauses: e.g. *Ich weiß, dass ich es nicht **habe** machen können* (see **21.4b**).

[122] If the following clause is a **relative** clause, however (i.e. a clause preceded by a relative pronoun), it may be kept together together with the noun to which it refers: e.g. *. . . obwohl ich <u>das Buch, das du mir empfohlen hast</u>, noch nicht gelesen **habe***.

26.1c (*Um*) . . . *zu* + infinitive

Constructions with *zu* + infinitive (with or without *um*, see **21.1–21.2**) are usually treated as a **separate clause**, which means that they **follow** the clause that introduces them. The infinitive itself always appears at the end of its clause (with *zu*): e.g. *Ich konnte es fast nicht mehr erwarten,*

*den ersten Schnee **zu sehen*** (7–8), NOT**ich konnte es fast nicht mehr, den ersten Schnee zu sehen,*
erwarten. Other examples are:

- *und ich musste mich ständig bemühen, meinen brasilianischen andante moderato **zu**
  beschleunigen* (13–15)
- *Trotz dieses überdimensionalen, unerwarteten Angebotes hatte ich nur wenige Sekunden, **um** mir
  eines **auszusuchen** und das Geld dafür bereit **zu halten*** (20–24)
- *Sie nehmen nichts persönlich, um ihre Gesprächspartner nicht **zu verletzen** und auch nicht **zu**
  verlieren* (34–35)
- *So dachte ich entsetzt an meinem ersten Abend in Deutschland, vollkommen ausgelaugt davon,
  den ganzen Tag nur diese Sprache **gehört zu haben*** (4–6)

However, if the *zu* + infinitive phrase is **short**, particularly if there are no other elements (e.g.
nouns, adjectives) involved, *zu* + infinitive may appear **inside** the clause instead of following it:
e.g. *Gleich in den ersten Tagen habe ich das **zu spüren** bekommen* (11).

26.2 ORDER OF SUBJECT AND OBJECTS

In German, the order of subjects and objects is much more flexible than in English. for instance,
if the speaker wishes to emphasise or shift the focus onto a particular subject or object, this is
often done by a change in word order. Therefore it is unwise to give hard-and-fast rules for the
position of subjects and objects within a German sentence, and only general tendencies will be
given which reflect the most common usage.

26.2a Subjects

Subjects usually begin a clause and precede the finite verb: e.g. ***Ich** fand es immer merkwürdig*
(29–30, and see **26.1a(i)** for more examples), unless another element begins the clause, in which
case the subject is placed after the verb: e.g. *plötzlich kam **ich**,* (1) (see **26.1a(ii)**). Being in a
subordinate clause does not affect the order of subjects and objects: e.g. ***Ich** fand **es** immer
merkwürdig* (29–30) → *weil **ich es** immer merkwürdig fand.*

26.2b Objects

i) **Accusative objects**[123] usually come later in the clause: after the subject and verb, and also
   after many expressions of time and some expressions of manner beginning with a
   preposition. On the other hand, they tend to precede *nicht* (see **Ch. 22**), and phrases
   beginning with a preposition that are not expressions of time or manner:

---

[123] For the relative order of accusative and dative objects, see **26.9**.

- *Wahrscheinlich würden die „komischen" Deutschen weiter das ganze Semester **Deutsch** mit
  mir sprechen* (3–4)
- *Trotz dieses überdimensionalen, unerwarteten Angebotes hatte ich nur **wenige Sekunden**
  (20–22)
- *Aber auch wenn ich später ohne größere Probleme **mein Brot** aus der Bäckerei holen konnte*
  (24–26)
- *. . . gab es jeden Tag **Situationen*** (26)

- *Er betrifft **den Umgang** der Deutschen . . .* (29)
- *So können sie nach einem heftigen Wortwechsel zusammen **einen gemütlichen Spaziergang** machen* (35–37)

ii) If the accusative object is a personal or reflexive **pronoun**, it usually immediately follows the subject and verb. This also applies to pronouns in the dative, e.g.:

- *Aber das hat **mich**, ehrlich gesagt, eher beruhigt* (7)
- *Ich konnte **es** fast nicht mehr erwarten* (7–8)
- *. . ., was **mir** in diesem Land immer wieder Schwierigkeiten bereiten würde* (12)
- *und ich musste **mich** ständig bemühen* (13–14)
- *Es wurde **mir** immer wieder bewusst* (33)

Other pronouns, e.g. the indefinite article functioning as a pronoun, meaning 'one', follow the personal and reflexive pronouns: *um **mir** eines auszusuchen* (22).

26.3 EXPRESSIONS OF TIME, MANNER AND PLACE

Again, the order of expressions of time, manner and place is quite flexible in German, depending on the focus that the speaker is using. Probably the most frequently used order is time–manner–place: e.g. *Ich fahre [jeden Tag]*_{Time (when?)} *[mit dem Bus]*_{Manner (how?)} *[zur Arbeit]*_{Place (where?)}. Examples from the text are:

- *[plötzlich_M] kam ich [in Deutschland_P] an* (1)
- *sollte [für ein ganzes Semester_T] [in diesem mir bis dahin fremden Land_P] bleiben* (1–2)
- *ich war [zum ersten Mal_T] [in Deutschland_P] richtig glücklich* (19–10)
- *ich bin [ohne Brot_M] wieder [nach Hause_P] gegangen* (24)
- *auch wenn ich [später_T] [ohne größere Probleme_M] mein Brot [aus der Bäckerei_P] holen konnte* (25–26)

26.4 PHRASES BEGINNING WITH PREPOSITIONS

If the preposition is required by the verb, e.g. *diskutieren **über***, its following phrase will tend to come late in the clause. If, however, the phrase beginning with a preposition is an expression of time, manner or place, and is not closely linked to the verb itself, then it follows the same tendencies as other expressions of time, manner and place (see **26.3** above). Consider the following examples in which the phrases in bold print occur with prepositions that are dependent on the verbs underlined:

- *Wahrscheinlich würden die „komischen" Deutschen weiter das ganze Semester Deutsch **mit mir** <u>sprechen</u>* (3–4).
- *So <u>dachte</u> ich entsetzt **an meinem ersten Abend*** (4–5) [NOT *So dachte ich an meinem ersten Abend entsetzt].
- *In der Bäckerei <u>hatte</u> ich beispielhafte <u>Schwierigkeiten</u> **damit*** (15–16).
- *. . ., wie sie stundenlang vollkommen objektiv **über ein bestimmtes Problem** <u>diskutieren</u> konnten* (30–31).

26.5 POSITION OF ADJECTIVES

Most predicative adjectives (i.e. those which do not precede a noun) occur at the **end** of the clause: e.g.

- *und ich war zum ersten Mal in Deutschland richtig* **glücklich** (9–10)
- *Es wurde mir immer wieder* **bewusst** (33)

In clauses where the verb has been sent to the end (**26.1b**) or there is a past participle or infinitive present (**26.1a(i)**), the adjective precedes these verbs: e.g. *dass ich zum ersten Mal in Deutschland richtig* **glücklich** <u>war</u>.

26.6 ELEMENTS PLACED AT THE BEGINNING OF THE CLAUSE

It is often the case that expressions of manner, place and particularly those of time are placed at the beginning of the clause. In some contexts this can be a way of emphasising the elements in question, while in others it is simply done without any special emphasis being intended. This 'fronting' of elements occurs extensively in our text: e.g. time *Nach drei Tagen* (8), *Gleich in den ersten Tagen* (11); manner *plötzlich* (1); place *In der Bäckerei* (15).

In addition to these expressions of time, manner and place, **objects** may also be 'fronted', e.g. *Einen letzten Eindruck aus dieser Zeit* (28), as can most other elements, e.g. adverbs *Wahrscheinlich* (3), *Außerdem* (6), *So* (4, 35), and phrases beginning with a preposition, e.g. *Bei meinem ersten Bäckereibesuch* (16), *Trotz dieses überdimensionalen, unerwarteten Angebotes* (20–21).

26.7 ELEMENTS PLACED AT THE END OF THE CLAUSE

It is also possible to place elements **after the final verb** in the clause (i.e. outside the verbal bracket). This is often done in the spoken language where these elements are added as an afterthought or by way of explanation or emphasis. This occurs much less in the written language and, where it does occur, it usually indicates emphasis:

- *. . . , was mir in diesem Land immer wieder Schwierigkeiten bereiten* <u>würde</u>: **der Rhythmus des Lebens** (11–13).
- *Situationen, in denen ich mich unter Tempo- oder Leistungsdruck gefühlt* <u>habe</u>, **sogar in der Freizeit** (26–27).

The placing of elements after the last verb in the clause is particularly common when they form a very long utterance whose inclusion within the verbal bracket would lead to a rather unwieldy sentence with the final verb being too far away from its subject: e.g. *. . . . dass Brot nicht einfach gleich Brot* <u>ist</u>, **sondern vielleicht gleich Fladenbrot, Krustenbrot, Roggenbrot, Roggenmischbrot, Gerstenbrot, Mehrkornbrot, Weizenbrot, Laugenbrot oder ein anderes von den mehr als 300 Brotsorten** (17–20).

Other points to note in the text

- Relative pronouns: *was* (11), *die* (20), *denen* (26) (see **Ch. 9**).
- Conditional: *würden . . . sprechen* (3–4), *bereiten würde* (12) (see **6.2a**).
- Negation: *nicht* (8, 33, 35), *nicht . . ., sondern* (17), *kein* (32), *nichts* (34) (see **Ch. 22**).
- Prepositions with explicit case: **für** + acc. (1, 32), **in** + dat. (2, 11, 12, 15, 20, 26, 27), **mit** + dat. (4, 29), **an** + dat. (4), **nach** + dat. (8, 36), **zu** + dat. (9), **bei** + dat. (16), **trotz** + gen. (20), **hinter** + dat. (23), **ohne** + acc. (25), **aus** + dat. (25, 28), **über** + acc. (30) (see **24.5**).
- Prepositions with *da-*: *davon* (5), *damit* (16), *dafür* (22) (see **24.3**).

▲ *Discover more about word order*

26.8 MULTIPLE SUBORDINATE CLAUSES

It is sometimes the case that an element that sends the following finite verb to the end, e.g. a subordinating conjunction or relative pronoun, has scope over more than one clause and therefore over more than one finite verb. This means that it is not sufficient to simply send the closest following verb to the end of the clause and leave the others. In this case, the finite verbs all go to **the end of their respective clauses**. Note that they do not 'pile up' at the end of the sentence: e.g.

*. . . weil sie kein Geld **hat**, ihre Miete nicht bezahlen **kann** und ihre Wohnung aufgeben **muss**.*

26.9 RELATIVE ORDER OF SUBJECT, ACCUSATIVE OBJECT AND DATIVE OBJECT

As with most aspects of word order in German, the relative position of subjects and objects is much more flexible than in English, depending on the focus which the speaker wants to give to these elements and on the wider context. Below are some basic guidelines for commonly used word order patterns in constructions where the subject and objects all **follow the finite verb**, as this is often problematic for English learners of German.

26.9a Nouns

The usual order for subjects and objects when they are all nouns following the verb is:
subject–dative object–accusative object:

- *Nachher erzählte der Vater$_S$ seinem Sohn$_D$ eine Geschichte$_A$.*
- *Gestern gab der Student$_S$ dem Lehrer$_D$ seinen Aufsatz$_A$.*[124]
- *Wie will dein Freund$_S$ seiner Mutter$_D$ diese Nachricht$_A$ beibringen?*

This does not apply when the objects are **personal pronouns**, however, as pronouns usually precede nouns which follow the finite verb, irrespective of case (see **26.9b**).

---

[124] And with the expression of time **not** at the beginning: *Der Student gab dem Lehrer **gestern** seinen Aufsatz.*

26.9b Personal pronouns

Personal pronouns following a finite verb usually come **immediately after the verb** (or, in subordinate clauses, the conjunction), which means that **personal pronouns tend to precede all nouns** in this position:

- *Trotzdem hat **ihr** der Chef eine Gehaltserhöhung gegeben.*[125]
- *Morgen muss **dich** dein Freund abholen. Mein Auto ist kaputt.*
- *Er weiß, dass **mir** der Kollege geholfen hat.*

That is not to say that placing the noun subject before the pronoun is incorrect, e.g. *Morgen muss dein Freund dich abholen . . .*, but it is less frequently used.

When the subject and both objects are all personal pronouns, the usual order is **subject–accusative–dative**.

- *Außerdem hat **er es ihr** nicht erzählt.*
- *Brauchst du heute deine Schlittschuhe? Kannst **du sie mir** leihen?*

---

[125] Reflexive pronouns occupy the same position as the personal pronouns: e.g. *Gestern hat **sich** der Chef geärgert.* By contrast, demonstrative pronouns and other types of pronoun tend to come after the noun: e.g. *Gestern hat sie dem Chef einen gegeben; Gestern hat sie dem Chef das gesagt* (OR *Gestern hat sie das dem Chef gesagt* for a different emphasis).

26.10 SOME COMMON GERMAN SENTENCE PATTERNS

Tables 30 and 31 illustrate some commonly used German sentence patterns. Students are advised to pay particular attention to the word order.

Table 30. Verbs and expressions of time, manner and place

Conj.	1st pos.	2nd pos.	Time	Manner	Place	Participle/ Infinitive	Verb sent to end
	Ute	fährt	heute	mit dem Zug	nach Berlin		
	Heute	fährt Ute		mit dem Zug	nach Berlin		
und	Ute	ist	heute	mit dem Zug	nach Berlin	gefahren	
weil	Ute		heute	mit dem Zug	nach Berlin	gefahren	ist

Table 31. Subjects, objects and prepositional phrases

1st pos.	2nd pos.	Pronouns	Inverted noun subj.	Dat. noun	Time	Acc. noun	Prepositional phrase
Ute	gab			ihrem Mann	heute	ein Buch	zum Geburtstag
Heute	gab		Ute	ihrem Mann		ein Buch	zum Geburtstag
Heute	gab	ihm	Ute			ein Buch	zum Geburtstag
Heute	gab	sie ihm				ein Buch	zum Geburtstag
Heute	gab	sie es ihm					zum Geburtstag

✎ EXERCISES

Vocabulary topic: *Zeit, Tage und Termine*

1 Insert the bracketed finite verbs into the correct place in the sentence:

1 Joachim am Samstag um acht Uhr eine Fete. [macht]
2 Diese Woche die Kinder zu ihren Großeltern. [fahren]
3 Leider es nicht möglich, vor dem vierundzwanzigsten Mai den Flug zu buchen. [ist]
4 Am 2. März ich bis sieben Uhr abends, aber den nächsten Tag ich frei. [arbeite, habe]
5 Karl, ich am Montag nicht kommen. [kann]
6 Stell dir vor, sie am 12. Februar hundert Jahre alt! [wird]
7 Wo du gestern Morgen um halb neun? [warst]
8 Ich glaube, er am 16. April Geburtstag [hat]
9 Schade, dass ich dich am ersten Januar nicht. [sah]
10 Der siebzehnte Juni der Tag, an dem wir uns. [war, kennenlernten]
11 Weißt du, ob deine englischen Freunde in Deutschland am 24. oder 25. Dezember Weihnachten und was sie an dem Tag? [feiern, essen]
12 Seine Mutter besorgt, weil er gestern Abend nicht nach Hause und sie auch nicht. [war, kam, anrief]
13 Ich froh, dass ich es jeden Tag, vor halb sechs mit meiner Arbeit fertig zu sein. [bin, schaffe]
14 Bevor ich dieses Jahr in den Urlaub, ich einen neuen Koffer. [fahre, brauche]
15 Da wir am 4. Juli unseren Hochzeitstag, wir abends in ein schönes Restaurant. [haben, gehen]

2 Return to question 1 above and put the bracketed verbs into the PERFECT tense, paying particular attention to where you place the auxiliary and past participle in the sentence.

3 Rearrange the following words and phrases to make proper sentences, paying particular attention to the order of the expressions of time, manner and place:

1 Jens, zur Arbeit, mit dem Auto, immer, fährt.
2 Mein Vater, am Bahnhof, morgen um halb acht, kommt, an.
3 Die Kinder, auf der Wiese, heute, fröhlich, spielen.
4 Wir, für vier Tage, nach Wien, dieses Wochenende, mit dem Schnellzug, fahren.
5 Meine Freundin, mit ihrem neuen Ehemann, auf Besuch, morgen Abend, kommt.
6 Ich, werde, warten, auf dich, auf dem Hauptplatz, um viertel vor drei.

✎ FURTHER EXERCISES

4 Put the bracketed subjects and objects into the correct order in the sentence:

1 Wollte schenken [er, Blumen, seiner Lehrerin].
2 Hat erklärt [sie, die Ursache des Problems, ihrem Chef].

3 Gestern habe gekauft [von H&M, ich, einen neuen Pulli, meinem Mann].

4 Ich hoffe, dass schon gegeben hast [du, die Nachricht, deinem Freund].

5 Hast schon gesagt [du, es, deiner Mutter]?

6 „Kannst leihen [du, einen Stift, mir]?" „Sicher. Ich kann geben [einen, dir]. Ich habe genug davon."

7 Ich glaube, dass schämt [wegen seines schlechten Benehmens, er, sich].

8 Ich weiß, dass zu sagen hast [du, etwas, mir]. Sag [es, mir]!

9 Dein Freund hat wegen seines Fahrrads angerufen. Kannst zurückgeben [du, es, ihm]?

10 „Was hält deine Mutter von unseren Urlaubsfotos?" „Habe noch nicht gezeigt [ich, sie, ihr]."

5 Make proper sentences out of the following dialogue by changing the order of the words and phrases where necessary:

Birgit: Du, meine Ohrringe, hast gesehen? Ich, sie, an, gehabt, gestern, habe, aber, ich, heute, sie, kann, finden, nicht mehr.

Kerstin: Ja, mir, du, sie, hast geliehen, gestern Abend. Du, sie, zurückhaben, willst?

Birgit: Nein, kein Problem, ist, das. Ich, vergessen, hatte, bloß[126], dass, ich, hatte, geliehen, dir, sie.

Kerstin: Und, hast, geliehen, auch[126], deine Goldkette, du, mir.

Birgit: Ja, das, ich, weiß.

Kerstin: Du, in die Disco, gehst, heute Abend?

Birgit: Nein, ich, ins Bett, gehe, früher, heute Abend, weil, ich, fahre, nach Frankfurt, mit meiner Schwester, morgen, und, muss, aufstehen, sehr früh.

Kerstin: OK, ich, versuchen, ruhig zu sein, werde, wenn, von der Disco, später, ich, zurückkomme, damit, ich, nicht, aufwecke, dich.

Birgit: Gut. Viel Spaß!

[126] The rules for the position of *bloß* and *auch* are similar to those for *nicht* (see **22.1a**).

☞ **Other word-order related exercises are: word order after conjunctions (Ch. 25, Exs. 1–2); word order after relative pronouns (Ch. 9, Exs. 2–4); word order with modals (Ch. 21, Exs. 3–4); position of *nicht* (Ch. 22, Exs. 1–3); position of separable prefixes (Ch. 19, Exs. 1–3); and position of reflexive pronouns (Ch. 20, Exs. 2–3). For further exercises on word order see Revision Texts 1 (Exs. 4 and 5), 2 (Ex. 3), 3 (Ex. 2), 4 (Ex. 4) and 5 (Ex. 5).**

27 | Word formation

Trieben Schweinekoteletts Mozart in den Tod?

Nierensteine? Rheumatisches Fieber? Lungenentzündung? Alles Quatsch,
sagt ein amerikanischer Forscher: Wolfgang Amadeus Mozart starb an
seiner Vorliebe für Schweinefleisch.

    Die Worte sprechen für sich: „Und was rieche ich? . . .

5 Schweinekoteletts! Was für ein wundervoller Geschmack." 44 Tage bevor
ihn seine letztlich tödliche Krankheit heimsuchte, gestand Wolfgang
Amadeus Mozart in einem Brief an die Gemahlin seine Vorliebe für
Schweinekoteletts. Mehr als 200 Jahre später glaubt der Mediziner Jan
Hirschmann aus Seattle, genau hierin die Ursache für den mysteriösen Tod

10 des Musikgenies gefunden zu haben.

    Wie der Spezialist für Immunerkrankungen in einer achtseitigen
Abhandlung im renommierten US-Fachblatt „Archives of Internal Medicine"
berichtet, starb der Meister vermutlich an Trichinose, einer oftmals tödlich
verlaufenden Wurmerkrankung. Dabei fressen sich die Würmer, als Larven

15 verspeist, durch das Muskelgewebe der betroffenen Patienten. In
Hirschmanns Augen spricht vieles für die durch nicht ausreichend erhitztes
Schweinefleisch hervorgerufene Krankheit. Die bei Mozart beschriebenen
Symptome – hohes Fieber, Gliederschmerzen oder Muskelschwellungen –
werden allesamt auch von der Wurmerkrankung hervorgerufen. Zudem sei

20 Ende des 18. Jahrhunderts in Wien eine unbekannte Epidemie aufgetreten;
möglicherweise Trichinose, die in Europa erst im 19. Jahrhundert endgültig
diagnostiziert werden konnte.

    Im Fall Mozart scheint auch der zeitliche Rahmen zu stimmen. Der
Komponist erkrankte exakt 44 Tage, nachdem er seine Ode an das

25 Schweinekotelett verfasst hatte. Die Inkubationszeit bei Trichinose kann bis
zu 46 Tage betragen. 15 Tage nach dem Ausbruch der Krankheit, am 5.
Dezember 1791, starb der Künstler schließlich – ein durchaus plausibler
Krankheitsverlauf bei Trichinose.

Aus: *Der Spiegel (Online)*. 11. Juni 2001.

♀ Word formation in the text

This chapter deals with the way in which words are derived from other words in German. This is a highly complex issue, as there are usually different ways of deriving words of a similar meaning and there often is no apparent 'reason' for the choice of derivation (e.g. if we say *schlafen* → *der Schlaf* why are *essen* → **der Ess* or *trinken* → **der Trink* incorrect, the correct forms being *das Essen* and *das Getränk*?). Moreover, it is hardly ever the case that a German derivation corresponds to a single English equivalent. For these reasons, this chapter does not set out hard-and-fast rules for word formation in German but simply lists the most common forms of derivation which the student is encouraged to recognise.

27.1 THE FORMATION OF NOUNS

In German, nouns can be formed from other words (nouns, adjectives, verbs), usually by adding a suffix. The noun formation processes used in our text are listed below. Note that they usually have a particular gender associated with them:

27.1a -er (less commonly: -ler) added to verb stems and many nouns (gender: masculine)

These are used to denote a person who does something, e.g. as a **profession**: *forschen* → *der Forscher* 'researcher' (2); *Medizin* → *der Mediziner* 'medic' (8), *Kunst* → *der Künstler* 'artist'. Sometimes, as the last example shows, the stressed vowel is umlauted. The *-er* formation is particularly productive.[127]

With many words of Latin origin, **-ist** tends to be used instead of *-er/-ler*: *komponieren* → *der Komponist* (24), *spezialisieren* → *der Spezialist* (11).

[127] This means that the rule is still in operation today, rather than being a relic from the past. Thus, if new words enter the language the rule will apply to them where appropriate: e.g. Programmierer.

27.1b -in added to nouns (gender: feminine)

This is used productively to denote the **female** equivalent of nouns referring to masculine people and animals: e.g. *Gemahl* → *die Gemahlin* 'wife' (7). Similarly, the nouns in **27.1a** above referring to professions all have equivalents in *-in*: *die Forscherin, Künstlerin, Komponistin* etc. The addition of *-in* very often triggers umlaut.

27.1c -heit (less commonly: -keit[128]) added to adjectives (gender: feminine)

These are added to **adjectives** to form nouns denoting a particular quality, often corresponding to English '-ness' or '-ity', and are also very productive: *krank* → *die Krankheit* 'illness' (6, 17, 26). Other examples are: *die Gesundheit* 'healthiness/health', *die Schönheit* 'beauty', *die Traurigkeit* 'sadness'.

[128] Usually after -bar, -ig, -lich, -sam and sometimes after -el, -er. Occasionally, -igkeit is used: e.g. genau → Genauigkeit 'exactness'.

27.1d -ung added to verb stems (gender: feminine)

This is a very frequently used and productive suffix which derives nouns from verbs. It sometimes renders English '-ing' or '-ion', referring to the action described by the verb: e.g. *entzünden* → *die Lungenentzündung* 'lung infection' (1), *erkranken* → *die Erkrankung* 'disease'

(11, 14), *die Abhandlung* 'treatise' (12), *schwellen → die Muskelschwellung* 'swelling of the muscles' (18).

27.1e -e added to verb stems[129] (gender: feminine)

When added to verb stems, this can denote an action: e.g. *lieben → die Liebe* 'love', which appears in the text as *Vorliebe* (3, 7) meaning 'preference'. It can also refer to the instrument of an action: e.g. (not in text) *bürsten → die Bürste* 'hairbrush'. Only the latter of these processes (i.e. denoting an instrument) is productive.

> [129] *-e* (with umlaut) can also be added to adjectives to denote a quality, often corresponding to English '-th', yet this is no longer productive: e.g. *lang → die Länge* 'length', *breit → die Breite* 'width', *stark → die Stärke* 'strength'.

27.1f Verb stems used as nouns (gender: masculine)

These also denote an action and tend to be tend to be used with prefixed verbs (i.e. verbs with separable or inseparable prefixes): e.g. *verlaufen → der Krankheits**verlauf*** 'course of the illness' (28). Other examples are *anfangen → der **Anfang*** 'beginning', *beginnen → der **Beginn*** 'beginning'; and examples with simple (i.e. non-prefixed) verbs *schlafen → der **Schlaf**, schlagen → der **Schlag***. This is less productive than the addition of *-ung* to form nouns from verbs denoting the action of the verb (see **27.1d**).

27.1g Irregular noun formations

There are irregular noun derivations in this text which must be learned as exceptions: *der **Ge**schm**ack*** 'taste' (5) from *schmecken; der Ausbr**uch*** 'outbreak' (26) from *ausbrechen*.

See **27.5** for more noun-forming processes.

27.2 THE FORMATION OF ADJECTIVES

In German, adjectives can be formed from nouns, verbs and other adjectives in the following ways, as illustrated in the text. Note that all of these are common and productive:

27.2a -lich added to nouns (where possible, umlaut is usually added)

This often roughly corresponds to English '-ly': *Tod → töd**lich*** (6, and functioning as adverb in line 13) 'fatal/deadly', *Zeit → zeit**lich*** 'temporal/time' (23).

Less commonly, *-lich* can be added to **adjectives** and **verb stems**: *letzt- → leztlich* (6) 'finally', *vermuten → vermut**lich*** (13) 'presumably', *schließen → schließ**lich*** (27) 'finally', all of which are used as adverbs here.

27.2b -isch added to nouns (umlaut is sometimes added, less so than with -lich)

This is often used with geographical names, *Amerikaner → amerikan**isch*** (2) 'American', and with nouns of foreign origin *Rheumatismus → rheumat**isch*** (1) 'rheumatic'. When used with nouns of German origin it denotes a particular characteristic associated with that noun (and is often pejorative): e.g. (not in text) *Kind → kind**isch*** 'childish'.

27.2c -ig added to nouns (where possible, umlaut is usually added)

This usually denotes possession of a particular characteristic associated with the noun: *acht Seiten → achtseit**ig*** (11).

27.2d *-voll* added to nouns (no umlaut is added)

This corresponds to English '-ful': *Wunder* → *wunder**voll*** (5) 'wonderful'. The opposite is *-**los*** meaning '-less': e.g. (not in text) *Mühe* → *mühe**los*** 'effortless'.

27.2e *un-* prefixed to adjectives

As in English, this is used to denote the **negative** of the meaning of the adjective: *bekannt* → ***un**bekannt* (20) 'unknown'.

27.2f Past and present participles

This can be used (unchanged) as adjectives (or adverbs). Examples from the text are: past participles *renommiert* (12) 'renowned', *betroffen* (15) 'affected, *erhitzt* (16) 'heated', *hervorgerufen* (17) 'caused', *beschrieben* (17) 'described', *unbekannt* (20) 'unknown'; present participles *verlaufend* (14) 'developing', *ausreichend* (16) 'sufficient'.

See **27.6** for more adjective-forming processes.

27.3 THE FORMATION OF VERBS

The infinitive forms of German verbs are formed from nouns and adjectives by the addition of *-(e)**n*** (e.g. *Knie* → *knie**n*** 'to kneel', *Email* → *email**en*** 'to email', and, with umlaut, *Hammer* → *hämmer**n*** 'to hammer')[130] or, with verbs of Latin origin, *-**ieren*** (e.g. *Telefon* → *telefon**ieren***).[131] In addition, however, many nouns and adjectives also need the addition of a **prefix** to form their verbal equivalent (e.g. *Wasser* → ***be**wässern* 'to water') and this is always the case when verbs are derived from other verbs (e.g. *stehen* → ***ver**stehen* 'to understand'). Verb-forming prefixes can be either **separable** or **inseparable**. The most commonly used separable prefixes have already been discussed in **Chapter 19**. This chapter will deal primarily with inseparable prefixes.

---

[130] *-n* occurs after *-e, -el* and *-er*, and *-en* occurs elsewhere.

[131] Some verbs can be formed by adding *-eln* (usually with umlaut). This conveys the meaning 'to a lesser degree': e.g. *lachen* 'to laugh' vs. *lächeln* 'to smile'.

27.3a Inseparable prefixes[132]

i) ***be-*** added to verbs, nouns and adjectives. This is commonly used to form **transitive** verbs: e.g. *steigen* → *den Berg **be**steigen* 'to climb the mountain'. The meaning of the derived verb often differs from that of the original verb, however, as we can see in the text: *richten* → ***be**richten* (13) 'report', *treffen* → ***be**treffen* (15) 'affect', *schreiben* → ***be**schreiben* (17) 'describe', *tragen* → ***be**tragen* (26) 'amount to'.

ii) ***er-*** added to verbs, nouns and adjectives. This often expresses the **achievement** or **conclusion** of an action: e.g. *stechen* and *schießen* mean 'stab' and 'shoot' respectively, while ***er**stechen* and ***er**schießen* mean 'to stab/shoot to death'. When added to adjectives and nouns, it often denotes a **change of state**, as in the text: *krank* → ***er**kranken* (24) 'to become ill', *Hitze* → ***er**hitzen* (16) 'to heat up'.

iii) ***ent-*** added to verbs, nouns and adjectives. This often denotes **escaping** (e.g. ***ent**laufen* 'run away') or **removing** something (e.g. ***ent**decken* 'discover'), although this is not the case in the text: *zünden* 'ignite' → ***ent**zünden* 'become inflamed' (in text: *Entzündung* (1) 'inflammation').

iv) **ver-** added to verbs, nouns and adjectives. This often expresses the meaning of **dying away** (e.g. **ver**gehen 'wear off/fade') or to do something **wrongly**, especially when reflexive (e.g. *sich* **ver**planen 'plan badly'). Alternatively, when added to adjectives, it expresses a change of state (e.g. **ver**größern 'to enlarge'). In the text, however, it has a variety of functions, ranging from hardly affecting the meaning at all, *speisen* 'eat' → **ver**speisen (15) 'consume', *laufen* 'run' → **ver**laufen 'run/take one's course', to completely changing the meaning of the verb, *fassen* 'grasp' → **ver**fassen (25) 'write/compose'.

v) **zer-** added to verbs. This usually conveys the meaning of **in pieces**: e.g. (not from text) *reißen* → **zer**reißen 'rip to pieces'.

vi) **ge-** added to verbs. This is no longer productive and occurs with relatively few verbs. It is not associated with a particular meaning. There is one example of *ge-* in the text: *stehen* → **ge**stehen 'admit'.

---

[132] Some other prefixes which are commonly used inseparably are *hinter-* 'behind' (e.g. **hinter**gehen 'go behind someone's back'), *miss-* '-mis' (e.g. **miss**verstehen 'misunderstand'), *wider-* 'against' (e.g. **wider**sprechen 'contradict').

27.3b Separable prefixes

Separable prefixes (see **19.2–19.3**) in the text are: **aus**reichend (16), **hervor**gerufen (17, 19), **auf**getreten (20), **Aus**bruch (26) from the verb **aus**brechen. Similarly, *Heim* in **heim**suchen (6) 'strike/fall upon' is also acting as a separable prefix.

27.4 COMPOUNDING

27.4a Types of compound

A compound is a word made up of two or more words that can also be used independently, e.g. *das Haus + die Frau = die Hausfrau* 'housewife', the gender and plural form being determined by the last word in the compound. Compounds can consist of nouns (e.g. *die Hausfrau*), adjectives (e.g. *blaugrün* 'bluey-green' or 'blue and green'), verbs (e.g. *kennenlernen* 'to get to know'[133]) or a combination of these (e.g. noun + adjective *tierliebend* 'animal-loving'). The most common type of compound in German is the noun compound which consists of two or more nouns. In fact, German is famous for its noun compounds, some of which can be very long. Examples of compounds from the text are:

noun + noun	*das* **Musikgenie** (10) 'musical genius', *die* **Immunerkrankung** (11) 'disease of the immune system', *das* **Fachblatt** (12) 'specialist journal', *die* **Wurmerkrankung** (14, 19) 'disease caused by worms', *das* **Muskelgewebe** (15) 'muscle tissue', *die* **Muskelschwellung** (18) 'swelling of the muscles'.
noun + adjective	**endgültig** (21) 'final'
numeral + adjective	**achtseitig** (11) 'eight-page'

---

[133] Here the infinitive form of the verb is used but it is much more common to have the verb stem as the first element of the compound: e.g. **Putz**frau 'cleaning lady'. Occasionally the verb stem may have an -e ending: e.g. *Bade*wanne 'bathtub', *Lese*brille 'reading glasses'.

As can be seen from the English translations, German compounds very often do not correspond to compounds in English but to hyphenated words or even whole phrases.

27.4b Linking elements

Compounding in German is further complicated by the fact that many compounds have a particular element linking the two halves of the compound, the use of which is not always predictable. For instance, the first word in the compound may have a suffix which looks like a noun plural ending (and have umlaut if the plural form has umlaut): e.g. 'bookshelf' is not *Buchregal but B**üch**e**r**regal. There are many examples of this type in the text:

der Niere**n**stein (1) 'gallstone'[134]   das Schwein**e**kotlett (5, 8, 25) 'pork chop'
die Lunge**n**entzündung (1) 'lung infection'   der Glied**er**schmerz (18) 'aching limbs'
das Schwein**e**fleisch (3, 17) 'pork'

Alternatively, a linking *-s* (or *-es* after words of one syllable) may appear: e.g. *Freund**es**kreis* 'circle of friends'[135]. Examples from the text are:

die Inkubation**s**zeit (25) 'incubation period', der Krankheit**s**verlauf (28) 'course of the illness'

[134] Nouns ending in -e regularly have -en in compounds if their plural also has -en.

[135] -s is the norm after noun-forming suffixes like -(k)eit, -ion, -ung, -ling and -tät.

Other points to note in the text

- Extended attributes: *einer **oftmals tödlich verlaufenden** Wurmerkrankung* (13–14), *die **durch nicht ausreichend erhitztes Schweinefleisch hervorgerufene** Krankheit* (16–17), *die **bei Mozart beschriebenen** Symptome* (17–18) (see **5.3**).
- *hier* + preposition, meaning 'this': *hierin* (9) (see **8.5**).
- Pluperfect: *verfasst hatte* (25) (see **Ch. 14**).
- Subjunctive: ***sei*** . . . *aufgetreten* (19–20) indicating reported speech (see **Ch. 17**).
- Prepositions with dative versus accusative: ***an*** + dat. (2–3, 13) vs. ***an*** + acc. (7); ***in*** + dat. (7, 11, 12, 21) vs. ***in*** + acc. (title) (see **24.1b**).
- *Was für* 'what (a)' always takes the nominative, even though *für* on its own takes the accusative: *Was für **ein** wundervoll**er** Geschmack* (5).
- Word order: i) accusative object is last element in the clause, *seine Vorliebe für Schweinekotletts* (7–8) (see **26.2b**); ii) pronoun precedes noun, *bevor **ihn** seine letztlich tödliche Krankheit heimsuchte* (5–6) (see **26.9b**); iii) expression of time precedes expression of place, *Ende des 18. Jahrhunderts in Wien* (20), but the opposite occurs later: *in Europa erst im 19. Jahrhundert* (21) to emphasise the expression of time – i.e. 'not until (as late as) the nineteenth century' (see **26.3**).

▲ *Discover more about word formation*

27.5 NOUNS

Other common ways of deriving nouns from other parts of speech are as follows:

27.5a Infinitive form of the verb (gender: neuter)

This is an extremely frequent and productive way of deriving nouns which refer to the action described by the verb. It very often corresponds to an English present participle in '-ing', e.g. *schlafen* → *das* **Schlafen** 'sleeping', and can apply to verbs which already have a derived noun (e.g. *der Schlaf* 'sleep') to make it clear that it is an **action** that is being referred to. Other examples are: *das* **Trinken** 'drinking', *das* **Rauchen** 'smoking', *das* **Essen**, meaning either 'eating' or 'food'.

27.5b *-chen* (or *-lein*[136]) added to nouns (gender: neuter)

These suffixes denote the **diminutive** form of a noun, meaning 'little', either in the literal sense of 'small' or when used as a term of endearment (or, in some contexts, condescension). The stressed vowel is umlauted where possible: e.g. *das Glas* → *das* **Glä**s**chen** 'little glass', *der Korb* → *das* **Körb**chen** 'little basket'. Nouns ending in *-e* drop it before the diminutive suffix: e.g. *die Tüte* → *das Tüt***chen** 'little bag'.

> [136] In standard German *-lein* is used after nouns ending in *-ch* and *-g* (e.g. *Bach* → *Bäch***lein** 'little stream'). In poetic language it is used more.

27.5c *-ei* added to nouns (gender: feminine)

This denotes the **place** where someone works: e.g. *der Bäcker* → *die Bäcker***ei** 'bakery', *der Abt* → *die Abt***ei** 'abbey'.

27.5d *-erei* added to verb stems (gender: feminine)

This denotes a repeated (often irritating) action, corresponding to English '-ing' used in a pejorative way: e.g. *herumfahren* → *die Herumfahr***erei** 'the driving around'.

27.5e Other less frequent suffixes

The following suffixes occur less frequently than those listed in **27.5b–d**:

i) *-***ling** (masc.) which productively denotes a person associated with a particular characteristic, e.g. *feige* → *der Feig***ling** 'coward';

ii) *-***nis** (fem. or neut.) which derives abstract nouns from verbs and adjectives but is no longer productive, e.g. *sich ereignen* → *das Ereig***nis** 'event';

iii) *-***schaft** (fem.) which is productively added to nouns (and to adjectives, but not productively) to denote a collective, e.g. *Mann* → *die Mann***schaft** 'team', or state, corresponding to English '-ship' or '-hood', e.g. *Mutter* → *die Mutter***schaft** 'motherhood';

iv) *-***tum** (neut.) which is productively added to nouns (and to adjectives, but not productively) referring to persons and expresses a characteristic or collective, e.g. *Heiden* → *das Heiden***tum** means both 'heathenism' and 'heathens'.

27.5f Ge- ... (-e) added to nouns (gender: neuter)

This denotes **collective nouns**. It is used with umlaut where possible (and *e* becomes *i*): e.g. *Berg* → *das Gebirge* 'mountain range', *Tier* → *das Getier* 'creatures', *Stein* → *das Gestein* '(layer of) stones'. Often the final -*e* is absent.

When used with a **verb** stem (and without umlaut), this has the same meaning as -*erei* (see **27.5d**): e.g. *schreien* → *das Geschrei* 'shouting/screaming'.

27.5g Prefixes

Some frequently used prefixes used to derive nouns from other nouns are: *mit*-, corresponding to English 'co-', 'fellow' etc. (e.g. *der Mitbewohner* 'fellow occupant/flatmate'), *nicht*-, corresponding to English 'non-' (e.g. *der Nichtraucher* 'non-smoker') and *scheiß*-, literally 'shit', which is often used in colloquial German to express displeasure (e.g. *die Scheißarbeit* 'the shitty job').

27.6 ADJECTIVES

Adjective formations not dealt with in the text are:

27.6a -*bar* added to verb stems (no umlaut)

This is extremely productive and usually corresponds to English '-able'/'-ible', e.g. *machen* → *machbar* 'doable', *lesen* → *lesbar* 'legible', or to a passive in English, e.g. *erreichen* → *Er ist nicht erreichbar* 'He cannot be reached'.

27.6b -*mäßig* added to nouns (no umlaut)

This is also very productive and has a variety of meanings, the most common being 'relating to/according to', e.g. *Gesetz* → *gezetzmäßig* 'according to the law/legal', and '-like', e.g. *Schüler* → *schülermäßig* 'like a school pupil'.

27.6c Less productive suffixes

There are a small number of less productive adjective-forming suffixes: -*en* (with some words -*ern* + umlaut) added to nouns denoting a material, e.g. *Gold* → *golden* 'golden', *Holz* → *hölzern* 'wooden'; -*haft* added to nouns to describe a quality associated with the noun, e.g. *Märchen* → *märchenhaft* 'like a fairy-tale'; -*sam* added to verb stems or nouns to express a tendency, *schweigen* → *schweigsam* 'taciturn/quiet'.

✎ EXERCISES

Vocabulary topic: *Berufe*

1 Form words for professions based on the verbs and nouns below. Give first the masculine and then the feminine form:

1 lehren	5 Garten	9 malen	13 Piano
2 arbeiten	6 Physik	10 Wissenschaft	14 Gitarre
3 backen	7 Sport	11 komponieren	15 Trommel
4 tanzen	8 übersetzen	12 Politik	16 Tisch

2 Give the female equivalent of the following professions:

1 Chef	4 Bauer	7 Professor	10 Psychologe
2 Arzt	5 Sänger	8 Putzmann	11 Anwalt
3 Koch	6 Dozent	9 Kellner	12 Schriftsteller

3 Find an appropriate compound noun to fit the description of the following professions. Note that some of these may require linking elements:

Example: Er pflegt Kranke.

Answer: Krankenpfleger.

1 Er spielt Fußball.

2 Er arbeitet in einem Büro.

3 Sie führt eine Gruppe.

4 Sie ist Professorin an der Universität.

5 Er ist ein Arzt, der sich auf Kinder spezialisiert.

6 Er ist ein Beamter, der für Sicherhheit verantwortlich ist.

7 Er fährt einen Bus.

8 Er verkauft Autos.

9 Sie lehrt Schwimmen.

10 Sie leitet eine Abteilung.

FURTHER EXERCISES

4 a Translate the following groups of words into English:

1 Haus, Häuschen, häuslich, Häuslichkeit.

2 Mann, männlich, Männlichkeit, mannhaft, Mannschaft, bemannen.

3 lesen, Leser, Lesung, lesbar, Lesbarkeit, Leserschaft, sich verlesen.

4 Freund, Freundin, unfreundlich, Freundlichkeit, befreunden.

5 Macht, machtlos, mächtig, Mächtigkeit, entmachten.

6 reden, Rede, Reden, Gerede, Rederei, Redner, rednerisch.

7 fühlen, fühlbar, Fühler, Gefühl, gefühlvoll, gefühllos.

8 brechen, unbrechbar, zerbrechen, zerbrechlich, Zerbrechlichkeit.

9 schlagen, Schlag, Schläger, Schlägerei, unschlagbar, erschlagen, zerschlagen.

10 sprechen, Sprecher, Sprache, sprachlos, Sprachlosigkeit, besprechen, Besprechung, entsprechen, versprechen, sich versprechen, widersprechen.

4 b Show the gender of the nouns above by adding the appropriate definite article.

5 Make compounds out of the following pairs of words, adding linking elements where required. Give the gender of the compound noun and translate your answers into English:

1 Haus, Tür	6 Kleid, Schrank	11 Buch, Regal
2 wohnen, Zimmer	7 bügeln, Brett	12 Sicherheit, Schloss
3 baden, Zimmer	8 Gast, Zimmer	13 alt, Papier
4 Straße, Lampe	9 Bett, Decke	14 Wohnung, Suche
5 Küche, Fenster	10 Hund, Haus	15 gefrieren, Truhe

☞ **For further exercises on deriving nouns see Revision Text 3, Ex. 4.**

28 | Punctuation and spelling

Text

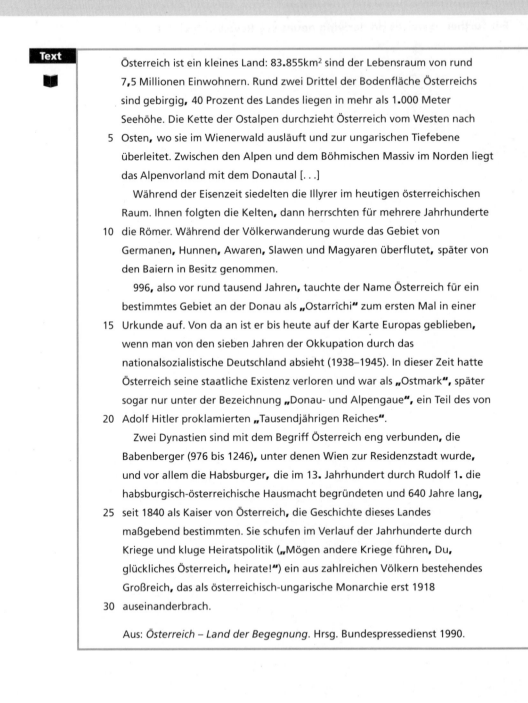

Österreich ist ein kleines Land: 83.855km² sind der Lebensraum von rund 7,5 Millionen Einwohnern. Rund zwei Drittel der Bodenfläche Österreichs sind gebirgig, 40 Prozent des Landes liegen in mehr als 1.000 Meter Seehöhe. Die Kette der Ostalpen durchzieht Österreich vom Westen nach
5 Osten, wo sie im Wienerwald ausläuft und zur ungarischen Tiefebene überleitet. Zwischen den Alpen und dem Böhmischen Massiv im Norden liegt das Alpenvorland mit dem Donautal [. . .]

Während der Eisenzeit siedelten die Illyrer im heutigen österreichischen Raum. Ihnen folgten die Kelten, dann herrschten für mehrere Jahrhunderte
10 die Römer. Während der Völkerwanderung wurde das Gebiet von Germanen, Hunnen, Awaren, Slawen und Magyaren überflutet, später von den Baiern in Besitz genommen.

996, also vor rund tausend Jahren, tauchte der Name Österreich für ein bestimmtes Gebiet an der Donau als „Ostarrîchi" zum ersten Mal in einer
15 Urkunde auf. Von da an ist er bis heute auf der Karte Europas geblieben, wenn man von den sieben Jahren der Okkupation durch das nationalsozialistische Deutschland absieht (1938–1945). In dieser Zeit hatte Österreich seine staatliche Existenz verloren und war als „Ostmark", später sogar nur unter der Bezeichnung „Donau- und Alpengaue", ein Teil des von
20 Adolf Hitler proklamierten „Tausendjährigen Reiches".

Zwei Dynastien sind mit dem Begriff Österreich eng verbunden, die Babenberger (976 bis 1246), unter denen Wien zur Residenzstadt wurde, und vor allem die Habsburger, die im 13. Jahrhundert durch Rudolf 1. die habsburgisch-österreichische Hausmacht begründeten und 640 Jahre lang,
25 seit 1840 als Kaiser von Österreich, die Geschichte dieses Landes maßgebend bestimmten. Sie schufen im Verlauf der Jahrhunderte durch Kriege und kluge Heiratspolitik („Mögen andere Kriege führen, Du, glückliches Österreich, heirate!") ein aus zahlreichen Völkern bestehendes Großreich, das als österreichisch-ungarische Monarchie erst 1918
30 auseinanderbrach.

Aus: *Österreich – Land der Begegnung.* Hrsg. Bundespressedienst 1990.

♀ **Punctuation and spelling in the text**

28.1 PUNCTUATION

On the whole, German punctuation is fairly similar to that of English: e.g. using a capital letter at the beginning of a sentence and a full stop at the end. There are, however, a couple of areas of divergence which may cause problems for English learners of German: the use of capitals for nouns, and the use of commas.

28.1a Use of capitals for nouns

In English, capital letters are used for proper nouns (i.e. names of people, places, titles etc., e.g. 'Mary', 'England', 'Prime Minister') while in German they are used for **all nouns** (including nouns derived from other parts of speech, such as adjectives and verbs). Some examples from the text are: **Ö**sterreich (line 1), **L**and (1), **L**ebensraum (1), **E**inwohnern (2), **B**odenfläche (2), **M**eter (3). This also applies to numerals and fractions used as nouns, e.g. **M**illionen (2), zwei **D**rittel (2), and to points of the compass used as nouns, e.g. vom **W**esten nach **O**sten (4–5), im **N**orden (6).

By contrast, with certain exceptions (see **28.3**), *adjectives* are usually not capitalised, even when they are derived from the names of countries: **ungarischen** Tiefebene (5), **österreichischen** Raum (8–9). Such adjectives would always have a capital letter in English: e.g. 'Austrian', 'English', 'French'. In German, they are only capitalised when they form part of a title: e.g. dem **B**öhmischen Massiv (6).

28.1b Commas

i) In general, commas are used in German to **separate one clause with a finite verb from another**. Examples from the text are (with the finite verbs underlined):

- *Rund zwei Drittel der Bodenfläche Österreichs <u>sind</u> gebirgig, 40 Prozent des Landes <u>liegen</u> in mehr als 1.000 Meter Seehöhe (2–4)*
- *Die Kette der Ostalpen <u>durchzieht</u> Österreich vom Westen nach Osten, wo sie im Wienerwald <u>ausläuft</u> . . . (4–5)*
- *Von da an <u>ist</u> er bis heute auf der Karte Europas geblieben, wenn man von den sieben Jahren der Okkupation durch das nationalsozialistische Deutschland <u>absieht</u> . . . (15–17)*

In English, commas may be used after introductory parts of the sentence not containing a finite verb: e.g. 'After a long discussion(,) they decided to go'. This is not permissible in German: *Während der Eisenzeit siedelten die Illyrer im heutigen österreichischen Raum* (8–9), where a comma after *Eisenzeit* would not be possible.

ii) Commas are not used before **und and oder** when the subject is **omitted** from the second clause but still understood: *wo sie im Wienerwald ausläuft und* [*sie* omitted] *zur ungarischen Tiefebene überleitet* (5–6).

iii) Commas always **precede relative pronouns** (see **Ch. 9**):[137]

- *die Habsburger, <u>die</u> im 13. Jahrhundert durch Rudolf 1. die habsburgisch-österreichische Hausmacht begründeten . . . (23–24)*

- *Großreich, das als österreichisch-ungarische Monarchie erst 1918 auseinanderbrach.* (29–30)
- *die Babenberger [...], unter denen Wien zur Residenzstadt wurde ...* (21–22)

iv) As in English, commas are often used in German to '**bracket off**' additional information or comments:

- *996, also vor rund tausend Jahren, tauchte der Name ...* (13)
- *und war als „Ostmark", später sogar nur unter der Bezeichnung „Donau- und Alpengaue", ein Teil des ... Reiches.* (18–20)

This does not apply to adverbial phrases such as 'however', 'above all', 'after all', 'incidentally' etc., which are often 'bracketed off' in English: *und **vor allem** die Habsburger* (23), contrast: 'and, above all, the Habsburgs'.

v) Commas are used to separate items on a **list**: *Während der Völkerwanderung wurde das Gebiet von Germanen, Hunnen, Awaren, Slawen und Magyaren überflutet* (10–11). This also happens with adjectives (e.g. *ein kalter, nasser Tag*).

vi) Where a **decimal point** is used in English, German uses a comma: *7,5 Millionen* (2). Conversely, full stops are used to indicate thousands, where English would use a comma: *1.000 Meter* (3).

> [137] Similarly, a comma is placed before subordinating conjunctions and interrogatives used indirectly, even where the preceding elements do not form a proper clause: e.g. *Egal, wer das gesagt hat.*

28.1c Further notes on punctuation

- Quotation marks in German usually take the form „ ", e.g. *„Ostmark"* (18) *„Donau- und Alpengaue"* (19). In some texts, however, « » or » « is preferred (see **Ch. 5, Ex. 4**, **Ch. 13, Ex. 4**).[138]
- Ordinal numbers, e.g. '1st', '2nd', '3rd', '4th', are indicated by placing a full stop after the number: *im 13. Jahrhundert durch Rudolf 1.* (23).
- The exclamation mark is used similarly in German and English. In the above text it follows a command: *Du, glückliches Österreich, heirate!* (27–28).
- Colons are used similarly in German and English, e.g. meaning 'that means': *ein kleines Land: 83.855km²* (1).[139] Semi-colons are much less frequent in German (note the lack of examples in the text).
- Hyphens are used to indicate that the second part of a compound word has been omitted to avoid repetition: *Donau- und Alpengaue* (instead of repeating *Donau**gaue** und Alpengaue* (19)). Otherwise they are used as in English, e.g. *österreichisch-ungarische Monarchie* (29).

> [138] The use of " ", as in English, is becoming increasingly common in German texts on the Internet.

> [139] And also before direct speech when the preceding verb is a verb of saying: e.g. *Er sagte: „Ich liebe dich"* (see also **Ch. 17, Ex. 1**).

28.2 SPELLING

The main difficulty for foreign learners of German is knowing when to use the letter *ß*, sometimes referred to as the *scharfes s* or the *eszet*, and when to use *ss*. The rules for the usage of these alternatives have recently been changed as part of the current spelling reform, which states that *ß* **should only be used after long vowels and diphthongs**. In the text there are two examples of this: *maßgebend* (26) and *Großreich* (29), both of which have *ß* following a long vowel. In older texts you will find uses of *ß* which do not conform to the above rules, i.e. after short vowels, for instance in *daß* and *muß* (now spelt *dass* and *muss*). The forms with *ß* after short vowels are now seen as older spellings and will soon no longer be permissible.

Other points to note in the text

- Plural verb with numerals and expressions of quantity: *83.855km² **sind*** (1), *40 Prozent des Landes **liegen*** (3).
- Use of plural with *Million*: *7,5 Million**en** Einwohnern* (7).
- Use of genitive with place names: *Bodenfläche Österreich**s*** (2), *Karte Europa**s*** (15) (see **3.1a(iv)** and footnote 13).
- Extended attributes: *ein Teil des **von Adolf Hitler proklamierten** „Tausendjährigen Reiches"* (19–20), *ein **aus zahlreichen Völkern bestehendes** Großreich* (28–29) (see **5.3**).
- Preposition with scope over two nouns: ***zwischen** <u>den</u> Alpen und <u>dem</u> Böhmischen Massiv* (6) (see **24.1c**).
- Dates used without the preposition *in*: *996* (13), *erst 1918* (29).[140]

---

[140] It is a common error of English speakers to include *in* before dates, as in English: e.g. *1914 brach der Krieg aus* (not **In 1914...*).

▲ *Discover more about punctuation and spelling*

28.3 PLACE NAMES AS ADJECTIVES

As stated above, adjectives are not capitalised unless they form part of a title, which means that adjectives derived from the names of **countries** have a small letter in German and a capital in English: e.g. *meine **d**eutsche Freundin* vs. 'my **G**erman friend'. Adjectives in *-er* derived from **town names** do begin with a capital letter, however: e.g. *meine **L**ondoner Kollegin* vs. *meine **e**nglische Kollegin*.

28.4 REFORM OF SPELLING AND PUNCTUATION[141]

Some aspects of punctuation and spelling have been affected by the recent German spelling reform. This book uses only the new spelling/punctuation, and students who have learned the older system should be aware of the new rules.

---

[141] For full details of the spelling/punctuation reform see DUDEN, *Die deutsche Rechtschreibung* (Mannheim: Bibliographisches Institut, 2000) or Hertha Beuschel-Menze and Frohmut Menze, *Die neue Rechtschreibung* (Reinbek: Rowholt, 1996).

i) Comma before **und**. A comma is no longer obligatory between clauses connected by *und*, even when the second clause contains an overt subject: e.g. *Er öffnete den Wein und <u>sie</u> holte die Gläser*. Formerly, the comma could only be dropped if the subject of the second clause was omitted (see **28.1b(ii)**). Of course, if *und* is followed by a subordinating conjunction, a comma must be used: e.g. *Ich gab ihm ein Bier, und <u>während</u> er trank . . .*

ii) Clauses with **infinitives** and **participles**. These were formerly divided off by commas: e.g. *Ich habe versucht, mit dir <u>zu sprechen</u>*. According to the new rules, however, commas are **no longer obligatory** before or after these types of clause, even when they are quite long, e.g. *Ich habe versucht(,) dich mit meinem neuen Handy <u>anzurufen</u>*, provided that their omission does not impede the reader's understanding of the sentence.

iii) Use of *ß*. As outlined in **28.2** above, this is to be used after long vowels and diphthongs: e.g. *Fuß* vs. *ich mu**ss***.

iv) Capitals. Nouns in set phrases which were formerly written with a small letter must be capitalised as part of the general rule that all nouns should begin with a capital letter: e.g. *in bezug auf* becomes *in **B**ezug auf*.

v) If three consonants come together in a compound it is no longer required to delete one: e.g. *Schiff* plus *Fahrt* becomes *Schi**fff**ahrt* (formerly *Schiffahrt*).

vi) Compounds ending in a verb or adjective tend to be written as two **separate** words, e.g. *radfahren, eislaufen* become *Rad fahren, Eis laufen*.

vii) The spelling of certain individual words has been changed to reflect their grammatical relatedness to other words: e.g. *potentiell* has become *poten**z**iell* because of *Potenz*.

28.5 PUNCTUATION IN LETTER WRITING

German letters, both formal and informal, have certain features of punctuation which English speakers must be aware of:

i) Formal headings of address may be followed by an **exclamation mark**, e.g. *Lieber Karl!*, although this is becoming slightly old-fashioned and is now usually replaced by a comma, as in English.

ii) If a comma is used after a form of address, the first sentence of the letter does **not begin with a capital letter**: e.g.

Lieber Karl,
es tut mir Leid, dass ich seit langem nicht geschrieben habe.

iii) One often finds the pronoun *du* (and related *dich, dein* etc.) capitalised in older letters. This practice has now been dropped as part of the spelling reform.

✎ EXERCISES

Vocabulary topic: *deutsche Geschichte*

1 Add the necessary punctuation: capital letters, full stops, commas, quotation marks, and change *ss* to *ß* where appropriate:

1914 In europa beginnt der erste weltkrieg.

1917 Nach der abdankung des zaren im frühjahr übernehmen in der oktoberrevolution die bolschewiki unter lenin die macht in russland.

1918 Deutschland wird republik.

1933 Hitler wird reichskanzler. Der aufbau des terroristischen führerstaates beginnt.

1939 Deutschland überfällt polen. Der zweite weltkrieg bricht aus.

1942 Auf der wannseekonferenz beschliessen die nazis die juden ganz europas systematisch zu ermorden.

1945 Hitler begeht selbstmord. Der zweite weltkrieg endet mit deutschlands bedingungsloser kapitulation.

1949 Das grundgesetz für die bundesrepublik deutschland wird verabschiedet. In ost-berlin nimmt der volkskongress die verfassung der deutschen demokratischen republik an.

1953 Im märz stirbt der sowjetische diktator josef stalin. Im juni wird ein arbeiteraufstand in der ddr von russischen truppen brutal niedergeschlagen.

1961 Die führung der ddr lässt die berliner mauer errichten.

1962 Die kuba-krise bringt die welt an den rand des atomkriegs.

1965 Die usa schicken verstärkt soldaten nach vietnam. Der krieg eskaliert.

1968 Schwere studentenunruhen in der bundesrepublik richten sich gegen notstandsgesetzgebung vietnamkrieg und spiesserrepublik.

1977 Der terror der RAF erreicht in einer beispiellosen serie von attentaten seinen höhepunkt.

1985 Michail gorbatschow generalsekretär des zk der kpdsu verkündet das reformprogramm der perestrojka.

1989 Das sozialistische regime der ddr bricht nach 40 jahren herrschaft zusammen.

1990 Die wiedererrichteten länder der ddr treten am 3 oktober der brd bei.

1991 In jugoslawien bricht der bürgerkrieg aus.

1993 Mit dem inkrafttreten des vertrags von maastricht entsteht die europäische union deren ziel ein wirtschaftlich und sozial geeintes europa ist.

Aus: *Der Stern – History (Online)*, 31 January 2001.

2 Insert commas where necessary:

Doch der Vormarsch der Alliierten ging an allen Fronten wenn auch von Stockungen begleitet etappenweise voran. Im Februar und März 1945 eroberten sie die linksrheinischen Gebiete Deutschlands. Nachdem amerikanische Truppen am 7. März bei Remagen und britische Einheiten am 24. März bei Wesel den Rhein überschritten hatten rückten die Amerikaner (zusammen mit der 1. französischen Armee) nach Süddeutschland vor. Sie besetzten auch Vorarlberg Tirol bis zum Brenner das Salzkammergut Oberösterreich und den Westen Böhmens bis zur Linie Karlsbad-Budweis-Linz. Im Norden erreichten die Engländer am 19. April 1945 die Elbe bei Lauenburg während amerikanische Verbände ins Zentrum des Reiches vorstießen und am 25. April 1945 mit den Sowjets bei Torgau zusammentrafen. Weiterzumarschieren lehnte der alliierte Oberbefehlshaber General Eisenhower jedoch aus politischen und militärischen Gründen ab da er sich mit der Masse seiner Streitkräfte der Eroberung des deutschen „Alpen-Reduit" einem von den Alliierten ernstgenommenen Propagandaprodukt der Nationalsozialismus zuwenden wollte.

Der Osten des Reiches wurde im Zeitraum vom Januar bis zum Mai 1945 von der sowjetischen Armee erobert vor der Millionen von Deutschen unter unsagbaren Leiden nach Westen zu fliehen versuchten. Dabei schützten die Reste des deutschen Ostheeres „in einem ganz elementaren Sinne die Menschen in . . . [den] preußisch-deutschen Ostprovinzen" [1099: A. Hillgruber] vor der furchtbaren Rache der heranrückenden Roten Armee und trugen damit unauflöslich verbunden doch gleichzeitig dazu bei die Existenz des nationalsozialistischen Unrechtsregimes zu verlängern.

Aus: Klaus Hildebrand, *Das Dritte Reich*. © 1987 R. Oldenbourg Verlag GmbH.

☞ **For further exercises on commas see Revision Text 4, Ex. 5.**

Appendix 1: Common strong and irregular verbs[142]

Infinitive[143]	Past Stem[144]	Past Participle[145]	
backen	backte[146]	gebacken	*bake*
befehlen (du befiehlst, er befiehlt)	befahl	befohlen	*command*
beginnen	begann	begonnen	*begin*
beißen	biss (bisse)	gebissen	*bite*
bersten (es birst *or* berstet)	barst	geborsten	*burst*
betrügen	betrog	betrogen	*deceive*
biegen	bog	(ist)$_{Int.}$ gebogen	*bend*
bieten	bot	geboten	*offer*
binden	band (bände)	gebunden	*bind*
bitten	bat (bäte)	gebeten	*ask for/request*
blasen (du bläst, er bläst)	blies	geblasen	*blow*
bleiben	blieb (bliebe)	ist geblieben	*stay*
braten (du brätst, er brät)	briet	gebraten	*roast/fry*
brechen (du brichst, er bricht)	brach (bräche)	(ist)$_{Int.}$ gebrochen	*break*
brennen	brannte	gebrannt	*burn*
bringen	brachte (brächte)	gebracht	*bring/take*
denken	dachte (dächte)	gedacht	*think*
dringen	drang	(ist)$_{Int.}$ gedrungen	*penetrate*
dürfen (ich/er darf, du darfst)	durfte (dürfte)	gedurft	*be allowed*

[142] Verbs beginning with a **prefix** are usually derived from basic verbs and, consequently, often have the same irregularities as the basic verbs: e.g. **ver**stehen is like stehen (ich verstand, ich habe verstanden), **an**kommen is like kommen (ich kam an, ich bin angekommen). For this reason, it is not necessary to include all prefixed verbs in the following list.

[143] Irregularities in the present tense are given in brackets after the infinitive. Note that the forms with er also occur with sie 'she' and es. The es-form is given instead of du and er where it is most appropriate to the context.

[144] This is used in the ich- and er/sie/es- forms. The other persons need additional endings: e.g. du befahl**st**, wir/sie/Sie befahl**en**, ihr befahl**t**. The same applies to the Konjunktiv II stems given in brackets after the past stems. Only Konjunktiv II stems which are still in use are included, although note that many of these sound stilted if used in spoken German (see **16.3b** for usage). Archaic forms are omitted.

[145] If a verb takes sein in the (plu)perfect, this is indicated by ist, otherwise it takes haben. Verbs which take haben when used transitively but sein when used intransitively (see **13.3b** for details) are marked (ist)$_{Int.}$.

[146] Older form: buk.

erschrecken (du erschrickst, er erschrickt)	erschrak	ist erschrocken	*be frightened*[147]
essen (du/er isst)	aß (äße)	gegessen	*eat*
fahren (du fährst, er fährt)	fuhr (führe)	(ist)_{Int.} gefahren	*go/drive*
fallen (du fällst, er fällt)	fiel (fiele)	ist gefallen	*fall*
fangen (du fängst, er fängt)	fing (finge)	gefangen	*catch*
finden	fand (fände)	gefunden	*find*
fliegen	flog (flöge)	(ist)_{Int.} geflogen	*fly*
fliehen	floh	ist geflohen	*flee*
fließen	floss	ist geflossen	*flow*
fressen (du/er frisst)	fraß	gefressen	*eat (of animals)*
frieren	fror	(ist)_{Int.} gefroren	*freeze*
gebären	gebar	geboren	*give birth*
geben (du gibst, er gibt)	gab (gäbe)	gegeben	*give*
gedeihen	gedieh	ist gediehen	*thrive*
gehen	ging (ginge)	ist gegangen	*go*
gelingen	gelang (gelänge)	ist gelungen	*succeed*
gelten (es gilt)	galt	gegolten	*be valid*
genießen	genoss	genossen	*enjoy*
geschehen (es geschieht)	geschah (geschähe)	ist geschehen	*happen*
gewinnen	gewann	gewonnen	*win*
gießen	goss	gegossen	*pour*
gleichen	glich (gliche)	geglichen	*resemble*
gleiten	glitt	ist geglitten	*slide/glide*
graben (du gräbst, er gräbt)	grub	gegraben	*dig*
greifen	griff (griffe)	gegriffen	*grasp/seize*
haben (du hast, er hat)	hatte (hätte)	gehabt	*have*
halten (du hältst, er hält)	hielt (hielte)	gehalten	*hold*
hängen[148] (du hängst, er hängt)	hing (hinge)	gehangen	*hang*
heben	hob	gehoben	*lift*
heißen	hieß (hieße)	geheißen	*be called*
helfen (du hilftst, er hilft)	half	geholfen	*help*
kennen	kannte	gekannt	*know*
klingen	klang (klänge)	geklungen	*sound*
kommen	kam (käme)	ist gekommen	*come*
können (ich/er kann, du kannst)	konnte (könnte)	gekonnt	be able
kriechen	kroch	ist gekrochen	*creep/crawl*
laden (du lädst, er lädt)	lud	geladen	*load*
lassen (du/er lässt)	ließ (ließe)	gelassen	*let*

---

[147] The transitive verb (*jemanden*) *erschrecken* 'to frighten (s.o.)' is regular: *erschreckte, erschreckt*.

[148] The transitive verb (*etwas*) *hängen* 'to hang (sth.)' is regular: *hängte, gehängt*.

laufen (du läufst, er läuft)	lief (liefe)	(ist)_{Int.} gelaufen	*run*
leiden	litt (litte)	gelitten	*suffer*
leihen	lieh (liehe)	geliehen	*lend/borrow*
lesen (du/er liest)	las	gelesen	*read*
liegen	lag	gelegen	*lie*
lügen	log	gelogen	*tell lies*
mahlen	mahlte	gemahlen	*grind*
meiden	mied (miede)	gemieden	*avoid*
messen (du/er misst)	maß	gemessen	*measure*
mögen (ich/er mag, du magst)	mochte (möchte)	gemocht	*like*
müssen (ich/er muss, du musst)	musste (müsste)	gemusst	*have to/must*
nehmen (du nimmst, er nimmt)	nahm (nähme)	genommen	*take*
nennen	nannte	gennant	*call/name*
pfeifen	pfiff (pfiffe)	gepfiffen	*whistle*
preisen	pries (priese)	gepriesen	*praise*
raten (du rätst, er rät)	riet (riete)	geraten	*advise*
reiben	rieb (riebe)	gerieben	*rub*
reißen	riss (risse)	(ist)_{Int.} gerissen	*tear/rip*
reiten	ritt (ritte)	(ist)_{Int.} geritten	*ride (a horse)*
rennen	rannte	(ist)_{Int.} gerannt	*run/race*
riechen	roch	gerochen	*smell*
rufen	rief (riefe)	gerufen	*shout/call*
salzen	salzte	gesalzen	*salt*
saufen	soff	gesoffen	*drink (of animals)/ booze*
saugen	saugte/sog	gesaugt/gesogen	*suck*
schaffen	schuf	geschaffen	*create*[149]
scheiden	schied (schiede)	(ist)_{Int.} geschieden	*separate/depart*
scheinen	schien (schiene)	geschienen	*shine/seem*
scheißen	schiss (schisse)	geschissen	*shit*
schelten (du schiltst, er schilt)	schalt	gescholten	*scold*
scheren	schor	geschoren	*shear/clip*
schieben	schob	geschoben	*shove/push*
schießen	schoss	(ist)_{Int.} geschossen	*shoot*
schlafen (du schläfst, er schläft)	schlief (schliefe)	geschlafen	*sleep*
schlagen (du schlägst, er schlägt)	schlug (schlüge)	geschlagen	*hit/strike/beat*
schleichen	schlich (schliche)	ist geschlichen	*creep*
schließen	schloss (schlösse)	geschlossen	*shut*
schmeißen	schmiss (schmisse)	geschmissen	*chuck*
schmelzen (es schmilzt)	schmolz	(ist)_{Int.} geschmolzen	*melt*

---

[149] *Schaffen* meaning 'to manage to do something' is regular: *schaffte, geschafft.*

schneiden	schnitt (schnitte)	geschnitten	*cut*
schreiben	schrieb (schriebe)	geschrieben	*write*
schreien	schrie	geschrie(e)n	*shout/scream*
schreiten	schritt (schritte)	ist geschritten	*stride*
schweigen	schwieg (schwiege)	geschwiegen	*be silent*
schwellen (es schwillt)	schwoll	ist geschwollen	*swell*
schwimmen	schwamm	(ist)_{Int.} geschwommen	*swim*
schwingen	schwang	geschwungen	*swing*
schwören	schwor	geschworen	*swear (an oath)*
sehen (du siehst, er sieht)	sah (sähe)	gesehen	*see*
sein (ich bin, du bist, er ist			
wir sind, ihr seid, sie sind)	war (wäre)	ist gewesen	*be*
singen	sang (sänge)	gesungen	*sing*
sinken	sank	ist gesunken	*sink*
sitzen	saß (säße)	gesessen	*sit*
sollen (ich/er soll, du sollst)	sollte (sollte)	gesollt	*should*
spinnen	spann	gesponnen	*spin/be stupid*
sprechen (du sprichst, er spricht)	sprach (spräche)	gesprochen	*speak*
springen	sprang (spränge)	ist gesprungen	*jump*
stechen (du stichst, er sticht)	stach	gestochen	*stab/prick/sting*
stehen	stand (stünde)	gestanden	*stand*
stehlen (du stiehlst, er stiehlt)	stahl	gestohlen	*steal*
steigen	stieg (stiege)	ist gestiegen	*rise/climb*
sterben (du stirbst, er stirbt)	starb (stürbe)	ist gestorben	*die*
stinken	stank	gestunken	*stink*
stoßen (du/er stößt)	stieß (stieße)	(ist)_{Int.} gestoßen	*bump/push*
streichen	strich (striche)	(ist)_{Int.} gestrichen	*stroke*
streiten	stritt (stritte)	gestritten	*quarrel*
tragen (du trägst, er trägt)	trug (trüge)	getragen	*carry/wear*
treffen (du triffst, er trifft)	traf (träfe)	getroffen	*meet/hit*
treiben	trieb (triebe)	(ist)_{Int.} getrieben	*drive/propel/ drift*
treten (du trittst, er tritt)	trat (träte)	(ist)_{Int.} getreten	*step/tread*
trinken	trank (tränke)	getrunken	*drink*
tun	tat (täte)	getan	*do*
verbergen (du verbirgst, er verbirgt)	verbarg	verborgen	*hide*
verderben (du verdirbst, er verdirbt)	verdarb	(ist)_{Int.} verdorben	*spoil*
vergessen (du/er vergisst)	vergaß (vergäße)	vergessen	*forget*
verlieren	verlor	verloren	*lose*
verschwinden	verschwand (verschwände)	ist verschwunden	*disappear*
verzeihen	verzieh (verziehe)	verziehen	*forgive*
wachsen (du/er wächst)	wuchs (wüchse)	ist gewachsen	*grow*

waschen (du wäschst, er wäscht)	wusch	gewaschen	*wash*
weichen	wich (wiche)	gewichen	*yield/give way*
weisen	wies (wiese)	gewiesen	*point*
werben (du wirbst, er wirbt)	warb	geworben	*recruit/advertise*
werden (du wirst, er wird)	wurde	ist geworden	*become*
werfen (du wirfst, er wirft)	warf	geworfen	*throw*
wiegen	wog	gewogen	*weigh*
wissen (ich/er weiß, du weißt)	wusste (wüsste)	gewusst	*know*
wollen (ich/er will, du willst)	wollte (wollte)	gewollt	*want*
ziehen	zog (zöge)	(ist)_{Int.} gezogen	*pull/move*
zwingen	zwang	gezwungen	*force*

Appendix 2: Article and adjective endings

Some students may find it easier to learn article and adjective endings together within the context of a whole sentence rather than as isolated words or endings. The following tables provide a list of simple sentences that should be learned by heart. This will enable students to generalise the different case and number ending patterns to other words, provided that the gender of the noun is known.

Adjectives without articles

MASC.	Nom.	Stark**ER** Kaffee schmeckt mir
	Acc.	Ich mag stark**EN** Kaffee
	Dat.	Brot mit stark**EM** Kaffee
	Gen.	Der Geschmack stark**EN** Kaffee**S**
FEM.	Nom.	Warm**E** Milch schmeckt mir
	Acc.	Ich mag warm**E** Milch
	Dat.	Brot mit warm**ER** Milch
	Gen.	Der Geschmack warm**ER** Milch
NEUT.	Nom.	Frisch**ES** Brot schmeckt mir
	Acc.	Ich mag frisch**ES** Brot
	Dat.	Käse mit frisch**EM** Brot
	Gen.	Der Geschmack frisch**EN** Brot**ES**
PLURAL	Nom.	Selbstgebacken**E** Kekse schmecken mir
	Acc.	Ich mag selbstgebacken**E** Kekse
	Dat.	Kaffee mit selbstgebacken**EN** Kekse**N**
	Gen.	Der Geschmack selbstgebacken**ER** Kekse

Definite article + adjective

MASC.	Nom.	**DER** stark**E** Kaffee schmeckt mir
	Acc.	Ich mag **DEN** stark**EN** Kaffee
	Dat.	Brot mit **DEM** stark**EN** Kaffee
	Gen.	Der Geschmack **DES** stark**EN** Kaffee**S**

FEM.	Nom.	**DIE** warm**E** Milch schmeckt mir
	Acc.	Ich mag **DIE** warm**E** Milch
	Dat.	Brot mit **DER** warm**EN** Milch
	Gen.	Der Geschmack **DER** warm**EN** Milch
NEUT.	Nom.	**DAS** frisch**E** Brot schmeckt mir
	Acc.	Ich mag **DAS** frisch**E** Brot
	Dat.	Käse mit **DEM** frisch**EN** Brot
	Gen.	Der Geschmack **DES** frisch**EN** Brot**ES**
PLURAL	Nom.	**DIE** selbstgebacken**EN** Kekse schmecken mir
	Acc.	Ich mag **DIE** selbstgebacken**EN** Kekse
	Dat.	Kaffee mit **DEN** sebstgebacken**EN** Kekse**N**
	Gen.	Der Geschmack **DER** selbstgebacken**EN** Kekse

Indefinite article + adjective

MASC.	Nom.	Das ist **EIN** stark**ER** Kaffee
	Acc.	Ich möchte **EINEN** stark**EN** Kaffee
	Dat.	Brot mit **EINEM** stark**EN** Kaffee
	Gen.	Der Geschmack **EINES** stark**EN** Kaffee**S**
FEM.	Nom.	Das ist **EINE** warm**E** Milch
	Acc.	Ich möchte **EINE** warm**E** Milch
	Dat.	Brot mit **EINER** warm**EN** Milch
	Gen.	Der Geschmack **EINER** warm**EN** Milch
NEUT.	Nom.	Das ist **EIN** frisch**ES** Brot
	Acc.	Ich möchte **EIN** frisch**ES** Brot
	Dat.	Käse mit **EINEM** frisch**EN** Brot
	Gen.	Der Geschmack **EINES** frisch**EN** Brot**ES**

Appendix 3: Revision texts

Revision
Text 1

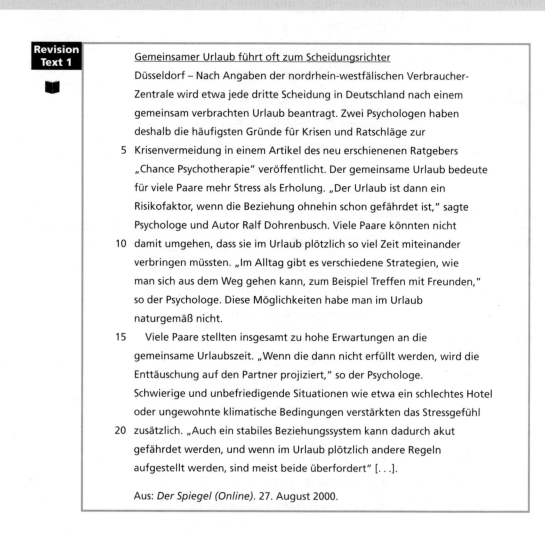

Gemeinsamer Urlaub führt oft zum Scheidungsrichter

Düsseldorf – Nach Angaben der nordrhein-westfälischen Verbraucher-
Zentrale wird etwa jede dritte Scheidung in Deutschland nach einem
gemeinsam verbrachten Urlaub beantragt. Zwei Psychologen haben
deshalb die häufigsten Gründe für Krisen und Ratschläge zur
5 Krisenvermeidung in einem Artikel des neu erschienenen Ratgebers
„Chance Psychotherapie" veröffentlicht. Der gemeinsame Urlaub bedeute
für viele Paare mehr Stress als Erholung. „Der Urlaub ist dann ein
Risikofaktor, wenn die Beziehung ohnehin schon gefährdet ist," sagte
Psychologe und Autor Ralf Dohrenbusch. Viele Paare könnten nicht
10 damit umgehen, dass sie im Urlaub plötzlich so viel Zeit miteinander
verbringen müssten. „Im Alltag gibt es verschiedene Strategien, wie
man sich aus dem Weg gehen kann, zum Beispiel Treffen mit Freunden,"
so der Psychologe. Diese Möglichkeiten habe man im Urlaub
naturgemäß nicht.
15   Viele Paare stellten insgesamt zu hohe Erwartungen an die
gemeinsame Urlaubszeit. „Wenn die dann nicht erfüllt werden, wird die
Enttäuschung auf den Partner projiziert," so der Psychologe.
Schwierige und unbefriedigende Situationen wie etwa ein schlechtes Hotel
oder ungewohnte klimatische Bedingungen verstärkten das Stressgefühl
20 zusätzlich. „Auch ein stabiles Beziehungssystem kann dadurch akut
gefährdet werden, und wenn im Urlaub plötzlich andere Regeln
aufgestellt werden, sind meist beide überfordert" [. . .].

Aus: *Der Spiegel (Online)*. 27. August 2000.

ANALYSIS

1 Identify the *werden*-passives in the text. There are in five in total. See Chapter 18.

2 Find the two *sein*-passives in the text and translate them literally into English, showing how
their meaning differs from that of their corresponding *werden*-passives. See Chapter 18.

3 Explain the use of the *Konjunktiv I* in lines 6 and 13 as opposed to the ordinary indicative in
lines 7–8. See Chapter 17.

4 Identify the forms *könnten* and *müssten* in lines 9 and 11 respectively, and explain their use. See Chapter 17.

5 Identify the forms *stellten* and *verstärkten* in lines 15 and 19 respectively, and explain their use. How do these forms compare with *könnten* and *müssten* mentioned in Question 4 above? See Chapter 17.

6 Explain the lack of ending on *gemeinsam* (line 3, contrast *gemeinsame* in line 16), *neu* (5) and *akut* (20). See Chapter 5.

7 What sort of adjective is *häufigsten* in line 4? What does it mean? See Chapter 6.

8 Identify the pronoun *sich* in line 12 and translate it into English. Why is it directly preceded by *man* in this text? See Chapter 20.

9 What sort of pronoun is *die* in line 16? Explain its use. See Chapter 8.

10 Explain the use of *damit* and *dadurch* in lines 10 and 20 respectively. How would you translate each one into English? See Chapters 24 and 8.

11 Why is *durch* used instead of *von* to refer to the agent of the passive clause in line 20? See Chapter 18.

12 In the title, why is the article absent before *Gemeinsamer Urlaub* but present in *zum Scheidungsrichter*? See Chapter 4.

EXERCISES

All exercises are based on Revision Text 1. Complete each of these without looking at the text or at the other exercises in this section:

1 Put the capitalised nouns into the plural (see Chapter 2), or into the dative plural if the context requires it (see Chapter 3):

Nach ANGABE; Zwei PSYCHOLOGE; die häufigsten GRUND für KRISE und RATSCHLAG; viele PAAR; verschiedene STRATEGIE; Treffen mit FREUND; Diese MÖGLICHKEIT; hohe ERWARTUNG; Schwierige SITUATION; klimatische BEDINGUNG; andere REGEL.

2 Put the italicised articles, pronouns and nouns into the correct case. Use the contracted forms of articles where appropriate (see Chapters 3 and 24):

Gemeinsamer Urlaub führt oft zu *der* Scheidungsrichter. Nach Angaben *die* nordrhein-westfälischen Verbraucher-Zentrale wird etwa *jede* dritte Scheidung in Deutschland nach *ein* gemeinsam verbrachten Urlaub beantragt. Zwei Psychologen haben deshalb *die* häufigsten Gründe für Krisen und Ratschläge zu *die* Krisenvermeidung in *ein* Artikel *der* neu erschienenen *Ratgeber* „Chance Psychotherapie" veröffentlicht. Viele Paare könnten nicht damit umgehen, dass sie in *der* Urlaub plötzlich so viel Zeit miteinander verbringen müssten. „In *der* Alltag gibt es verschiedene Strategien, wie man sich aus *der* Weg gehen kann, zum Beispiel Treffen mit *Freunde*", so *der* Psychologe. Viele Paare stellten insgesamt zu hohe

Erwartungen an *die* gemeinsame Urlaubszeit. „Wenn *die* dann nicht erfüllt werden, wird *die* Enttäuschung auf *der* Partner projiziert".

3   Insert the correct adjective endings where appropriate (see Chapter 5 and Appendix 2):

Gemeinsam__ Urlaub führt oft zum Scheidungsrichter. Nach Angaben der nordrhein__-westfälisch__ Verbraucher-Zentrale wird etwa jede dritt__ Scheidung in Deutschland nach einem gemeinsam__ verbracht__ Urlaub beantragt. Zwei Psychologen haben deshalb die häufigst__ Gründe für Krisenvermeidung in einem Artikel des neu erschienen__ Ratgebers . . . . veröffentlicht. Der gemeinsam__ Urlaub bedeute für viele Paare mehr Stress als Erholung[. . .]. Schwierig__ und unbefriedigend__ Situationen wie etwa ein schlecht__ Hotel oder ungewohnt__ klimatisch__ Bedingungen verstärkten das Stressgefühl zusätzlich.

4   Insert the bracketed verb forms in the correct position in the following sentences (see Chapter 26):

1   Nach Angaben der nordrhein-westfälischen Verbraucher-Zentrale etwa jede dritte Scheidung in Deutschland nach einem gemeinsam verbrachten Urlaub. (wird beantragt)
2   Zwei Psychologen deshalb die häufigsten Gründe für Krisen und Ratschläge zur Krisenvermeidung in einem Artikel des neu erschienenen Ratgebers „Chance Psychotherapie". (haben veröffentlicht)
3   Der Urlaub ist dann ein Risikofaktor, wenn die Beziehung ohnehin schon. (ist gefährdet)
4   Viele Paare könnten nicht damit umgehen, dass sie im Urlaub plötzlich so viel Zeit miteinander. (müssten verbringen)
5   Im Alltag es verschiedene Strategien (gibt), wie man sich aus dem Weg, zum Beispiel Treffen mit Freunden. (kann gehen)
6   „Wenn die dann nicht (werden erfüllt), die Enttäuschung auf den Partner." (wird projiziert)
7   Auch ein stabiles Beziehungssystem dadurch akut. (kann werden gefährdet)
8   Und wenn im Urlaub plötzlich andere Regeln (werden aufgestellt), meist beide. (sind überfordert)

5   Insert the bracketed words in the correct position in the following clauses. Note that *oft* and *schon* often follow the same word order rules as *nicht* (see Chapter 22):

1   Gemeinsamer Urlaub führt zum Scheidungsrichter. (oft)
2   . . ., wenn die Beziehung ohnehin gefährdet ist. (schon)
3   Viele Paare könnten damit umgehen, . . . (nicht)
4   Diese Möglichkeiten habe man im Urlaub naturgemäß. (nicht)
5   Wenn die dann erfüllt werden, . . . (nicht)

Revision Text 2

Brief 1. Fremdenverkehr: Seitenhiebe gegen die Deutschen

Da wird in Österreich seit längerem darüber geredet, warum denn vor allem der Gästestrom aus Deutschland immer stärker nachlässt und wesentlich weniger deutsche Urlauber kommen. Es werden alle nur denkbaren Ursachen diskutiert, nur eines wird geflissentlich übergangen -
5 obwohl es doch so klar auf der Hand liegt -, nämlich die latente Feindlichkeit der Österreicher gegenüber den Deutschen.

Ich halte mich oft in Österreich auf und muss auch im KURIER immer und immer wieder böswillige Seitenhiebe gegen Deutsche feststellen. Der latente Chauvinismus ist sehr arg. Es ist ja auch nicht so, dass wir
10 Deutsche uns ständig „anpinkeln" lassen müssen. Die Folgen davon sind ganz zwangsläufig, dass in den Medien eine ablehnende Stimmung gegen uns Deutsche erzeugt wird. Jeder, der sich länger in Österreich aufhält, merkt das recht wohl.

Uns Deutschen liegt es fern, mit gleicher Münze zurückzuzahlen, wir
15 stehen den Österreichern mehr als ein gutmütiger „großer Bruder" gegenüber. Aber alles hat auch seine Grenzen. Von den Preisen, die deutsche Urlauber zahlen müssen, gar nicht zu reden: In Österreich sind Lebensmittel und vor allem technische Gegenstände wesentlich teurer. Und schöne Landschaft gibt es auch in Deutschland genug.

Oswald Pirl, Frankfurt. In: *Der Kurier*. August 1995.

ANALYSIS

1 What sort of word is *eines* in line 4 and what does it mean here? See Chapter 3.

2 Find examples of relative pronouns in the text and explain their form in terms of gender, number and case. There are two examples in total. See Chapter 9.

3 What sort of pronouns are *mich*, *uns* and *sich* in lines 7, 10 and 12 respectively? Account for their position in the sentence. See Chapter 20.

4 Consider the first two passive constructions in lines 1–4. Explain why the verb *werden* is singular in the first example and plural in the second. Why does *es* appear in the second example but not in the first? See Chapter 18.

5 Explain the use of the nominative case in *ein gutmütiger großer Bruder* in line 15. See Chapter 3.

6 Explain the form and meaning of *der* in line 6. See Chapter 3.

7 Identify the five comparatives in the text and state which adjectives/adverbs they have been derived from. Why have some simply added endings while others have changed the form of the original adjective? See Chapter 6.

8 What sort of word is *auf* in line 7 and why does it occur in this position in the sentence? See Chapter 19.

9 Account for the position of *nachlässt* and *kommen* in the first three lines of the text. See Chapter 23.

10 Explain the word order in the last sentence (line 19). See Chapter 26.

11 Why does the noun *Deutschen* in the title have a different ending to *Deutsche* in lines 8, 10 and 12? See Chapter 3.

12 Account for the capital letter in *Deutsche* (line 10) versus the small letter in *deutsche* (line 17). Chapter 28.

✎ EXERCISES

All exercises are based on Revision Text 2. Complete each of these without looking at the text or at the other exercises in this section:

1 Put the capitalised nouns, pronouns, articles and adjectives into the correct case (see Chapter 3):

1 Da wird in Österreich seit längerem darüber geredet, warum denn vor allem DER GÄSTESTROM aus Deutschland immer stärker nachlässt.

2 Die latente Feindlichkeit DIE ÖSTERREICHER.

3 WIR DEUTSCHE liegt es fern, mit gleicher Münze zurückzuzahlen.

4 Wir stehen DIE ÖSTERREICHER mehr als ein gutmütiger „großer Bruder" gegenüber.

2 Put the capitalised nouns, pronouns, articles and adjectives into the case required by the underlined prepositions (see Chapter 24):

1 Da wird in Österreich <u>seit</u> LÄNGER darüber geredet, warum denn <u>vor</u> ALLES der Gästestrom aus Deutschland immer stärker nachlässt.

2 Nur eines wird geflissentlich übergangen – obwohl es doch so klar <u>auf</u> DIE HAND liegt -, nämlich die latente Feindlichkeit der Österreicher <u>gegenüber</u> DIE DEUTSCHEN.

3 Ich halte mich oft in Österreich auf und muss auch <u>in</u> DER KURIER immer und immer wieder böswillige Seitenhiebe <u>gegen</u> DEUTSCHE feststellen.

4 Die Folgen davon sind ganz zwangsläufig, dass <u>in</u> DIE MEDIEN eine ablehnende Stimmung <u>gegen</u> WIR DEUTSCHE erzeugt wird.

5 Uns Deutschen liegt es fern, <u>mit</u> GLEICHE MÜNZE zurückzuzahlen.

6 <u>Von</u> DIE PREISE, die deutsche Urlauber zahlen müssen, gar nicht zu reden.

3 Move the bracketed phrases to the front of each sentence and change the word order of the following verbs where necessary (see Chapter 25):

1 Vor allem der Gästestrom aus Deutschland lässt immer stärker nach und wesentlich weniger deutsche Urlauber kommen. (da wird in Österreich darüber geredet, warum denn)

2 Es liegt doch so klar auf der Hand. (obwohl)

3 Wir Deutsche müssen uns ständig „anpinkeln" lassen. (es ist ja auch nicht so, dass)
4 In den Medien wird eine ablehnende Stimmung gegen uns Deutsche erzeugt. (die Folgen davon sind ganz zwangsläufig, dass)
5 Alles hat auch seine Grenzen. (aber)
6 Schöne Landschaft gibt es auch in Deutschland genug. (und)

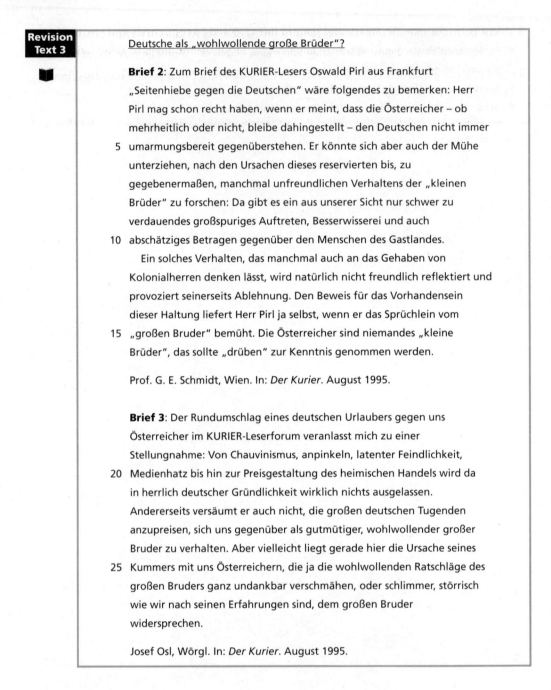

Deutsche als „wohlwollende große Brüder"?

Brief 2: Zum Brief des KURIER-Lesers Oswald Pirl aus Frankfurt „Seitenhiebe gegen die Deutschen" wäre folgendes zu bemerken: Herr Pirl mag schon recht haben, wenn er meint, dass die Österreicher – ob mehrheitlich oder nicht, bleibe dahingestellt – den Deutschen nicht immer
5 umarmungsbereit gegenüberstehen. Er könnte sich aber auch der Mühe unterziehen, nach den Ursachen dieses reservierten bis, zu gegebenermaßen, manchmal unfreundlichen Verhaltens der „kleinen Brüder" zu forschen: Da gibt es ein aus unserer Sicht nur schwer zu verdauendes großspuriges Auftreten, Besserwisserei und auch
10 abschätziges Betragen gegenüber den Menschen des Gastlandes.
Ein solches Verhalten, das manchmal auch an das Gehaben von Kolonialherren denken lässt, wird natürlich nicht freundlich reflektiert und provoziert seinerseits Ablehnung. Den Beweis für das Vorhandensein dieser Haltung liefert Herr Pirl ja selbst, wenn er das Sprüchlein vom
15 „großen Bruder" bemüht. Die Österreicher sind niemandes „kleine Brüder", das sollte „drüben" zur Kenntnis genommen werden.

Prof. G. E. Schmidt, Wien. In: *Der Kurier*. August 1995.

Brief 3: Der Rundumschlag eines deutschen Urlaubers gegen uns Österreicher im KURIER-Leserforum veranlasst mich zu einer Stellungnahme: Von Chauvinismus, anpinkeln, latenter Feindlichkeit,
20 Medienhatz bis hin zur Preisgestaltung des heimischen Handels wird da in herrlich deutscher Gründlichkeit wirklich nichts ausgelassen. Andererseits versäumt er auch nicht, die großen deutschen Tugenden anzupreisen, sich uns gegenüber als gutmütiger, wohlwollender großer Bruder zu verhalten. Aber vielleicht liegt gerade hier die Ursache seines
25 Kummers mit uns Österreichern, die ja die wohlwollenden Ratschläge des großen Bruders ganz undankbar verschmähen, oder schlimmer, störrisch wie wir nach seinen Erfahrungen sind, dem großen Bruder widersprechen.

Josef Osl, Wörgl. In: *Der Kurier*. August 1995.

ANALYSIS

1 Find the two extended attributes in the text and paraphrase them using relative pronouns (the appropriate form for 'which/that') plus a finite verb: e.g. *Der **vor Freude springende** Hund → Der Hund, **der** vor Freude **springt**.* See Chapter 5.

2 Find the three verbs in the text which take a dative object. See Chapter 3.

3 Identify the forms *wäre*, *könnte* and *sollte* in lines 2, 5 and 16 respectively and give their English equivalents. See Chapter 16 (and Chapter 21 for the meanings of *könnte* and *sollte*).

4 What sort of construction is *zu bemerken* in line 2 and how can it best be translated into English? See Chapter 18.

5 What does *lassen* usually mean when it is used with another verb? What does it mean in line 12? See Chapter 21.

6 Identify the form *mag* in line 3. How would you translate *Herr Pirl mag schon recht haben* into English? See Chapter 21.

7 Identify the form *Österreichern* in line 25 and explain why it is used here. See Chapter 24.

8 What does the ending *-er* signify on the adjective *latent* in line 19 and why is it there? See Chapter 24.

9 What case does the preposition *an* take in line 11 and why? See Chapter 24.

10 What type of word is *Sprüchlein* in line 14 and how would you translate it into English? See Chapter 27.

✎ EXERCISES

All exercises are based on Revision Text 3. Complete each of these without looking at the text or at the other exercises in this section:

1 Put the italicised phrases into the genitive, changing only those words which have to be changed (see Chapters 3 and 5, also Appendix 2):

Example: Das Haus: *mein bester Freund*.

Answer: Das Haus mein**es** best**en** Freund**es**.

   1 Zum Brief: *der KURIER-Leser Oswald Pirl*.
   2 Die Ursachen: *dieses reservierte bis, zu gegebenermaßen, manchmal unfreundliche Verhalten*.
   3 Das Verhalten: *die kleinen Brüder*.
   4 Die Menschen: *das Gastland*.
   5 Das Vorhandensein: *diese Haltung*.
   6 *Niemand*: kleine Brüder.
   7 Der Rundumschlag: *ein deutscher Urlauber*.
   8 Die Preisgestaltung: *der heimische Handel*.
   9 Die Ursache: *sein Kummer*.
   10 Die wohlwollenden Ratschläge: *der große Bruder*.

2 Put the bracketed infinitives into the present tense, taking care to insert them into the correct position in the phrase or sentence (see Chapter 10):

   1 Herr Pirl schon recht haben. (mögen)
   2 . . . wenn er, dass die Österreicher den Deutschen nicht immer umarmungsbereit gegenüberstehen. (meinen)

3 Da es ein aus unserer Sicht nur schwer zu verdauendes großspuriges Auftreten. (geben)

4 Ein solches Verhalten, das manchmal auch an das Gehaben von Kolonialherren denken (lassen), nicht freundlich reflektiert (werden) und seinerseits Ablehnung. (provozieren)

5 Den Beweis für das Vorhandensein dieser Haltung Herr Pirl ja selbst. (liefern)

6 ... wenn er das Sprüchlein vom „großen Bruder". (bemühen)

7 Die Österreicher niemandes „kleine Brüder". (sein)

8 Der Rundumschlag eines deutschen Urlaubers gegen uns Österreicher im KURIER-Leserforum mich zu einer Stellungnahme. (veranlassen)

9 Andererseits er auch nicht, die großen deutschen Tugenden anzupreisen. (versäumen)

10 Aber vielleicht gerade hier die Ursache seines Kummers mit uns Österreichern. (liegen)

11 ... mit uns Österreichern, die ja die wohlwollenden Ratschläge des großen Bruders ganz undankbar (verschmähen), oder schlimmer, dem großen Bruder. (widersprechen)

12 Störrisch, wie wir nach seinen Erfahrungen. (sein).

3 Fill in the missing preposition and change the capitalised articles etc. as appropriate. Use the contracted forms of the articles where appropriate (see Chapter 24):

1 _____ DER Brief des KURIER-Lesers Oswald Pirl _____ Frankfurt „Seitenhiebe _____ DIE Deutschen" wäre folgendes zu bemerken: [. . .].

2 Er könnte sich aber auch der Mühe unterziehen, _____ DIE Ursachen dieses reservierten [. . .] Verhaltens der „kleinen Brüder" zu forschen.

3 Da gibt es ein _____ UNSER Sicht nur schwer zu verdauendes großspuriges Auftreten, Besserwisserei und auch abschätziges Betragen _____ DIE Menschen des Gastlandes.

4 Ein solches Verhalten, das manchmal auch _____ DAS Gehaben von Kolonialherren denken lässt.

5 Den Beweis _____ DAS Vorhandensein dieser Haltung liefert Herr Pirl ja selbst, wenn er das Sprüchlein _____ DER „GROSSE Bruder" bemüht.

6 Das sollte „drüben" _____ DIE Kenntnis genommen werden.

7 Der Rundumschlag eines deutschen Urlaubers _____ WIR Österreicher _____ DAS KURIER-Leserforum veranlasst mich _____ EINE Stellungnahme.

8 Von Chauvinismus, anpinkeln, latenter Feindlichkeit, Medienhatz bis hin _____ DIE Preisgestaltung des heimischen Handels wird da _____ herrlich DEUTSCHE Gründlichkeit wirklich nichts ausgelassen.

9 Störisch wie wir _____ SEINE Erfahrungen sind.

4 Derive nouns from the following adjectives and verbs and add the definite article to each one to show its gender (see Chapter 27). Use the nouns that appear in the text:

1 deutsch	6 sich betragen	11 kennen
2 sich verhalten	7 ablehnen	12 Stellung nehmen
3 sehen	8 beweisen	13 feindlich
4 auftreten	9 vorhanden sein	14 gründlich
5 besser wissen	10 halten	15 erfahren

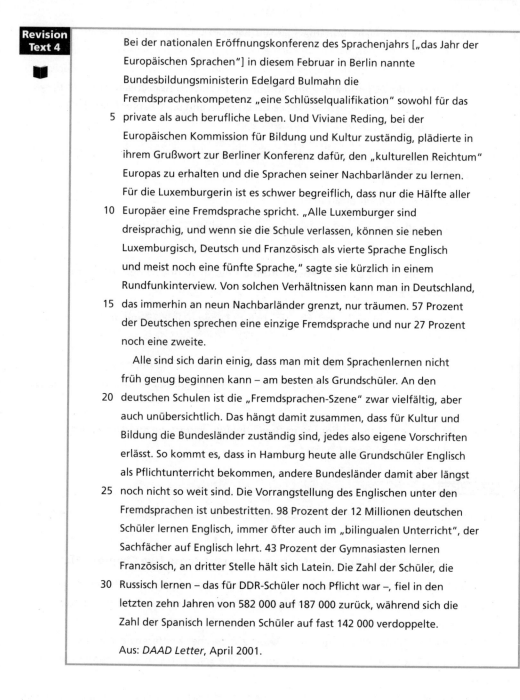

Revision Text 4

Bei der nationalen Eröffnungskonferenz des Sprachenjahrs [„das Jahr der Europäischen Sprachen"] in diesem Februar in Berlin nannte Bundesbildungsministerin Edelgard Bulmahn die Fremdsprachenkompetenz „eine Schlüsselqualifikation" sowohl für das

5   private als auch berufliche Leben. Und Viviane Reding, bei der Europäischen Kommission für Bildung und Kultur zuständig, plädierte in ihrem Grußwort zur Berliner Konferenz dafür, den „kulturellen Reichtum" Europas zu erhalten und die Sprachen seiner Nachbarländer zu lernen. Für die Luxemburgerin ist es schwer begreiflich, dass nur die Hälfte aller

10 Europäer eine Fremdsprache spricht. „Alle Luxemburger sind dreisprachig, und wenn sie die Schule verlassen, können sie neben Luxemburgisch, Deutsch und Französisch als vierte Sprache Englisch und meist noch eine fünfte Sprache," sagte sie kürzlich in einem Rundfunkinterview. Von solchen Verhältnissen kann man in Deutschland,

15 das immerhin an neun Nachbarländer grenzt, nur träumen. 57 Prozent der Deutschen sprechen eine einzige Fremdsprache und nur 27 Prozent noch eine zweite.

   Alle sind sich darin einig, dass man mit dem Sprachenlernen nicht früh genug beginnen kann – am besten als Grundschüler. An den

20 deutschen Schulen ist die „Fremdsprachen-Szene" zwar vielfältig, aber auch unübersichtlich. Das hängt damit zusammen, dass für Kultur und Bildung die Bundesländer zuständig sind, jedes also eigene Vorschriften erlässt. So kommt es, dass in Hamburg heute alle Grundschüler Englisch als Pflichtunterricht bekommen, andere Bundesländer damit aber längst

25 noch nicht so weit sind. Die Vorrangstellung des Englischen unter den Fremdsprachen ist unbestritten. 98 Prozent der 12 Millionen deutschen Schüler lernen Englisch, immer öfter auch im „bilingualen Unterricht", der Sachfächer auf Englisch lehrt. 43 Prozent der Gymnasiasten lernen Französisch, an dritter Stelle hält sich Latein. Die Zahl der Schüler, die

30 Russisch lernen – das für DDR-Schüler noch Pflicht war –, fiel in den letzten zehn Jahren von 582 000 auf 187 000 zurück, während sich die Zahl der Spanisch lernenden Schüler auf fast 142 000 verdoppelte.

Aus: *DAAD Letter*, April 2001.

ANALYSIS

1   Which tense is used in this text to refer to past events: the simple past or the perfect? Explain why. See Chapter 12.

2   Why are the infinitives *erhalten* and *lernen* in line 8 preceded by *zu* while *träumen* in line 15 is not? See Chapter 21.

3 What type of word is *lernenden* in line 32? See Chapter 10.

4 Account for the ending on *Berliner* in line 7. See Chapter 5.

5 Identify the forms *dafür*, *darin* and *damit* in lines 7, 18 and 21, respectively. How do these differ in function from *damit* in line 24? See Chapter 24, and see Chapter 8 for the last occurrence of *damit* in line 24.

6 Why is *dass* spelt with two *s*'s in line 9 but only with one (*das*) in lines 15 and 30? See Chapters 9 and 25.

7 What does the verb *können* mean in line 11?

8 Which case does the preposition *an* take in lines 15 and 19? Explain the reason for the difference. See Chapter 24.

9 Why is the definite article used with the word for 'English' in line 25 but not in lines 12, 23, 27 and 28? See Chapter 4.

10 Account for the position of the reflexive *sich* before *Latein* in line 29 and *die Zahl* in line 31. See Chapter 26.

11 Account for the word order *in diesem Februar in Berlin* (line 2), as opposed to **in Berlin in diesem Februar*. Why is the word order in *in Hamburg heute* (line 23) different? See Chapter 26.

12 What is the function of the ending *-in* in *Bundesbildungsministerin* and *Luxemburgerin* in lines 3 and 9 respectively? See Chapter 27.

✎ **EXERCISES**

All exercises are based on Revision Text 4. Complete each of these without looking at the text or at the other exercises in this section:

1 a Put the capitalised infinitives into the simple past tense (see Chapter 12):

1 Bei der nationalen Eröffnungskonferenz des Sprachenjahrs in diesem Februar in Berlin NENNEN Bundesbildungsministerin Edelgard Bulmahn die Fremdsprachenkompetenz „eine Schlüsselqualifikation".

2 Viviane Reding PLÄDIEREN in ihrem Grußwort zur Berliner Konferenz dafür, den „kulturellen Reichtum" Europas zu erhalten und die Sprachen seiner Nachbarländer zu lernen.

3 „Alle Luxemburger sind dreisprachig, und wenn sie die Schule verlassen, können sie neben Luxemburgisch, Deutsch und Französisch als vierte Sprache Englisch und meist noch eine fünfte Sprache," SAGEN sie kürzlich in einem Rundfunkinterview.

4 Die Zahl der Schüler, die Russisch lernen, ZURÜCKFALLEN in den letzten zehn Jahren, während sich die Zahl der Spanisch lernenden Schüler auf fast 142 000 VERDOPPELN.

1 b Take your answer to question 1a(1) above and find four other verbs with a similar past tense form.

2 Write down the gender of the following nouns (see Chapter 1):

1 Eröffnungskonferenz
2 Jahr
3 Schlüsselqualifikation
4 Leben
5 Grußwort
6 Reichtum

7 Luxemburgerin
8 Hälfte
9 Fremdsprache
10 Schule
11 Deutschland
12 Szene

13 Kultur
14 Bundesland
15 Vorrangstellung
16 Schüler
17 Unterricht
18 Zahl

3 Put the capitalised words into the correct case (see Chapters 3 and 5, and for case after prepositions see Chapter 24). Use the contracted form of the articles where appropriate:

1 Bei DIE NATIONAL__ Eröffnungskonferenz DAS SPRACHENJAHR in DIESER Februar in Berlin nannte Bundesbildungsministerin Edelgard Bulmahn DIE Fremdsprachenkompetenz „EINE Schlüsselqualifikation" sowohl für DAS PRIVAT__ als auch für DAS BERUFLICH__ Leben.

2 Viviane Reding plädierte in IHR Grußwort zur Berliner Konferenz dafür, DER „kulturellen Reichtum" EUROPA zu erhalten und DIE Sprachen SEINE Nachbarländer zu lernen.

3 Nur DIE Hälfte ALLE Europäer spricht EINE Fremdsprache.

4 „Alle Luxemburger sind dreisprachig [. . .]," sagte SIE kürzlich in EIN Rundfunkinterview.

5 Von SOLCHE VERHÄLTNISSE kann man in Deutschland nur träumen.

6 Alle sind sich darin einig, dass man mit DAS Sprachenlernen nicht früh genug beginnen kann.

7 An DIE DEUTSCH__ Schulen ist die „Fremdsprachen-Szene" zwar vielfältig, aber auch unübersichtlich.

8 Die Vorrangstellung DAS ENGLISCH__ unter DIE Fremdsprachen ist unbestritten.

9 98 Prozent DIE 12 Millionen DEUTSCH__ Schüler lernen Englisch, immer öfter auch in DER „BILINGUAL__ Unterricht", DER Sachfächer auf Englisch lehrt.

10 An DRITTE Stelle hält sich Latein.

11 Die Zahl DIE Schüler, DIE Russisch lernen, fiel in DIE LETZT__ zehn JAHRE.

12 . . . während sich die Zahl DIE Spanisch LERNEND__ Schüler auf fast 142 000 verdoppelte.

4 Move the italicised words to the appropriate position in the sentence where necessary (see Chapter 26):

1 Bei der nationalen Eröffnungskonferenz des Sprachenjahrs Bundesbildungsministerin Edelgard Bulmahn *nannte* die Fremdsprachenkompetenz „eine Schlüsselqualifikation".

2 Viviane Reding, *zuständig* bei der Europäischen Kommission für Bildung und Kultur.

3 Viviane Reding plädierte dafür, *zu erhalten* den „kulturellen Reichtum" Europas und *zu lernen* die Sprachen seiner Nachbarländer.

4 Für die Luxemburgerin es *ist* schwer begreiflich, dass nur die Hälfte aller Europäer *spricht* eine Fremdsprache.

5 Alle Luxemburger *sind* dreisprachig, und wenn sie *verlassen* die Schule, sie *können* neben Luxemburgisch, Deutsch und Französisch als vierte Sprache Englisch.

6 Von solchen Verhältnissen man *kann nur träumen* in Deutschland, das *grenzt* immerhin an neun Nachbarländer.

7 Alle *sind sich* darin einig, dass man *kann beginnen* mit dem Sprachenlernen nicht früh genug.

8 Das *zusammenhängt* damit, dass für Kultur und Bildung die Bundesländer *sind* zuständig, jedes *erlässt* also eigene Vorschriften.

9 So es *kommt*, dass in Hamburg heute alle Grundschüler *bekommen* Englisch als Pflichtunterricht, andere Bundesländer *sind* damit aber längst noch nicht so weit.

10 Die Zahl der Schüler, die *lernen* Russisch – das *war* für DDR-Schüler noch Pflicht –, *zurückfiel* in den letzten zehn Jahren von 582 000 auf 187 000, während die Zahl der Spanisch lernenden Schüler *sich verdoppelte* auf fast 142 000.

5 Decide where it is necessary to add commas and explain the reasons for your decisions (see Chapter 28):

1 Bei der nationalen Eröffnungskonferenz des Sprachenjahrs in diesem Februar in Berlin nannte Bundesbildungsministerin Edelgard Bulmahn die Fremdsprachenkompetenz „eine Schlüsselqualifikation" sowohl für das private als auch berufliche Leben.

2 Und Viviane Reding bei der Europäischen Kommission für Bildung und Kultur zuständig plädierte in ihrem Grußwort zur Berliner Konferenz.

3 Für die Luxemburgerin ist es schwer begreiflich dass nur die Hälfte aller aller Europäer eine Fremdsprache spricht.

4 „Alle Luxemburger sind dreisprachig und wenn sie die Schule verlassen können sie neben Luxemburgisch Deutsch und Französisch als vierte Sprache Englisch."

5 Das hängt damit zusammen dass für Kultur und Bildung die Bundesländer zuständig sind jedes also eigene Vorschriften erlässt.

6 . . . immer öfter auch im „bilingualen Unterricht" der Sachfächer auf Englisch lehrt.

7 Die Zahl der Schüler die Russisch lernen fiel in den letzten Jahren zurück während sich die Zahl der Spanisch lernenden Schüler auf fast 142 000 verdoppelte.

Revision Text 5

Wie man eine Frau kennenlernt. Trick 1: Der Abschiedsbrief-Köder.

Sind Sie nicht gut drauf? Fühlen Sie sich ausgelaugt und abgespannt?
Haben Sie Ränder unter den Augen und ist Ihre Kleidung zerknittert?
Ideal! Genau mit diesem Aussehen gehen Sie jetzt in die nächste Kneipe
und setzen sich in die unmittelbare Nähe einer attraktiven Frau [. . .].
5 Jetzt stöhnen Sie leise, seufzen schwer, bestellen sich einen
doppelten Whiskey (auch wenn Sie keinen Whiskey mögen), stoßen
vielleicht ein Glas um. Aus den Augenwinkeln beobachten Sie, ob Sie der
attraktiven Frau auffallen. Falls ja: Wenden Sie sich an sie, indem Sie
einen zerknitterten Brief aus der Tasche ziehen. Ideal wäre es, wenn Sie
10 ein Stück einer kaputten Brille (bei Woolworth gibt es ab 10 Mark eine
Zweit-Lese-Brille, die Sie zerbrechen können) in der anderen Hand halten
könnten, denn Sie werden jetzt zu ihr mit tränenerstickter Stimme
folgenden Satz sagen: „Entschuldigen Sie, ich möchte Sie wirklich nicht
belästigen. Aber dieser Brief ist unheimlich wichtig für mich. Und gerade
15 jetzt ist meine Brille . . . Würden (schluck) könnten Sie ihn mir vorlesen?
Bitte!" Sie haben den Brief natürlich selbst geschrieben. Zerknittern Sie
ihn etwas. Achten Sie darauf, dass die Schrift leserlich ist. Der Brief sollte
ungefähr folgenden Inhalt haben:

Lieber Stephan,
20 *ich verlasse dich! Ja, gewiss, wir hatten eine wundervolle Zeit! Niemand*
hatte bisher so viele Dinge wie du mit mir unternommen. Ob Theater,
Kino oder Konzerte – immer hattest du eine Überraschung für mich bereit.
Es war wunderbar, wie du dich um den Haushalt gekümmert hast.
Wirklich, ich habe deinen sprühenden Charme, deinen Humor aber auch
25 *deine Besonnenheit sehr genossen. Nie werde ich die langen*
Waldspaziergänge in Schweden vergessen, nie die Segel-Turns bei
Griechenland, nie die plötzlichen Wochenendtrips nach London, Paris
oder Sidney [sic]. Und dass du trotz deiner Position als Chefarzt in der
Uniklinik immer Zeit für mich hattest, ist wirklich unglaublich. Doch du
30 *hast mir einfach zuviel Freiheit gelassen. Karl, du weißt schon, der Body-*
Builder aus meinem Fitness-Club ist völlig anders. Bitte, vergiss mich!
Claudia.

Aus: *Herberts Männerseiten* [www.maennerseiten.de]

ANALYSIS

1 In the title, why is the verb *kennenlernt* at the end of the sentence? See Chapter 23.

2 Identify the form *der* in line 7 and explain its use. See Chapter 3.

3 Identify the form *Ihre* in line 2 and explain its use. See Chapter 7.

4 What do *den* and *der* in lines 2, 7, 9 and 11 have in common, apart from being definite articles? How would you translate them into English? See Chapter 4.

5 Identify the form *die* in line 11. See Chapter 9.

6 Which case does the preposition *in* take in lines 3, 4, 11 and 28? What is the reason for the difference? See Chapter 24.

7 Explain the form and function of the verbs *seufzen*, *bestellen* and *umstoßen* in lines 5, 6 and 7. See Chapter 11.

8 Why is *keinen* used in line 6 and not *nicht*, as in line 13? See Chapter 22.

9 What does the pronoun *ihn* refer to in line 15 and how would we translate it into English? See Chapter 7. Account for its position immediately before *mir*. See Chapter 26.

10 Identify the tense of the verbs *kümmern*, *geniessen* and *lassen* in lines 23, 25 and 30 respectively and explain its use. Which tense would you use to translate these into English? See Chapter 13.

11 Explain the use of the simple past tense form *hatte* in lines 20, 22 and 29 instead of the perfect tense. See Chapter 13.

12 Identify the tense of the verb *unternehmen* in line 21 and explain its use. See Chapter 14.

13 Identify the tense of the verbs *sagen* and *vergessen* in lines 13 and 26 and explain its use. See Chapter 15.

14 Find examples of verbs used reflexively in the text (five in total) and comment on the form (i.e. case) of their reflexive pronouns. Why can't *selbst* in line 16 be replaced by the reflexive pronoun *sich*, even though both mean 'yourself'? See Chapter 20.

15 Consider the italicised section of the text. Apart from the use of capital letters with nouns in German, can you spot any other difference in the use of capitals in English and German letter-writing? See Chapter 28.

✎ **EXERCISES**

All exercises are based on Revision Text 5. Complete each of these without looking at the text or at the other exercises in this section:

1 Make questions out of the following statements (see Chapter 23):

1 Sie sind nicht gut drauf.
2 Sie fühlen sich ausgelaugt und abgespannt.
3 Sie haben Ränder unter den Augen und Ihre Kleidung ist zerknittert.
4 Sie könnten ihn mir vorlesen.

2 Put the following imperatives into the polite or informal form as requested in the brackets (see Chapter 11):

1 Geh jetzt in die nächste Kneipe. (polite)
2 Setz dich in die unmittelbare Nähe einer attraktiven Frau. (polite)
3 Jetzt stöhne leise. (polite)
4 Bestell dir ein Glas Whiskey. (polite)
5 Zerknitter ihn etwas. (polite)
6 Vergessen Sie mich. (informal)

3 Fill in the gaps with the correct German translations of the bracketed personal pronouns and possessives (see Chapter 7) or, where 'reflex.' is stated, with the appropriate reflexive pronoun (see Chapter 20):

1 Wie _____ ('one') eine Frau kennenlernt.
2 Fühlen _____ ('you', *polite*) _____ (*reflex.*) ausgelaugt und abgespannt?
3 Ist __ ('your', *polite*) Kleidung zerknittert?
4 Wenden _____ ('you', *polite*) _____ (*reflex.*) an _____ ('her').
5 _____ ('you', *polite*) werden jetzt zu _____ ('her') mit tränenerstickter Stimme folgenden Satz sagen.
6 _____ ('I') möchte _____ ('you', *polite*) wirklich nicht belästigen.
7 Dieser Brief ist unheimlich wichtig für _____ ('me').
8 Und gerade jetzt ist _____ ('my') Brille . . .
9 Könnten _____ ('you', *polite*) _____ ('it') _____ ('me') vorlesen? ['it' = 'der Brief']
10 _____ ('I') verlasse _____ ('you', *informal*).
11 _____ ('we') hatten eine wundervolle Zeit.
12 Niemand hatte bisher so viele Dinge wie _____ ('you', *informal*) mit _____ ('me') unternommen.
13 Immer hattest _____ ('you', informal) eine Überraschung für _____ ('me') bereit.
14 Es war wunderbar, wie _____ ('you', *informal*), _____ (*reflex.*) um den Haushalt gekümmert hast.
15 Wirklich, _____ ('I') habe _____ ('your', *informal*) sprühenden Charme, _____ ('your') Humor aber auch _____ ('your') Besonnenheit sehr genossen.
16 Und dass _____ ('you', *informal*) trotz _____ ('your') Position als Chefarzt in der Uniklinik immer Zeit für _____ ('me') hattest, ist wirklich unglaublich.
17 Doch _____ ('you', *informal*) hast _____ ('me') einfach zuviel Freiheit gelassen.
18 Der Body-Builder aus _____ ('my') Fitness-Club ist völlig anders.
19 Bitte, vergiss _____ ('me')!

4 Put the capitalised infinitives into the appropriate form of the conditional. Decide whether to use the *würde* + infinitive conditional or the *Konjuntiv II* form (see Chapter 16):

1 Ideal SEIN es, wenn Sie ein Stück einer kaputten Brille in der Hand halten KÖNNEN.
2 Ich MÖGEN Sie wirklich nicht belästigen.

3 VORLESEN Sie ihn mir?

4 KÖNNEN Sie ihn mir vorlesen?

5 Der Brief SOLLEN ungefähr folgenden Inhalt haben.

5 Join the following clauses using the conjunctions in brackets, changing the word order where necessary and paying attention to commas (see Chapter 25):

1 Haben Sie Ränder unter den Augen? Ist Ihre Kleidung zerknittert? (und)

2 Bestellen Sie sich einen doppelten Whiskey. Sie mögen keinen Whiskey. (auch wenn)

3 Aus den Augenwinkeln beobachten Sie. Sie fallen der attraktiven Frau auf. (ob)

4 Wenden Sie sich an sie. Sie ziehen einen zerknitterten Brief aus der Tasche. (indem)

5 Ideal wäre es. Sie könnten ein Stück einer kaputten Brille in der anderen Hand halten. (wenn). Sie werden jetzt zu ihr mit tränenerstickter Stimme folgenden Satz sagen. (denn)

6 Entschuldigen Sie, ich möchte Sie wirklich nicht belästigen. Dieser Brief ist unheimlich wichtig für mich. (aber)

7 Achten Sie darauf. Die Schrift ist leserlich. (dass)

8 Es war wunderbar. Du hast dich um den Haushalt gekümmert. (wie)

9 Es ist wirklich unglaublich. Du hattest trotz deiner Polition als Chefarzt in der Uniklinik immer Zeit für mich. (dass)

Appendix 4: Key to exercises

● **1 GENDER**

1. 1. der, die. 2. die, der. 3. das, das. 4. das. 5. der. 6. der. 7. das, die. 8. der, der.

2. Column 1: der Bruder, der Schnee, der Liebling, der Frühling, der Whisky, der Lehrer, der Tourismus, der Polizist, der Osten, der Motor. Column 2: die Blume, die Regierung, die Politik, die Gesundheit, die Universität, die Natur, die Höhe, die Erde, die Freundin, die Bäckerei. Comlumn 3: das Foto, das Ereignis, das Kind, das Französisch, das Viertel, das Lesen, das Grün, das Geräusch, das Fräulein, das Klima.

● **2 NOUN PLURALS**

1. Tomaten, Äpfel, 12 Eier, Vollwertnudeln, Zwiebeln, Weintrauben, 6 Brötchen, 2 Dosen Thunfisch, Kartoffeln, Erdbeeren, 4 Joghurts (or Joghurt), Kaffeefilter, Champignons, Pfirsiche, Pizzas, 2 Kisten Bier, Kräuter, Datteln, Bonbons, 4 Flaschen Wein, Gewürze, Erdnüsse, Muesliriegel, verschiedene Fruchtsäfte.

2. Rosinen, Esslöffel, Klümpchen, Rosinen, Zutaten, Minuten, Stückchen, Lauchzwiebeln, Paprikaschoten, Zucchini, Lauchzwiebeln, Stücke, Schoten, Streifen, Zucchini, Stifte, Kichererbsen, Rosinen, Mandeln, Mandeln, Häufchen, Portionen, Kalorien, Joule, Ballaststoffe, Stunden.

3. 1. Ossis. 2. Schuhe. 3. Zeitungen. 4. Kekse. 5. Scheiben. 6. Schlüssel (Schluessel). 7. Hüte (Huete).

● **3 CASE**

1. 1. den Mann meiner Schwester. 2. der Junge. 3. den Chef. 4. mein Vater. 5. den Freund des Nachbarmädchens. 6. den Kindern einen Kuss. 7. einer von den Nachbarn. 8. der Assistentin . . . der Chef. 9. der Junge seinen Vater. 10. des Lehrers.

2. 1. Er hat Angst vor den Lehrern. 2. Sie schrie die Hunde wütend an. 3. Ich sagte den Müttern, dass die Kinder böse waren. 4. Verärgert erklärte ich den Arbeitern die Ursache der Probleme. 5. Warum müssen die Frauen in diesem Büro immer über ihre Gefühle reden? 6. Er macht seinen Freunden Sorgen.

3. 1. den Kollegen. 2. den Arzt. 3. dem Lehrer. 4. seinem Vater einen Pullover. 5. meiner Nachbarin. 6. meine Frau. 7. eines/eins. 8. einer der Studentinnen. 9. den Kindern. 10. den Eltern. 11. einen. 12. seinem Onkel. 13. einer Freundin. 14. einen Ausflug . . . den Schülern. 15. dem Kind diesen Witz.

4. 1. Das ist das Auto eines Freundes. 2. Das ist Peters Frau. 3. Es war die Idee der Chefin. 4. Hast du Annas Bücher gesehen? 5. Was ist die Hauptstadt Brasiliens? (*or* Was ist Brasiliens Hauptstadt?) 6. Ich bin mit dem Fortschritt der Kinder sehr zufrieden. 7. Der Film handelt sich vom Untergang der „Titanic".

5. 1. Nachbarn. 2. Kunden. 3. Taxifahrer. 4. Herrn . . . Journalisten. 5. Löwen, Tiger, Elephanten, Bären, Hund. 6. Kommissar . . . Kollegen. 7. Studenten. 8. des Professors. [NOTE: In colloquial German the weak -(e)n can be omitted.]

6. der Prokurist, Ihrem Zimmer, Ihren Eltern, Ihre geschäftlichen Pflichten, einer eigentlich unerhörten Weise, Ihrer Eltern und Ihres Chefs, eine augenblickliche, deutliche Erklärung, einen ruhigen, vernünftigen Menschen, den Prokuristen, dieser Stimmung, seine Stellung, die Eltern, den langen Jahren, die Überzeugung, diesem Geschäft, sein Leben, den augenblicklichen Sorgen, diese Voraussicht, der Prokurist, Gregors und seiner Familie.

● **4 USE OF ARTICLES**

1. 1. no article. 2. no article (*because of* werden), no article, ein. 3. einen, eine. 4. ein, no article, eine, no article. 5. einer, einen. 6. no article (*after* als '*as*'), no article. 7. ein, ein, ein (*here* als *means* '*than*'). 8. no article, no article. 9. no article, no article (*after* als '*as*'). 10. no article. 11. einen. 12. einem, no article, no article, ein.

2. 1. zum. 2. im, no article, no article. 3. im, die. 4. no article. 5. den, die, zum, die. 6. den, am. 7. der. 8. das. 9. no article, no article (*because idiom: 'age before beauty'*). 10. no article, no article, no article. 11. der, no article. 12. no article, der. 13. der (*genitive*). 14. no article, dem. 15. am, no article, no article.

● **5 ADJECTIVES**

1. deutsches Bier, der englische Tee, diese schwedischen Fleischklöße, holländischer Käse, ein schottischer Lachs, welcher österreichische Wein?, spanische Oliven, keine belgischen Pralinen, das frische französische Brot, mein griechischer Schafskäse.

2. 1. guten. 2. schönes, großen, heutigen. 3. europaweiten, riesigen. 4. weltberühmte, hoher. 5. schicken italienischen. 6. kleine, teuren französischen, vierzigsten.

3. 1. Meine schönen alten Häuser haben zwei besonders große Schlafzimmer. 2. Die schwarzen Hemden mit den weißen Streifen hingen im Kleiderschrank. 3. Gute Weine sind selten billig. Nimm diese zwei französischen, zum Beispiel. 4. Diese frischgepflückten Blumen sind für meine neuen Freundinnen. 5. Sie ist trotz der verspäteten Züge relativ früh nach Hause gekommen.

4. unruhigen, ungeheueren, harten, gewölbten, braunen, bogenförmigen, geteilten, gänzlichen, vielen, sonstigen, dünnen, richtiges, kleines, wohlbekannten, auseinandergepackte, illustrierten, hübschen, vergoldeten, schweren, ganzer, trübe.

5. a 1. panzerartig <u>harten</u>. 2. von bogenförmigen Versteifungen <u>geteilten</u>. 3. im Vergleich zu seinem sonstigen Umfang kläglich <u>dünnen</u>. 4. nur etwas zu <u>kleines</u>.

5. b 1. Seine vor zwei Tagen achtzig gewordene Mutter. 2. Ein von mehreren Akademikern viel gelobter Schriftsteller. 3. Ein von den Deutschen eingeführtes Gesetz. 4. Sie bieten vier von der Gemeinde finanzierte Arbeitsplätze an. 5. Sie haben keinen für die Stelle geeigneten Kandidaten gefunden.

6. 1. Hier kommt die Unfreundliche. 2. Sie spielte mit dem Kleinen. 3. Der Chef feuerte den Angestellten. 4. Sie war die Freundin des Gestorbenen. 5. Wir müssen für die Armen mehr spenden. 6. Ich habe etwas Interessantes gelesen. 7. Ich muss dir leider etwas Trauriges mitteilen.

7. 1. Er hat eine ungewöhnlich große Nase. 2. Was für ein unglaublich schmutziges Zimmer! 3. Sie hat eine geschmackvoll eingerichtete Wohnung. 4. Es war ein unangenehm heißer Tag.

● **6 COMPARATIVES AND SUPERLATIVES**

1. a) niedriger, breiter, dicker, schmaler/schmäler, höher, schlanker, fetter, flacher; b) niedrigst, breitest, dickst, schmalst/schmälst, höchst, schlankst, fettest, flachst.

2. 1. längeren, längsten. 2. kürzere, kürzeste. 3. kleinere, kleinste. 4. größeren, größten. 5. dünnere, dünnste.

3. 1. jünger. 2. Älteste. 3. älter, langsamer. 4. beste. 5. reicher, arroganter. 6. wärmer, kälter. 7. klügsten. 8. Beste. 9. billigeren *or* billigsten. 10. stärker.

4. 1. das teuerste/am teuersten. 2. am besten. 3. am liebsten. 4. am lautesten. 5. nasseste/nässeste.

• 7 PERSONAL PRONOUNS AND POSSESSIVES

1. 1. du, mir. 2. ihr, wir, ihm. 3. ich, Sie. 4. sie, ihn, er. 5. dich, sie, dir. 6. wir, euch. 7. du, sie, ich, ihr. 8. Sie, mich, Ihnen.

2. 1. dein, deinem. 2. ihr, eure, wir, ihnen. 3. mir, meiner. 4. deine, sie, ihrem. 5. mein, deinen. 6. ich, meine (*more commonly*: mir die Haare). 7. uns, sein. 8. er, unser(e)s. 9. ihrer, ihrem (= Marions Mann) *or* deren (= der Mann ihrer Freundin). 10. euch, ihm.

3. 1. Das ist mein Lippenstift – Das ist meiner. 2. Das ist dein Zimmer – Das ist dein(e)s. 3. Das sind seine Schuhe – Das sind seine. 4. Das ist unser Wagen – Das ist unserer. 5. Das sind eure Bücher – Das sind eure. 6. Das sind ihre Ohrringe – Das sind ihre. 7. Das ist ihr Baby – Das ist ihr(e)s. 8. Das ist Ihr Kaffee – Das ist Ihrer.

4. 1. sie. 2. sie. 3. er. 4. ihn. 5. es *or* er. 6. es *or* er. 7. dafür. 8. darauf *or* auf sie. 9. davon. 10. ihn.

5. 1. You can't/aren't allowed to smoke here. 2. A new bridge has just been built *or* They've just built a new bridge. 3. That can really get on your nerves. 4. The Germans are considered to be very hard-working/industrious. 5. The weather here can really depress you.

• 8 DEMONSTRATIVES

1. 1. den, diesen. 2. der, dieser. 3. der, dieser. 4. den, diesen. 5. des, dieses. 6. den, diesen.

2. 1. die da, diese da. 2. der da, dieser da. 3. zu denen da, zu diesen da (Note: the preposition is usually repeated.). 4. den da, diesen da. 5. von der da, von dieser da. 6. von denen da, von diesen da. 7. der da, dieser da. 8. die da, diese da.

3. 1. den. 2. das. 3. das. 4. derjenige. 5. demjenigen. 6. von dem *or better:* davon. 7. an das *or better:* daran.

4. 1. Ich weiß es nicht. Den habe ich seit langem nicht gesehen. 2. Der ist im urlaub. 3. Ja, von denen habe ich diese Uhr gekriegt. 4. Der habe ich eine CD gegeben. 5. Dem schmecken Fisch und Meeresfrüchte überhaupt nicht.

• 9 RELATIVE PRONOUNS

1. 1. die. 2. der. 3. den. 4. das. 5. der. 6. was. 7. der. 8. den. 9. was. 10. dem.

2. 1. Mein Chef, von dem ich eine Gehaltserhöhung bekommen habe. 2. Die Assistentin, auf die ich mich verlassen kann. 3. Der Kunde, auf den er seit einer halben Stunde wartet. 4. Der Abteilungsleiter, dessen Papiere auf dem Tisch liegen. 5. Die Sekretärin, deren Computer nicht funktioniert. 6. Das Vorstellungsgespräch, an dem ich gescheitert bin. 7. Der Computer, mit dem du arbeitest. 8. Der neue Drucker, auf den er gewartet hat. 9. Die neuen Arbeitsbedingungen, über die ich nicht viel weiß. 10. Die flexiblen Arbeitszeiten, von denen der Manager geredet hat.

3. 1. Wir haben nur zehn Minuten Kaffeepause, was viel zu wenig ist. 2. Ich muss heute Abend lange arbeiten, worauf ich mich nicht freue. 3. Mein Kollege ist heute auf Abruf, womit er nicht sehr glücklich ist. 4. Ich kriege keine Überstunden mehr bezahlt, was ich nicht richtig finde. 5. Wir können morgens früher anfangen und abends früher nach Hause gehen, wogegen ich nichts habe.

4. einen gut erinnerten Traum, <u>den</u> (in the accusative because the following *er* is the subject), der Notar, <u>bei dem</u> (preposition plus relative pronoun in the dative, as *bei* takes the dative), Kaiserbirnen, <u>von denen</u> (preposition plus plural relative pronoun in dative), alter Herr, <u>der</u> (nominative masculine = 'who'), die Brüste der Mutter, <u>die</u> (plural nominative referring back to 'Brüste'), die Brust, <u>an der</u> (preposition plus relative pronoun in dative).

• 10 PRESENT TENSE

1. a 1. kannst. 2. findet, gefällt. 3. Wie spricht man „Chrysantheme" aus? 4. liest. 5. denke, sind, ist.

1. **b** ist, macht, fühlt sich, bin, glaubt, anführt, wird, denkt, wappnet sich auf (*in this text the separable prefixes precede the prepositional object of the verb, as the object is placed outside the verbal bracket; see 26.7 on word order*), hat, heißt, vertraut, setzen.

2. 1. fischt. 2. hängen hundert Hemden raus. 3. entwächst. 4. magst. 5. bremst, brennt. 6. tut, tut er seine Tute wieder in den Tutkasten rein. 7. ist, besitzt. 8. schwitzt, schweißt.

3. 1. geht, bringt es auch zwei Flaschen Apfelsaft mit, fragt, wollen, antwortet, trinken. 2. sitzt, meint, weiß, glaubst, soll. 3. fragt, sprechen, spreche, schlafen, bin. 4. müssen, befiehlt, singen. 5. sagt, steht, ist (sind *is also possible*), sind, herumstehen, haben. 6. fragt, bist, geht, bist, habe. 7. läuft, kommt, bin.

4. 1. *remains perfect*. 2. wohnt. 3. *remains perfect*. 4. sind. 5. habe.

5. 1. spricht. 2. fängt [faengt]. 3. rettet. 4. betrachte. 5. steuerst. 6. regnet. 7. hängt [haengt].

● 11 IMPERATIVE

1. Komm (*less frequently* komme) heute Abend mit! 2. Gib mir einen Kuss! 3. Bleibt brav zu Hause! 4. Sagen Sie mir Bescheid! 5. Räumt euer Zimmer auf! 6. Entschuldigen Sie mich, bitte! 7. Iss dein Gemüse! 8. Sag (*less frequently* sage) das noch einmal! 9. Nimm deinen Regenschirm mit! 10. Wasch dir die Hände! 11. Ruh (*less frequently* ruhe) dich aus! 12. Stell (*less frequently* stelle) dir die Situation vor! 13. Gehen wir ins Kino! 14. Setzen wir uns! 15. Den Rasen nicht betreten [*general imperative*].

● 12 PAST TENSE

1. 1. buchten. 2. reservierten. 3. übernachtete. 4. wolltest. 5. amüsiertet. 6. kaufte. 7. spielten. 8. dauerte. 9. wanderten. 10. frühstückten.

2. 1. hatte. 2. schwammen. 3. flogen. 4. kamen um halb elf am Flughafen an. 5. aßen. 6. kostete. 7. nahm alles mit der Videokamera auf. 8. waren. 9. reiste um 16 Uhr ab. 10. sahen uns die schönsten Städte an.

3. 1. tranken. 2. redete. 3. starrte. 4. fanden. 5. tadelten. 6. antwortete. 7. endeten.

4. kamen, traten, sagte, gebar, waren, war, waren, starb, stand mitten in der Nacht auf, nahm mir mein Kind weg, schlief, legte, legte, aufstand, war, ansah, war, rief, entgegnete, stritten, begann, fuhr fort, brachte, entschied, bat, regte, rief, befahl, hörte, schauten mit Ehrfurcht zu ihm auf, erkannten, war, sprach.

13 PERFECT TENSE

1. 1. Wir haben auf den Bus gewartet. 2. Der Zug hat Verspätung gehabt. 3. Ich habe eine Rückfahrkarte gebraucht. 4. Habt ihr ein neues Auto gekauft? 5. Wir haben unser altes Motorrad verkauft. 6. Sie haben sich am Bahnhof getroffen. 7. Wir haben im Nichtrauchercoupé gesessen. 8. Hast du die Straßenbahn gesehen?

2. 1. sind. 2. bin. 3. hat. 4. ist. 5. habe. 6. hast. 7. habe. 8. ist. 9. hat. 10. sind. 11. hat. 12. bist, bin.

3. 1. Der Junge ist nach Hause gelaufen. 2. Die Teekanne ist zu Boden gefallen und ist gebrochen. 3. Es tut mir leid, ich habe das Weinglas zerbrochen. 4. Die Kinder sind in ihrem Zimmer geblieben und haben gespielt. 5. Wir sind mit KLM nach Amsterdam geflogen. 6. Er hat heute zum ersten Mal sein Modellflugzeug geflogen, aber leider ist es abgestürzt. 7. Der Schüler hat einen Mitschüler in den Bauch getreten. 8. Der Lehrer ist ins Zimmer getreten. 9. Pass auf! Du bist (hast *is also possible*) mir auf den Fuß getreten. 10. Der Dieb ist in das Haus eingebrochen.

4. stattgefunden hat, gegeben hat, musste, habe Näheres darüber einmal auf Urlaub von einem aus jener Klasse erfahren, haben einen hübschen Burschen unter sich gehabt, waren*, haben damals die

Sache zu weit getrieben, verstand, handelte, fühlte, wusste, zuckte, ist dir nicht aufgefallen, geworden ist, hat er kaum mehr etwas sagen lassen (*see footnote* 60), hieß*, hat er sich wahrscheinlich gedacht, versprochen haben (*this is a future perfect, see* **15.4**), geirrt haben, bist du darauf gekommen, bin ihnen einmal nachgegangen.

* Past is used in original but perfect is also possible: gewesen sind; hat ... geheissen.

• 14 PLUPERFECT TENSE

1. 1. geregnet hatte. 2. hatte es geschneit. 3. war untergegangen. 4. hatte einen Sturm gegeben, waren umgefallen. 5. war in letzter Zeit am Meer sehr windig gewesen. 6. gehagelt hatte.

2. Ex. 2 1. waren. 2. war. 3. hatte. 4. war. 5. hatte. 6. hattest. 7. hatte. 8. war. 9. hatte. 10. waren. 11. hatte. 12. warst, war. **Ex. 3.** 1. Der Junge war nach Hause gelaufen. 2. Die Teekanne war zu Boden gefallen und war gebrochen. 3. Ich hatte das Weinglas zerbrochen. 4. Die Kinder waren in ihrem Zimmer geblieben und hatten gespielt. 5. Wir waren mit KLM nach Amsterdam geflogen. 6. Er hatte heute zum ersten Mal sein Modellflugzeug geflogen, aber leider war es abgestürzt. 7. Der Schüler hatte einen Mitschüler in den Bauch getreten. 8. Der Lehrer war ins Zimmer getreten. 9. Du warst (hattest *is also possible*) mir auf den Fuß getreten. 10. Der Dieb war in das Haus eingebrochen.

3. 1. Ich war im Nebel nach Hause gefahren. 2. Ich fuhr (gerade) von der Arbeit nach Hause, als das Gewitter anfing. 3. Es war ziemlich warm gewesen und das Eis war geschmolzen. 4. Ich sonnte mich (gerade) im Garten, als das Telefon klingelte. 5. Es war den ganzen Tag bewölkt gewesen.

• 15 FUTURE

1. 1. Welche Partei wird nächstes Jahr an der Macht sein? 2. Es wird wahrscheinlich eine Koalition geben. 3. Welchen Kandidaten wirst du wählen? 4. Die nächste Wahl wird im Juni dieses Jahres stattfinden. 5. Alle Parteien werden das Verhältniswahlrecht unterstützen. 6. In welchem Wahlkreis werdet ihr nächstes Jahr sein? 7. Ich werde dem Innenminister schreiben. 8. Er wird wahrscheinlich Außenminister werden. 9. Der Abgeordnete wird seine Wähler vertreten. 10. Die Politiker, die an die Macht kommen werden, sind die, die dem Publikum zuhören werden.

2. 1. Die Regierung wird ihre Ausgaben reduziert haben. 2. Die Linken werden mehr in das Schulwesen investiert haben. 3. Der Bundeskanzler wird zurückgetreten sein. 4. Die Rechten werden sich aufgelöst haben. 5. Er wird Mitglied des Europaparlaments gewesen sein.

3. 1. treffen (*future expressed by* um drei Uhr). 2. fahrt (*future expressed by* wann). 3. wird schön sein (ist *would be ambiguous here: 'it is nice/it will be nice'*). 4. wird regnen (*future used for predictions*). 5. kommt um 18 Uhr an (*future expressed by* um 18 Uhr). 6. Morgen wird es schneien (*future used for predictions*). 7. machst (*future expressed by* morgen Abend). 8. wird er machen (*present would be ambiguous: 'what is he doing/what will he do'*).

4. 1. Klaus wird wahrscheinlich noch arbeiten. 2. Er wird wahrscheinlich noch schlafen. 3. Peter wird es wahrscheinlich schon gemacht haben. 4. Die Nachbarn werden wahrscheinlich schon abgereist sein. 5. Er wird es wahrscheinlich seiner Frau erzählt haben.

• 16 CONDITIONAL

1. 1. Ich würde die Blumen gießen. 2. Er würde die neuen Pflanzen eingraben. 3. Wir möchten auf der Terasse frühstücken. 4. Es wäre schön beim Brunnen zu sitzen. 5. Ich würde es schwierig finden, den großen Busch zurückzuschneiden. 6. Wir müssten eigentlich den Rosenstrauch düngen. 7. Der Baum würde im Winter seine Blätter verlieren. 8. Könntest du Unkraut jäten? Ich hätte eine Schaufel. 9. Ich sollte einen richtigen Komposthaufen machen. 10. Wüsstest du zufällig (*or* würdest du zufällig wissen), wo der Rechen sein könnte?

2. 1. Der Gärtner hätte es besser gemacht. 2. Ich hätte eine Regentonne gekauft, aber sie war zu groß zu transportieren. 3. Ein guter Spaten wäre zu teuer gewesen. Deshalb habe ich die Schaufel genommen. 4. Ich hätte den Gartenzaun streichen sollen, aber es war zu viel Arbeit. 5. Rhododendrons haben eigentlich sehr kleine Wurzeln. Du hättest sie in einen Topf pflanzen können. 6. Eine schöne Elster wäre in den Garten geflogen, aber die Katze hat sie weggescheucht.

3. 1. Wenn es nicht regnen würde, wäre die Erde sehr trocken 'If it didn't rain, the soil would be very dry'. 2. Wenn sie Geld hätten, würden sie einen Wintergarten kaufen 'If they had money, they would buy a conservatory'. 3. Wenn ich ein Glashaus hätte, könnte ich Tomaten ziehen 'If I had a greenhouse, I would be able to grow tomatoes (*or 'I could grow tomatoes'*)'. 4. Wenn das Wetter besser wäre, würden die Kletterpflanzen höher wachsen 'If the weather was better, the climbers would grow higher'. 5. Wenn du mir den Gartenschlauch geben würdest, würde ich den Rasen spritzen 'If you gave me the hose, I would water the grass'. 6. Wenn wir jetzt die Zwiebeln pflanzen würden, würden die Krokusse und Narzissen im Frühling kommen (*also possible:* kämen die Krokusse und Narzissen im Frühling) 'If we planted the bulbs now, the crocuses and daffodils would come in the spring'. 7. Wenn der Blumenstock verwelken würde, müsste ich ihn umtopfen 'If the pot plant wilted, I would have to repot it'. 8. Wenn du mir helfen wolltest, könntest du den Gartenschuppen aufbauen 'If you wanted to help me, you could put up the garden shed.'

4. 1. Wenn es nicht geregnet hätte, wäre die Erde sehr trocken gewesen 'If it hadn't rained the soil would have been very dry'. 2. Wenn sie Geld gehabt hätten, hätten sie einen Wintergarten gekauft 'If they had had money, they would have bought a conservatory'. 3. Wenn ich ein Glashaus gehabt hätte, hätte ich Tomaten ziehen können 'If I had had a greenhouse, I would have been able to grow tomatoes (*or 'could have grown tomatoes'*)'. 4. Wenn das Wetter besser gewesen wäre, wären die Kletterpflanzen höher gewachsen 'If the weather had been better, the climbers would have grown higher'. 5. Wenn du mir den Gartenschlauch gegeben hättest, hätte ich den Rasen gespritzt 'If you had given me the hose, I would have watered the grass'. 6. Wenn wir jetzt die Zwiebeln gepflanzt hätten, wären die Krokusse und Narzissen im Frühling gekommen 'If we had planted the bulbs now, the crocuses and daffodils would have come in the spring'. 7. Wenn der Blumenstock verwelkt wäre, hätte ich ihn umtopfen müssen 'If the pot plant had wilted, I would have had to repot it'. 8. Wenn du mir hättest helfen wollen, hättest du den Gartenschuppen aufbauen können 'If you had wanted to help me, you could have put up the garden shed'.

• 17 SUBJUNCTIVE IN REPORTED SPEECH

1. a 1. Das Formel 1 Team teilte mit, Eddie Irvine könne voraussichtlich aus dem Krankenhaus entlassen werden. Kein medizinischer Eingriff sei nötig, stellten die Ärzte nach eingehenden Untersuchungen fest. 2. Der jüngere der beiden Klitschko-Brüder sagte, er wolle diesen Kampf unbedingt und er hoffe, dass er bald diese Chance bekomme. Klitschko sagte, er warte auf große Kämpfe. Zu 70 Prozent sei er zufrieden, 30 Prozent müsse er sich noch erarbeiten. 3. Wenn der Vertrag unter Dach und Fach sei, ergänzte Schaaf, komme Verlaat bereits in der nächsten Woche mit ins Trainingslager nach Österreich. 4. Es könne nicht sein, betonte Völler, dass es nur als Pflichtübung gelte, in der Nationalmannschaft zu spielen. Jeder müsse es wollen. Es müsse eine Ehre sein. 5. Die dreimalige Olympiasiegerin sagte, sie sei froh, das sie es versucht habe. Sie werde nichts in Zweifel ziehen, jetzt liege alles hinter ihr. 6. Als sie über die Ziellinie gelaufen sei, seien jahrelang angestaute Gefühle aufgekommen, jubelte Anna Jones. Seit sie neun sei, habe sie davon geträumt, im Olympia-Team zu stehen. Jetzt sei der Traum wahr. 7. Eigentlich habe er gar nicht so recht mit diesem Sieg gerechnet, weil er diese Rallye nicht gekannt habe, erklärte der 32 Jahre alte Finne. Daher freue er sich umsomehr darüber.

1. b 1. Werder-Trainer Thomas Schaaf sagte am Sonntag, sie hätten sich am Wochenende mit Verlaat und Ajax so weit geeinigt, dass man davon ausgehen könne, er komme zu ihnen. 2. Baumanns Anwalt Michael Lehner kommentierte, Dieter Baumann solle sich erst einmal in Ruhe auf Sydney vorbereiten, dann würden sie weitersehen. 3. Rüdiger Nickel, Vorsitzender des DLV-Bundesausschusses Leistungssport, sagte, natürlich fehlten die großen Reißer. Aber sie hätten eine sehr ausgeglichene Mannschaft, wobei die Frauen gegenüber dem letzten Jahr deutlich im Aufwind seien. Bei den Männern müsse man sehen. Der erste Tag sei nie der Tag der Deutschen gewesen. Die big points würden sicher morgen kommen. 4. Völler fügte hinzu, nach einer EM oder großenTurnieren habe es immer einen Schnitt gegeben. Einige hörten aus Altersgründen auf, andere würden durch das Sieb fallen. Wenn ein neuer Trainer komme, habe man andere Vorstellungen. 5. Die Australier würden zu 90 Prozent damit rechnen, dass sie zum Endspiel nach Spanien reisen müssten und nicht gegen die USA im heimischen National Tennis Centre in Melbourne antreten könnten, berichtete die dpa. 6. Der Coach meinte, die MetroStars würden die Entscheidung treffen. Lothar habe da nur noch wenig zu sagen [. . .] Er glaube, dass er (*or, to make it clear,* Der Coach glaube, dass Lothar) die falsche Einstellung habe. Es drehe sich hier nicht alles um Lothar Matthäus, das habe es nie getan. Der Coach erklärte, sie hätten einige Fragen an Lothar zu seiner Verletzung und seiner Einstellung zur Mannschaft gehabt. Alle hätten ihre Meinung gesagt.

2. 1. Paul sagte, er würde lieber Squash als Tennis spielen. 2. Mein Bruder sagte, Matthäus hätte zwei Tore innerhalb fünf Minuten geschossen. 3. Meine Freundin meinte, sie würde sich überhaupt nicht für Autorennen interessieren. 4. Benno sagte, der Schiedsrichter hätte ihm die gelbe Karte gezeigt. 5. Unsere Gegner drohten uns, sie würden uns mit fünf zu null schlagen. 6. Anton sagte, er müsste sich beeilen. Er würde gleich ins Fußballstadion gehen. 7. Sabine sagte, sie wüsste nicht, ob er gewonnen hätte. 8. Mein Schilehrer sagte, man müsste beim Schifahren immer auf der Piste bleiben, sonst könnte ein Unfall passieren. 9. Mein Vater sagte, es würde nichts schöneres als Pferderennen geben! (*less commonly in speech*: es gäbe). 10. Ulrike sagte, sie hätte mit ihm Badminton spielen wollen, aber er hätte keine Zeit gehabt.

3. könne, wisse, sei, einleuchte, sei, hätten, könne, herausstelle, gebe, werde, könne, gestorben sei, grolle, habe, stehe, sei, werde, habe sich aus . . . für Katharina ergeben, habe mit großer Zuneigung . . . über sie gesprochen, sei, vorliege, seien, verachte, sei.

4. Was gilt überhaupt als Diät? Jede zweite Frau in Deutschland möchte weniger wiegen. 44 Prozent der Frauen zwischen 20 und 60 Jahren wollten kalorienbewusst essen. Fast die Hälfte der befragten Frauen habe angegeben, schon einmal eine Diät gemacht zu haben, sagte Miglietti. Allerdings würden 88 Prozent so genannte *Formula-Diäten*, also das Ersetzen einer Mahlzeit durch einen Drink, nicht als Diät ansehen. Auch eine Mahlzeit ausfallen zu lassen, werde von 80 Prozent nicht als Abmagerungskur empfunden. Der Griff zur Tüte: Miglietti erklärte, dass jede siebte Frau zur Gruppe der *unkritischen Pflichtesserinnen* gehöre. Diese *Trash-Fress-Frauen* würden häufig zu Fertiggerichten greifen oder beschäftigten sich neben dem Essen noch mit anderen Dingen. Vor allem junge Singles im Alter von 20 bis 30 Jahren gehörten zu dieser Gruppe. 43 Prozent der Frauen würden beim Fernsehen essen ('äßen' would be stilted), 42 Prozent würden sich vom leckeren Anblick der Speisen verleiten lassen ('ließen sich' is also possible), erklärte die Journalistin. 80 Prozent der Frauen hätten angegeben, gesundheitsbewusst zu kochen. Demgegenüber hätten allerdings 54 Prozent erklärt, sie benutzten auch Halbfertig- oder Fertigprodukte wie Soßenpulver. 62 Prozent müssten immer Salziges oder Süßes zum Knabbern zu Hause haben. Ein entspanntes Verhältnis zum Essen hätten nur 40 Prozent der 20- bis 60-Jährigen. Sie seien auch eher mit ihrem Gewicht zufrieden.

• **18 PASSIVE**

1. 1. Musik wird oft als Wahlfach genommen. 2. Die Hausarbeit muss bis Montag abgegeben werden. 3. Fragen können während der Gruppenarbeit gestellt werden. 4. Das Klassenzimmer wird aufgeräumt. 5. Wie viele Fächer werden hier unterrichtet?

2. 1. Der Unterricht wurde gestört. 2. Die Prüfungen sind verschoben worden. 3. Dieses Thema war schon drei Mal besprochen worden, aber trotzdem fanden es die Schüler sehr schwierig zu verstehen. 4. Die Übungen sind nicht gemacht worden. 5. Keine Taschenrechner dürfen benutzt werden. 6. Die Schüler werden nächsten Monat in diesem Fach geprüft (werden).

3. 1. Der Lehrer wurde von den Schülern beleidigt. 2. Das Problem ist von dem Klassensprecher erwähnt worden. 3. Klaus war vom Sportlehrer für die Fußballmannschaft der Schule ausgewählt worden. 4. Das Hockeyturnier wurde durch das schlechte Wetter ruiniert. 5. Die Konzentration der Prüfungskandidaten ist durch das Geräusch des Rasenmähers gestört worden. 6. Der Unruhestifter wird vom Direktor aus der Schule herausgeschmissen werden. 7. Peter wurde wegen seiner schlechten Noten von den Lehrern gezwungen sitzenzubleiben. 8. Sechs Auszeichnungen sind von den Prüfern erteilt worden. 9. Der Schüleraustausch war von den Organisatoren wegen Mangel an Interesse gestrichen worden. (NB *Placing the agent after* Mangel an Interesse *would make the sentence ambiguous: i.e. 'lack of interest from the organisers'*). 10. Er kann wegen Schwänzerei der Schule verwiesen werden.

4. 1. Meinem Sohn ist geholfen worden. 2. Mein Mann ist mitten in der Nacht angerufen worden. 3. Auf keinen wird bei uns in der Firma Rücksicht genommen. 4. Über Geld wird oft geredet, aber es gibt wichtigere Dinge im Leben. 5. Meiner Freundin wurde nach Hause gefolgt. 6. Die Nachbarn waren nicht eingeladen worden. 7. Den Angestellten ist nichts gesagt worden. 8. Mit Elektrizität wird nicht herumgespielt! 9. Schau, mir sind diese leckeren Pralinen geschenkt worden! 10. Der Brief war noch nicht weggeschickt worden.

5. a 1. Man störte den Unterricht. 2. Man hat die Prüfungen verschoben. 3. Man hatte dieses Thema schon dreimal besprochen . . . 4. Man hat die Übungen nicht gemacht. 5. Man darf keine Taschenrechner benutzen. 6. Man wird die Schüler nächsten Monat in diesem Fach prüfen.

5. b 1. Man hat meine Handtasche gestohlen! 2. Was kann man machen? 3. Man hat mir einen Scheck gegeben. (*or* Man gab mir einen Scheck). 4. Man beschreibt ihn oft als arrogant.

6. 1. Die Tasse ist gebrochen 'The cup is broken'. 2. Der Nagel ist gebogen 'The nail is bent'. 3. Mein Bruder ist gesehen worden 'My brother has been seen'. 4. Maria ist eben geküsst worden 'Maria has just been kissed'. 5. Das Kind ist angezogen 'The child is dressed'. 6. Die Zeitung ist gelesen worden 'The newspaper has been read'.

7. Werden-passives: Unbeschadet des staatlichen Aufsichtsrechtes <u>wird</u> der Religionsunterricht in Übereinstimmung mit den Grundsätzen der Religionsgemeinschaften <u>erteilt</u>; Kein Lehrer darf . . . <u>verpflichtet werden</u>; <u>wird gewährleistet</u>; <u>gefördert wird</u>; <u>errichtet werden</u> soll. Sein-passive: nicht genügend <u>versichert ist</u>. Zu+infinitive-passives Die Genehmigung <u>ist zu erteilen</u>; Die Genehmigung <u>ist zu versagen</u>; <u>ist</u> nur <u>zuzulassen</u>.

• 19 SEPARABLE VERBS

1. 1. Wir ziehen am Samstag in unser neues Haus ein. 2. Ich ziehe heute um. 3. Wann ziehst du aus? 4. Die Männer streichen gerade die Wand an. 5. Die Gäste setzten sich hin. 6. Ich versuche durch das Küchenfenster hinauszuschauen, aber es ist zu schmutzig. 7. Wir haben vor die neuen Gardinen aufzuhängen. 8. Drehst du den Wasserhahn auf?

2. 1. Wir sind am Samstag in unser neues Haus eingezogen. 2. Ich bin heute umgezogen. 3. Wann bist du ausgezogen? 4. Die Männer haben gerade die Wand angestrichen. 5. Die Gäste haben sich hingesetzt. 6. Ich habe versucht durch das Küchenfenster hinauszuschauen, aber es ist zu schmutzig gewesen. 7. Wir haben vorgehabt die neuen Gardinen aufzuhängen. 8. Hast du den Wasserhahn aufgedreht?

3. 1. Er war müde und legte sich aufs Sofa hin. 2. Als er ins Badezimmer hereinkam, saß sie schon im Bad. 3. Ich ersetze diesen alten Teppich. 4. Wir richten eine neue Küche ein. 5. Hast du die alte Tapete im Wohnzimmer weggerissen? 6. Die Katze hat meine neue Bettdecke zerrissen. 7. Wenn du das Fenster aufmachst . . . 8. Der Maurer versucht die Wand zu verputzen. 9. Ich habe keine Zeit dieses Geschirr abzutrocknen. 10. Man hat das Zimmer noch nicht hergerichtet. 11. Schalt den Fernseher aus! 12. Er überzieht den Esstisch mit einer bunten Tischdecke.

• 20 REFLEXIVE VERBS

1. 1. Er bemüht sich sehr das Rauchen aufzugeben. 2. Du hast dich erkältet. 3. Wir haben uns mit dem Whiskeytrinken krank gemacht. 4. Als ich schwanger war, habe ich mich jeden Morgen übergeben. 5. Die Kinder hatten vor zwei Wochen eine Grippe, aber jetzt haben sie sich erholt. 6. Ihr müsst euch warm anziehen, sonst bekommt ihr einen Schnupfen.

2. 1. Habt ihr euch die Zähne geputzt? 2. Ich werde mich duschen und mir die Haare waschen. 3. Du hast einen Unfall gehabt? Hast du dir wehgetan? 4. Du bist ganz schmutzig. Hast du dich heute nicht gewaschen? 5. Ich habe mir das Bein gebrochen. 6. Ich muss mich beeilen. Ich habe einen Arzttermin. 7. Sie müssen sich ärztlich untersuchen lassen. 8. Er hat aufgehört sich zu rasieren. Der Stoppelbart passt ihm sehr gut. 9. Wir schämen uns beide wegen unseres Gewichts. 10. Hast du dir das Handgelenk verstaucht?

2. 1. Interessierst du dich für Fußball? 2. Er arbeitet für eine andere Firma. 3. Ich freue mich sehr auf die Sommerferien. 4. Erinnert ihr euch an letzten Silvester? 5. Ich habe vergessen, wieviel ich für das Auto bezahlt habe. 6. Nein, das stimmt nicht. Sie müssen sich geirrt haben. 7. Er langweilt sich zu Hause. 8. Kannst du dir vorstellen, wie ich mich gefühlt habe? 9. Er hat erzählt, dass ihn seine Frau verlassen habe. 10. Wir wollten uns irgendwo hinsetzen, aber es gab keinen Platz.

• 21 INFINITIVES AND MODAL VERBS

1. 1. Es ist zu spät zu essen. Ich gehe bald schlafen. 2. Ich habe heute keine Zeit einkaufen zu gehen. 3. Ich habe die Absicht morgen um 6 Uhr aufzustehen. 4. *No change*. 5. Hast du Lust heute Abend auszugehen? 6. Willst du bei mir zu Abend essen? Oder willst du, dass wir in ein Café gehen? 7. Ich habe versucht meine Zeitung zu lesen, aber ich war zu müde. 8. *No change*. 9. Wie lange brauchst du, um das Mittagessen vorzubereiten? 10. Er möchte jetzt teilzeit arbeiten, um mehr Zeit zu Hause mit seinen Kindern verbringen zu können. 11. Ich freue mich darauf mich heute Abend vor dem Fernseher zu entspannen. 12. Ich freue mich darauf, dass du heute Abend kochst. 13. Sie ist zu krank, um (*or, colloquially, without* um) zur Arbeit zu gehen. 14. Er hat vorgeschlagen einen Spaziergang zu machen. 15. Ich brauche nur 15 Minuten um mich zu duschen und mir die Haare zu waschen [*You don't need to repeat* um]. 16 Ich habe nichts mehr anzuziehen. Alles muss gewaschen werden. 17. Es ist sehr nett von dir uns einzuladen. Um wieviel Uhr sollten wir kommen?.

2. 1. wollten. 2. musste. 3. könntest. 4. musst. 5. darf. 6. will. 7. durften. 8. ließ.

3. 1. Wir haben Musik hören wollen. 2. Ich habe mich zuerst waschen (müssen) und mir die Haare bürsten müssen. 3. Hast du das Abendbrot herrichten können? 4. Hast du heute tanken müssen? 5. Hat er dein Fahrrad benutzen dürfen? 6. Er hat den Rasen mähen wolllen. 7. Die Kinder wussten, dass sie keine Computerspiele haben spielen dürfen. 8. Er hat sein Auto reparieren lassen.

4. 1. Ich möchte vier Brötchen. 2. Darf ich hier rauchen. 3. Musst du heute arbeiten? 4. Du darfst deine Schlüssel nicht vergessen. 5. Du musst nicht auf mich warten. 6. Er soll ziemlich reich sein. 7. Ich sollte ihn anrufen, aber ich habe es vergessen. 8. Wo ist Peter? Er könnte bei seiner Freundin sein. 9. Er müsste um halb sechs kommen. 10. Ich wollte eben (*or* gerade) einen Tee machen. 11. Du hättest mich gestern anrufen sollen. 12. Er hätte länger bleiben können, aber er wollte nicht. 13. Wer hat mein Bier getrunken? Es könnte Peter gewesen sein. 14. Ich hätte nicht gehen können. 15. Sie hätten sowieso nicht kommen wollen. 16. Normalerweise hätte ich an einem Samstag nicht arbeiten müssen, aber mein Kollege war krank.

• 22 NEGATION

1. 1. Wolfgang tanzt nicht. 2. Er geht nicht in die Disco. 3. Jutta hat das neueste Buch von Martin Walser nicht gelesen. 4. Mein Vater liest nicht oft Zeitung, weil er nicht viel Freizeit hat. 5. Ich habe diese Schmuckschachtel nicht für dich gebastelt. 6. Meine Eltern sehen nicht fern. 7. Meine Mutter will mir den selbstgebackenen Marmorkuchen nicht geben. 8. Mit dieser alten Nähmaschine kannst du nicht nähen. 9. Ich will nicht, dass du in einer Band spielst. 10. Er ist nicht der beste Sänger im Chor.

2. 1. Er treibt keinen Sport. 2. Hast du die Briefmarkensammlung nicht mit? 3. Er hat die zwei Modellschiffe nicht selber gebaut. 4. Es kommt keine neue Folge von „Tatort" im Fernsehen. 5. Natürlich habe ich den neuen Film von Heiner Lauterbach nicht gesehen. Du weißt doch, dass ich nicht ins Kino gegangen bin. 6. Wir sammeln keine Schmetterlinge. 7. Ich male nicht mit Ölfarben.

3. 1. Nein, ich habe deinen Mann nicht im Fitnesszentrum gesehen, sondern in der Kneipe. 2. Nein, ich habe nicht mit Bernhard Tennis gespielt, sondern mit Fredi. 3. Nein, ich war mit Klaus nicht im Theater, sondern in der Oper. 4. Nein, ich habe keinen CD-Spieler gekauft, sondern einen Mini-Disc-

Spieler. 5. Nein, ich zeichne nicht die Landschaft, sondern die Pferde in dem Feld da. 6. Nein, er möchte keine Bücher zum Geburtstag, sondern Computerspiele.

4. 1. Nein, ich habe keines (*or* keins). 2. Nein, er hat keinen. 3. Nein, sie sind mit keinen von ihren Freunden joggen gegangen. 4. Keiner gefällt mir. 5. Nein, ich brauche keine.

● **23 QUESTIONS**

---

1. 1. Wo liegt das Krankenhaus? 2. Was ist der kürzeste Weg zum Postamt? 3. Wie muss man fahren? (*or* Womit muss man fahren? *to indicate means of transport*). 4. Wie lange dauert es zu Fuß? 5. Wie weit muss man zum Bahnhof gehen? 6. Wann (*or* um wieviel Uhr) muss man losfahren um am Flughafen rechtzeitig anzukommen?

2. 1. wie. 2. warum. 3. welche. 4. welcher. 5. wer. 6. wem.

3. 1. Muss man geradeaus fahren um in die Stadtmitte zu kommen? 2. Kann ich einfach auf der Straße bis zum großen Kreisverkehr bleiben? 3. Ist der Taxifahrer in die dritte Straße rechts abgebogen? 4. Nimmst du die zweite Straße links nach den Zebrastreifen? 5. Darf man nur beim Fußgängerübergang über die Straße gehen? 6. Sind wir auf dem falschen Weg? Müssen wir umdrehen?

4. Ex. 1. 1. Ich weiß, wo das Krankenhaus liegt. 2. Ich weiß, was der kürzeste Weg zum Postamt ist. 3. Ich weiß, wie (*or* womit) man fahren muss. 4. Ich weiß, wie lange es zu Fuß dauert. 5. Ich weiß, wie weit man zum Bahnhof gehen muss. 6. Ich weiß, wann (*or* um wieviel Uhr) man losfahren muss um am Flughafen rechtzeitig anzukommen. **Ex. 2.** 1. Ich weiß, wie ich am besten zum Markt komme. 2. Ich weiß, warum man hier nicht rechts abbiegen darf. Weil das eine Einbahnstraße ist. 3. Ich weiß, welche Richtung ich nehmen muss. 4. Ich weiß, in welcher Straße er sein Geschäft hat. 5. Ich weiß, wer mir am besten den Weg zum Fußballstadion erklären kann. 6. Ich weiß, von wem du den Straßenplan bekommen hast. Von Peter.

● **24 PREPOSITIONS**

---

1. 1. einer deutschen. 2. den. 3. dem ersten. 4. die. 5. der. 6. den, die. 7. seinem. 8. dem.

2. 1. mit Computern. 2. bei dem (*or* von dem). 3. bei der mündlichen. 4. in der (*or* vor der, hinter der, neben der, bei der), auf meinen Kommilitonen (*'weak' noun, see* **3.3b**). 5. von dem. 6. auf die. 7. in den (*or* für die, während der – *colloquial* während den). 8. an seiner. 9. von den. 10. mit ihren. 11. mit dem, mit dem, in die, mit dem, auf dem. 12. an vier Hauptseminaren und zwei Proseminaren.

3. in die, für die, nach, an der LSE, nach, vor den Preisen (fliehen **vor** = 'to flee from'), in der fünfteuersten, für einen Studenten, auf (schätzen **auf** = 'to estimate at'), wegen des Kursverlusts, für das (*or* fürs), zum.

4. 1. im. 2. mit seiner, auf ein. 3. ins. 4. in dem, auf dem. 5. auf eine, bei ihm. 6. über seine. 7. im, zu uns. 8. in die, mit dem. 9. in der, vor vielen. 10. an unserem (*or* zu unserem), ins.

5. mit dem Bus in die Stadt, im Bus, an meine Ex-Freundin, in sie, neben sie (*or* zu ihr), mit ihr, (*either* für *or* no preposition before eine halbe Stunde), über Fußball, aus Dortmund, von Borussia, für Fußball, über Fußball (*or* von Fußball), an unserem Gespräch, nach einer Weile, zum Eishockey, über die verschiedenen Positionen im Spiel, an die, an Sport, in ihrer Stimme, auf etwas Neutrales, an ein neues Thema, im Fernsehen, über die verschiedenen Kreidesorten, auf den Billardstock, zu ihr (*or* mit ihr), mit mir ins Bett, auf den Kopf mit ihrem Regenschirm.

6. 1. „Ich freue mich sehr auf deinen Besuch." „Ja, ich freue mich auch darauf, dich wiederzusehen." 2. „Kommst du heute Abend zum Essen?" „Es hängt davon ab, ob ich länger arbeiten muss oder nicht." 3. Er ist sehr stolz darauf, dass seine Frau einen Bestseller geschrieben hat (*Here,* darauf *can be omitted in spoken German*). 4. Du bist selber daran schuld, dass du dich mit deinen Freunden gestritten hast (*Here,* daran *can be omitted in spoken German*). 5. Ich bin daran (*or* daran *can be omitted in speech*) gewöhnt, meinen eigenen Weg zu gehen, aber jetzt muss ich mich auf andere

Leute verlassen. 6. Kannst du mich daran erinnern, die Telefonrechnung zu bezahlen, bevor wir in den Urlaub (*colloquial* auf Urlaub) fahren? 7. „Was ist das Problem?" „Es handelt sich darum, dass zwei Jugendliche bei einer alten Frau eingebrochen sind und viertausend Mark von ihren Ersparnissen gestohlen haben, die unter ihrer Matratze versteckt waren." 8. Der Gedanke daran, dass er seit einem Jahr seine Frau betrügt, gefällt mir überhaupt nicht (*Here,* daran *can be omitted in spoken German*).

25 CONJUNCTIONS

1. 1. Ich habe staubgesaugt und (ich habe) den Boden gewischt. 2. Entweder du kochst, oder du musst abwaschen. 3. Ich muss einkaufen gehen, weil ich kein Brot und keine Milch habe (*colloquial* weil ich habe kein Brot . . .). 4. Kannst du die Kerze anzünden, nachdem du den Tisch gedeckt hast? 5. Er hatte die Fenster geputzt, aber sie sahen immer noch ziemlich dreckig aus. 6. Kannst du deine Wäsche aufhängen, bevor du weggehst? 7. Ich wusste nicht, dass du eine Mikrowelle hast. 8. Du kannst den Kaffee machen, während ich das Frühstück vorbereite. 9. Er versucht die Waschmaschine zu reparieren, obwohl er das richtige Werkzeug nicht hat. 10. Dieses Fleisch darf man nicht einfrieren, sondern (man) muss es innerhalb von zwei Tagen kochen.

2. 3. Weil ich kein Brot und keine Milch habe, muss ich einkaufen gehen. 4. Nachdem du den Tisch gedeckt hast, kannst du die Kerze anzünden? 6. Bevor du weggehst, kannst du deine Wäsche aufhängen? 7. Dass du eine Mikrowelle hast, wusste ich nicht. 8. Während ich das Frühstück vorbereite, kannst du den Kaffee machen. 9. Obwohl er das richtige Werkzeug nicht hat, versucht er die Waschmaschine zu reparieren.

3. 1. Bis der Ofen repariert wird, kann ich keinen Rostbraten machen. 2. Abwaschen ist die reine Hölle, es sei denn, dass man einen Geschirrspüler hat. 3. Als wir unser Haus gekauft haben, haben wir uns kein Möbel leisten können. 4. Wenn ich Staub wische, benutze ich immer einen nassen Fetzen. 5. Wenn du mehr Zeit hättest, könntest du ein paar Regale aufstellen. 6. Ich weiß nicht, ob er mit einer Bohrmaschine umgehen kann. 7. Mann muss die Wand zweimal streichen, damit die ursprüngliche Farbe nicht durchscheint. 8. Er hatte die Tassen nicht richtig gespühlt, so daß mein Kaffee nach Seife schmeckte. 9. Ich hasse es, wenn er auf dem Sofa lümmelt und seine Füße auf den Tisch legt. 10. Ich habe bemerkt, dass mein Putzmann das Klo nicht gründlich geputzt (hat) und eine Zigarettenkippe im Waschbecken gelassen hat (*the auxiliary can be omitted if it appears later in the same sentence*).

4. 1. Sie sitzt am Tisch und schneidet Brot. 2. Da ich wusste, dass er nicht gut kochen konnte, schlug ich ein gutes Restaurant vor (weil *can also be used instead of* da). 3. Ich schnitt mir in den Finger, als ich gestern Abend das Abendessen vorbereitete (während *can also be used*). 4. Ich machte ihn krank, indem ich zu viel Chilli in sein Essen tat.

26 WORD ORDER

1. 1. Joachim macht am Samstag um acht Uhr eine Fete. 2. Diese Woche fahren die Kinder zu ihren Großeltern. 3. Leider ist es nicht möglich, vor dem vierundzwanzigsten Mai den Flug zu buchen. 4. Am 2. März arbeite ich bis sieben Uhr abends, aber den nächsten Tag habe ich frei. 5. Karl, ich kann am Montag nicht kommen. 6. Stell dir vor, sie wird am 12. Februar hundert Jahre alt! 7. Wo warst du gestern Morgen um halb neun? 8. Ich glaube, er hat am 16. April Geburtstag. 9. Schade, dass ich dich am ersten Januar nicht sah. 10. Der siebzehnte Juni war der Tag, an dem wir uns kennenlernten. 11. Weißt du, ob deine englischen Freunde in Deutschland am 24. oder 25. Dezember Weihnachten feiern und was sie an dem Tag essen? 12. Seine Mutter war besorgt, weil er gestern Abend nicht nach Hause kam und sie auch nicht anrief. 13. Ich bin froh, dass ich es jeden Tag schaffe, vor halb sechs mit meiner Arbeit fertig zu sein. 14. Bevor ich dieses Jahr in den Urlaub fahre, brauche ich einen neuen Koffer. 15. Da wir am 4. Juli unseren Hochzeitstag haben, gehen wir abends in ein schönes Restaurant.

2. 1. Joachim hat am Samstag um acht Uhr eine Fete gemacht. 2. Diese Woche sind die Kinder zu ihren Großeltern gefahren. 3. Leider ist es nicht möglich gewesen, vor dem vierundzwanzigsten Mai den Flug zu buchen. 4. Am 2. März habe ich bis sieben Uhr abends gearbeitet, aber den nächsten Tag habe ich frei gehabt. 5. Karl, ich habe am Montag nicht kommen können. 6. Stell dir vor, sie ist am 12. Februar hundert Jahre alt geworden! 7. Wo bist du gestern Morgen um halb neun gewesen? 8. Ich glaube, er hat am 16. April Geburtstag gehabt. 9. Schade, dass ich dich am ersten Januar nicht gesehen habe. 10. Der siebzehnte Juni ist der Tag gewesen, an dem wir uns kennengelernt haben. 11. Weißt du, ob deine englischen Freunde in Deutschland am 24. oder 25. Dezember Weihnachten gefeiert haben und was sie an dem Tag gegessen haben? 12. Seine Mutter ist besorgt gewesen, weil er gestern Abend nicht nach Hause gekommen ist und sie auch nicht angerufen hat. 13. Ich bin froh gewesen, dass ich es jeden Tag geschafft habe, vor halb sechs mit meiner Arbeit fertig zu sein. 14. Bevor ich dieses Jahr in den Urlaub gefahren bin, habe ich einen neuen Koffer gebraucht. 15. Da wir am 4. Juli unseren Hochzeitstag gehabt haben, sind wir abends in ein schönes Restaurant gegangen.

3. 1. Jens fährt immer mit dem Auto zur Arbeit. 2. Mein Vater kommt morgen um halb acht am Bahnhof an (*or* Morgen kommt mein Vater um halb acht am Bahnhof an). 3. Die Kinder spielen heute fröhlich auf der Wiese (*or* Heute spielen die Kinder fröhlich auf der Wiese). 4. Wir fahren dieses Wochenende für vier Tage mit dem Schnellzug nach Wien (*or* Dieses Wochenende fahren wir für vier Tage mit dem Schnellzug nach Wien). 5. Meine Freundin kommt morgen Abend mit ihrem neuen Ehemann auf Besuch (*or* Morgen Abend kommt meine Freundin mit ihrem neuen Ehemann auf Besuch). 6. Ich werde um viertel vor drei auf dem Hauptplatz auf dich warten (*or* Um viertel vor drei werde ich auf dem Hauptplatz auf dich warten).

4. 1. Er wollte seiner Lehrerin Blumen schenken. 2. Sie hat ihrem Chef die Ursache des Problems erklärt. 3. Gestern habe ich meinem Mann einen neuen Pulli von H&M gekauft (*or* Gestern habe ich meinem Mann von H&M einen neuen Pulli gekauft). 4. Ich hoffe, dass du deinem Freund die Nachricht schon gegeben hast. 5. Hast du es deiner Mutter schon gesagt? 6. „Kannst du mir einen Stift leihen?" „Sicher. Ich kann dir einen geben. Ich habe genug davon." 7. Ich glaube, dass er sich wegen seines schlechten Benehmens schämt. 8. Ich weiß, dass du mir etwas zu sagen hast. Sag es mir! 9. Dein Freund hat wegen seines Fahrrads angerufen. Kannst du es ihm zurückgeben? 10. „Was hält deine Mutter von unseren Urlaubsfotos?" „Ich habe sie ihr noch nicht gezeigt."

5. 1. B: Hast du meine Ohrringe gesehen? Ich habe sie gestern an gehabt, aber ich kann sie heute nicht mehr finden (*or* Gestern habe ich sie an gehabt, aber heute kann ich sie nicht mehr finden). K: Ja, du hast sie mir gestern Abend geliehen (*or* Ja, gestern Abend hast du sie mir geliehen). Willst du sie zurückhaben? B: Nein, das ist kein Problem. Ich hatte bloß vergessen, dass ich sie dir geliehen hatte. K: Und du hast mir deine Goldkette auch geliehen. (*To place emphasis on* Goldkette *we could say:* Und du hast mir auch deine Goldkette geliehen *or* Und deine Goldkette hast du mir auch geliehen). B: Ja, das weiß ich. K: Gehst du heute Abend in die Disco? B: Nein, ich gehe heute Abend früher ins Bett, weil ich morgen mit meiner Schwester nach Frankfurt fahre und sehr früh aufstehen muss. K: OK. Ich werde versuchen ruhig zu sein, wenn ich später von der Disco zurückkomme, damit ich dich nicht aufwecke. B: Gut. Viel Spaß!

- **27 WORD FORMATION**

1. 1. Lehrer, Lehrerin. 2. Arbeiter, Arbeiterin. 3. Bäcker, Bäckerin. 4. Tänzer, Tänzerin. 5. Gärtner, Gärtnerin. 6. Physiker, Physikerin. 7. Sportler, Sportlerin. 8. Übersetzer, Übersetzerin. 9. Maler, Malerin. 10. Wissenschaftler, Wissenschaftlerin. 11. Komponist, Komponistin. 12. Politiker, Politikerin. 13. Pianist, Pianistin. 14. Gitarist, Gitaristin. 15. Trommler, Trommlerin. 16. Tischler, Tischlerin.

2. 1. Chefin. 2. Ärztin. 3. Köchin. 4. Bäuerin. 5. Sängerin. 6. Dozentin. 7. Professorin. 8. Putzfrau. 9. Kellnerin. 10. Psychologin. 11. Anwältin. 12. Schriftstellerin.

3. 1. Fußballspieler. 2. Büroarbeiter. 3. Gruppenführerin. 4. Universitätsprofessorin. 5. Kinderarzt. 6. Sicherheitsbeamter. 7. Busfahrer. 8. Autoverkäufer. 9. Schwimmlehrerin. 10. Abteilungsleiterin.

4. a 1. house, little house (cottage), domestic, domesticity. 2. man, manly (or masculine), manliness (or masculinity), manful/valiant, team, to man (or staff, or crew, e.g. a ship). 3. to read, reader, a reading, legible, legibility, readership, to misread. 4. friend, girlfriend, unfriendly, friendliness, to befriend. 5. power, powerless, powerful/mighty, powerfulness/mightiness, to remove power. 6. to speak/talk/give a speech, speech, speaking (the act of), talk (pejorative), chatter (pejorative), speaker/orator, oratorical. 7. to feel, perceptible, feeler (of insect), feeling, sensitive, insensitive/without feeling. 8. to break, unbreakable, to break into pieces/shatter, fragile/breakable, fragility. 9. to hit/strike a blow/beat, blow, hitter (*or* raquet in sports), fight, unbeatable, to beat to death, to smash to pieces. 10. to speak, speaker, speech/language, speechless, speechlessness, to discuss, discussion, to correspond, to promise, to say wrongly/make a slip of the tongue, to contradict.

4. b 1. das Haus, das Häuschen, die Häuslichkeit. 2. der Mann, die Männlichkeit, die Mannschaft. 3. der Leser, die Lesung, die Lesbarbeit, die Leserschaft. 4. der Freund, die Freundin, die Freundlichkeit. 5. die Macht, die Mächtigkeit. 6. die Rede, das Reden, das Gerede, die Rederei, der Redner. 7. der Fühler, das Gefühl. 8. die Zerbrechlichkeit. 9. der Schlag, der Schläger, die Schlägerei. 10. der Sprecher, die Sprache, die Sprachlosigkeit, die Besprechung.

5. 1. die Haustür 'front door'. 2. das Wohnzimmer 'living room'. 3. das Badezimmer 'bathroom'. 4. die Straßenlampe 'street lamp'. 5. das Küchenfenster 'kitchen window'. 6. der Kleiderschrank 'wardrobe'. 7. das Bügelbrett 'ironing board'. 8. das Gästezimmer 'guest room'. 9. die Bettdecke 'blanket/bedcover'. 10. das Hundehaus 'kennel'. 11. das Bücherregal 'bookshelf'. 12. das Sicherheitsschloss 'safety lock'. 13. das Altpapier 'paper for recycling'. 14. die Wohnungssuche 'flat hunting'. 15. die Gefriertrühe 'freezer/deep freeze'.

● 28 PUNCTUATION AND SPELLING

1. 1914 In Europa beginnt der Erste Weltkrieg. **1917** Nach der Abdankung des Zaren im Frühjahr übernehmen in der Oktoberrevolution die Bolschewiki unter Lenin die Macht in Russland. **1918** Deutschland wird Republik. **1933** Hitler wird Reichskanzler. Der Aufbau des terroristischen Führerstaates beginnt. **1939** Deutschland überfällt Polen. Der Zweite Weltkrieg bricht aus. **1942** Auf der Wannseekonferenz beschließen die Nazis die Juden ganz Europas systematisch zu ermorden. **1945** Hitler begeht Selbstmord. Der Zweite Weltkrieg endet mit Deutschlands bedingungsloser Kapitulation. **1949** Das Grundgesetz für die Bundesrepublik Deutschland wird verabschiedet. In Ost-Berlin nimmt der Volkskongress die Verfassung der Deutschen Demokratischen Republik an. **1953** Im März stirbt der sowjetische Diktator Josef Stalin. Im Juni wird ein Arbeiteraufstand in der DDR von russischen Truppen brutal niedergeschlagen. **1961** Die Führung der DDR lässt die Berliner Mauer errichten. **1962** Die Kuba-Krise bringt die Welt an den Rand des Atomkriegs. **1965** Die USA schicken verstärkt Soldaten nach Vietnam. Der Krieg eskaliert. **1968** Schwere Studentenunruhen in der Bundesrepublik richten sich gegen Notstandsgesetzgebung, Vietnamkrieg und Spießerrepublik. **1977** Der Terror der RAF erreicht in einer beispiellosen Serie von Attentaten seinen Höhepunkt. **1985** Michail Gorbatschow, Generalsekretär des ZK der KPdSU, verkündet das Reformprogramm der Perestrojka. **1989** Das sozialistische Regime der DDR bricht nach 40 Jahren Herrschaft zusammen. **1990** Die wiedererrichteten Länder der DDR treten am 3. Oktober der BRD bei. **1991** In Jugoslawien bricht der Bürgerkrieg aus. **1993** Mit dem Inkrafttreten des Vertrags von Maastricht entsteht die Europäische Union, deren Ziel ein wirtschaftlich und sozial geeintes Europa ist.

2. Doch der Vormarsch der Alliierten ging an allen Fronten, wenn auch von Stockungen begleitet, etappenweise voran. Im Februar und März 1945 eroberten sie die linksrheinischen Gebiete Deutschlands. Nachdem amerikanische Truppen am 7. März bei Remagen und britische Einheiten am 24. März bei Wesel den Rhein überschritten hatten, rückten die Amerikaner (zusammen mit der 1. französischen Armee) nach Süddeutschland vor. Sie besetzten auch Vorarlberg, Tirol bis zum Brenner, das Salzkammergut, Oberösterreich und den Westen Böhmens bis zur Linie Karlsbad-Budweis-Linz. Im Norden erreichten die Engländer am 19. April 1945 die Elbe bei Lauenburg, während amerikanische Verbände ins Zentrum des Reiches vorstießen und am 25. April 1945 mit den Sowjets bei Torgau zusammentrafen. Weiterzumarschieren lehnte der alliierte Oberbefehlshaber General Eisenhower jedoch aus politischen und militärischen Gründen ab, da er sich mit der Masse seiner Streitkräfte der Eroberung des deutschen „Alpen-Reduit", einem von den Alliierten ernstgenommenen Propagandaprodukt der Nationalsozialismus, zuwenden wollte. Der Osten des Reiches wurde im Zeitraum vom Januar bis zum Mai 1945 von der sowjetischen Armee erobert, vor der Millionen von Deutschen unter unsagbaren Leiden nach Westen zu fliehen versuchten. Dabei schützten die Reste des deutschen Ostheeres „in einem ganz elementaren Sinne die Menschen in . . . [den] preußisch-deutschen Ostprovinzen" [1099: A. Hillgruber] vor der furchtbaren Rache der heranrückenden Roten Armee und trugen, damit unauflöslich verbunden, doch gleichzeitig dazu bei(,) die Existenz des nationalsozialistischen Unrechtsregimes zu verlängern.

Appendix 5: Key to revision texts

● **REVISION TEXT 1**

Analysis

1. wird . . . beantragt (lines 2–3), erfüllt werden (16), wird . . . projiziert (16–17), kann . . . gefährdet werden (20–21), aufgestellt werden (22).

2. gefährdet ist (8) literally: 'is endangered' (or, more naturally, 'at risk'), sind . . . überfordert (22) 'are overstretched'. These both express a **state**. If *sein* was replaced by *werden* then an **action** would be expressed: i.e. 'is being endangered' (or 'put at risk'), 'are being overstretched' (see line 21 for an example of *gefährdet* with *werden*).

3. The *Konjunktiv I* is used, primarily in written German, to express reported (otherwise known as 'indirect') speech; here it conveys what was said by the psychologists in their article. By contrast, where the speech is direct (i.e. a direct quotation indicated by inverted commas) the ordinary indicative is used.

4. These are *Konjunktiv II* forms and are used to indicate reported speech in contexts where the *Konjunktiv I* form would be identical to the indicative. For instance, the *Konjunktiv I* form of *können* in the plural is *können*, which looks like an indicative. *Könnten* is used to make it clear that this is a subjunctive which is used to report what the psychologist is saying.

5. These are also *Konjunktiv II* forms, but as they are regular verbs these forms appear identical to the ordinary past tense forms. We know that these are *Konjunktiv II* forms because they appear in reported speech where some sort of subjunctive is needed (and the *Konjunktiv I* would not be possible as it is identical to the indicative in the plural, see Answer 4 above). They cannot be ordinary past tense forms because the article is written largely in the present, as it expresses a general present-day trend. In spoken German, the *Konjunktiv II* forms of regular verbs are usually replaced with *würde* + infinitive: e.g. *Viele Paare würden zu hohe Erwartungen . . . stellen*.

6. There is no grammatical ending on these forms because they are used as adverbs.

7. This is the superlative form of the adjective *häufig*, meaning 'most frequent'.

8. This is a reflexive pronoun in the third person singular form. As the expression *jemandem aus dem Weg gehen* takes the dative (e.g. *Er ging mir aus dem Weg*) we know that *sich* must be in the dative, although this third person form is identical to the accusative. In this context it has a reciprocal rather than a reflexive meaning – it means 'each other' rather than 'oneself' if translated into English: 'there are different strategies for avoiding each other'. With regard to word order, the reflexive pronoun occupies the same position as the direct object: i.e. it follows the subject (and verb, but in this sentence the verb has been sent to the end of the clause because of *wie*).

9. It is a demonstrative pronoun, meaning literally 'those' (= 'those expectations'). It occurs instead of the personal pronoun *sie* 'they' for extra emphasis.

10. Because the verb *umgehen* takes the preposition *mit* 'to deal with', it is necessary to have *damit* before a following clause (see 24.6b). Literally this means 'Many couples cannot deal **with it** that on holiday they have to spend so much time with each other'. A more natural translation would be 'deal with the fact that . . .'. *Dadurch* is slightly different in that it is not linked to a particular verb but *da* refers specifically to what has been said before (= 'this' or 'that'): 'Difficult and unsatisfactory situations such as a bad hotel or unaccustomed weather conditions further increase stress levels. Even a strong relationship can be acutely jeopardised **by this**'.

11. *Durch* refers back to an idea (i.e. 'difficult situations') rather than to a person who is the direct agent of the verb.

12. The definite article tends to be used more when it appears in its contracted form after a preposition, even in contexts which allow it to be dropped (in this case, in a news headline).

Exercises

1. Angaben [*dat. pl., same as nom. pl.*], Psychologen, Gründe, Krisen, Ratschläge, Paare, Strategien, Freunden [*dat. pl., contrast nom. pl.* = Freunde], Möglichkeiten, Erwartungen, Situationen, Bedingungen, Regeln.

2. zum, der, jede, einem, die, zur, einem, des, Ratgebers, im, im, dem, Freunden, der, die, die, die, den.

3. Gemeinsamer, nordrhein-westfälischen, dritte, gemeinsam [*adverb so no ending*], verbrachten, häufigsten, erschienenen, gemeinsame, schwierige, unbefriedigende, schlechtes, ungewohnte, klimatische.

4. 1. Nach Angaben der nordrhein-westfälischen Verbraucher-Zentrale wird etwa jede dritte Scheidung in Deutschland nach einem gemeinsam verbrachten Urlaub beantragt. 2. Zwei Psychologen haben deshalb die häufigsten Gründe für Krisen und Ratschläge zur Krisenvermeidung in einem Artikel des neu erschienenen Ratgebers „Chance Psychotherapie" veröffentlicht. 3. Der Urlaub ist dann ein Risikofaktor, wenn die Beziehung ohnehin schon gefährdet ist. 4. Viele Paare könnten nicht damit umgehen, dass sie im Urlaub plötzlich so viel Zeit miteinander verbringen müssten. 5. Im Alltag gibt es verschiedene Strategien, wie man sich aus dem Weg gehen kann, zum Beispiel Treffen mit Freunden. 6. „Wenn die dann nicht erfüllt werden, wird die Enttäuschung auf den Partner projiziert". 7. Auch ein stabiles Beziehungssystem kann dadurch akut gefährdet werden. 8. Und wenn im Urlaub plötzlich andere Regeln aufgestellt werden, sind meist beide überfordert.

5. 1. führt oft zum. 2. ohnehin schon gefärdet. 3. könnten nicht damit. 4. naturgemäß nicht. 5. dann nicht erfüllt.

● REVISION TEXT 2

Analysis

1. It is an indefinite article (nominative neuter singular) functioning as a pronoun. It means 'one thing': 'only one thing is deliberately overlooked'.

2. *Jeder,* **der** *sich länger in Österreich aufhält* (line 12). This is masculine singular because it refers back to *jeder* which is also masculine singular. It is in the nominative case because it is the subject of its following verb: 'anyone **who** <u>has</u> spent a reasonable length of time in Austria'. *Von den Preisen,* **die** *deutsche Urlauber zahlen müssen* (line 16). The relative pronoun is plural because it refers back to a plural noun, *Preise*. It is accusative as it is the direct object of its following verb (*deutsche Urlauber* is the subject): 'the prices **that/which** German holidaymakers have to pay'.

3. They are reflexive pronouns (first person singular, first person plural and third person singular, respectively) and are all in the accusative case. They follow the same word order as direct objects, thus they immediately follow the subject and verb (except when the verb has been sent to the end, as is the case in lines 12–13, where, the reflexive pronoun follows the subject *der*).

4. The first example of *werden* is in the singular because the clause has no proper subject and in this case the 'default' third person singular form is used. The clause has a general meaning: 'there has been much discussion'. By contrast, the second occurrence of *werden* is in the plural because the clause has a plural subject: *alle nur denkbaren Ursachen*: 'all causes imaginable are being discussed'. The *es* is not a proper subject but is added at the beginning of the clause when the subject **follows** the verb (contrast *es werden alle Ursachen diskutiert* with *alle Ursachen werden diskutiert*). Similarly, we would expect *es* to begin the very first sentence, yet it is absent because the writer uses *da* instead, which in this context has a similar function to *es* – as an element placed at the beginning of the sentence where the subject should be but which has no real meaning and is therefore not translated into English.

5. This is in the nominative because it is, together with *wir*, the subject of the sentence, despite the fact that it comes quite late in the sentence and is preceded by *als*. We know it is the subject because it refers to the same person (or, in this case, persons) as the subject *wir*: i.e. the Germans.

6. It is a definite article in the genitive plural form, meaning '**of** the': 'The latent hostility of the Austrians towards the Germans' (or 'the Austrians' latent hostility . . .'). It is plural because of the following noun: 'Austrians'.

7. *länger* (lines 1, 12) from *lang*; *stärker* (2) from *stark*; *weniger* (3) from *wenig*; *mehr* (16) from *viel*; *teurer* (18) from *teuer*. *Weniger* has simply added the comparative ending *-er* while the others have changed the form of the adjective, too: *länger* and *stärker* have umlauted their vowel as well, which is very common in adjectives with *-a-*; *teurer* has dropped the last *-e*, *teuer* → *teur-* before adding the comparative ending, which is the case with all adjectives/adverbs ending in unstressed *-er*; *mehr* is a completely irregular comparative deriving from *viel* (compare the irregular 'many → more' in English).

8. It is the separable prefix of the verb *aufhalten*. Like all separable prefixes, it appears at the end of the clause when its verb is in the present (or past) tense. Note that it appears at the end of the *clause* and not at the end of the whole sentence, which would be incorrect here.

9. These are finite verb forms and consequently appear at the end of their respective clauses when preceded by a subordinating conjunction or, as in this case, an interrogative used indirectly, i.e. *warum*.

10. The accusative object of the verb *gibt* is placed at the beginning of the sentence for emphasis. If the standard subject–verb word order was used, *es gibt . . .* the sentence would lose its force. Similarly, the placing of *genug* at the end also emphasises its meaning.

11. This is an adjectival noun and therefore requires the same endings as an adjective: e.g. *-en* after the plural definite article *die* versus *-e* where no article is used.

12. The first example is a noun and, in German, all nouns are capitalised. By contrast, the second example is an adjective which, as a proper noun, would be capitalised in English but not in German, as adjectives in German never have a capital letter (unless they occur in titles etc.).

Exercises

1. 1. der Gästestrom. 2. der Österreicher. 3. Uns Deutschen. 4. den Österreichern.

2. 1. seit längerem, vor allem. 2. auf der Hand, gegenüber den Deutschen. 3. in dem (*or* im) KURIER, gegen Deutsche. 4. in den Medien, uns Deutsche. 5. mit gleicher Münze. 6. Von den Preisen.

3. 1. Da wird in Österreich darüber geredet, warum denn vor allem der Gästestrom aus Deutschland immer stärker nachlässt und wesentlich weniger deutsche Urlauber kommen. 2. Obwohl es doch so klar auf der Hand liegt. 3. Es ist ja auch nicht so, dass wir Deutsche uns ständig „anpinkeln" lassen müssen. 4. Die Folgen davon sind ganz zwangsläufig, dass in den Medien eine ablehnende Stimmung gegen uns Deutsche erzeugt wird. 5. Aber alles hat auch seine Grenzen. 6. Und schöne Landschaft gibt es auch in Deutschland genug.

● **REVISION TEXT 3**

Analysis

1. dieses <u>reservierten bis, zu gegebenermaßen, manchmal unfreundlichen</u> Verhaltens (lines 6–7) → dieses Verhaltens, das reserviert bis, zu gegebenermaßen, manchmal unfreundlich ist; ein <u>aus</u>

unserer Sicht nur schwer zu verdauendes großspuriges Auftreten (8–9) → ein großspuriges Auftreten, das aus unserer Sicht nur schwer zu verdauen ist.

2. den Deutschen ... gegenüberstehen (4–5); sich der Mühe unterziehen (5–6); dem großen Bruder widersprechen (27–28).

3. These are all *Konjunktiv II* forms used with a conditional meaning (see **16.3**). They mean 'would be', 'could' and 'should/ought to be' respectively.

4. It is a *zu* + infinitive construction which corresponds to a passive in English: 'the following would have to be said'.

5. It usually means 'to let', but in this context it means 'to make' in the sense of 'to cause to': 'Such conduct, which sometimes makes one think of the behaviour of colonial rulers'. Note that an object (in the English translation 'one' or 'us') is not necessary with this construction in German.

6. This is the third person singular present form of the modal verb *mögen*. It usually means 'like' but in this context it means 'may', 'Herr Pirl may well be right', and is used here to indicate that the speaker will use a 'but' or 'however' later on: 'but he should make the effort to investigate the causes of this ...'.

7. It is a dative plural (the nominative/accusative/genitive plural is *Österreicher*). It is in the dative because it is affected by the preceding preposition *mit*, despite the fact that another word (*uns*, also in the dative) intervenes.

8. This is a dative ending (feminine and singular agreeing with the noun *Feindlichkeit*) because the adjective is affected by the preposition *von*, which has scope over all the items in the list which follows it.

9. *An* is one of those prepositions which can take the accusative or dative. Here, it takes the accusative because it is occurring in combination with the verb *denken* (see **Table 26**).

10. It is a diminutive. The diminutive ending *-chen* is not possible here as the noun ends in *ch*, therefore the alternative *-lein* is used. In this context the word has a pejorative, belittling effect: 'when he brings in his **little saying** about the 'big brother' (= 'stupid little saying').

Exercises

1. 1. Zum Brief des KURIER-Lesers Oswald Pirl. 2. Die Ursachen dieses reservierten bis, zu gegebenermaßen, manchmal unfreundlichen Verhaltens. 3. Das Verhalten der kleinen Brüder. 4. Die Menschen des Gastlandes. 5. Das Vorhandensein dieser Haltung. 6. Niemandes kleine Brüder (*also possible:* niemands). 7. Der Rundumschlag eines deutschen Urlaubers. 8. Die Preisgestaltung des heimischen Handels. 9. Die Ursache seines Kummers. 10. Die wohlwollenden Ratschläge des großen Bruders.

2. 1. Herr Pirl mag schon recht haben. 2. ... wenn er meint, dass die Österreicher den Deutschen nicht immer umarmungsbereit gegenüberstehen. 3. Da gibt es ein aus unserer Sicht nur schwer zu verdauendes großspuriges Auftreten. 4. Ein solches Verhalten, das manchmal auch an das Gehaben von Kolonialherren denken lässt, wird nicht freundlich reflektiert und provoziert seinerseits Ablehnung. 5. Den Beweis für das Vorhandensein dieser Haltung liefert Herr Pirl ja selbst. 6. ... wenn er das Sprüchlein vom „großen Bruder" bemüht. 7. Die Österreicher sind niemandes „kleine Brüder". 8. Der Rundumschlag eines deutschen Urlaubers gegen uns Österreicher im KURIER-Leserforum veranlasst mich zu einer Stellungnahme. 9. Andererseits versäumt er auch nicht, die großen deutschen Tugenden anzupreisen. 10. Aber vielleicht liegt gerade hier die Ursache seines Kummers mit uns Österreichern. 11. ... mit uns Österreichern, die ja die wohlwollenden Ratschläge des großen Bruders ganz undankbar verschmähen, oder schlimmer, dem großen Bruder widersprechen. 12. Störisch, wie wir nach seinen Erfahrungen sind.

3. 1. zum, aus, gegen die. 2. nach den. 3. aus unserer, gegenüber den. 4. an das (ans *is also possible*). 5. für das (*colloquial:* fürs), vom großen. 6. zur. 7. gegen uns, im, zu einer. 8. zur, in herrlich deutscher. 9. nach seinen.

4. 1. der Deutsche (*plural:* die Deutschen). 2. das Verhalten. 3. die Sicht. 4. das Auftreten. 5. die Besserwisserei. 6. das Betragen. 7. die Ablehnung. 8. der Beweis. 9. das Vorhandensein. 10. die

Haltung. 11. die Kenntnis. 12. die Stellungnahme. 13. die Feindlichkeit. 14. die Gründlichkeit. 15. die Erfahrung.

• REVISION TEXT 4

Analysis

1. The simple past is used (e.g. *nannte, plädierte*) because this is a written report. The perfect is mainly used in the spoken language.

2. Infinitives are always preceded by *zu* unless they co-occur with a modal verb (and a few other verbs such as *lassen, sehen* etc.). In line 15, *träumen* co-occurs with *kann* in line 14 which is a modal verb.

3. It is a present participle, *lernend*, functioning as an adjective, hence the ending *-en*.

4. The ending *-er* is always used with the names of towns when they function as adjectives.

5. The first three occurrences show a prepositional phrase with *da-* being used because the co-occurring verb takes that particular preposition: e.g. *plädieren **für** etwas, **in** etwas einig sein* etc. Often, these *da-* + preposition forms are not translated into English (see **24.6b**). By contrast, in line 24, the *da-* in *damit* refers to a demonstrative *das* 'that', which denotes what has been mentioned before, i.e. *dass in Hamburg heute alle Grundschüler Englisch als Pflichtunterricht bekommen*. Thus, in English the equivalent would be 'but other federal states are nowhere near **that**' (see **8.5**).

6. Because *dass* is a conjunction while *das* is a relative pronoun. The latter means 'that' in the sense of 'which' and refers back to a preceding noun (e.g. *Deutschland* or *Russisch*).

7. In this context, the verb *können* is used to mean 'know' or 'can speak'. It is often used when talking about foreign languages: e.g. *Kannst du Deutsch?*

8. It takes the accusative in line 15 because it is dependent on the verb *grenzen* and the dative in line 19 because it is not dependent on a particular verb, which means that the usual rules for the use of accusative vs. dative apply: i.e. it takes the dative to denote position (rather than movement).

9. The definite article is used with the names of foreign languages when the speaker is talking of translating from one into another, or when they appear in the genitive; the latter applies in line 25.

10. As *sich* is a pronoun while *Latein* and *die Zahl* are nouns it comes first, as pronouns usually precede nouns.

11. In an ordinary sentence expressions of time (e.g. *in diesem Februar*) usually precede expressions of place (e.g. *in Berlin*). The reason why this is reversed in line 23 is that the writer wants to emphasise *Hamburg*: i.e. that is the state where English is compulsory while the other states still have some way to go. Thus, the word order expresses a contrast (see **26.6**).

12. It denotes female humans and animals. Thus, we know that the minister for education and the Luxembourger referred to in the text are women.

Exercises

1. a 1. nannte. 2. plädierte. 3. sagte. 4. fiel in den letzten zehn Jahren zurück, . . . verdoppelte.

1. b nennen – nannte: brennen – brannte, kennen – kannte, rennen – rannte (*also similar*: denken – dachte).

2. 1. die Eröffnungskonferenz. 2. das Jahr. 3. die Schlüsselqualifikation. 4. das Leben. 5. das Grußwort. 6. der Reichtum. 7. die Luxemburgerin. 8. die Hälfte. 9. die Fremdsprache. 10. die Schule. 11. das Deutschland. 12. die Szene. 13. die Kultur. 14. das Bundesland. 15. die Vorrangstellung. 16. der Schüler. 17. der Unterricht. 18. die Zahl.

3. 1. der nationalen, des Sprachenjahrs, diesem, die, eine, das private, das berufliche. 2. ihrem, den, Europas, die, seiner. 3. die, aller, eine. 4. sie, einem. 5. solchen Verhältnissen. 6. dem. 7. den deutschen. 8. des Englischen, den. 9. der, deutschen, im, bilingualen, der. 10. dritter. 11. der, die, den letzten, Jahren. 12. der, lernenden.

4. 1. Bei der nationalen Eröffnungskonferenz des Sprachenjahrs *nannte* Bundesbildungsministerin Edelgard Bulmahn die Fremdsprachenkompetenz „eine Schlüsselqualifikation". 2. Viviane Reding, bei der Europäischen Kommission für Bildung und Kultur *zuständig*. 3. Viviane Reding plädierte dafür, den „kulturellen Reichtum" Europas *zu erhalten* und die Sprachen seiner Nachbarländer *zu lernen*. 4. Für die Luxemburgerin *ist* es schwer begreiflich, dass nur die Hälfte aller Europäer eine Fremdsprache *spricht*. 5. Alle Luxemburger *sind* dreisprachig, und wenn sie die Schule *verlassen*, *können* sie neben Luxemburgisch, Deutsch und Französisch als vierte Sprache Englisch. 6. Von solchen Verhältnissen *kann* man in Deutschland, das immerhin an neun Nachbarländer *grenzt, nur träumen*. 7. Alle *sind sich* darin einig, dass man mit dem Sprachenlernen nicht früh genug *beginnen kann*. 8. Das *hängt* damit *zusammen*, dass für Kultur und Bildung die Bundesländer zuständig *sind*, jedes also eigene Vorschriften *erlässt*. 9. So *kommt* es, dass in Hamburg heute alle Grundschüler Englisch als Pflichtunterricht *bekommen*, andere Bundesländer damit aber längst noch nicht so weit *sind*. 10. Die Zahl der Schüler, die Russisch *lernen* – das für DDR-Schüler noch Pflicht *war* –, *fiel* in den letzten zehn Jahren von 582 000 auf 187 000 *zurück*, während *sich* die Zahl der Spanisch lernenden Schüler auf fast 142 000 *verdoppelte*.

5. 1. No commas necessary because this is just one clause: the only verb is *nannte*. 2. Comma after *Reding* and *zuständig* to bracket off this incidental information. 3. Comma before the conjunction *dass*, to separate the two clauses. 4. Comma before *und* because it is followed by the conjunction *wenn*. In this case, *und* begins the next clause as it is seen as occurring together with *wenn*. Comma after *verlassen* to separate the two finite verbs *verlassen* and *können* which each belong to separate clauses. 5. As in (3) above, comma before *dass*. Comma before *sind* to separate that clause from the following clause with *erlässt*. 6. Comma before *der* because it is a relative pronoun. 7. Comma after *Schüler* before the relative pronoun *die* and after *lernen* to separate that relative clause from the following clause with *fiel*. Comma before the conjunction *während* to separate the clause with *fiel* from the following clause with *verdoppelte*.

● **REVISION TEXT 5**

Analysis

1. Because it has been affected by *wie* 'how', which is an interrogative used indirectly.

2. It is a definite article in the feminine singular **dative** form, as the verb *auffallen* takes a dative object.

3. It is a possessive (in the nominative feminine singular agreeing with the following noun *Kleidung*), meaning 'your', which corresponds to the pronoun *Sie*, the polite form of address meaning 'you'. The informal *du*-possessive would be *deine*.

4. They are definite articles used instead of possessives (i.e. instead of *unter deinen Augen, in deiner Tasche* etc.). This is very common in German when the following noun refers to parts of the body or clothing. In English, we would usually use a possessive here, thus *den, der* etc. would be translated by 'your' in these cases.

5. This is a relative pronoun meaning 'which' and it refers back to the previous noun *Brille*, hence the feminine singular form. It is in the accusative.

6. The first two occurrences take an accusative and the last two take a dative. In the first two cases the meaning denotes movement towards the following noun: 'go in**to** the nearest pub', 'sit **down** next to an attractive woman'. In the last two the meaning denotes position: 'hold in (not *into) your other hand', 'chief consultant in (not *into) the university hospital'.

7. They are imperatives (not infinitives!) in the *Sie*-form. The *Sie* is omitted here to avoid repetition.

8. Because the clause contains an indefinite noun, 'whiskey', that is being negated (i.e. a noun not preceded by a definite article, a demonstrative or a possessive; contrast *Sie mögen* **den** *Whiskey* *nicht* 'you don't like the whiskey'). In line 13 there is no noun in the negative sentence: *nicht* refers to the verb *belästigen*.

9. It refers back to *der Brief* and is therefore masculine. In English we would use 'it'. It immediately precedes *mir* because the usual order of personal pronouns is nominative–accusative–dative, and *ihn* is in the accusative while *mir* is in the dative.

10. These verbs are in the perfect tense because this is the tense used to refer to past events in spoken German. Although this is a letter, and therefore written, it is informal and consequently has many grammatical features in common with the spoken language. In English we would use the simple past tense, not the perfect, to translate these forms: 'You dealt with the housework', 'I appreciated your dazzling charm etc.', 'You gave me too much freedom'.

11. Very common verbs like *haben*, *sein* and the modals often tend to appear in the simple past tense where other verbs would be in the perfect.

12. This is a pluperfect tense and is used to refer to the period *before* the couple were together: i.e. a past within the past.

13. These verbs are in the future tense. In German, the present is often used to refer to the future unless the speaker is making a prediction (line 13) or a promise (line 26).

14. *fühlen Sie sich* (accusative pronoun), *setzen sich* (accusative pronoun), *bestellen sich einen Whiskey* (dative pronoun because an accusative object is also present), *wenden Sie sich* (accusative pronoun), *wie du dich . . . gekümmert hast* (accusative pronoun). We cannot replace *selbst* with *sich* as the object of the sentence is *den Brief* and we cannot have two different accusative objects. If we did use *sich* it would be interpreted as a dative: i.e. 'You have written a letter to yourself', which has a completely different meaning.

15. The first sentence of the letter (*ich verlasse dich!*) does not begin with a capital letter, as you would expect in English. This is because the address, *Lieber Stephan*, was followed by a comma (not an exclamation mark) and therefore the next line is not considered to be the beginning of a new sentence.

Exercises

1. 1. Sind Sie nicht gut drauf? 2. Fühlen Sie sich ausgelaugt und abgespannt? 3. Haben Sie Ränder unter den Augen und ist Ihre Kleidung zerknittert? 4. Könnten Sie ihn mir vorlesen?

2. 1. Gehen Sie jetzt in die nächste Kneipe. 2. Setzen Sie sich in die unmittelbare Nähe einer attraktiven Frau. 3. Jetzt stöhnen Sie leise. 4. Bestellen Sie sich ein Glas Whiskey. 5. Zerknittern Sie ihn etwas. 6. Vergiss mich.

3. 1. man. 2. Sie sich. 3. Ihre. 4. Sie sich, sie. 5. Sie, ihr. 6. ich, Sie. 7. mich. 8. meine. 9. Sie, ihn, mir. 10. ich, dich. 11. wir. 12. du, mir. 13. du, mich. 14. du dich. 15. ich, deinen, deinen, deine. 16. du, deiner, mich. 17. du, mir. 18. meinem. 19. mich.

4. 1. wäre, könnten. 2. möchte. 3. Würden Sie ihn mir vorlesen? 4. könnten. 5. sollte.

5. 1. Haben Sie Ränder unter den Augen und ist Ihre Kleidung zerknittert? 2. Bestellen Sie sich einen doppelten Whiskey, auch wenn Sie keinen Whiskey mögen. 3. Aus den Augenwinkeln beobachten Sie, ob Sie der attraktiven Frau auffallen. 4. Wenden Sie sich an sie, indem Sie einen zerknitterten Brief aus der Tasche ziehen. 5. Ideal wäre es, wenn Sie ein Stück einer kaputten Brille in der anderen Hand halten könnten, denn Sie werden jetzt zu ihr mit tränenerstickter Stimme folgenden Satz sagen. 6. Entschuldigen Sie, ich möchte Sie wirklich nicht belästigen, aber dieser Brief ist unheimlich wichtig für mich [*or with a new sentence,* Aber dieser Brief . . ., *as in the text*]. 7. Achten Sie darauf, dass die Schrift leserlich ist. 8. Es war wunderbar, wie du dich um den Haushalt gekümmert hast. 9. Es ist wirklich unglaublich, dass du trotz deiner Polition als Chefarzt in der Uniklinik immer Zeit für mich hattest.

Recommended reading

For further details on aspects of German grammar covered in this book and information on more specific grammatical topics not dealt with here I recommend the following:

DUDEN (1998) *DUDEN Band 4. Grammatik der deutschen Gegenwartssprache, neue Rechtschreibung*. Mannheim: Bibliographisches Institut.

Dodd, Bill *et al.* (1996) *Modern German Grammar. A Practical Guide*. London: Routledge.

Eisenberg, Peter (1998) *Grundriss der deutschen Grammatik. Band 1: Das Wort*. Stuttgart: Metzler.

Eisenberg, Peter (1999) *Grundriss der deutschen Grammatik. Band 2: Der Satz*. Stuttgart: Metzler.

Durrell, Martin (1992) *Using German*. Cambridge: Cambridge University Press.

Durrell, Martin (2002) *Hammer's German Grammar and Usage*. Revised version with new spelling. London: Edward Arnold.

Fleischer, Wolfgang and Irmhild Barz (1995) *Wortbildung der deuschen Gegenwartssprache*. Tübingen: Max Niemeyer.

Fox, Anthony (1990) *The Structure of German*. Oxford: Clarendon Press.

Lockwood, W. B. (1987) *German Today: The Advanced Learner's Guide*. Oxford: Clarendon Press.

West, Jonathan (1992) *Progressive Grammar of German 2: Sentences and Their Realisation*. Dublin: Authentik.

West, Jonathan (1994) *Progressive Grammar of German 5: Words and Their Constituents*. Dublin: Authentik.

West, Jonathan, Stephen Crain and Diane Lillo-Martin (forthcoming) *A Comprehensive German Grammar*. Oxford and Cambridge, MA: Blackwell.

Index

Bold is used to highlight the pages which deal with the topic in more detail.